Global Muslims in
the Age of Steam and Print

The publisher gratefully acknowledges the generous support of the Philip E. Lilienthal Asian Studies Endowment Fund of the University of California Press Foundation, which was established by a major gift from Sally Lilienthal.

Global Muslims in the Age of Steam and Print

Edited by

James L. Gelvin and Nile Green

UNIVERSITY OF CALIFORNIA PRESS

Berkeley   Los Angeles   London

University of California Press, one of the most distinguished university presses in the United States, enriches lives around the world by advancing scholarship in the humanities, social sciences, and natural sciences. Its activities are supported by the UC Press Foundation and by philanthropic contributions from individuals and institutions. For more information, visit www.ucpress.edu.

University of California Press
Berkeley and Los Angeles, California

University of California Press, Ltd.
London, England

Library of Congress Cataloging-in-Publication Data
  Global Muslims in the age of steam and print / [edited by]
James L. Gelvin, Nile Green.
    pages cm
  Includes bibliographical references and index.
  ISBN 978-0-520-27501-0 (hardback)
  ISBN 978-0-520-27502-7 (paper)
  ISBN 978-0-520-95722-0 (ebook)
  1. Islamic countries—History—19th century. 2. Islamic civilization—
19th century. 3. Technology—Islamic countries—History—19th century.
I. Gelvin, James L., 1951– II. Green, Nile.
  DS34.G46 2014
  909′.09767081—dc23   2013031181

23   22   21   20   19   18   17   16   15   14
10   9   8   7   6   5   4   3   2   1

CONTENTS

ILLUSTRATIONS

MAPS

FIGURES

ACKNOWLEDGMENTS

Global Muslims in the Age of Steam and Print had its origins in the two-day conference "Circuits and Networks: Muslim Interactions in the First Age of Globalization," held at the University of California, Los Angeles, on February 25–26, 2009. Co-organized by James Gelvin and Nile Green, the conference was hosted by UCLA's G. E. von Grunebaum Center for Near Eastern Studies. The organizers—now editors—acknowledge the generous financial support of the Center for Near Eastern Studies, which made the conference possible, and thank in particular the center's director, Professor Susan Slyomovics. For help in organizing the conference, we also express our gratitude to the center's staff members, especially Amy Bruinooge, Hanna Petro, Mona Ramezani, and Megan Rancier. Among the various UCLA colleagues and graduate students with whom we have shared ideas related to this book's themes, we give thanks to Ziad Abu-Rish, Ned Alpers, Sebouh Aslanian, Michael Morony, Gabriel Piterberg, Geoffrey Robinson, Michael Salman, Sarah Stein, Sanjay Subrahmanyam, and Bin Wong. At University of California Press, we are obliged to our commissioning editor, Niels Hooper, for his faith in and enthusiasm for the project, and to Kim Hogeland and Chalon Emmons, for overseeing the editorial process. Thanks also to copy editor Juliana Froggatt. Most of all, we are grateful to the speakers who traveled to the conference and who, in contributing to the final book, are allowing us to share with more people the rich and strange fruits of their research.

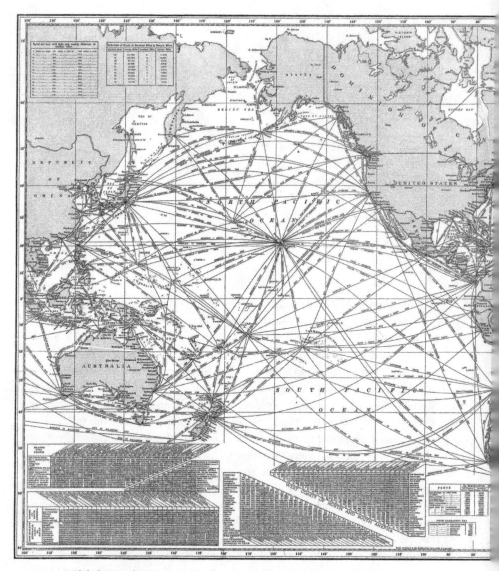

MAP 1. Global steamship routes.

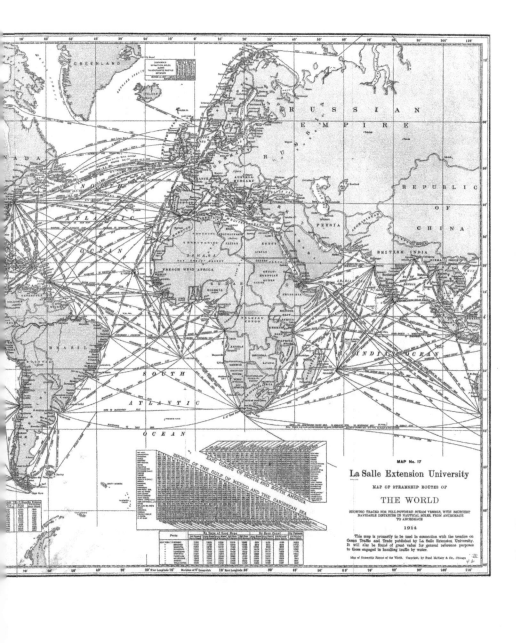

MAP No. 17

La Salle Extension University

MAP OF STEAMSHIP ROUTES OF

THE WORLD

SHOWING TRACKS FOR FULL-POWERED STEAM VESSELS, WITH SHORTEST
NAVIGABLE DISTANCES IN NAUTICAL MILES, FROM ANCHORAGE
TO ANCHORAGE

1914

This map is primarily to be used in connection with the treatise on
Ocean Traffic and Trade published by La Salle Extension University.
It will also be found of great value for general reference purposes
to those engaged in handling traffic by water.

Map of Steamship Routes of the World. Copyright, by Rand McNally & Co., Chicago

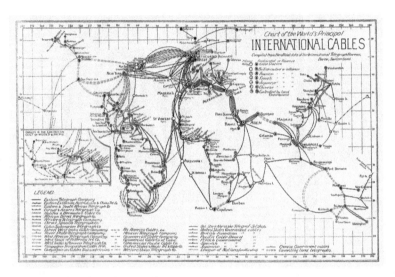

MAP 2. Global telegraph networks.

Introduction

Global Muslims in the Age of Steam and Print

James L. Gelvin and Nile Green

DEFINING "GLOBAL" PARAMETERS

At the end of the twentieth century, the term *globalization* entered both the social science lexicon and the popular imagination. While it has become a commonplace to say that we live in an era of globalization, there is little agreement on the exact parameters and processes that define this era.[1] The fundamental assumption of this book is that, however defined, the current age of globalization did not begin with the fall of the Berlin Wall or the invention of the microchip. Rather, this era was made possible and in many ways was defined by earlier globalizing events, such as those of "the Age of Steam and Print."[2] In using this phrase in the title of this book, we do not seek to add another vague abstraction to debates about globalization. For if in its cultural, commercial, or even epidemiological aspects, globalization is an outcome of intensified and accelerated interactions, then the basic enablers of such interaction must be placed at the center of analysis.[3] During much of the nineteenth and early twentieth centuries, the two most fundamental—and indeed, most global—of these enablers were the technologies of steam and print. Whether through quickening the production and distribution of commodities, facilitating mass migrations and private pilgrimages, or disseminating learned tracts and proletarian newspapers worldwide, these technologies were prime movers that set in motion further cycles of human interaction. By focusing on steam and print, we are better able to discern a specific phase of global history that is set apart from the more nebulous periods of "modernity/early modernity" on the one hand and unqualified "globalization" on the other.

In relation to what came before, what was distinctive about this period was the sheer scale of interaction that technology enabled, in terms of both the numbers of people moving across land and sea and the range of ethnic, religious, and language groups now able to print, publicize and exchange their ideas. Because the defining technologies emerged from European and American societies (albeit with precursors elsewhere), the notion of an Age of Steam and Print by necessity connects the history of Euro-American societies to that of other (in this case, Muslim) societies. If the Age of Steam and Print was therefore an intrinsically global age, for Muslims it was also an age of discovery and differentiation, creativity and crisis. Muslims discovered both other Muslim and non-Muslim societies, defined themselves in relation to these contacts, and synthesized new ideologies and rethought older doctrines. The Age of Steam and Print was the foundational sine qua non of the contemporary Islamic world.

When, though, did this "age" begin, and when did it end? In Islamic regions and elsewhere, the Age of Steam and Print can be dated from around 1850 to 1930. This period intersects with what is commonly referred to as "the long nineteenth century," though the latter both begins and ends earlier. Since our study highlights the technological rather than the political or military, we focus on the mid-nineteenth century, when the global diffusion of enabling technologies began, through 1930, when automobile and air travel, along with telephonic and televisual/radio communications, ushered in a new (because more intensified) phase of globalization. Indeed, the phase of interaction that followed the Age of Steam and Print—a period of decolonization, economic nationalism, ideological contestation, and Third World assertion that closed in the 1970s—was not merely subsequent to that age but was both its apotheosis and its logical culmination.[4]

The year 1850 also marked the beginning of the Second Industrial Revolution. In terms of steam, we are therefore dealing with the era of railroads and of oceanic rather than river steamship travel. And although print technology had been around since the days of Johannes Gutenberg, it is important to recognize the reinvention of printing that occurred during the industrial nineteenth century. As we shall see in more detail below, it was through the distribution of mass-produced iron Stanhope presses and the spread of lithographic (or, as the process was originally known, chemical) printing—first introduced to the Islamic world in 1820 but not in widespread use until about 1850—that the Islamic world came to feel the full effects of the Gutenberg (or even Stanhope) revolution.[5] Once again, the broader parameters of these processes were global, for Muslims were first exposed to steam travel and print technology at the same time as non-Muslim peoples in Africa, South and Central Asia, and Australasia.[6] The Muslim story is therefore part of a larger, global history told from a non-Western perspective, albeit one that must recognize the transformative impact of Western technologies and the power they lent their controllers.

The model of an Age of Steam and Print therefore allows us to frame the temporal parameters and technological processes that defined the realm of the possible during a particular phase of global history, although these processes by no means determined the outcomes. Looking at this phase of history through the lens of these two technologies points to another aspect of the period. This was, after all, an age of increasing Western domination of the globe, and these two technologies not only emerged from the West but continued to be constructed in and sold by the West as its technological, commercial, political, and military powers expanded worldwide. However, focusing on these technologies also highlights the fundamental problem of ascribing agency solely to one part of the globe. Technologies are simply tools, and once tools leave the workshop their inventors can no longer determine how they will be used. Soon after he patented his telegraph in 1847, Samuel F. B. Morse predicted that his invention would "annihilat[e] space and time . . . bringing mankind into a common brotherhood." Little did he foresee that the telegraph would become an indispensible tool both for imperial reassertion in the Ottoman and (to a lesser extent) Qajar Persian Empires and, along with the steamship and the Gatling gun, for the spread and maintenance of informal and formal European empires.[7] In the same vein, it seems unlikely that such steamboat pioneers as Thomas Dundas and Robert Fulton imagined that their inventions would enable more Muslims to make the hajj than had gone in the previous twelve centuries, but this is precisely what took place. Likewise, the spread of Western technologies among Muslim communities enabled an assortment of Muslim intellectuals and activists to disseminate their ideas and mobilize the general population around them. The "controllers" of technology were by no means always the representatives of the colonial powers. Muslims worldwide quickly adopted "the tools of empire," to borrow a phrase from Daniel Headrick's well-known study, for purposes that their initial inventors and disseminators did not intend.[8] As later chapters in this volume show, with regard to printing presses, steamships, and even mass-produced weapons, the circulating tools of empire were not only tools for imperialists.

Rather than tell a simple story of imperial hegemony or technological determinism, the chapters that follow recount a tremendous variety of Muslim responses to a world transformed. Some of these responses were in the realm of ideas that ranged from the self-consciously "modernist" to the no less self-consciously "traditionalist."[9] Others were in the realm of economics, including the commodification of cultural production and the adoption of new forms of production and distribution and hybrid forms of economic exploitation. Although the Age of Steam and Print had certain uniform parameters and even structures (whether the stopping points on steamship routes or the medium of newspaper reports), there were no predetermined, uniform, or teleological outcomes.

Steam and print also enabled Muslims to redefine the geographies they inhabited, on both the concrete and conceptual levels.[10] Old travel routes gave way to steam routes whose nodes were newly industrialized or colonized port cities such as Port Said, Aden, Beirut, Bombay, Singapore, and Mombasa, or for that matter London, Marseilles, Rio de Janeiro, and Yokohama. Old knowledge centers similarly declined in importance when faced with competition from new centers of printing, which commonly overlapped with hubs for steam transportation (Cairo and Lucknow, perhaps, being the rare exceptions to the rule). For Muslim and other global citizens, steam and print were geographically coterminous technologies which in turn triggered transformations in the conceptual arenas of religion, politics, and culture. Port cities were often the bridgeheads for the power of print as well steam.

In a sense, Muslim thinkers have always worked with categories of global scale: Throughout history, Muslim clerics have conceived of a universal Muslim community, or *umma*. Yet if the intellectual genealogy of the umma stretches back to the beginnings of Islam, then the notion of an "Islamic world" is of much more recent provenance and cannot be equated with its antecedent. As far as the evidence suggests, it appears that the latter formulation first appeared in the period with which this book is concerned. That age saw the global dissemination of the term through a polyglottal range of publications, from the American missionary periodical *The Moslem World* (1911), which was edited in Cairo but published in New York, to the Turkish, Urdu, and Arabic newspaper *Jahan-i Islam* (Istanbul, 1914), the German-language journal *Die Islamische Welt* (Berlin, 1916), and the expatriate Urdu magazine *Islami Dunya* (Cairo, 1929).[11] It was also a time when Muslims were increasingly subjected to the Western gaze through imperial projects, professionalized academic disciplines, and the mass tourism of the Thomas Cook Company, which briefly even ventured into the hajj business. Muslim communities were subsumed within the post-Enlightenment categories of "culture" and "civilization"—categories in turn adopted, and adapted, by Muslim scholars themselves (and sometimes in spite of themselves).[12] Like such terms as *farhang* (Persian for "culture") and *medeniyet* (Turkish for "civilization"), the concept of an Islamic world is a product of a specific and relatively recent conjuncture, when steam and print allowed for the synthesis of new social imaginaries, which were in turn validated by new social practices.

On the most fundamental level, these new social practices resulted from a broadening and deepening of the twin systems identified with the modern period: the world system of nation-states and the modern world economic system. The nation-state system came to Islamic regions in two ways: In such cases as India, Indonesia, Transcaucasia, and the Transjordanian frontier, the structures and institutions associated with the nation-state were imposed by nonindigenous rulers throughout their overseas and continental empires. However, in the Egypt of Mehmet Ali, the Tunisia of Ahmad Bey, and the Ottoman Empire during and subsequent to the *tanzimat* (reorganization) period, local rulers directly borrowed instruments of governance from Europe to strengthen state power and protect the domains they governed from outside interference. Whatever the efficacy of individual programs initiated by colonial powers or indigenous potentates, the disciplinary and representational regimens they imposed engaged populations in practices that reinforced the notion that those populations were real or potential citizen-participants in unified societies and that those societies had discrete histories and transhistorical identities of their own.

The world economic system also came to Muslim regions as a result of exogenous factors (such as informal and formal imperialism) and indigenous factors (such as the pull of the market). As Immanuel Wallerstein and several generations of world-systems theorists have pointed out, a hierarchical structure and a transnational division of labor defined this system, unlike the systems that had preceded it. Neither this structure nor division of labor worked to the benefit of worldwide Muslims, either postcontact or postintegration. In 1750, states outside Europe and North America accounted for 73 percent of world manufacturing; by 1913 that share had dropped to 7.5 percent. To cite a specific example, in the eighteenth century the Indian textile industry was unrivalled in both quality and quantity of production and exports. By the end of the century, India imported more than 70 percent of its textiles.[13] Of course, the effects of what world-systems analysts call integration and peripheralization were uneven, and as often as not, these processes solidified retrograde labor relationships, such as slavery, not usually associated with a capitalist system. Nevertheless, market, enclave, and mixed economies catering to a trade in primary commodities replaced marketplace economies in many Muslim regions.

The impact of the expanding world economy was as momentous as it was unforeseeable. Driven by new markets and increasing profits, Egyptians planted cotton and Iranians cultivated opium. Thus it an event at Appomattox Court House in Virginia could wreak havoc on the Egyptian economy; the discovery of the Comstock Lode in Nevada and the exploitation of the Albert Mine in Bronkhorstspruit, South Africa, could devastate a silver-based Persian economy that had been buoyed by wars between Britain and China; and Muslim communities worldwide would feel the toxic effects of the global depression of 1873.[14] Even so, these effects were uneven too: the economies of inland cities associated with the caravan trade declined (as in Bukhara) while the economies of port cities boomed (as in Bombay). Peasant and tribal labor was increasingly a commodity to be bought and sold as landlords and tribal leaders profited from cultivating cash crops. So was the labor of women wherever the household economy lost ground. And even as the Ottoman Empire and its province of Egypt declared separate bankruptcies in 1875 and 1876, respectively, and as European creditors subjected their budgets to oversight, certain groups of Muslim traders grew wealthy as middlemen, particularly in regions where they had formerly been predominant, such as the vast littoral of the Indian Ocean.[15]

GLOBAL MUSLIM STEAM TRAVEL

One of the defining features of the Age of Steam and Print was the contraction of space through swifter and cheaper travel.[16] This led to the diffusion of ideas, techniques, commodities, and technologies with an unprecedented rapidity across a span of unparalleled breadth. It took no more than a few decades for James Watt's steam engine to be harnessed for practical purposes in the form of steamships and railroads. Steam-powered boats were being tested in Britain as early as 1801, when William Symington successfully crossed a Scottish loch in his *Charlotte Dundas*.[17] By 1812 the first regular steamship service in Europe had begun, although the adaptation of the boats from their early lake and river runs to the stronger currents of the high seas presented huge mechanical problems. As a result, when the first steamship passage was made from Britain to India, in 1825, it was achieved more through sailing than steaming, proving to investors for several decades that middle-distance journeys were more feasible.[18] Even so, these middle distances were in many cases between cosmopolitan port cities—Bombay, Suez, Istanbul, Beirut, Singapore, Hong Kong, Marseilles, London—where Muslims congregated in increasing numbers.[19]

With the adaptation of the screw propeller, iron plating, and the compound engine around 1880, far larger steamships were able to sail on smaller quantities of coal, resulting in cheap intercontinental travel for larger numbers of passengers. Oceanic travel was no longer reliant on and regulated by the rhythm of the monsoons. It was now governed by the ever-rolling propellers of the ocean liners. Industrial travel revolutionized oceanic time, replacing the uncertain schedules of the monsoon winds—the *mawsim*, or season, of the old Arab navigators—with the tabulated departures of the P&O steamer. This age of capacious ocean liners and secondhand tramp steamers, sailed by the motley international crews described in the novels of Joseph Conrad, transformed the lives of African and Asian Muslims no less than those of European Jews and Christians. Cheap tickets on such vessels enabled migration and pilgrimage, trade and tourism, in ways that were out of reach a generation before.[20] The construction and use of steamships (and, as we shall see, railroads) expanded with extraordinary speed, in large measure because they were quintessential tools of empire. Only two decades after Symington tested his *Charlotte Dundas* in Scotland, steamboats were plying the Hooghly River in India, and by mid-century there was regular steam service on the Black Sea, on the Caspian Sea, on the Tigris and Euphrates Rivers, and in the Persian Gulf.[21] As a result, the Ottoman Empire and Persia were able to enjoy the "full benefits" of the commercial treaties imposed on them by Russia and Britain.

Railroads followed a similar trajectory. The first practical railroad was built in 1825. Fifteen years later there were four thousand kilometers (2,485 miles) of rail worldwide; by World War I there were one million (621,371 miles), including four thousand kilometers in Egypt and another six thousand (3,728 miles) in the rest of the Ottoman Empire.[22] India was particularly prominent in the expansion of rail travel. The first railroad in Asia opened in Bombay in 1853, and by 1900 there were almost forty thousand kilometers (24,855 miles) of track across India.[23] The Trans-Siberian Railway, completed in 1916, was a similar feat in the Russian Empire.[24] Cheap rail and steamship travel allowed Muslims to discover the world with unprecedented ease. To take just one example, during the Age of Steam and Print the Siberian Tatar ʿAbd al-Rashid Ibrahim crisscrossed Eurasia on the Russian, British Indian, and Ottoman imperial rail networks. In the course of his journeys, he helped found a pan-Islamist newspaper and the first mosque in Japan and met Muslims in every port from Hong Kong to Bombay, where he successfully converted a Japanese man, with whom he then made the hajj via steamer. Soon thereafter, he moved via the Hijaz Railway to Istanbul, where he printed the long tale of his travels in Turkish.[25]

The effects of steam travel were varied for both Muslims themselves and the Islam they practiced. One of the most widely observed transformations was the massive increase in the numbers of Muslims making the hajj, particularly those traveling from such regions as India and the Malay archipelago.[26] Not only did this spark the emergence and spread of religious and quasi-religious movements, from pan-Islamism to varieties of Sufism,[27] but the sheer number of Muslims converging on Mecca from so many regions became a major factor in the global spread of cholera from the 1830s onward, forcing Muslims to confront in medical or theological terms the globalized diseases of the nineteenth century.[28] Contagion resulting from the overcrowding of poorer passengers on ocean crossings triggered new forms of religious writings, including maritime hagiographies celebrating Muslim holy men capable of curing outbreaks of cholera aboard steamships.[29] In such ways, the steam-powered hajj encouraged the creation of cults venerating these holy men as well as Mecca-centric religious uniformity.[30]

The advent of railroads and steamships also made Muslim societies accessible to European adventurers, missionaries, settlers, scholars, and tourists (a term coined in the second decade of the nineteenth century).[31] In some cases, as with the British Arabist Edward Lane (1801–76), evidence survives of European correspondence in Arabic and other Islamic languages with Muslim scholars.[32] For our purposes, the more important traffic took place in the opposite direction. Rifaʿa al-Tahtawi (1801–73), for example, led the first Egyptian educational mission to Paris, in 1826, and on his return home oversaw the translation of French works into Arabic at the School of Languages that had been founded for that purpose.[33] Around the same time, the Persian government sponsored two parties of students who spent almost five years in England learning languages, printing, medicine, and cannon founding. Returning to Persia, they became the touchstone for later generations who also imported European learning and technology.[34]

As a result of these new connections, innovative hybrid schools appeared in other Muslim regions. These included the Dar al-Funun polytechnic (which housed one of the most important printing presses in Persia), founded in Tehran in 1851 on the French model, and the Muhammadan Anglo-Oriental College, founded in 1875 at Aligarh in North India and modeled on Oxford in its architecture no less than in its syllabi.[35] Muslim proponents of scientific learning were joined by those interested in applying European-style educational techniques to the transmission of the traditional sciences. In such new madrassas as that founded at Deoband, India, in 1866, the instructors of scripture, Hadith, and law adopted such Eurogenic techniques as prescheduled classes, written examinations, and visiting examiners to test their charges.[36] Over the following decades, this madrassa developed a large network of subsidiary schools, whose classes were enabled by mass-produced printed textbooks.

Many Muslim travelers wrote in praise of various aspects of technology. According to Albert Hourani, Tahtawi was so enamored of the marvels of the age that he wrote a poem extolling the virtues of the steam engine, in the process joining the ranks of those like Samuel F. B. Morse who predicted—and continue to predict—a reign of universal peace as the result of the invention of one gadget or another.[37] In his Persian-language account of his journey from Hyderabad to England in 1888, the Indian grand tourist La'iq 'Ali Khan, Salar Jang II (1868–89), wrote elegiacally of a Bombay hotel built entirely of iron, of the engine room of the steamship *Peshawar*, and of the fountain pen and rifle factories he toured in the industrial city of Birmingham.[38] Travel as a means to access and experience technology was a major theme of the new Muslim literature of actual and imagined travel that emerged in the Age of Steam and Print. In the years either side of 1900, the modernist Muslim reformers Ahmad Ihsan Tokgöz (1868–1942), an Ottoman, and the Afghan Mahmud Tarzi (1865–1933) even translated into Turkish and Persian, respectively, the *voyages fantastiques* novels of Jules Verne, which celebrate steam and electrical technologies through the journeys of such characters as Phileas Fogg and Captain Nemo.[39]

The flip side of this infatuation with technology was a current of Muslim anti-technologism that was self-consciously framed in Islamic terms.[40] The Damascus-based advocates of a neoorthodox Islam, for example, protested against the inevitable mixing of men and women in railroad cars that would follow the expansion of the Ottoman rail system in Syria, the use of the telegraph to relay the sighting of the new moon that signals the start of Ramadan, the simplification of the holy language of Arabic necessitated by the spread of print media and telegraphy, and the digging of an artesian well for their home city, which would oblige Muslims to violate the Qur'anic injunction against drinking from stagnant pools. Yet they did all this on the pages of a printed newspaper circulated to influence public opinion.[41]

Technological change was not just a marvel for Muslims to behold; it provided useful tools to be exploited. Rail and steam enabled the expansion of trade and migration to a degree never before achieved. In the 1830s it took forty-eight days to travel from Liverpool to New York under sail and thirty-six days to return. With steam, the voyage took fourteen days each way. As a result of greater speed and capacity, the cost of shipping a bushel of wheat from New York to Liverpool halved between 1830 and 1880, then halved again between 1880 and 1913.[42] The decline of transport costs stimulated increased trade during the nineteenth century by a factor of twenty. By enabling the exploitation of previously unexploitable areas, by integrating local and regional markets, by connecting those markets to markets worldwide, and by reducing costs and travel time, rail and steam joined most of the Islamic world to the world economy. Responding to the economic disruptions of the American Civil War, both khedival Egypt and tsarist Central Asia emerged as globalized cotton economies. In the former case, income from cotton exports underwrote the Egyptian subscription to the Suez Canal, which halved the travel distance between Liverpool and Bombay. In reducing the number of and distance between coaling stations en route from Europe to India and points east, the canal has been credited with driving the final nail into the coffin of the Age of Sail.[43] The technological and educational infrastructure that Egypt's short-lived boom afforded rendered it, for a brief period, a kind of modernist Muslim utopia for travelers from other (particularly colonized) regions, such as the Indian intellectual Shibli Nuʿmani (1857–1914), who visited Egypt in 1892.[44] In Russian Central Asia, the transformations of technology and economy inspired modernist religious reform among groups of educated Muslims who self-consciously named themselves Jadid, or New, Muslims.[45]

Steam-powered transport and the resulting contraction of distance also set loose the greatest period of migration in human history. Before the nineteenth century, enslaved Africans made up the vast majority of long-distance travelers, followed distantly by a small rivulet of merchants, settlers, and others. During the nineteenth century that rivulet turned into a torrent. On the one hand, there was the pull of new territories opened up for settlement, as well as the pull of a global labor market. On the other hand, there was the push of more-intrusive states demanding more of their populations, ethnonationalist conflicts, demographic pressures, and a twenty-five-year-long agricultural depression. Demographers have identified three main paths taken by nineteenth-century migrants. The best known carried fifty-five to fifty-eight million Europeans to North America between 1870 and 1940. During the same period, however, almost as many migrants traveled from India and southern China to Southeast Asia, the Indian Ocean rim, and the South Pacific, and from northeastern Asia and Russia to Manchuria, Siberia, Central Asia, and Japan. Some of this migration was undertaken by free labor; much was not. By the start of the twentieth century, eleven million Chinese had settled in the British-controlled Straits Settlements, three million Italians and French were in North Africa, three hundred thousand Persian workers resided in

Baku, four to six million Muslims had entered the Ottoman Empire from South-east Europe and Russia, and as much as a third of the population of Mount Lebanon had decamped elsewhere in one of the highest emigration rates in the world.[46]

Syrians and Lebanese mingled with Italy's single largest nineteenth-century export—anarchists—in Beirut, Cairo, Alexandria, and Rio de Janeiro, as well as New Jersey and Massachusetts.[47] Levantines thus came to participate in a global radical movement—really more of an ethos than a movement—that emerged in opposition to the nation-state and world-economic systems. Some of these migrants returned home; others found permanent residence abroad. Eighty per cent of the Persians who worked in Baku's oil fields rotated home, bringing with them experiences gleaned from the Russian social democratic and trade union movements. They made the northern Persian city of Tabriz one of the two epicenters of the 1905 Persian constitutional revolution.[48]

Ideologies enabled by capitalism, such as trade unionism and social democracy, and those that opposed it, such as anarchism, provided unprecedented foundations for claims to social justice in Muslim regions worldwide. Other ideologies also spread in response to the social and political disjunctures of the age. Hence, constitutionalism in the Ottoman Empire and Persia, and nationalist movements any-where touched by the worldwide spread of the nation-state system.[49] Feminism also enjoyed its mythic founding moment in Africa during the Age of Steam and Print, when three Egyptian feminists—Huda Shaarawi (1879–1947), Saiza Nabarawi (1897–?), and Nabawiyya Musa (1886–1951)—publically unveiled after returning home from a feminist conference in Rome in 1923. (In fact, the roots of feminism in Egypt—and elsewhere in the Islamic world—might be traced back another three decades or so.)[50] In some cases—such as the aforementioned spread, in tandem, of constitutionalism in Russia and Persia—ideologies followed migratory routes. (The peculiarity of the assumption underlying constitutionalism—that the only way to reverse imperial decay is to compel rulers to enter into written contracts with their subjects—along with the timing of events in Russia and Persia makes the diffusion of this idea across borders at least as likely as its independent invention within them.) In other cases—such as feminism and the synthesis of particular nationalist movements—travel and transnational contacts delivered content to movements whose social and cultural foundations might be found at home. Hence, for example, Indian and Egyptian nationalist exiles living in London, Paris, Brussels, Geneva, and elsewhere forged collaborative bonds and shared ideas and strategies before returning home to struggle against their common enemy.[51] Hence also, as we have seen, the connection between the celebrated birth of Egyptian feminism and the convergence of feminists from around the globe in Rome.

While the spread of constitutional and even secularist ideas was one outcome of migration, the dissemination and reproduction or adaptation of customary social and religious forms was another. In the second half of the nineteenth century, for example, Afghans began migrating to Australia, where they took advantage of their long expertise in overland trade to establish—by camel—the first trans-Australian transport route.[52] When the transcontinental railroad eventually came to Australia, it was dubbed "the Ghan" in their memory. In Durban and Singapore, Muslim immigrants re-created the cults of saints they had venerated at home.[53] In the Caribbean, indentured laborers from India adopted carnivalesque forms for the performance of their Muharram rites.[54] The experience of travel by increasing numbers of Muslims from different classes and regions and with different educations and agendas triggered the invention of a multiplicity of old/new social patterns, religious practices, and traditions.

In 1841 the Catholic traditionalist François-René de Chateaubriand wrote, "When steam power will be perfected, when together with telegraphy and railways, it will have made distances disappear, it will not only be commodities which travel, but also ideas which will have wings."[55] The reactionary Chateaubriand would not have been amused to discover that those winged ideas descended on Beirut in 1909 in the form of a play celebrating the life and work of the Spanish anarchist Francisco Ferrer, or that steam power enabled an Ottoman representative to join his comrades at the founding of the Second International in 1889.[56] Steam travel likewise enabled new Sufi networks to expand, many through itineraries identical to those of steamships. Such wider itineraries brought together strange companions, not only enabling the Sudanese shaykh Ahmad Muhammad Surkitti (d. 1943) to establish himself as a religious authority in distant Southeast Asia but also making it possible for the Iranian Sufi Hajji Pirzada (d. 1904) to converse with the Orientalist E. G. Browne in the drawing rooms of Cambridge.[57] Individual travelers, as well as and groups of migrant laborers forged enclave communities throughout the world, including those of Iranians in Istanbul and of Indians and Indonesians in Cairo. From these cities, their expatriate journals in their native languages connected Muslims globally.[58] The new multiethnic and self-consciously Muslim communities that formed in such cities as London and Berlin around the start of the twentieth century also contributed books and journals in English and German to the new global Islamic public sphere.[59] For the first time the languages of Europe were rendered part of the linguistic currency of Islam.

GLOBAL MUSLIM PRINTING

While Muslims had experimented with printing as early as the eighteenth century (the most famous example being Ibrahim Müteferrika [1674–1745] in Istanbul), they began using print technology in a sustained way only in the early 1800s, as a result of increased interaction with Europe. Although Europeans had sponsored Arabic, Turkish, and Persian printing in such cities as Cairo, Kazan, and Calcutta between the 1780s and 1800s, it was not until Arab and Iranian journeymen traveled to

Europe that printing technology transferred into Muslim hands in Iran and Egypt, around 1820.[60] In more distant Calcutta and Lucknow in India and Singapore and Riau in Southeast Asia, pioneer Muslim printers such as Munshi ʿAbdullah (1796–1854) acquired printing skills from commercial or missionary presses closer to home. In 1817–18, Muslim printing ventures simultaneously appeared hundreds of miles apart, in Cairo, Tabriz, and Lucknow. During the ensuing decades, the spread of cheap, mass-produced printing presses modeled on the Stanhope iron handpress of 1801 extended the reach of print even farther.[61] Although print technology—from presses and type to machine-made paper and lithographic stones quarried in Solenhofen, Bavaria—was a by-product of the Industrial Revolution in Europe, Muslims swiftly adapted it to their needs.

Some scholars have argued that print had a "protestantizing" effect on Muslim religiosity, allowing individuals to interpret on their own Qur'ans that frequently had been translated into local languages.[62] There is no doubt that the distribution of cheap, printed Qur'ans did at times result in lay interpretations of scripture, which occasionally provoked scandal, particularly when those interpretations pertained to women's issues. When a Beiruti Druze woman, Nazira Zain al-Din (1905?–1976?), argued in print in 1928 that only a particularly misogynistic interpretation of Islamic law could support veiling, public protests erupted and she joined the ranks of other vilified feminists, such as the Baghdadi poet and essayist Jamil Sidqi al-Zahawi (1863–1936) and the Tunisian socialist al-Tahir al-Haddad (1899–1935), whose arguments also drew from printed copies of Islam's foundational texts. (One of al-Zahawi's polemics, written in Baghdad, was first published in an Egyptian newspaper and critiqued one month later in a Syrian journal that cited sociological data on divorce in Massachusetts, Pennsylvania, and California to bolster its demand that Islamic traditions be observed.)[63]

In the first decades of the twentieth century, printing enabled both charismatic and reformist Muslims to disseminate their messages. This was in large measure a result of the mass production of printing machines, as from about 1850 the technology began to spread to a far wider range of commercial and religious organizations. But there was another side to the story. Print also became a powerful weapon in the hands of rulers seeking better control over their subjects through the standardization of their beliefs and practices and through the promulgation of official, religiously tinged nationalisms. Such attempts at control were certainly evident in the Ottoman Empire of Abdulhamid II, who took the title of caliph and promoted an Ottoman-Islamic nationalism. During his reign (1876–1909), the state sponsored missionary activity to convert antinomian Sufis and heterodox Muslims to the officially sanctioned Hanafi rite of Sunni Islam. It also made the printing of the Qur'an a state monopoly and established a Commission for the Inspection of Qur'ans, which was overseen by the office of the highest imperial religious official, the shaykh al-Islam in Istanbul. In at least one case, the sultan himself used his personal funds to underwrite the cost of printing these Qur'ans, which were then distributed gratis at the request of a provincial governor. The state supported the publication of a variety of other books as well—four thousand in the first fifteen years of Abdulhamid II's reign alone. These included not only classic Islamic legal and religious texts but also works that the state associated with Islamic culture, such as epics depicting the exploits of Muslim heroes like Saladin.[64]

Three characteristics of the Muslim print revolution are particularly germane to our concerns. First, beginning around 1850 the number of newspapers published by Muslims—many of whom were political exiles or living in enclave communities—increased dramatically, in line with the globalizing trajectories of the age. For example, between 1908 and the end of 1916, forty-one daily newspapers and seven journals competed for readership in Damascus, a significant increase from the three daily newspapers and two journals published in the city during the final three decades of the nineteenth century.[65] Persian-language newspapers circulating during this period ranged from the *Qanun* (Law) published in London by the exiled reformist Mirza Malkum Khan (1833–1908) to the *Akhtar-e Istanbul* (Istanbul Star) published in the large Iranian community of Istanbul in the late 1800s.[66] Not only did New World cities such as Boston, Buenos Aires, Tucumán (Argentina), and Rio de Janeiro host Arabic-language newspapers, but during World War I New York alone had at least five.[67] And in distant Tokyo the globetrotting Indian pan-Islamist Muhammad Barakatullah (1854–1927) published his English-language journal, *Islamic Fraternity*, from 1909 to 1913.[68] Printed in a wide variety of languages and typically using newly simplified idioms designed, in large measure, to reach a broader public, the newspapers created a transnational public sphere where news of world events and the fortunes of other communities of Muslims could be disseminated.

This revolution also fostered the creation of information hubs in cities where print was concentrated. Often these were port cities, such as Beirut, Istanbul, and, to a lesser extent, Alexandria and Valletta, which few would have identified as centers of Islamic learning in earlier periods. Bombay and Singapore, with their large and diverse oceanic marketplaces of Muslim readers and with transportation links to other port cities throughout the Indian Ocean, became major producers of books for export. These books were in languages ranging from Arabic, Persian, Urdu, and Swahili to Gujarati, Malay, Javanese, and Arabic-script Tamil. It was a testament to the globalization of printed knowledge that as often as not, Malay books were printed in Bombay and Tamil books in Singapore.

Finally, the Muslim print revolution enabled new religious movements to disseminate their messages and compete with more-established groups, which were, in many cases, slower to adapt to the new era of printed knowledge. These developments too had global provenance. Best known, perhaps, was the case of the Mediterranean-based Salafi movement and its journal *Al-Manar*, which found an audience as far away as Southeast Asia.[69] No less ambitious than the reformists in their use of print were new charismatic and even messianic groups. Among them were many Sufi organizations that printed hagiographical advertisements of the miraculous powers of their saints for popular readerships.[70] From the 1880s the North Indian Muslim renewer (*mujaddid*) and messiah (*masih*) Mirza Ghulam Ahmad (1835–1908) took advantage of the culture of cheap print introduced by missionaries and reformists to announce his message of revelation to the world.[71] Through vernacular newspaper advertisements, printed forms used by adherents to pledge their allegiance, and scores of stern treatises, he poured out his revelations across continents and oceans. His expansive reach points to the extraordinary potential of printing to bring new Muslim movements from, for example, the provinces of India to a worldwide audience. It points no less to a process that Alfred Gell has called "the enchantment of technology," by which charismatic no less than reformist Muslim groups were able to make use of the new technologies.[72]

MUSLIM EXPERIENCES IN THE AGE OF STEAM AND PRINT

This book presents twelve case studies, divided into three parts. The first part deals with the creation of new communities and networks in varying political contexts during the Age of Steam and Print. The expansion of a Western-dominated world order had diverse effects on the Islamic world, from the decline of the indigenous Muslim sultanates of Southeast Asia and the waning of the Ottoman Empire's ability to project power abroad to the creation of heterogenous Muslim communities in British imperial port cities and the emergence of a far-flung Syro-Lebanese diaspora. In each case, Muslims and the non-Muslim and heterodox populations that lived among them were obliged to reconceptualize their relationships to one another and to the outside world. In some cases, they took what might be termed a traditionalist course, falling back on familiar structures—no matter how much changing circumstances might have transformed the meaning and function of those structures. In other cases, they consciously adapted those structures to the brave new world in which they found themselves. In still others, they attempted to redefine or even abolish communal boundaries, finding community in a far-flung empire of the mind or even in the global order—both of which the world of steam and print enabled.

Michael Laffan's chapter examines the debates surrounding Sufi practices in Indonesia during the Age of Steam and Print. These debates took place within an emerging Muslim public sphere inside and outside Indonesia in the context of new technologies, particularly printing. The chapter closely reads those debates to trace their role in defining an Islamic Indonesia that was reintegrated into a transnational Islamic framework and integrated into the global economy. As a result of the Sufi orders' connections to the Middle East and use of print, they not only engaged with a newly constituted public but also created audiences for later Islamic reformers.

Amal Ghazal probes the centrality of networks of religious reform in the formation and continuity of a transnational Muslim identity. Using the life of Sulayman al-Baruni (1870–1940), an Ibadi from the Nafusa Mountains in Tripolitania, to encapsulate the linkages among Salafism, pan-Islamism, and globalization, Ghazal argues that discourses of Islamic religious reform allowed for the development of a Muslim identity that transcended parochial sectarian identities and embraced a more encompassing cosmopolitanism. Thus, for al-Baruni the end of the Ottoman Empire meant the replacement of an imperial identity with a pan-Islamic one.

Focusing on the British settlement of Aden, Scott S. Reese examines the development of Muslim communities in spaces that imperial rule created. In particular, he explores how individual Muslims from widely disparate backgrounds brought together by the networks of empire created a cohesive community using the one commonality at their disposal: Islam. According to Reese, religious institutions and ideas served as the framework for the creation of community and provided the kinds of symbolic capital that people needed to attain influence as "leading Muslims" within the confines of empire.

Ilham Khuri-Makdisi looks at a very different phenomenon of the Age of Steam and Print. In the late nineteenth and early twentieth centuries, radical leftist ideas began circulating in Cairo and Alexandria. These adaptations of socialist and anarchist principles included calls for social justice, workers' rights, and mass secular education, challenging the existing sociopolitical order at home and abroad. Khuri-Makdisi focuses on two particular networks that espoused leftist ideas: an Arab diasporic network of intellectuals exchanging ideas between Egypt, Brazil, and North America, and an Italian anarchist network active in Egypt. While most network members were non-Muslims, they were pivotal in disseminating leftist ideas in a predominantly Muslim society.

The expansion of the world economic system in the Age of Steam and Print, along with the spread of European empires, unleashed an unprecedented period of linkage and exchange among peoples of the globe. In terms of the novelty of commodities that changed hands, the age is rivaled only by the Columbian Exchange, which began in the last years of the fifteenth century. In terms of their quantity and the number of people involved in their production and trade, no other era comes close. The exchange of goods and the movement of people had dramatic cultural and social consequences for the Islamic world, ranging from the commodification of cultural products and the spread of mass cultures and a global genteel cosmopolitanism, through the introduction of new relationships of labor and the reintroduction of retrograde ones, to the enforcement of new norms of sanitation and public health that came in response to new epidemics and new paradigms of sanitation and epidemiology. These topics are the subject of the second section of this book, "Contagions and Commodities."

In the first chapter of this section, Eric Tagliacozzo examines the nexus between the hajj and health through the lens of cholera, which traveled on steamships transporting pilgrims to Mecca from Southeast Asia. During the Age of Steam and Print, millions of hajjis made this journey by ship, and the prospect of contagion traveling with them became one of the great health issues of the late nineteenth and early twentieth centuries. The fight against cholera on the hajj was global in scope, since the disease was terrifying to behold and Europeans feared its spread to the West. Contagion intersected with the age in two ways: the dangers posed by rapid diffusion of disease, and the globalization of distinctly European forms of biopower.

Robert Crews looks at the global arms trade and the clandestine activities that knitted together manufacturers, traders, and consumers in the Islamic world and elsewhere around the globe between the 1880s and 1920s. His chapter reconstructs the activities of a diverse collection of individuals involved in the trade, from German gunmakers, Belgian commercial intermediaries, administrators of British steamship companies, and Persian officials to Afghan nomads, Armenian revolutionaries, and Persian racketeers. From Birmingham in the English Midlands to Dera Isma'il Khan on the Afghan-Indian frontier and from Tbilisi in the Caucasus Mountains to Bandar 'Abbas on the Persian Gulf, the circuits that gave shape to the arms trade were shifting and dynamic. And like other commodities, guns took on new meanings in particular cultural contexts, even as these networks tied communities to the worldwide flow of illicit goods.

Ann E. Lucas focuses on another commodity from the Age of Steam and Print: music. Around the time when the Persian constitutional movement was gaining traction, Qajar court musicians popularized their unique style of musical practice, promoting it through their institutions for education and performance. By doing so, they placed their music at the center of Persia/Iran's emerging national consciousness. The arrival of the gramophone and music companies from Europe further encouraged these new initiatives by enabling the preservation and sharing of music by Iranian musicians. Overall, the efforts of both the musicians and their sponsors created a canon, privileging a particular group and their practice, as a distinct Persian "national music," which played a key role in the formulation of a Persian/Iranian national identity.

In the final chapter of this section, Matthew S. Hopper examines the global dimensions of the Arabian date trade from the mid-nineteenth century through the third decade of the twentieth century. Arabian dates had fed Indian Ocean markets for hundreds of years, but in the early nineteenth century, American merchants helped globalize the trade by bringing dates from Oman to the United States. While Americans offered new sources of wealth for producers, they could not dictate terms of trade and were dependent on local merchants' knowledge. Ultimately, the same forces of globalization that brought Arabian dates to new global markets also led to the demise of the trade. For the very technologies that made date shipments to the United States possible enabled American producers to bring offshoots of Arabian palms to California, eliminating the need for imported dates.

In the final section of the book, "Nodes and Routes," the contributors narrow their gazes to a single text or corpus of texts to access the big picture of one of our key themes: the effects on intellectual production of the transformations brought about by steam and print. In particular, this section looks at intellectual cross-fertilization, the transformation of subjectivities, and the reconstruction of identity and remembrance fostered by print and translation, travel and migration, in the Age of Steam and Print.

In the first chapter of this section, Ronit Ricci looks at the ways the small Malay community in Sri Lanka at the turn of the twentieth century imagined and remembered Java's Islamization. Dating back to the mid-seventeenth century, this community maintained its Muslim-Malay identity through an adherence to the Malay language and its rich tradition of literary production. By focusing on the "Hikayat Tuan Gusti," a Sri Lankan manuscript composed in Arabic-script Malay in 1897, Ricci explores Sri Lankan Malay Muslims' reimagination of and attachment to experiences of an earlier era of globalization in the context of a later one.

Turning from one Indian Ocean island to another, the next chapter deals with Muslim globalization from the perspective of Zanzibar. During the late nineteenth century, Zanzibar's relationships with western India, southern Arabia, and the Mediterranean were intensifying through trade, migration, and networks of Islamic learning. Against this background, Jeremy Prestholdt's chapter investigates globalism in Zanzibari public discourse and its influence in the formation of individual cognitive maps, highlighting shifting world views in an age of rapidly increasing interdependence. Prestholdt concentrates on the voluminous writings of Emily Ruete (born Sayyida Salme bint Said), the first Zanzibari and Arab woman to publish an autobiography, *Memoirs of an Arabian Princess* (1886). In considering the particularities of Ruete's experiences, the chapter views the local systemically and comparatively within the framework of both imperial and lateral connectivities.

Homayra Ziad considers a different genre of writing, which took on a distinctive form in the Age of Steam and Print: the hajj narrative. The specific text that Ziad analyzes is the *Safar-i Hijaz* (Journey to the Hijaz), composed in 1929 as forty journal installments by the North Indian Muslim modernist and pan-Islamist ʿAbd al-Majid Daryabadi (1892–1977). According to Ziad, Daryabadi's Urdu text reflects both his modernism and his commitment to the pan-Islamic Khilafat movement in colonial India. The *Safar-i Hijaz* thus combines a compendium of geographic and scientific fact with a personal testament of faith (reflecting the same modern subjectivity as contemporaneous biography). It is also a moralizing travelogue aimed at demonstrating to its readers the essential unity of the Islamic world and the necessity for Muslims to embrace that unity to withstand a Western-dominated world order.

The final chapter in the book, by Zvi Ben-Dor Benite, takes us the farthest afield: to China. Despite the long history of Islam in China, Chinese exchanges with the Middle East reignited only toward the end of the nineteenth century, and mostly as random and isolated linkages. Then, at the beginning of the twentieth century, connections and communications began to intensify as Chinese imams, and later delegations of students, were sent to Cairo's Al-Azhar University. As a result, the number of Chinese able to speak and read Arabic increased, facilitating a two-way traffic in translated texts. Around the same time that the first Arabic translation of Confucius appeared in Egypt, a translation of Muhammad ʿAbduh's influential *Theology of Unity* appeared in China. This translation into a Chinese language of an Arabic text that argued for the compatibility of Western epistemic assumptions with Islamic theology thus rendered a two-way exchange of ideas into a three-way exchange. Built on the mobility of books and bodies made possible by new technologies, the layers of intellectual fusion found in the "Chinese ʿAbduh" were part of the larger global exchanges that characterized the Age of Steam and Print.

NOTES

1. For example, the economist Paul Streeten lists thirty-five published definitions of *globalization*. See Streeten, *Globalisation: Threat or Opportunity?* (Copenhagen: Copenhagen Business School Press, 2001).

2. Here we depart from studies of Muslim globalization that focus on the late twentieth century. See, for example, Roel Meijer, ed., *Global Salafism: Islam's New Religious Movement* (New York: Columbia University Press, 2009); Oliver Roy, *Globalized Islam: The Search for a New Umma* (New York: Columbia University Press, 2004); Birgit Schaebler and Leif Stenberg, eds., *Globalization and the Muslim World* (Syracuse, NY: Syracuse University Press, 2004).

3. John Tomlinson, *Globalization and Culture* (Chicago: University of Chicago Press, 1999), 20.

4. James L. Gelvin, "American Global Economic Policy and the Civic Order in the Middle East," in *Is There a Middle East?*, ed. Michael Bonine, Abbas Amanat, and Michael Gasper (Stanford: Stanford University Press, 2011), 191–206, esp. 192–95.

5. Nile Green, "Persian Print and the Stanhope Revolution: Industrialization, Evangelicalism, and the Birth of Printing in Early Qajar Iran," *Comparative Studies of South Asia, Africa and the Middle East* 30, no. 3 (2010): 473–90.

6. Here we build on recent work examining connectivity across large maritime areas. See, for example, Amal Ghazal, *Islamic Reform and Arab Nationalism: Expanding the Crescent from the Mediterranean to the Indian Ocean (1880s–1930s)* (New York: Routledge, 2010); Nile Green, *Bombay Islam: The Religious Economy of the West Indian Ocean, 1840–1915* (Cambridge: Cambridge University Press, 2011); Michael F. Laffan, *Islamic Nationhood and Colonial Indonesia: The Umma below the Winds* (New York: RoutledgeCurzon, 2003).

7. Kenneth Silverman, *Lightning Man: The Accursed Life of Samuel F. B. Morse* (New York: Knopf, 2003), 240–41; Yakup Bektas, "The Sultan's Messenger: Cultural Constructions of Ottoman Telegraphy, 1847–1880," *Technology and Culture* 41, no. 4 (2000): 669–96; Michael Rubin, "The Making of Modern Iran, 1858–1909: Communications, Telegraph and Society" (PhD dissertation, Yale University, 1999).

8. Daniel R. Headrick, *The Tools of Empire: Technology and European Imperialism in the Nineteenth Century* (New York: Oxford University Press, 1981).

9. On the use of these terms, see Barbara D. Metcalf, "'Traditionalist' Islamic Activism: Deoband, Tablighis, and Talibs," in *Understanding September 11*, ed. Craig Calhoun, Paul Price, and Ashley Timmer (New York: New Press, 2002), 53–66.

10. Nile Green, "Spacetime and the Muslim Journey West: Industrial Communications in the Making of the 'Muslim World,'" *American Historical Review* 118, no. 2 (2013): 401–29.

11. Ibid.

12. See, for example, Mustafa al-Galayini, *Al-Islam: Ruh al-Madaniya, au al-Islam wa-Krumar (Islam: Spirit of Civilization, or Islam and Cromer)* (Beirut: n.p., 1908).

13. See, inter alia, Immanuel Wallerstein, "World Systems Analysis: The Second Phase," in *Unthinking Social Science: The Limits of Nineteenth-Century Paradigms*, ed. Wallerstein (Philadelphia: Temple University Press, 2001), 266–72; Patrick Karl O'Brien, "Intercontinental Trade and the Development of the Third World since the Industrial Revolution," *Journal of World History* 8, no. 1 (1997): 75–133; Anthoni Estevadeordal, Brian Frantz, and Alan M. Taylor, "The Rise and Fall of World Trade, 1870–1939," *Quarterly Journal of Economics* 118 (2003): 359–407; Kirti N. Chaudhuri, *The Trading World of India and the English East India Company, 1660–1760* (Cambridge: Cambridge University Press, 1978).

14. James L. Gelvin, *The Modern Middle East: A History* (New York: Oxford University Press, 2011), 76, 154.

15. William G. Clarence-Smith, "The Rise and Fall of Hadhrami Shipping in the Indian Ocean, c. 1750–c. 1940," in *Ships and the Development of Maritime Technology across the Indian Ocean*, ed. D. Parkin and R. Barnes (London: RoutledgeCurzon, 2002), 227–58; Donald Quataert, *Ottoman Manufacturing in the Age of the Industrial Revolution* (Cambridge: Cambridge University Press, 2002), 96–104; Takashi Oishi, "Indian Muslim Merchants in Mozambique and South Africa: Intra-regional Networks in Strategic Association with State Institutions, 1870s–1930s," Journal of the Economic and Social History of the Orient 50, nos. 2–3 (2007): 287–324; Roger Owen, *The Middle East in the World Economy, 1800–1914* (London: I. B. Taurus, 1993); Judith E. Tucker, *Women in Nineteenth Century Egypt* (Cambridge: Cambridge University Press, 2002).

16. Wolfgang Kaschuba, *Die Überwindung der Distanz: Zeit und Raum in der europäischen Moderne* (Frankfurt am Main: Fischer, 2004).

17. Sarah Searight, *Steaming East: The Forging of Steamship and Rail Links between Europe and Asia* (London: Bodley Head, 1991).

18. Robert J. Blyth, "Aden, British India and the Development of Steam Power in the Red Sea, 1825–1839," in *Maritime Empires: British Imperial Maritime Trade in the Nineteenth Century*, ed. David Killingray, Margarette Lincoln, and Nigel Rigby (Rochester, NY: Boydell, 2004), 68–83.

19. See, for example, Humayun Ansari, "Making Transnational Connections: Muslim Networks in Early Twentieth Century Britain," in *Islam in Inter-war Europe*, ed. Nathalie Clayer and Eric Germain (London: Hurst, 2008), 31–63; L. Tarazi Fawaz, *Merchants and Migrants in Nineteenth-Century Beirut* (Cambridge, MA: Harvard University Press, 1983); Robin Ostle, "Alexandria: A Mediterranean Cosmopolitan Center of Cultural Production," in *Modernity and Culture: From the Mediterranean to the Indian Ocean*, ed. L. Tarazi Fawaz and Christopher A. Bayly (New York: Columbia University Press, 2002), 314–43.

20. Christopher Clay, "Labour Migration and Economic Conditions in Nineteenth-Century Anatolia," *Middle Eastern Studies* 34, no. 4 (1998): 1–32; Eileen Kane, "Odessa as a Hajj Hub, 1880s–1910s,"

in *Russia in Motion: Essays on the Politics, Society, and Culture of Human Mobility since 1850*, ed. John Randolph and Eugene Avrutin (Champagne: University of Illinois Press, 2012), 107–25; Michael B. Miller, "Pilgrims' Progress: The Business of the Hajj," *Past and Present* 191, no. 1 (2006): 189–228.

21. Nitish K. Sengupta, *Land of Two Rivers: A History of Bengal from the Mahabharata to Mujib* (London: Penguin Books, 2011), 211–12.

22. Peter Mentzel, *Transportation Technology and Imperialism in the Ottoman Empire, 1800–1923* (Washington DC: American Historical Association, 2006).

23. Ian J. Kerr, *Building the Railways of the Raj, 1850–1900* (Delhi: Oxford University Press, 1997), 1.

24. Nile Green, "The Rail Hajjis: The Trans-Siberian Railway and the Long Way to Mecca," in *Hajj: Collected Essays,* ed. Venetia Porter (London: British Museum, 2013), 000–000.

25. Abdürrechid Ibrahim, *Un Tatar au Japon: Voyage en Asie (1908–1910)*, trans. Francois Georgeon and Işık Tamdoğan-Abel (Paris: Sindbad–Actes Sud, 2004).

26. Mary Byrne McDonnell, "Patterns of Muslim Pilgrimage from Malaysia, 1885–1985," in *Muslim Travellers: Pilgrimage, Migration, and the Religious Imagination,* ed. Dale F. Eickelman and James Piscatori (Berkeley: University of California Press, 1990), 111–30; F. E. Peters, *The Hajj: The Muslim Pilgrimage to Mecca and the Holy Places* (Princeton, NJ: Princeton University Press, 1994), 266–315.

27. R. Sean O'Fahey, "'Small World': Neo-Sufi Interconnexions between the Maghrib, the Hijaz and Southeast Asia," in *The Transmission of Learning in Islamic Africa,* ed. Scott S. Reese (Leiden: Brill, 2004), 274–88; Merle Ricklefs, "The Middle East Connection and Reform and Revival Movements among the *Putihan* in 19th-Century Java," in *Southeast Asia and the Middle East: Islam, Movement, and the Longue Durée,* ed. Eric Tagliacozzo (Singapore: NUS Press, 2009), 111–34.

28. Michael C. Low, "Empire and the Hajj: Pilgrims, Plagues, and Pan-Islam under British Surveillance, 1865–1908," *International Journal of Middle East Studies* 40, no. 2 (2008): 269–90; Sheldon Watts, "From Rapid Change to Stasis: Official Responses to Cholera in British-Ruled India and Egypt: 1860 to c. 1921," *Journal of World History* 12, no. 2 (2001): 321–74.

29. Nile Green, "The Dilemmas of the Pious Biographer: Missionary Islam and the Oceanic Hagiography," *Journal of Religious History* 34, no. 4 (2010): 383–97.

30. For broader discussions of the phenomenon, see C. A. Bayly, *The Birth of the Modern World, 1780–1914: Global Connections and Comparisons* (Oxford: Blackwell, 2004), 325–65; James L. Gelvin, "Secularism and Religion in the Arab Middle East: Reinventing Islam in a World of Nation States," in *The Invention of Religion: Rethinking Belief and Politics in History,* ed. Derek R. Peterson and Darren Walhof (New Brunswick, NJ: Rutgers University Press, 2002), 115–32.

31. Mahdi Naderpour, Armin Rajabzadeh, and Mahdi Namazi Shabestari, "Tourism Industry: A Tourism Development System Approach," *Australian Journal of Basic and Applied Sciences* 5 (2011): 1409–15.

32. D. S. Richards, "Edward Lane's Surviving Arabic Correspondence," Journal of the Royal Asiatic Society 9, no. 1 (1999): 1–25.

33. Daniel Newman, *Rifa'a al-Tahtawi: A Nineteenth-Century Egyptian Educationalist and Reformer* (Edinburgh: Edinburgh University Press, forthcoming).

34. Nile Green, "The Madrasas of Oxford: Iranian Interactions with the English Universities in the Early Nineteenth Century," *Iranian Studies* 44, no. 6 (2011): 807–29.

35. Maryam Ekhtiar, *Modern Science, Education and Reform in Qajar Iran: The Dar al-Funun* (Richmond, Surrey: Curzon, 2005); David Lelyveld, *Aligarh's First Generation: Muslim Solidarity in British India* (Princeton, NJ: Princeton University Press, 1978).

36. Barbara D. Metcalf, "The Madrasa at Deoband: A Model for Religious Education in Modern India," *Modern Asian Studies* 12, no. 1 (1978): 111–34.

37. Albert Hourani, *Arabic Thought in the Liberal Age, 1798–1939* (Cambridge: Cambridge University Press, 1962), 81.

38. Mir Laʾiq ʿAli Khan ʿImad al-Saltana, *Safarnama-yi ʿImad al-Saltana bih Urupa* (repr., Tehran: Nashr-i Paband, 1383 AH [2005]), 54–57, 205–6.

39. Nile Green, "The Afghan Afterlife of Phileas Fogg: Space and Time in the Literature of Afghan Travel," in *Afghanistan in Ink: Literature between Diaspora and Nation,* ed. Green and Nushin Arbabza-dah (New York: Columbia University Press, 2013), 67–90.

40. Rudolf Peters, "Religious Attitudes towards Modernization in the Ottoman Empire: A Nine-teenth Century Pious Text on Steamships, Factories and the Telegraph," *Die Welt des Islams* 26, nos. 1–4 (1986): 76–105.

41. James L. Gelvin, "'Modernity,' 'Tradition,' and the Battleground of Gender in Early Twentieth-Century Damascus," *Die Welt des Islams* 52 (2012): 1–22.

42. Guillaume Daudin, Matthias Morys, and Kevin H. O'Rourke, "Globalization, 1870–1914" (Oxford University Department of Economics Discussion Paper Series, May 2008), available online at http://ideas.repec.org/p/oxf/wpaper/395.html (accessed 5 June 2012).

43. Max E. Fletcher, "The Suez Canal and World Shipping, 1869–1914," *Journal of Economic History* 18, no. 4 (1958): 556–73.

44. On the rise and collapse of the nineteenth-century Egyptian economy, see Roger Owen, *Cotton and the Egyptian Economy, 1820–1914: A Study in Trade and Development* (London: Oxford University Press, 1969); Trevor Mostyn, *Egypt's Belle Epoque: Cairo and the Age of the Hedonists* (repr., London: I. B. Tauris, 2006).

45. Adeeb Khalid, *The Politics of Muslim Cultural Reform: Jadidism in Central Asia* (Berkeley: Uni-versity of California Press, 1998).

46. Adam McKeown, "Global Migration, 1846–1940," *Journal of World History* 15, no. 2 (2004): 155–89; H. Hakimian, "Persians in the Russian Empire," *Encyclopaedia Iranica,* www.iranian.com/Dec96/Iranica/Russian/Russian.html (accessed 5 June 2012); Kemal H. Karpat, "The *Hijra* from Russia and the Balkans: The Process of Self-Definition in the Late Ottoman State," in Eickelman and Piscatori, *Muslim Travellers,* 131–52; Akram Khater, *Inventing Home: Emigration, Gender, and the Middle Class in Lebanon, 1870–1920* (Berkeley: University of California Press, 2001), 48–70.

47. Ilham Khuri-Makdisi, *The Eastern Mediterranean and the Making of Global Radicalism, 1860–1914* (Berkeley: University of California Press, 2010).

48. Janet Afary, *The Iranian Constitutional Revolution, 1906–1911* (New York: Columbia University Press, 1996).

49. On constitutionalism, see Gelvin, *Modern Middle East,* 150–57. On the origins of nationalism in the Arab and Islamic world, see James L. Gelvin, "'Arab Nationalism': Has a New Framework Emerged?," *International Journal of Middle East Studies* 41, no. 1 (2009): 10–12.

50. Leila Ahmed, *Women and Gender in Islam: Historical Roots of a Modern Debate* (New Haven, CT: Yale University Press, 1993).

51. K. Humayun Ansari, "Pan-Islam and the Making of the Early Indian Muslim Socialists," *Mod-ern Asian Studies* 20, no. 3 (1986): 509–37; Noor-Aiman I. Khan, *Egyptian-Indian Nationalist Collabora-tion and the British Empire* (New York: Palgrave-MacMillan, 2011); Fariba Zarinebaf, "From Istanbul to Tabriz: Modernity and Constitutionalism in the Ottoman Empire and Iran," *Comparative Studies of South Asia, Africa, and the Middle East* 28, no. 1 (2008): 154–69.

52. Christine Stevens, *Tin Mosques and Ghan Towns: A History of Afghan Camel Drivers in Austra-lia* (Melbourne: Oxford University Press, 1989).

53. Nile Green, "Islam for the Indentured Indian: A Muslim Missionary in Colonial South Africa," *Bulletin of the School of Oriental and African Studies* 71, no. 3 (2008): 529–53; Torsten Tschacher, "From Local Practice to Transnational Network: Saints, Shrines and Sufis among Tamil Muslims in Singa-pore," *Asian Journal of Social Science* 34, no. 2 (2006): 225–42.

54. Frank J. Korom, *Hosay Trinidad: Muharram Performances in an Indo-Caribbean Diaspora* (Philadelphia: University of Pennsylvania Press, 2003).

55. François-René de Chateaubriand, *Mémoires d'outre-tombe* (Paris: Le Livre de Poche, 1973), trans. Emma Rothschild, quoted in David Singh Grewal, *Network Power: The Social Dynamics of Globalization* (New Haven, CT: Yale University Press, 2008), 18.

56. Khuri-Makdisi, *The Eastern Mediterranean*, 60–62; Dikran Mesrob Kaligian, *Armenian Organization and Ideology under Ottoman Rule, 1908–1914* (Piscataway, NJ: Transaction Publishers, 2011), 14.

57. O'Fahey, "'Small World,'" 285–86; Hajji Muhammad ʿAli Pirzada, *Safarnama-yi Hajji Pirzada*, ed. Hafiz Farmanfarmaʾiyan, 2 vols. (Tehran: Danishgah-i Tihran, 1342–43 AH [1963–65]), 1:317–18.

58. Jalal al-Hafnawi, "'Islami Dunyaʾ Misr se Shaʾiʿ Shoda Urdu ka Akhbar," *Khuda Bakhsh Library Journal* 110 (1994): 135–46; Thierry Zarcone and Fariba Zarinebaf-Shahr, eds., *Les Iraniens d'Istanbul* (Paris: Institut Français d'Études Anatoliennes, 1993); Michael F. Laffan, "An Indonesian Community in Cairo: Continuity and Change in a Cosmopolitan Islamic Milieu," *Indonesia* 77 (2004): 1–26.

59. Humayun Ansari, *The Infidel Within: Muslims in Britain since 1800* (London: Hurst, 2004); Green, "Spacetime and the Muslim Journey West"; Gerdien Jonker and Gerhard Höpp, eds., *In fremder Erde: zur Geschichte und Gegenwart der islamischen Bestattung in Deutschland* (Berlin: Das Arabische Buch, 1996).

60. Nile Green, "Journeymen, Middlemen: Travel, Trans-culture and Technology in the Origins of Muslim Printing," *International Journal of Middle East Studies* 41, no. 2 (2009): 203–24.

61. Green, "Persian Print."

62. Francis Robinson, "Technology and Religious Change: Islam and the Impact of Print," *Modern Asian Studies* 27, no. 1 (1993): 229–51.

63. Gelvin, "'Modernity,' 'Tradition,'" 10–14, 19.

64. Selim Deringil, *The Well-Protected Domains: Ideology and the Legitimation of Power in the Ottoman Empire, 1876–1909* (London: I. B. Taurus, 2011); Kemal H. Karpat, "The Mass Media: Turkey," in *Political Modernization in Japan and Turkey*, ed. Robert E. Ward and Dankwart A. Rustow (Princeton, NJ: Princeton University Press, 1964), 265; Selim Deringil, "The Invention of Tradition as Public Image in the Late Ottoman Empire, 1808 to 1908," *Comparative Studies in Society and History* 35, no. 1 (1993): 3–29, esp. 24.

65. Iskandar Luqa, *Al-Haraka al-Adabiya fi Dimashq, 1800–1918* (Damascus: n.p., 1976), 158–59.

66. Hamid Algar, *Mirza Malkum Khan: A Study in the History of Iranian Modernism* (Berkeley: University of California Press, 1973); Anja Pistor-Hatam, *Nachrichtenblatt, Informationsbörse und Diskussionsforum: Ahtar-e Estanbul (1876–1896): Anstöße zur frühen persischen Moderne* (Munich: Lit, 1999).

67. "Arabic Newspapers Held by the British Library," www.bl.uk/reshelp/pdfs/ArabicNewspapers. pdf (accessed 11 June 2012).

68. Cemil Aydin, *The Politics of Anti-Westernism in Asia: Visions of World Order in Pan-Islamic and Pan-Asian Thought* (New York: Columbia University Press, 2007), 113–14.

69. Laffan, *Islamic Nationhood*.

70. Amal Ghazal, "Sufism, *Ijtihad* and Modernity: Yusuf al-Nabhani in the Age of ʿAbd al-Hamid II," *Archivum Ottomanicum* 19 (2001): 239–72; Green, *Bombay Islam*, 90–117.

71. Iqbal Singh Sevea, "The Ahmadiyya Print Jihad in South and Southeast Asia," in *Islamic Connections: Muslim Societies in South and Southeast Asia*, ed. R. Michael Feener and Terenjit Sevea (Singapore: Institute of Southeast Asian Studies, 2009), 134–48.

72. Alfred Gell, "The Technology of Enchantment and the Enchantment of Technology," in *Anthropology, Art and Aesthetics,* ed. Jeremy Coote and Anthony Shelton (Oxford: Clarendon, 1992), 40–66; Green, *Bombay Islam*.

PART ONE

Communities and Networks

1

A Sufi Century?

The Modern Spread of the Sufi Orders in Southeast Asia

Michael Laffan

PLACING SOUTHEAST ASIA IN A GLOBAL *UMMA* AND A SUFI CENTURY

With the global spread of Western power and the ensuing decline of indigenous polities in monsoonal Asia throughout the nineteenth century, members of key transregional Sufi brotherhoods, known individually as *tariqa* (from the Arabic word for "way" or "path") and divided by specific techniques and genealogies, engaged in active competition across the Indian Ocean. They did so in the name of broader orthodoxy and their putative founders alike, whether as Shattaris, linked to the heritage of Siraj al-Din ʿAbdallah Shattar (d. 1406), who had been active in India, or as Naqshbandis, committed to the teachings of the earlier, Bukhara-born Baha' al-Din Naqshband (d. 1389). This chapter shows how the outcome of contestation between such groups was decided both by their relative connection to the holy cities of Mecca and Medina in the Hijaz, which startlingly swifter modes of steam travel increasingly facilitated, and by the new forms of print technology being engaged at modernizing sites from Istanbul and Cairo to Bombay and Singapore. Certainly this is not a uniquely Southeast Asian story, as can be gathered from Nile Green's *Bombay Islam* and this volume's chapters 2 (by Amal Ghazal) and 11 (by Homayra Ziad), which cross the threshold of the twentieth century to show the ongoing repercussions of the use of print in conceptualizing the global *umma* and its seemingly universal concerns. Even so, there is still much to be gained by highlighting this region (now home to the second-largest concentration of Muslims on earth) as a locus of wider social changes that swept across Afrasia, and by seeing how what Green labels "Customary Islam" prepared the way for modernist action.[1] As such, it is a story that helps us place an often overlooked region into a worldwide Muslim community that was reconceiving itself across oceans and, just as important, against the Western hegemony to which it was beholden for territorial definition.

Prior to leaping straight into the Age of Steam and Print, however, it is worth taking brief stock of how Southeast Asia engaged with the umma in the first place. Certainly Islam came late to the region. It was only from around the thirteenth century that the rulers of the many polities that dotted the sprawling archipelagic crossroads adopted the faith of some of the great dynasties to the West, joining a religious tradition whose adherents had long been found in the cosmopolitan ports of southern India and China and taking on a universal system of script, titulature, and rituals that connected every believer to the focal node of Mecca and the example of the Prophet. By the time Europeans began to arrive in Southeast Asia in the sixteenth century in quest of the lucrative spices of the famed Moluccan archipelago, they found a network of Muslim-dominated ports, stretching almost the whole way from India to China, where daily prayers were a regular part of popular praxis. Europeans also saw how the mosques built from Aceh in the west to Ternate and Manila in the east acted as sites of instruction in the basic principles of belief and, for those with the financial capacity and time, instruction in the texts of Islamic jurisprudence intended to regulate all aspects of social congress.

That said, beyond the occasional observation in later European sources of prayer beads in the hands of local rulers and visiting scholars, whether Malays, Egyptians, or even Rumis (as many Turkic speakers were known), we have little clear sense of what role the Sufi tariqas played in the process of conversion and then in the maintenance of Mecca-conscious orthodoxy. Still, struck by the powerful weight of evidence from later periods, coupled with the crucial observations of missionaries in the nineteenth century, Orientalist scholars of the high colonial era began to suspect that some sort of pantheistic Indic Sufism must once have provided inspiration for converts eager to throw off the old faiths of their ancestors, which an inherently austere faith of the Arabian desert supplanted.[2]

Yet there is quite some irony in the fact that aside from a brief period of Saʿudi dominance early in the nineteenth century, Mecca and Medina had long been redoubts of the Sufi orders. Hence any aspirant mystic worth his (or her) salt claimed a connection to both cities, as indeed did many Southeast Asian Muslims, whom Arabic speakers knew collectively as Jawa and individually as Jawi. The latter term remains in use today, to designate Arabic-script Malay, a language that has long served as the key scholarly link of the archipelago. From the seventeenth century at the latest, Jawi sojourners supported by their distant sovereigns would often return home with the latest or supposedly purest form of Meccan knowledge, embodied for the elect in Sufi tariqa rituals. These rites were often differentiated by the manner of their *dhikr* (remembrance of God) and the specific *silsila* (chain) of authority that allowed their brotherhoods to assert that such practices had been sanctioned by the Prophet, whose mantle so many local rulers claimed as exclusive protectors of the faith. The orders furthermore at times policed the spread of alleged heterodoxy within the community at large, challenging any rival mystical teachers as flouters of the law and enablers of sin, especially if they could be shown to be heedless propounders of the doctrine of the Wujudiyya, which posited an essential indivisibility of God and creation (*wujud*).

Scholars often situate such campaigns within a long history of Islamic "reform-ism," as the trend of policing the public bounds of belief is often termed.[3] Reform-ist or not, these campaigners were able to make their pronouncements only because they enjoyed the backing of key rulers. This was clearly the case with the spread of the Shattariyya in seventeenth-century Aceh and then of the Egyptian-oriented Sammaniyya in eighteenth-century Palembang, farther south on the Sumatran coast.

However, as we shall see, matters would change, and quite radically, given that the Age of Steam and Print overlapped and served to define what I term an inher-ently populist Sufi century. For much as ʿAmir al-Naggar has declared the thir-teenth century—which he characterizes as lacking in ties between the rulers and the ruled—to be that of the Sufi orders in Egypt, I propose a similar reading for the nineteenth century in Southeast Asia.[4] The spread of European power and the con-sequent weakening of local court authority allowed new pietist movements to attract greater public participation in Sufi ritual and to cast the dances and litanies, not to mention the associated social practices, of their regally backed rivals as anathema or simply outdated.

It is equally worth noting that even if the genealogies of Islamic reformism allow us to connect the scholarly dots between eighteenth- and nineteenth-cen-tury Jawi and Arab intellectuals moving on the transoceanic paths linking the port of Makassar on Sulawesi, say, with Shihr in Yemen or even with Sri Lanka and the Cape of Good Hope, the sources say little of peoples outside the courts. Popular participation in Sufi movements seems to appear only when particular teachers are finally wedded by the teleology of nationalist historiography to what are now cast as anticolonial struggles against the Dutch, who had usurped, and thereby united, much of the Southeast Asian archipelago by the First World War.

An oft-cited example of a specifically Sufi struggle in quest of "national" indepen-dence is the so-called Banten Jihad, which broke out in the West Javanese town of Cilegon in 1888.[5] Instead of investigating it, however, I prefer to open the temporal bounds of this chapter by reconsidering the much earlier Padri Movement of West Sumatra, which is said to have coalesced around three returning pilgrims inspired by the occupation of Mecca by the first Saʿudi state in 1803.[6] Even if this movement declared at an end with the Dutch taking of the highland fort of Bonjol in 1837, has retrospectively obtained a Wahhabi tint in popular memory and scholarship, there are good reasons to see it as a vehicle for the manifestation of the new populist and puritanical Sufism in island Southeast Asia.

By starting with the Padri events on Sumatra and moving forward in time in the region at large, beyond the period of the revival of Sufi fortunes at Mecca after the Ottoman-backed expulsion of the Wahhabiyya in 1818, one can see that the new populist push exacerbated intertariqa contestation in Southeast Asia, especially on the neighboring isle of Java. I also note that such Sufi challengers harnessed the crucial means of modern modes of travel and the transmission of knowledge through printing by the 1870s, inadvertently laying the groundwork for the expansion of the Salafiyya movement that—as may be seen in chapters 2, 3, and 11—finally condemned so much Sufi-related activity as backward heterodoxy.

SHATTARIS REMEMBERED AS NAQSHBANDIS, NAQSHBANDIS REMEMBERED AS PADRIS

In 1986, Imam Maulana Abdul Manaf Amin, a scholar of Batang Kabung in the Minangkabau Highlands of West Sumatra, completed his *Kitab al-Taqwim wa-l-Siyam* (Book of rectification and fasting). In this work, Abdul Manaf lays out the method for determining the new moon by calculation (*hisab*) in preference to observation (*ru'ya*). He could appeal to long local precedent in this respect, though matters had not always been thus. In what seems an unrelated diversion in his book, Abdul Manaf writes of how the Shattari Sufi lineage once prevailed in West Sumatra, after the sainted Burhan al-Din (1646–1704) established it at the town of Ulakan at the end of the seventeenth century. Abdul Manaf makes this interpolation to point out that whereas the various scholarly descendants of Burhan al-Din used calculation for determining most dates, they preferred observation of the crescent moon to mark the commencement of the fasting month of Ramadan. However, the arrival of the rival Naqshbandi Sufi order in the highlands around 1792 shattered the regional consensus. For it was at this juncture that the new master of the school at Cangking, Tuan Shaykh Kota Tua (also known as Tuanku Nan Tua; d. 1824), proclaimed that the commencement of Ramadan should also be calculated rather than witnessed. Beyond this, Abdul Manaf implied that Shaykh Kota Tua had attacked many of the Shattari teachers for claiming that Shaykh Burhan al-Din had been a proponent of Wujudi pantheism.[7]

On the face of it, here we have recorded memories of a specific date signaling the introduction of the Naqshbandiyya in West Sumatra and the outline of a doctrinal difference that separated them, quite publicly, from their Shattari rivals. After all, the start of the fast a day early or late is a profound marker of social distance in Muslim societies. Yet there are problems with taking Abdul Manaf's modern account at face value, for a yawning gulf of decades separates it from the events it describes. I also suggest that it backdates later doctrinal concerns that overlaid and amplified earlier political ones. Indeed, it is clear from an account written in the 1820s by Shaykh Kota Tua's immediate successor, Faqih Saghir (also known as Jalal al-Din Ahmad of Samiang), that his master had been a leading proponent of the Shattariyya and had instituted a program in the 1790s for the eradication not of Wujudi ideology but of the popular social practices of cock fighting, gambling, tooth filing, and consuming opium and alcohol. In the process he and his agents stirred up the remnants of the royal family and their supporters at Ulakan. Hostilities soon commenced in what its participants long knew as "the war of religion," whose partisans some ulama agitators termed "white ones" (like themselves) and "black ones."[8]

This all began beyond the gaze of most Europeans, who were in the process of reassigning parts of the region for exploitation in the wake of the Napoleonic Wars. When the British based at nearby Bencoolen (Bengkulu) started to hear about the new movement and the violence it initiated, they cast it as led by Mecca-inspired returnees and preachers, whom they dubbed "Padres" or "Padris." This was their long-standing parlance for Muslim (and other non-Christian) priests, by analogy with the Catholic clergy.[9] It appears too in Faqih Saghir's account, written at the behest of the Dutch after their first interventions in the conflict, in the early 1820s, on the side of the traditional elite and the Shattari masters who remained loyal to them.

A full-scale uprising on Java led by Prince Dipanagara of Yogyakarta (c. 1785–1855) forced the Dutch to take their time in tackling their priestly foes. In what became known as the Java War (1825–30), Dipanagara called on the island's expanding community of self-declared white ones in a war against the court and the Dutch, whose power supported it.[10] Galvanized by the sight in the ranks of their enemies of so many members of the burgeoning network of Islamic schools (known on Java as *pesantren*), the Dutch began to wonder about the nature of Islamic power. Even so, they did not yet have the ability to ask detailed questions about the doctrinal inspiration of their foes and chose rather to collect manuscripts for subsequent study, as was the case in Sumatra after the fall of the last redoubt of Imam Bonjol, in 1837. It was only in the 1840s that metropolitan scholars began to moot their identification as fellow-travelers of the Wahhabis of Arabia.[11]

This is not to say that *Wahhabi* was the only appellation that subsequent observers suggested. Another term brought into focus by people familiar with the terrain of the old jihadists and their descendants but with little training in Islam or Islamology was *Hanafi*. In 1871, for example, A. W. P. Verkerk Pistorius (1838–93) described an Islamic teacher he had known on Sumatra's west coast in the 1860s, Shaykh Muhammad of Silungkang, as a member of the Hanafi legal school (*madhhab*).[12] This was the official juridical school of the Ottoman State and one at clear variance with the Shafi'i line, to which practically all Southeast Asians adhere. Certainly Pistorius believed that this teaching, which he suggested a Shaykh Barudah (or Barulah) of Tanah Datar was also advocating, was sharply different from most local practices, with its periods of sequestration known as *suluk* and the commencement of Ramadan a day early. Similarly, Arnold Snackey wrote in the 1880s about the late Shaykh Da'ud of Sunur as a member of the Padri movement, who, having been dislodged by his (apparently Shattari) rival in the 1820s, had returned to Sumatra from Mecca as an advocate of the Hanafi school.[13]

I suggest, however, that none of these West Sumatrans were Hanafis. Shaykh Da'ud expressly declared himself to be Shafi'i in his own writings.[14] Rather, the appellation *Hanafi* indicates their having affirmed their Meccan credentials by advocating Ottoman-backed calendrical practices. And members of the Naqshbandi Sufi order who moved into Southeast Asia after the Ottoman restoration of the holy places certainly favored such methods. Beyond this, the Malay world used *suluk*—the term that Verkerk Pistorius noted in his articles—to refer to the Naqshbandi practice of sequestration in their rituals of initiation. And while we cannot necessarily identify either the Padri instigator Shaykh Kota Tua or his disciple Faqih Saghir as Naqshbandis, there is clear evidence that the returned Shaykh Da'ud and then Faqih Saghir's son, who studied under Da'ud in Mecca, were proponents of the Naqshbandiyya for which the school at Cangking ultimately became known.[15]

HINTS OF SUFI RIVALRIES ELSEWHERE

We know that the reforms attempted by a once-Shattari shaykh and his Mecca-oriented disciples resulted in violent contestation and a shift in allegiance to a Sufi order that was active once more in the holy places with the vanquishing of the Wahhabiyya in 1818. As we have already noted, one of the ways the new and explicitly Mecca-connected Naqshbandis distinguished their practices from those of the Shattari Sufis was in advocating (Hanafi) calculation rather than the sighting of the new moon. And while we do not necessarily find the explicit claim of Hanafi influence on Southeast Asian Muslims in the dilettante observations of diplomats and missionaries, similar debates were observed in other parts of the archipelago. In the 1850s, for example, the British consul at Brunei wrote about how the court had become doctrinally divided from the surrounding countryside once a certain hajji returned from Ottoman Mecca around 1840 and challenged the state-sponsored philosophy, which had been twinned to some form of Sufi praxis. We also learn from this observer that the rival parties, which engaged in heated theological arguments about whether or not God could be assigned a personality, marked themselves off from each other by publicly commencing the fasting month on different days.[16]

Similar dissent had occurred in the 1840s in the former sultanate of Banten, West Java. According to one account of the affair, a Dutch official had been forced to intervene in a public spat when a group of new ulama challenged the officially sanctioned commencement of Ramadan.[17] While the precise details of the case are elusive, these teachers may well have been connected to the same web of concerns, as, perhaps, was another movement noted much farther east, at Madiun in 1855, where a Dutch observer referred to members of a sect known locally as the Agama Dul. Apparently a new group of sectarians said to be followers of teachings propounded by the caliph Abu Bakr (573–634) were gathering under "priests" to perform ecstatic dances to the beat of a drum and in the presence of women and the young. The observer further noted the disdain for this new group evinced by "the chiefs and the priests of the orthodox Islamic faith" who had doubtless informed him of the movement's existence and who similarly hoped that it would soon die out.[18]

In his important work *Mystic Synthesis in Java*, Merle C. Ricklefs proposes that these sectarians were followers of an Arab teacher buried at Jepara, on Java's north coast.[19] As we have seen, the members of the indigenous bureaucracy (who were generally Shattari if they had any Sufi linkage) claimed that the new "priests" followed the teachings of the first caliph, Abu Bakr. This assertion likely rested on Naqshbandi declarations that both Abu Bakr and ʿAli ibn Abi Talib (d. 661) had transmitted their method of dhikr, one of the more unusual claims vested in the pedigree of the Naqshbandiyya. Beyond this, their dances sound rather more Naqshbandi than Shattari. Indeed, the exertions they required were cited thirty years later in widespread rumors of an impending uprising led by the Sufi masters of Mecca and as explicit justification for the suppression of the Naqshbandiyya in central Java, after which the Orientalist C. Snouck Hurgronje (1857–1936) was engaged to make a study of the Sufi orders and their impact on the Netherlands Indies.[20]

Certainly, by the 1880s the Dutch believed they had much to fear from Mecca, whether in terms of doctrine or the vectors of disease, the combatting of which has been the subject of work by William R. Roff and now Eric Tagliacozzo (see chapter 5).[21] Some had even suggested that the Well of Zamzam, in the Grand Mosque itself, was a major source of cholera. This was an allegation that Snouck Hurgronje debunked, having seen fit to collect water samples from Zamzam in between playing the part of a sincere convert and student of religion in Mecca, albeit one who looked somewhat askance at the activities of the Naqshbandis.[22] In any event, as a result of his time in that city in 1885, followed by a tour of Java from mid-1889 to early 1891, Snouck Hurgronje saw that town after town of Java had informal schools with teachers with links to the Meccan Naqshbandiyya or one of its Southeast Asian offshoots.[23]

There was, however, a crucial difference on Java from what had obtained in West Sumatra, given that the rise of the once-scorned Naqshbandis had not come on the heels of fraternal violence. For in the wake of the catastrophic Java War, the surviving Javanese courts had been driven closer to the Dutch and well away from the networks of Islamic learning that had supported Dipanegara (who was sent into exile on Sulawesi, where he copied down the litanies of both the Shattariyya and the Naqshbandiyya).[24] For his part, Snouck Hurgronje was a scholarly witness to the tail end of a process by which many Javanese had made the hajj and joined the long queues of aspirant Naqshbandis visiting the masters ensconced in Mecca. The emissaries of the great Daghestani teacher Sulayman Affandi had been particularly effective over the previous decades in leading a Mecca-centric transition from a Shattari Sufi orthodoxy tied to the moribund courts to the more populist interpretation of the Naqshbandi Sufis. In some cases, formerly Shattari teachers would even return to Southeast Asia and offer training in the new forms of dhikr in addition to the Shattariyya, easing the transition and recognizing that they were becoming part of a global community. Perhaps one of the most interesting men in this respect whom Snouck Hurgronje met in Java was Muhammad Talha of Kalisapu, Cirebon. Shaykh Talha claimed not only to teach at least two Sufi rites, the Khalidyya and the Qadiriyya wa-Naqshbandiyya (see below), at his well-appointed school but even to have had training in "Hanafi" law.[25]

STEAM AND PRINT: THE CRUCIAL CONJUNCTION

Much of what the Dutch colonial official Snouck Hurgronje saw was connected to the exponential rise in Southeast Asian participation in the hajj that resulted from the opening of the Suez Canal in 1869 and the ensuing increase in steam shipping between Arabia and the hubs of Penang, Singapore, Batavia, and Surabaya. It was further facilitated by the internal development on Java in particular of roads and train lines intended to secure both Dutch control of the island and the rapid transport of crops to the same ports where increasing numbers of scholars—Javanese and Arab—were establishing independent schools. One particularly famous teacher of the late nineteenth century was Kyai Salih of Darat (d. 1904), whose *pesantren* was near the busy port of Semarang, the end point of Java's first train line. He was well known for his Javanese glossings of Arabic works—though not necessarily Sufi works, for not all of the teachers active in the traditional schools necessarily advocated tariqa activities.[26]

These schools formed a natural, and often lucrative, opportunity. They were often designated as tax-free holdings or ancestral endowments by their patrons, and many of their leaders—regardless of whether they offered additional training to the elect in the form of Sufi praxis—were able to gain the support of members of the indigenous bureaucracy who had their feet in two worlds: the Jawi- and Arabic-literate Muslim one that was rapidly adopting lithographic technology, and the typographic Roman-script one advancing under Dutch rule. Certainly Muslim scholars were aware of the opportunities opened by knowledge of colonial scripts and structures of power, which they could use to their advantage in shaping the bounds of the orthodox community.[27] One should not ignore the impact and dissemination of literature in the spread of the new teachings. In the course of carrying out his surveys of the many schools of Java, with their frequent connections to Sufi teachers of one group or another, Snouck Hurgronje often noted the presence of printed works in the hands of various shaykhs. Muhammad Talha, for example, had a two-volume edition of Ibrahim al-Jaylani's *Al-Insan al-kamil* (The perfect man) that had been published in Cairo in 1876, in addition to an edition of epistles composed by Sulayman Affandi in Mecca and then lithographed in Istanbul in 1883/84. I suggest that, by the 1880s, the possession of such prestigious texts was often a mark of teachers of rank, who were also able to hand out (or sell) printed copies of their (very Meccan) pedigrees and commend the manuals that would be made available from places such as Singapore.[28]

The story of Sufism and print in Southeast Asia still requires serious attention, much as it does in China and West Africa. The current holdings in library collections are limited, to say the least, reflecting the concerns of older generations of collectors and officials, who often sought evidence of manuscript continuities with an imagined past rather than quotidian print affirmations of a modern present. Additionally, much of the sometimes ephemeral material that was connected with the orders was brought in from beyond local shores rather than being produced on the lithographic presses of Singapore and Surabaya that began to function in earnest in the 1850s.[29] Perhaps the first work from those presses with a bearing on questions of Sufism was not a manual for its practice but rather a pamphlet condemning its excesses. This was released in 1852/53 by Salim ibn Sumayr (d. 1853), a leading Hadrami-born Yemeni scholar and long-term resident of Batavia.[30] In his tract, which reflects the general concerns of the Arabocentric 'Alawiyya Sufi order, Ibn Sumayr attacked a certain Jawi called Isma'il al-Minankabawi, who had recently arrived in Singapore and enjoyed success in gathering disciples for the Naqshbandiyya there and in nearby Riau and Kedah on the peninsula.[31] Isma'il al-Minankabawi was most likely a follower of Da'ud of Sunur, referred to earlier, given that he had been involved in the redaction of a work by that scholar in Mecca that extolled the practices of the holy city as compared with the putative backwardness of those of their Sumatran homeland. This was reprinted several times in Singapore, although in the misleading form of a guide to the hajj, alongside al-Minankabawi's guides to the Naqshbandiyya.[32]

In time the presses of Singapore spilled forth other books that might be seen as relevant to Sufi readers, augmenting such prestigious works as the latest compilations of saintly biographies or do-it-yourself manuals such as the *Jami' Usul al-Awliya'* (Compilation of the principles of the saints), a conveniently indexed treatise on the Naqshbandiyya order composed by Ahmad ibn Mustafa al-Kumushkhanawi (also called Gümüşhanevi; c. 1812–c. 1893). Some of the most popular texts were compilations of odes in praise of the Prophet, such as those of Ibn al-Dayba'i (1461–1537) and Ja'far al-Barzanji (1690–1764), at whose recitation it was popularly believed that the Prophet himself would join the believers.[33] There were also numerous ephemeral tracts confirming the Sufi path as one for all believers rather than just a small elite. One cheap and frequently reprinted pamphlet, the *Sha'ir Shari'a Dan Tariqa* (Poem of Shari'a and tariqa), announced to the general reader (who was increasingly aware of the possibilities of travel) that the struggle with the self in the face of the world was incumbent on all, not just the saints. In addition, it warned of the dangers of being captured and made a coolie at any number of foreign ports from Bombay to Tokyo![34]

Beyond such general calls for the believer to cultivate the self and fend off base passions (and rapacious sea captains), Muslims literate in Malay would have been able to access printed works from Mecca itself starting in 1884, when the prominent Southeast Asian scholar (and noted Sufi) Ahmad al-Fatani (1856–1906/7) began to oversee the production of Malay works on that city's new typographic press. This press also saw the issuance of a fatwa by the Meccan jurist Ahmad ibn Zayni Dahlan (1816–86) condemning Sulayman Affandi and his activities.[35] Indeed, the scholastic and regal elites of Mecca and the Malay world had not thrown their hands up in the face of the thousands of aspirant Sufi hajjis. They still sought to cultivate and channel popular manifestations of belief. Along the coasts of East Sumatra and the Malay Peninsula, the still-active sultans of so many small polities, such as Deli, Serdang, and Kedah, remained (or tried to remain) the ultimate arbiters of what was allowed. In Kelantan in 1905, for example, the young Muhammad IV, whose lands were under Thai suzerainty, wrote to Ahmad al-Fatani for advice in regard to the nocturnal meetings and dancing of a new teacher who represented the Ahmadiyya Sufi order, a fraternity that was as popular in the northern Malay Peninsula as the Naqshbandiyya order was in the straits and on Java.[36]

There were also controversial orders that sought to ride the coattails of the Naqshbandiyya Sufis' popularity or obtain the opportunities gained by the Ahmadiyya. Of particular influence was the Qadiriyya wa-Naqshbandiyya, a hybrid order established in Mecca in the 1860s or 1870s by Ahmad Khatib of Sambas, on the west coast of Borneo. His networks subsequently spread across the archipelago and were strengthened by his successor, 'Abd al-Karim of Banten. Snouck Hurgronje even met the latter in the holy city and identified him as influential and potentially dangerous to the Dutch, if not for the content of his statements then for the power attributed to him by his followers, who often carried his printed manuals or used them as the basis of their own manuscript copies.[37]

We may recall that after the scare of the early 1880s the Dutch became far more alive to the potential inspiration of Islam in the expanding web of their Asian possessions and to the activities of the seemingly ubiquitous and still illegible Sufi orders. Such concerns led to Snouck Hurgronje's dispatch to Arabia and then, after the infamous Cilegon massacre by some of 'Abd al-Karim's followers in 1888, to Java. It is somewhat ironic, then, that after making his studies of Java, Snouck Hurgronje downplayed the fears that he had peddled in the press on either side of his journey to Mecca. He had come to see tariqa Sufism as less a globally coordinated threat than an antiquated form of folk practice. Indeed, it appears from his letters that he believed it had more to tell the Dutch about the origins of Islam in the region than about any threat they might face in the future.[38]

SUFISM SUPPLANTED

Like libertines they sway
yet like donkeys they bray.
Thinking themselves on the path of the devout,
they are more in error than those who doubt.

AHMAD IBN ZAYNI DAHLAN, *RISALA RADDIYYA 'ALA*
RISALAT AL-SHAYKH SULAYMAN AFANDI, 5

As Snouck Hurgronje built up his network of contacts in the Indies, he came to rely heavily on informants to whom he was introduced in Mecca or who had already made themselves known to the Dutch authorities. One particularly active figure was the Arab polemicist and printer Sayyid 'Uthman ibn Yahya (1822–1914) of Batavia, who was well known for his many tracts attacking the Naqshbandiyya, which the state subsidized after the disaster at Cilegon. Indeed, he saw himself as a follower of Salim ibn Sumayr.[39] Beyond this he sought to affirm his position by echoing the printed admonitions of Ahmad Dahlan in Mecca.

But if Sayyid 'Uthman campaigned ceaselessly in the name of both Islam and colonial security for the curtailment of the many mystical teachers, his works—even with their references to contemporary authorities in Mecca—lack the punch of a much more forceful antagonist active in the holy city in the 1890s. This was Ahmad Khatib al-Minankabawi (1860–1916), the descendant of a Padri judge, and a claimant to the salaried post of imam in Mecca's Holy Mosque. Of course he was but one of many prayer leaders within the sacred precinct, but he made sure to advertise his title on each of the many works he sent to the archipelago for printing and dissemination. At first he attracted the hostility of Snouck Hurgronje for his attacks on matrilineal law in West Sumatra and then of Sayyid 'Uthman for opposing the building of a Friday mosque in Palembang. However, he subsequently gained the plaudits of the latter polemicist when he released the first of three tracts excoriating the emissaries of the Naqshbandiyya in his place of birth.[40]

Ahmad Khatib al-Minankabawi published this tract at Padang in 1906, initiating a print war with his Naqshbandi opponents, during which he often ripped through their printed texts, from the *'Awarif al-Ma'arif* (Knowers of the sciences) of al-Suhrawardi to the aforementioned *Jami' Usul al-Awliya'* of Gümüşhanevi and the *Fath al-'Arifin* (Victory of the Gnostics) of Ahmad Khatib of Sambas. That said, it should be emphasized that Ahmad Khatib al-Minankabawi was not technically a foe of all forms of tariqa mysticism. As he confesses near the close of his third such tract, he had been drawn to the Naqshbandiyya in his youth, though he became incensed at the fact that so many of his Southeast Asian kin were streaming to Mecca to be inducted (in *that* order) without proper attention to their knowledge of the law.

> For years I sought people of gnosis . . . so I made myself their slave, and took "the path of the people" [*tariqat al-qawm*] and joined their program. Yet I found none other than tricksters who sold religion for the world, seeking a livelihood by using the name *tariqa*. Thus did I learn the truth of the words of the writer of the recent *Hayat al-Qulub* [Life of the hearts], namely that its people were sundered [from true knowledge] in the fourth century. Yet here we are now in the fourteenth century, a century in which there is nothing other than empty propaganda, much like yours![41]

Given Ahmad Khatib al-Minankabawi's otherwise moderate tone toward the ideal of Sufism, his critiques do not form a break in the long history of Sufi polemics but rather mark the typographed continuation of contests in which scholars attempt to restrict sober tariqa knowledge to the elect.

Yet by the time he released his polemics, the latest group of self-declared reformers—Malays and Arabs—active in Singapore, and thus freer to write in some senses, had begun in 1908 to take aim at various practices related to the Naqshbandiyya, the Ahmadiyya, and the Qadiriyya wa-Naqshbandiyya. They did so in a key monthly periodical, *Al-Imam*, which had commenced operations in 1906 and which soon cast the vast bulk of the shaykhs of the Naqshbandiyya as mere purveyors of talismans who had discouraged Muslims from the path of advancement and competition on the global stage. The editors certainly mocked any teaching that held that the Prophet had urged that the old and the young should lock themselves away for days on end or that men and women should gather together to recite odes to the beat of a drum or commit outrages of propriety when the lamps were dimmed. This was the time of a rising Asia: Japan had vanquished Russia in war, and great things were promised in the form of the Hijaz Railway and the new reformist teachings of Muhammad 'Abduh and Rashid Rida in Cairo.[42]

Beyond this, it was clear that, rather like Emily Ruete, whom Jeremy Prestholdt discusses in chapter 10, *Al-Imam*'s reformers felt the need for both an awareness of and representation in a world larger than the umma. Indeed, they cited the opinions of the colonizing British at times, to attest to their own backwardness and to stimulate the Malays into action against their old masters, be they talisman-selling shaykhs or supposedly idle aristocrats. Still, a great many readers were perplexed. For even if *Al-Imam*'s champions cast their polemics in a way that invited distinction between valid and invalid Sufi practices, their charged language led a great many Sufi shaykhs to urge their students and extended family networks to desist reading the pages of this upstart journal. It also seems that the board split between its Arab and Malay members, with the former continuing to extol their natural leadership potential in a new series of papers while the latter took their critiques of the Sufi orders a step further, earning them the epithet *Wahhabi* and reifying an imagined lineage that stretched back to the Padris of Sumatra. In the near future the rhetoric of a great many Muslim organizations that sprang up in colonial Southeast Asia would be one of action and similar discontent with the Sufi orders, whose shaykhs sometimes watched in anger as their youthful disciples gravitated toward new forms of mass participation, such as welfare societies, associations, and eventually political parties, which ultimately absorbed the Sufis of Southeast Asia's long nineteenth century.

NOTES

Unless otherwise stated, all translations are mine.

1. Nile Green, *Bombay Islam: The Religious Economy of the West Indian Ocean, 1840–1915* (New York: Cambridge University Press, 2011). Cf. Michael Laffan, *The Makings of Indonesian Islam: Orientalism and the Narration of a Sufi Past* (Princeton, NJ: Princeton University Press, 2011).

2. Western scholars were taken with the idea of some sort of syncretic Sufi genesis because older Indic or indigenous praxis appeared to imbue many of the practices that they witnessed. Perhaps the apotheosis of such imaginings, or at least of their infusion into elegant prose, is Clifford Geertz's widely influential book *The Religion of Java* (Glencoe, IL: Free Press, 1960).

3. Azyumardi Azra has used this framework in his work tracking critical attitudes toward ecstatic or antinomian Sufism voiced by elite ulama who were often Sufis themselves and even proponents of Wujudi thought limited to the elect: *The Origins of Islamic Reformism in Southeast Asia: Networks of Malay-Indonesian and Middle Eastern 'Ulamā' in the Seventeenth and Eighteenth Centuries* (Leiden, Netherlands: KITLV, 2004).

4. 'Amir al-Najjar, *Al-Turuq al-Sufiyya fi Misr: Nasha'atuha wa-Nuzumuha wa-Rawwaduha* (Cairo: Dar al-Ma'arif, 1992).

5. Sartono Kartodirdjo, *The Peasants' Revolt in Banten in 1888: Its Conditions, Course and Sequel: A Case Study of Social Movements in Indonesia* (The Hague: Nijhoff, 1966).

6. Christine Dobbin, *Islamic Revivalism in a Changing Peasant Economy: Central Sumatra, 1784–1847* (London: Curzon, 1983); Jeffrey Hadler, *Muslims and Matriarchs: Cultural Resilience in Indonesia through Jihad and Colonialism* (Ithaca, NY: Cornell University Press, 2008). Together these works provide the best window onto events surrounding the Padri Wars.

7. Oman Fathurahman, *Tarekat Syattariyah di Minangkabau: Teks dan Konteks* (Jakarta: EFEO/PPIM/KITLV, 2008), 76–77, though see also 45–48, for it appears that Abdul Manaf dated the change to 1786 in another work.

8. Jalal al-Din's account has appeared in various editions. See, for example, J. J. de Hollander, ed., *Maleisch leesboek voor eerstbeginnenden en meergevorderden; Vijfde stukje; Bevattende een verhaal van den aanvang der Padri-onlusten op Sumatra, door Sjech Djilâl-Eddîn*, (Leiden, Netherlands: Brill, 1857); E. Ulrich Kratz and Adriyetti Amir, eds., *Surat Keterangan Syeikh Jalaluddin Karangan Fakih Saghir* (Kuala Lumpur: Dewan Bahasa dan Pustaka, 2002).

9. G. W. J. Drewes, "De Etymologie van *Padri*," *Bijdragen tot de Taal-, Land- en Volkenkunde* 138, nos. 2–3 (1982): 346–50; J. Kathirithamby-Wells, "The Origin of the Term *Padri*: Some Historical Evidence," *Indonesia Circle* 41 (November 1986): 3–9.

10. For the definitive account of the Java War, see Peter Carey, *The Power of Prophecy: Prince Dipanagara and the End of an Old Order in Java, 1785–1855* (Leiden, Netherlands: KITLV, 2008).

11. H. J. J. L. de Stuers, *De vestiging en uitbreiding der Nederlanders ter westkust van Sumatra*, 2 vols. (Amsterdam: van Kampen, 1849–50), 1:xcix, 33–34, 36.

12. A. W. P. Verkerk Pistorius, *Studiën over de Inlandsche huishouding in de Padangsche Bovenlanden* (Zalt-Bommel, Netherlands: Noman, 1871), esp. 188–240.

13. Arnold Snackey, ed., *Sair Soenoer Ditoeroenkan dari ABC Melajoe-Arab dan Diterangkan oleh Arnold Snackey* (Batavia: Albrecht, 1888), 14.

14. Ms. Or. [Oriental manuscript] 12.161, folio 17, Leiden University Library, Netherlands.

15. Hamka (Hajji Abdul Malik Karim Amrullah), *Ajahku: Riwayat hidup Dr. H. Abd. Karim Amrullah dan Perdjuangan Kaum Agama di Sumatera* (Jakarta: Widjaja, 1967), 34–35. Cf. Snackey, *Sair Soenoer*, 12.

16. Spencer St. John, *Life in the Forests of the Far East*, 2 vols. (Kuala Lumpur: Oxford University Press, 1974), 2:258–59. For earlier observations of *tariqa dhikr* at Brunei, see [J. T. Dickinson], "Notices of the City of Borneo and Its Inhabitants, Made during the Voyage of the American Brig Himmaleh in the Indian Archipelago, in 1837," *Chinese Repository* 7 (1838): 121–36, 177–93.

17. [W. R. van Hoëvell], "Verdraagzaamheid der Mohammedanen op Java," *Tijdschrift voor Neêrlands Indië* 12, no. 2 (1850): 74–75.

18. J. L. V., "Bijdrage tot de kennis der residentie Madioen," *Tijdschrift voor Neêrlands Indië* 17, no. 2 (1855): 1–17, esp. 14–15.

19. Merle C. Ricklefs, *Mystic Synthesis in Java: A History of Islamization from the Fourteenth to the Early Nineteenth Centuries* (Norwalk, CT: EastBridge, 2006), 203–4.

20. Michael Laffan, "'A Watchful Eye': The Meccan Plot of 1881 and Changing Dutch Perceptions of Islam in Indonesia," *Archipel* 63, no. 1 (2002): 79–108.

21. William R. Roff, "Sanitation and Security: The Imperial Powers and the Nineteenth Century Hajj," *Arabian Studies* 6 (1982): 143–60.

22. J. J. Witkam, introduction to C. Snouck Hurgronje, *Mekka in de tweede helft van de negentiende eeuw: Schetsen uit het dagelijks leven*, ed. and trans. Witkam (Amsterdam: Atlas, 2007), 15–175.

23. Michael Laffan, "The New Turn to Mecca: Snapshots of Arabic Printing and Sufi Networks in Late 19th Century Java," in "Langues, religion et modernité," ed. Catherine Miller and Niloofar Haeri, special issue, *Revue des Mondes Musulmans et de la Mediterranée* 124, no. 2 (2008): 113–31.

24. Carey, *Power of Prophecy*, 113–14, 744–45.

25. Snouck Hurgronje, Ms. Or. 7931, 22b, 77, 78b–79b, Leiden University Library.

26. Martin van Bruinessen, "Saleh Darat," in *Dictionnaire biographique des savants et grandes figures du monde musulman périphérique, du XIXe siècle à nos jours* (Paris: CNRS-EHESS, 1998), fasc. 2, 25–26.

27. Nile Green, "Journeymen, Middlemen: Travel, Trans-culture and Technology in the Origins of Muslim Printing," *International Journal of Middle East Studies* 41, no. 2 (2009): 203–24. For later parallels in colonial Aden, see ch. 3.

28. This observation was made at numerous points in a conference on Sufism and nineteenth-century literary production held at Cairo in March 2010 under the auspices of the Institut français d'archéologie orientale du Caire. A volume is in preparation.

29. Ian Proudfoot, *Early Malay Printed Books: A Provisional Account of Materials Published in the Singapore-Malaysia Area up to 1920, Noting Holdings in Major Public Collections* (Kuala Lumpur: Academy of Malay Studies and the Library, University of Malaya, 1993).

30. K. F. Holle, "Mededeelingen over de devotie der Naqsjibendijah in den Ned. Indischen Archipel," *Tijdschrift voor Indische Taal-, Land- en Volkenkunde* 31 (1886): 67–81, esp. 67, 69–76; Martin van Bruinessen, "Controversies and Polemics Involving the Sufi Orders in Twentieth-Century Indonesia," in *Islamic Mysticism Contested: Thirteen Centuries of Controversies and Polemics*, ed. Frederick de Jong and Bernd Radtke (Leiden, Netherlands: E. J. Brill, 1999), 705–28, at 710–12; 'Uthman ibn 'Abdallah ibn 'Aqil, *Al-Nasiha al-Aniqa lil-Mutalabbisin bi-l-Tariqa* (Batavia, n.d.), 2.

31. H. W. Muhd. Shaghir Abdullah, *Syeikh Ismail Al Minangkabawi: Penyiar Thariqat Naqsyabandi-yah Khalidiyah* (Solo [Surakarta], Indonesia: Ramadhani, 1985).

32. See E. P. Wieringa, "A Tale of Two Cities and Two Modes of Reading: A Transformation of the Intended Function of the *Syair Makah dan Madinah,*" *Die Welt des Islams* 42, no. 2 (2002): 174–206.

33. Nico Kaptein, "The *Berdiri Mawlid* Issue among Indonesian Muslims in the Period from circa 1875 to 1930," *Bijdragen tot de Taal-, Land- en Volkenkunde* 149, no. 1 (1993): 124–53.

34. Anonymous, *Sha'ir Shari'a Dan Tariqa* (Singapore: Arshad Semarang, [c. 1880s]), 8.

35. Ahmad ibn Zayni Dahlan, *Risala Raddiyya 'ala Risalat al-Shaykh Sulayman Afandi* (Mecca: Al-Miriyya, A.H. 1301 [1883/84]).

36. Ahmad ibn Muhammad Zayn ibn Mustafa al-Fatani, *Al-Fatawa al-Fataniyya* (Thailand: Al-Fataniyya, 1957), 179–80. Cf. Werner Kraus, "Sufis und ihre widersacher in Kelantan/Malaysia: Die polemik gegen de Ahmadiyya zu beginn des 20. Jahrhunderts," in de Jong and Radtke, *Islamic Mysticism Contested,* 744; Mark Sedgwick, *Saints and Sons: The Making and Remaking of the Rashidi Ahmadi Sufi Order, 1799–2000* (Leiden, Netherlands: Brill, 2005).

37. Snouck Hurgronje, quoted in K. F. Holle, to GG, Waspada, 14 October 1888, secret, Ministerie van Koloniën, *Mailrapporten* 1869–1900, nummer toegang 2.10.02, 1888, no. 727, National Achives, The Hague,.

38. I take these issues up at greater length in my *Makings of Indonesian Islam.*

39. Some of Sayyid 'Uthman's concerns and activities anticipated those of the Comoros-born reformist Ibn Sumayt, on whom see Anne K. Bang, *Sufis and Scholars of the Sea: Family Networks in East Africa, 1860–1925* (London: RoutledgeCurzon, 2003); Jeremy Prestholdt's ch. 10.

40. Laffan, *Makings of Indonesian Islam,* 162–64.

41. Ahmad Khatib ibn 'Abd al-Latif, *Al-Sayf al-Battar fi Mahq Kalimat ba'd Ahl al-Ightirar* (Misr [Egypt]: Al-Taqaddum al-'Ilmiyya, A.H. 1326 [1908/9]), 25.

42. For further, perhaps overly technical, details, see Michael Laffan, "Understanding *Al-Imam's* Critique of *Tariqa* Sufism," in *Varieties of Religious Authority: Changes and Challenges in 20th Century Indonesian Islam,* ed. Azyumardi Azra, Nico Kaptein, and Kees Van Dijk (Singapore: Institute of South East Asian Studies, 2010), 17–53.

2

An Ottoman Pasha and the End of Empire

Sulayman al-Baruni and the Networks of Islamic Reform

Amal Ghazal

INTRODUCTION

In a photograph taken in 1913, Sulayman al-Baruni (1872/73–1940), a native of the Nafusa Mountains in what is now Libya, has donned an Ottoman army uniform and a fez and poses with an Ottoman officer.[1] His appearance and his career epitomized the cosmopolitan Muslim reformer at the beginning of the twentieth century. Educated in Tunisia, Egypt, and Algeria, elected to the Ottoman parliament in Istanbul, dispatched to Tripolitania to fight Italian invaders, and spending the end of his life in exile in Oman with intermittent visits to Baghdad, al-Baruni had a career resembling that of many of his contemporaries who zigzagged the Ottoman realm, defended its borders, and then watched as their world crumbled into fragments. But al-Baruni was distinctive among Ottoman officials. He was a member of the minority Ibadi sect who turned into a modernist reformer, a pan-Ottomanist, and, later on, a pan-Arabist.

At the heart of al-Baruni's experience lay a web of transformations and developments peculiar to the age. By the late nineteenth century, the movement of modernist Islamic reform known as Harakat al-Islah (later to be labeled the Salafi movement of reform), which sought Muslim unity across sects and schools of jurisprudence, as well as Ottoman pan-Islamism and anticolonialism, provided someone like al-Baruni, as an Ibadi, with the opportunity to transcend his parochial sectarian identity and find a place in the world of transnational politics. A globalized world order, with new and faster means of transportation and communication, including steam and print respectively, turned the possible into a living reality and the world of reformist ideals into a concrete experience. The steamship facilitated al-Baruni's movements and gave him access to individuals who shared his ideas and politics. It was also fundamental in shaping a cosmopolitan experience tied to his travels between the cities of Tunis, Cairo, Istanbul, Algiers, Marseilles, Muscat, and Baghdad. The printing press connected him to a world of ideas he came to advocate and help disseminate; it also connected him to like-minded individuals who also used it to communicate across a wide geography and propagate their ideas of religious reform, Muslim unity, and liberation from colonialism.

Both the steamship and the printing press created new forms of connectivity and reconfigured existent ones. One particular form of connectivity affected by this new wave of globalization was the network. A network consists of an interrelated group of people who come together around social, political, economic, or intellectual concerns. What distinguishes the network from other forms of connectivity is the clear and conscious decision made by individuals to join a specific one, whose members share their interests, goals, and beliefs.[2] Tracing networks and using them as analytical tools provide us with an opportunity to follow the movement of ideas and people horizontally and through any cross-regional links that might exist. They also create a framework of analysis that looks at the levels of interaction and fusion between the local and the global and, more significantly for studies encompassing the late nineteenth and early twentieth centuries, at traces of continuity between the Ottoman and the post-Ottoman eras. Networks function as bridges between the two, providing connections across borders constructed by colonial realities and by new political entities, the nation-states. Because the erection of these new borders has also had an effect on our research methodologies in the post-Ottoman order, networks are a reminder and a proof that the fragmented Ottoman polity and the newly erected geographic borders and boundaries mischaracterize intellectual fluidity and continuity between the two eras. Transnational networks such as al-Baruni's, encompassing Istanbul, Algeria, Tunisia, Libya, Egypt, Syria, and Iraq, permeated borders and pulled people together, providing some intellectual cohesiveness to the fragmented geography in the post-Ottoman period.[3] Some of those networks formed an intellectually and politically subversive power that tried to formulate a new reality to undo the colonial one.

This biographical approach, however, is not meant to highlight the uniqueness of al-Baruni's experience. Some aspects of his political career, such as his membership in the Ottoman parliament, might have been exceptional, but he was not the only one to cross sectarian boundaries and join a reformist network defined by pan-Islamism and/or pan-Arabism and by anticolonialism. Far from being an isolated case, al-Baruni rather represented a trend among many Muslim intellectuals and political activists—Ibadis and non-Ibadis—whose careers were shaped by their membership in Muslim networks and who bore witness to dramatic changes and transformations in their societies starting in the late nineteenth century. Tracing his life opens the door to this larger network, within which he operated. The biography of al-Baruni thus becomes a mirror of many biographies and a reflection of dramatic times that shaped him as they shaped many like him.[4]

THE NETWORKS OF ISLAMIC REFORM

Muslim networks, as Miriam Cooke and Bruce Lawrence have observed, inform the span of Islamic civilization.[5] Within the Ottoman realm, Muslim networks traditionally functioned as bridges connecting distant communities and, more significantly, as conduits of ideas adhered to by individuals or groups that may have been far apart geographically but close intellectually and ideologically. The emergence of a new phase of the globalized order in the late nineteenth century breathed new life into these networks. As a form of connectivity, they changed at an unprecedented level. The steamship made movements of people and material faster and more frequent, and print functioned as a more efficient medium for communicating and disseminating ideas among members of the same network, as evident in the previous chapter, by Michael Laffan. Newspapers and periodicals in particular played a formidable role in cementing intellectual networks whose members used them as tools of communication among themselves and with their readers and proponents, with Muslim reformers making especially effective use of the press.[6] The press also defined the networks' political or ideological platforms. At the heart of those networks were cities linked to global circuits of connection and communication. Playing an important role similar to that of cities in contemporary economic networks, Tunis, Cairo, Istanbul, Baghdad, and others were nodal points for Muslim intellectual and activist networks, whose members could now more easily and frequently travel and converge in such cosmopolitan cities.[7]

Ilham Khuri-Makdisi's chapter 4 illustrates the role of both the network and the press in circulating and disseminating anarchist ideas in Mediterranean cities and in exposing Muslim societies to the thought of non-Muslims. However, as Scott S. Reese reminds us in chapter 3, on colonial Aden, interaction with fellow Muslims remained of utmost importance. This interaction, increased by a greater ability to travel and connect, had its own discourse, idioms, and dynamics, which altered the world view of Muslims and their attitudes vis-à-vis one another. Muslim-Muslim encounters defined the network to which al-Baruni belonged. This network was essential to the movement of modernist reform initiated by the teachings of Jamal al-Din al-Afghani and Muhammad 'Abduh, whose historiography has focused on this movement's attempts to overcome an intellectual rift between Islam and the West, overlooking its quest to overcome a Muslim-Muslim rift. While it was certainly preoccupied with reconciliation with the West, it was equally preoccupied with reconciliation among Muslims. The emphasis on the Salaf (the early Muslim community, hence the later appellation Salafiyya) and its adoption as a reference point served the goal of creating a framework of unity for Muslims. Invoking the Salaf referred to a community imagined to have been free of discord. This unity transcended *madhahib* (schools of religious jurisprudence) and sects and acted as the catalyst for forging a reformist network whose members were both Ibadis and Sunnis.

Ibadism is the only surviving sect from the Kharijite legacy in Islamic history. The Kharijites (or Khawarij) constituted a movement of Muslims dissatisfied with the politics and policies of Caliph ʿUthman, which they considered a deviation from the ideals of Islam.[8] They supported ʿAli's bid for the caliphate as a means to restore social and political justice. When ʿAli accepted arbitration with Muʿawiya at the Battle of Siffin in 657, those Muslims, then known as the Muhakkima, objected and defected. Their opposition to ʿAli earned them his wrath, and their antagonism toward the Umayyads and later the ʿAbbasids led to their persecution. Violence both carried out by and inflicted on the Kharijites divided the movement between radical militants and those who refused to legitimize the killing of other Muslims. Among the latter were the Ibadis, who established the Rustumid dynasty in North Africa, destroyed by the Fatimids in 909. By then a wide sectarian gap separated the Ibadis from the Sunnis (and the Shiʿis), so the Ibadis sought refuge in peripheral areas, also suiting their goal of preserving their beliefs and traditions, away from the urban centers of the Sunni- or Shiʿi-dominated world.[9]

Ibadi Muslim communities are now found in the Mzab Valley in Algeria, on Jerba Island in Tunisia, in the Nafusa Mountains in modern-day Libya, in Oman, and in East Africa, the last the result of Omani influence and rule there in the nineteenth and twentieth centuries. Through travel, Ibadi traders and seekers of ʿilm (knowledge) connected the Ibadi communities. Ibadis' relationships with other Muslims, especially their Sunni compatriots and neighbors, however, remained cautious at best and hostile at worst. Perhaps other forms of connection between these groups developed in Andalusia, but this requires further investigation. Whatever the Andalusian space might have offered the Ibadi community in terms of a more cordial interaction with Sunnis, it is only in the late nineteenth century that Sunni-Ibadi interaction took a different shape and Ibadis sought to reinterpret their history and identity to create more common ground with other Muslims. That reinterpretation was made possible by the reformist discourse emphasizing Muslim unity in the face of Western hegemony and colonialism, to which many prominent and influential Ibadi scholars, writers, and intellectuals responded by reconstructing the history of their sect, and with it their identity as Ibadis.[10]

Ibadis, like members of other religious communities, saw their share of revitalization in the nineteenth century. One form taken by the Ibadi *nahda* (renewal) was a literary renaissance. That nahda, drawing on existing networks of scholarship, took place simultaneously in Oman, North Africa, and East Africa. Thanks to the central role of the Ibadi community in the Sultanate of Zanzibar in sponsoring and funding Ibadi scholars and, later on, publishing their works, this renaissance went unabated throughout the nineteenth century. It coincided, however, with European imperial and colonial dominance over North Africa and the Indian Ocean, where the Omani Empire was also stretching its wings. The Ibadi religious nahda thus transformed itself into a political force and developed an anticolonial discourse and movements in Oman, Zanzibar, and North Africa. It is in reaction to a common colonial experience, including threats to religious values and political sovereignty, and in response to calls for religious reform and Muslim unity that Ibadis and Sunnis found common ground.

The early traces of this rapprochement can be seen in the writings of leaders of the Ibadi literary nahda in the late nineteenth century who experienced the effects of European colonialism firsthand. Muhammad Atfiyyash (d. 1914) witnessed and opposed the annexation of the Mzab, his home, by France; Nur al-Din al-Salimi (d. 1914) led a coup d'état against al-Busaʿidi rule in Muscat and its British protectors; and Nasir al-Rawahi in Zanzibar (d. 1920) wrote extensively lamenting the loss of Zanzibar and Oman to the British.[11] They were sympathetic to both Ottoman pan-Islamism and the pan-Islamic cause promoted by Sunni reformers, and supported downplaying sectarian differences for the sake of Muslim unity. Many Ibadis also joined Sunni reformers in attacking what they considered excessive Sufi practices and beliefs and in accusing Sufi orders of causing divisions among Muslims.[12] Qasim bin Saʿid al-Shammakhi, an Ibadi from Jerba Island residing in turn-of-the-century Egypt and integrated into the reformist circles of ʿAbduh and al-Afghani, was articulate in his support for ʿAbduh's program and revisionist in his approach to the history and identity of Ibadism, whose association with Kharijism he redefined to highlight the commonalities, if not the absence of differences, between Ibadis and Sunnis.[13]

Abu-Ishaq Ibrahim Atfiyyash, a nephew and a pupil of Muhammad Atfiyyash who was exiled to Egypt in 1923, went further, totally dismissing the association between Ibadism and Kharijism and publishing his revisionist views in the newspapers of the prominent Salafi reformer Muhibb al-Din al-Khatib, a Syrian resident of Egypt.[14] Both al-Shammakhi and Atfiyyash could establish themselves in Egypt, publish in the Egyptian press, and even start their own newspapers mainly because of their association with Salafis such as al-Khatib, who provided them with moral and material assistance. By the early twentieth century, several prominent Ibadi scholars, political activists, and writers had moved from their geographic peripheries into Algiers, Tunis, and Cairo—a trend that was intensified after World War I—where they formed a small network integral to a broader one comprising Salafi reformers and their supporters in those cities. It was there—in the halls of their universities and mosques, libraries and clubs, among their ulama and activists—that Ibadis developed a Salafi-reformist identity.

AL-BARUNI: FROM PERIPHERY TO CENTER

Al-Baruni's life and career illustrate and capture the transformation of the Islamic intellectual sphere and the production of an Islamic reformist movement championed by a cross-regional and cross-sectarian network that promoted a pan-Islamic identity at the expense of a parochial one defined by sect. Al-Baruni belonged to a notable family of Jabal Nafusa known for its line of Ibadi ulama and scholarly contributions to Ibadi literature. Raised and educated in his hometown, al-Baruni began his odyssey at Al-Zaytuna University in Tunisia. His father had studied there and wanted his son to receive a similar experience and acquire more knowledge in Islamic disciplines than Jabal Nafusa or Tripolitania could offer.[15] But little did al-Baruni's father know that the Zaytuna of his age was different from that of his son's, especially after the French occupation of Tunisia in 1881. The university was witnessing a fierce debate between Muslim reformers and their opponents and had become a center of intellectual and political activities led by a generation of Algerian and Tunisian students who were to form the backbone of anticolonial and nationalist movements in their homelands.[16] Algerians had been seeking refuge in the Regency of Tunis since the French occupation, beginning in 1830, of what would become Algeria. In the 1870s, there were about sixteen thousand Algerians in the regency.[17] After 1881, the fate of the Algerians in Tunisia met that of their hosts, as both experienced colonialism and occupation firsthand. The history of the two countries, and with it their anticolonial movements and networks of resistance, now became even more entangled than before. Al-Zaytuna and later Al-Khalduniyya (founded in Tunis in 1896) became sites of bitter reform-antireform rivalry and of anticolonial movements led by both Tunisians and Algerians. Al-Baruni came to Tunisia in 1887, where he was tutored by, among others, two prominent reformist ulama, Muhammad al-Nakhli and ʿUthman al-Makki, critics of Sufism and colonialism credited with the dissemination of reformist ideas among the students of Al-Zaytuna.[18] Al-Nakhli in particular seems to have had the most influence on al-Baruni, who, eulogizing his teacher, promised to continue on the path of resistance to colonialism.[19]

While our sources do not shed much light on al-Baruni's time in Tunisia, the career of one of his close associates in Tunis, ʿAbd al-Aziz al-Thaʿalibi (1876–1944)—who attended Al-Zaytuna around the same time, became part of al-Baruni's intellectual and social network, suffered from the intimidation of antireform Sufis, and endured exile like al-Baruni,—provides a clear picture of the political and intellectual environment prevalent then. Al-Thaʿalibi studied at Al-Zaytuna between 1889 and 1896, founded (in 1895) one of the earliest anticolonial newspapers in Tunisia, *Sabil al-Rashad,* and established the first Tunisian nationalist party, Al-Hizb al-Dusturi al-Hurr (The free constitutional party), in 1920. His political activities and antireform Sufi intrigues against him led to his exile by the

French authorities in 1912 and again in 1923. He spent two years in Egypt and then went to Baghdad, where King Faysal I hosted him between 1925 and 1931, as al-Baruni was hosted later on. Al-Tha'alibi spent his years of exile moving from one place to another, until he was allowed to go back to Tunisia in 1937.[20] One can infer from his itinerary that there was in Tunis, and particularly at Al-Zaytuna, a highly charged environment of anti-French politics and religious currents, which formed the basis of Tunisia's future nationalist movement and to which al-Baruni was exposed. In any case, during his stay in Tunis, al-Baruni forged long-lasting friendships with a number of reformers, both Sunnis and Ibadis.

In 1893, al-Baruni left Tunis for Egypt to study at Al-Azhar University for three years. There he was part of an active front of modernist religious reformism and was exposed to a wide spectrum of anticolonial movements in an even more politically and intellectually charged atmosphere than in Tunis. The anticolonial politics of Mustafa Kamil, especially his call for Egyptian independence from British rule, seemed to have had a particular impact on al-Baruni, who heroized him.[21] After Egypt, al-Baruni spent three years in the Mzab Valley, learning at the feet of one of the most prominent Ibadi scholars of the time, Muhammad Atfiyyash. While this immersed al-Baruni more in Arabic studies, theology, and traditional Ibadi literature and served to raise his stature in the larger Ibadi community, it did not provide him with the same exposure to anticolonial politics as Tunis and Cairo had done. But although the Mzab was not yet a hub of such activities, it was not unaffected by them or uninfluenced by religious reform and calls for Muslim unity. With the French annexation of the valley in 1882, Mzabis gradually integrated into the larger Algerian and regional networks of anticolonial politics.

Atfiyyash himself was known for his hostility toward the French and his support for anticolonial movements, including the Omani one that sought to overthrow the al-Busa'idis in Muscat, accused by the leaders of the Ibadi nahda of collaboration with and submission to the British.[22] Atfiyyash's time in Mecca from 1886 to 1888 brought him closer to Sunni circles, some of whose scholars he befriended, and this might have been when he got a close glimpse of Sunni reformist currents that advocated Muslim unity. He also corresponded with Muhammad 'Abduh, who seems to have held him in high esteem, and Rashid Rida's Al-Manar journal featured his scholarship. The impact of these experiences is evident in his increased interest in pan-Islamic affairs on his return home and in his treatise explaining Ibadism to non-Ibadi Muslims, reducing the points of contention between Ibadis and Sunnis to only four points.[23] Al-Baruni played a similar role, exposing Mzabis to the ideas and movements he experienced in Tunis and Cairo, including religious reform and Ottoman pan-Islamism. It is reported that he explained the Ottoman-Greek war of 1897 to Atfiyyash, describing the heroic acts of Ottoman troops against the Greeks and showing him newspaper illustrations of retreating Greek troops. In response, Atfiyyash asked his students to raise their hands in prayer for the victory of the Ottomans.[24]

Al-Baruni's introduction into reformist networks seems to have earned him the enmity of the antireform group in Tripolitania. On his way home from the Mzab in 1900, he was arrested, charged with subversive activities against Sultan 'Abd al-Hamid II, including attempting to establish an independent Ibadi emirate in Nafusa, and sentenced to five years in prison.[25] There is no evidence in the writings, career, or thought of al-Baruni that he was guilty. It is instead likely that he had become known as a Muslim reformer after criticizing the "obscurantists" in Tripolitania, who, it seems, framed him, as their counterparts in Egypt and Syria did to reformers such as al-Tha'alibi. There was no doubt of al-Baruni's allegiance to the Ottoman Empire and to its pan-Islamic policy. He praised 'Abd al-Hamid II for his drive to modernize, to improve communications among Muslims, and to build schools and mosques; for his pan-Islamic policy; and for his resolve against European powers and against "treaties aimed at subjugating the [Ottoman] dynasty." Only after the Young Turk Revolution of 1908 did al-Baruni criticize as despotic 'Abd al-Hamid II's regime, as well as the conservative Sufis on the sultan's advisory team, such as Abu al-Huda al-Sayyadi, who were hostile to reformers.[26]

Mediating parties secured al-Baruni's release two years into his sentence, when he received a pardon from the Sublime Porte in August 1902.[27] One of those mediators was Atfiyyash. He wrote a letter to 'Abd al-Hamid II indicating that al-Baruni was his student, whom he had recommended as an aid to the sultan, and had been unjustly accused and imprisoned.[28] This was one of seven letters that Atfiyyash sent to 'Abd al-Hamid II pleading for al-Baruni's release, though he doubted they reached the sultan.[29] It is not clear what impact—if any—this correspondence had, but it testifies to the integration of the Mzab and its reformist ulama into Ottoman pan-Islamist networks and to Ibadi support for ideas of unity and cooperation among Muslims and solidarity with the Ottoman government. Two years after his release the case was reopened, and al-Baruni was charged again and imprisoned for six months.

In 1906 he returned to Cairo and established a publishing house, Al-Azhar al-Baruniyya. In addition to printing Ibadi books and disseminating them in both the Mashreq (Arab East) and the Maghreb (Arab West), he produced a newspaper, Al-Asad al-Islami. By then Muslim reformers had realized the full potential of the press, and al-Baruni, believing in its enlightening mission and its ability to be a better medium of communication between Muslims and having experienced its potential in both Tunis and Cairo, was the second Ibadi to establish a newspaper with a reformist orientation in Egypt, after Qasim al-Shammakhi's Nibras al-Mashariqa wa-l-Maghariba. Al-Asad al-Islami not only served as a platform for al-Baruni's ideals of Muslim unity and religious reform but also marked him as part of an expanding network that was coalescing around the press.

The newspaper did not survive more than two years, and only three volumes appeared. From the few excerpts of *Al-Asad al-Islami* in Za'ima al-Baruni's biography of her father, it is clear that the paper had a fiery pan-Islamic tone.[30] The following excerpt from a letter sent to "the notables of this *umma*, the representatives of the Islamic groups" and titled "Al-Jami'a al-Islamiyya" (Islamic unity) serves as a good example of the newspaper's preoccupations:

> Do you agree that one of the main reasons behind the division among Muslims is the numerous madhahib and their disparities?
>
> If you do not agree, what is the main reason behind their division?
>
> If you do agree, is it possible to unite [the madhahib] and eliminate the differences since we are in a critical need of unity at all levels?
>
> If it is impossible to unite the madhahib, why is it so and how can we solve the problem?
>
> If it is possible to unite the madhahib, what is the easiest way to achieve this unity, in what country should we attempt it first, and approximately how much money do we need?
>
> How do we organize it? And how do you judge the person seeking to achieve this? Is he a reformer or a corrupt [Muslim]?[31]

Al-Baruni had no doubt of the need for such unity, which was a recurrent theme in this newspaper and in his writings published and reprinted in other newspapers. His emphasis on Muslim unity and reform also mirrored his concerns for the Ottoman Empire, whose territorial integrity and strength he sought to preserve. The need for reforms and modernization in all of the empire's provinces, including his own, were a top priority. Al-Baruni hoped to see Tripolitania on par with Egypt and Tunisia in terms of educational opportunities, infrastructure, and technologies.[32]

Publishing was not the only domain in which he defined his Ottoman identity and his allegiance to the Ottoman Empire. The political career he pursued until 1919 marked that identity too. Al-Baruni's prestigious background and reputation in Tripolitania, as well as his troubles with the Hamidian regime, earned him a seat in the restored Ottoman parliament in Istanbul after the Young Turk Revolution in 1908. He then became a field commander and was dispatched to defend his homeland against the Italian invasion in 1911. But Tripolitania was lost, and he retreated to Tunisia in the spring of 1913 before returning a year later, via London, to Istanbul, where he was appointed to the Chamber of Deputies in recognition of his efforts in the war against the Italians. In the wake of World War I, he lobbied the Ottoman government to send him back to Tripolitania to organize and reignite resistance against the Italians. For that purpose, he was appointed governor of the province in 1916; his mission was to secure its independence. When the Ottomans completely lost their grip on Tripolitania, in 1919, al-Baruni and others led negotiations with the Italians and secured, through a formal declaration at the Paris Peace Conference, its independence, as the first, though short-lived, Arab republic, with al-Baruni a member of its supervisory Council of Four. Nevertheless, al-Baruni's activities shortly after 1919 indicate that he, like many others at the time, still had faith in an Ottoman future: he was assisting the new Turkish government in Ankara in its activities of interference in Tripolitania.[33]

The French authorities in Algeria, aware of al-Baruni's connections and their significance, were monitoring his activities for fear of their implications in the Mzab. They recalled that during the war against the Italians, Ibadis in the Mzab and in Tripolitania were constantly in touch with one another, and that the former offered al-Baruni financial and moral support. The French believed that whatever ephemeral success Ibadis had had at the time in the Nafusa Mountains, it reverberated among Mzabis who hoped for independence from French rule. They also noted al-Baruni's association with the Tunisian nationalist party, among whose members were Mzabis.[34] In 1923, al-Baruni left Tripolitania, never to be able to visit it again, and headed to Istanbul.

From Istanbul he went to Ankara and then to Europe, where he attended the Conference of Lausanne in an unofficial capacity. Once he was in France, the French authorities prevented him from leaving, fearing he might continue his anticolonial agitation in one or another of their North African possessions. He wanted to go to Egypt, but the British did not permit him to enter. His Mzabi friend Ibrahim Atfiyyash, now in exile there, corresponded with the British consulate in Cairo on his behalf, but to no avail.[35] Al-Baruni's forced exile in France was a bitter one, about which he complained incessantly, continuously pleading, without any success, with the French and the British authorities to allow him to return to any Arab country. Whether Algeria, Tunisia, or Egypt, they had all become part of the world to which he belonged and from which colonial authorities wanted to keep him. Al-Baruni's yearning for Tripolitania was no stronger than that for Algeria, Tunisia, or Egypt. In fact, the last two were his preferred choices, the location of the nexus of his network of friends and fellow activists. That same network, with its press, provided al-Baruni with a window onto current events in the Arab world, practically his life support during his two years of exile in France. While there, he corresponded with several newspapers and received some as well. His main link was his Mzabi friend Abu al-Yaqzan Ibrahim, who was then in Tunis, attending Al-Zaytuna and supervising the Mzabi student mission at that university and at Al-Khalduniyya. Ibrahim was one of his main correspondents and was also in charge of subscribing al-Baruni to Arabic newspapers. Without significant financial resources, al-Baruni received material support from the Mzabi community in France and from individuals who were familiar with his anticolonial history, including his actions against the Italians.[36]

In 1923, al-Baruni pleaded with the French to be allowed to settle in Algeria. He had previously asked them for permission to settle in Tunisia, but they had refused, citing Italian objections: Tunisia was close to Tripolitania, and he thus remained a threat. He promised the French to abandon any correspondence with the Turkish government and not to be involved in politics.[37] His tone was one of despair, of someone tired of a life in exile and bewildered by a new world order with no anchor; with the collapse of the Ottoman imperial order, he had lost his center of political gravity. The government of Ankara interceded on his behalf, assuring the French that he would cause no harm to them in Algeria.[38] The French refused.

Between Tripolitania, Tunis, Cairo, the Mzab, and Istanbul, al-Baruni's world was defined by an allegiance to the Ottoman Empire, by modern reformism as an ideology of Muslim unity, and by anticolonialism. Those intellectual and political circuits merged and formed a framework for a new identity, with Islamic reform and unity at its core. For those from the geographic and intellectual peripheries of the Muslim world, membership in the intellectual networks forged by anticolonialists and people with Salafi and pro-Salafi orientations facilitated an affiliation with those currents and the cities in which they thrived. The press was one of the available tools for identifying with and even expanding such networks. Al-Baruni, a product of those cities and a member of their pan-Islamic and reformist networks, had become a cosmopolitan Muslim who, although still an Ibadi, had transcended the boundaries of such an identity while making it part of a larger one.

AL-BARUNI IN EXILE: A LIFE HELD TOGETHER BY NETWORKS

Al-Baruni's exile in France came to an end when Sharif Hussein in Mecca granted him permission to make a pilgrimage in June 1924. He boarded a ship from Marseilles to Alexandria, Port Said, and eventually Beirut. From there, he took a train to Jedda. As a guest of Sharif Hussein, al-Baruni was treated to a trip to Mecca by automobile.[39] On his return to Jedda, he traveled by sea to Muscat, where he arrived in early August and spent the next few months visiting different parts of Oman, then divided into two political entities: the Sultanate of Muscat and the Imamate of Oman, in the interior. Oman's imam Muhammad al-Khalili persuaded al-Baruni to move to the interior and work for him, appointing him an adviser and prime minister. Known for his experience in state affairs, al-Baruni was assigned the tasks of administering the imamate's finances and implementing reforms in that arena, governance, and education. He also hoped to help mend fences between the imam and Sultan Saʿid bin Taymur of Muscat.

Ibadi communities everywhere celebrated both his arrival in Oman and his new responsibilities, a testimony to the prestige he had earned as a reformist and a political leader well recognized in his network. The Ibadi press in Cairo and in the Mzab kept receiving congratulatory letters from readers in Oman, Zanzibar, and North Africa, who also occasionally requested updates on al-Baruni's stay and activities in Oman.[40] They were celebrating the end of his exile in France but also, and more significantly, the contributions that this former Ottoman statesman could make to the Omani Imamate to help it progress and modernize. Although it is beyond the scope of this study to assess the degree to which he was able to introduce significant changes in Oman, it is clear that al-Baruni sowed seeds of reform and provided the imamate with a more international outlook, despite the opposition he faced from conservative imamites which resulted in his resignation as the imam's adviser. Ibrahim commented that "he intended to reform and modernize all administrative units, to make the imamate in Oman compete with developed and modern nations."[41] This might have been an exaggeration, but it is also an indication of what Ibadis expected from him and from Oman.

Other significant and relevant aspects of al-Baruni's stay in Oman are the ways in which he, as an exile, managed his communications and remained involved in regional affairs and connected to his network. The colonial policy of exile, a widening phenomenon after World War I, defeated its own purpose. Exiles, forced to relocate, spread their anticolonial activities with them. Their world had to stretch beyond their locality, to engulf all the distance between themselves and the places they called home. The reality of exile made the network wider and more elastic. Some exiles even became the nexus of their networks, as their banishment and subsequent experiences only enhanced their reputation as anticolonial activists. Paramount here again was the role of the press in keeping up the integrity and vitality of such networks, despite newly erected borders, distance, and censorship.

In al-Baruni's case, this is most evident in his stay in Oman. What we know about him during those years we know primarily from the press that either reported on his activities or published his opinions on a variety of topics. The number of issues on which he wrote for newspapers is staggering, and the geographic scope of discussion about his ideas also speaks to the power of the press. Al-Baruni published in a number of newspapers, including Ibadi ones such as *Al-Minhaj* in Cairo, *Wadi Mzab* and *Al-Umma* in Algeria, and *Al-Falaq* in Zanzibar and non-Ibadi ones such as *Al-Shura*, *Al-Zahra*ʾ, and *Al-Fath* in Cairo, from which the Ibadi newspapers also reprinted his submissions.[42] His correspondence with *Al-Fath* in particular is significant. Muhibb al-Din al-Khatib, the owner and editor of both that paper and *Al-Zahra*ʾ, played a key role in providing Ibadi reformers with all possible assistance to publish their works and even establish their own newspapers.[43] He had much respect for al-Baruni, including his role in opposing colonialism, and wrote to defend him against accusations by some rivals of mismanaging the war against the Italians.[44] Al-Khatib praised al-Baruni as a leading notable in the Muslim world and twice printed a photo of him in the pages of *Al-Fath*, in an Ottoman military coat and a fez and with a sword in his hand.

Through the press, al-Baruni remained involved in discussions about several regional issues, the most important for him being the unity of the Arab world. For him, and for many of his generation, a political unity defined by Islam, Arabism, or a conflation of both was the best alternative to the shattered Ottoman order and a guard against the European colonial order in the region. Arab unity was certainly the number one issue that preoccupied al-Baruni in the late 1920s and the 1930s, around which revolved most of the commentaries he sent to the press. His constant elaborations on ways to unite the Arab countries led people to consult him on related matters. Following the General Islamic Congress in Jerusalem in December 1931, he received a letter from a group of "prominent Arabs" dated February 26, 1932, asking for his input on the policies and priorities of that meeting. In his reply, he listed the liberation of Arab countries from colonialism as the top priority, advising his correspondents to consider this the first necessary step toward the union of all Arab countries.[45] Hashil al-Maskari, a leader of the Arab Association in Zanzibar, which represented Omani interests on the island, and the editor of *Al-Falaq* for eleven years, frequently consulted al-Baruni on matters relating to the association and to Arabs in Zanzibar. On launching *Al-Falaq*, he sent al-Baruni a letter, on December 23, 1928, informing him of the news. Al-Baruni replied on February 13, 1929, congratulating the Arabs in Zanzibar on that step and praising their efforts to resurrect "the glory of Arabs in Zanzibar."[46]

Al-Baruni was thus no obscure figure among intellectuals and political activists in the Arab world. Ibadis and non-Ibadis constantly sought his advice on political affairs, and his contributions to newspapers were often the subject of discussion and debate.[47] He defended himself against accusations of collaboration with the Italians, described the sacrifices of Tripolitanians during the war, elaborated on the role of the League of Nations in world affairs, warned about the consequences of the war in the Arabian Peninsula between Imam Yahya in Yemen and Saudi Arabia's King ʿAbd al-ʿAziz ibn Saʿud, stood up for the rights of the Palestinians in Palestine, and preached unity among Arabs and Muslims.[48] Arab unity for him was part and parcel of Muslim unity and included all Arabic-speaking countries, from Morocco to Iraq, Oman, and Yemen. Islam, the Arabic language, and movements of liberation from European domination and colonialism gave a form to that unity. Al-Baruni therefore lamented all actions and decisions by Arab leaders that, in his opinion, undermined such unity. Thus he criticized the Arabic press for taking sides in the war between Ibn Saʿud and Imam Yahya. He shunned both parties, as he considered their actions a war against Islam and Arabism.[49]

Al-Baruni clashed with Shakib Arslan when the latter suggested in a 1936 speech at the Arab Club in Damascus that Arab unity could be confined, temporarily, to the Mashreq, to the exclusion of the Maghreb. This generated much criticism from Maghrebis, especially Libyans, who, as William Cleveland notes, felt that "Arslan had abandoned his anti-imperial campaign in exchange for Italian gold."[50] Al-Baruni condemned Arslan in an article published in the Tunisian periodical *Al-Rabita al-ʿArabiyya* and reprinted in the Mzabi newspaper *Al-Umma*. Al-Baruni believed that one pillar of Arab unity was Islam. North Africans, as

Muslims and speakers of Arabic, should naturally be included in this unity. Arslan, he contended, had abandoned them not only to please the Italian and the French governments but also because North African countries were poor, lacking the wealth of countries such as Egypt, which Arslan included in his plan.[51]

Despite their different opinions, al-Baruni's career was strikingly similar to that of Arslan. Both belonged to fringe Muslim sects—Arslan hailing from a notable Druze family from Mount Lebanon but a convert to Sunni Islam—and both fought against the Italian invasion of Libya, were elected to the Ottoman parliament in 1913, defended the Ottoman order during World War I, and were denied entry into territories occupied by the French and the British. Both spent their careers in exile campaigning for Arab unity and Islamic reform, battling colonialism, and bridging intellectual networks in the Maghreb and the Mashreq. Cleveland's words about Arslan—that "independence was his objective in dealing with Europeans, the reconstruction of a true Islamic society in confronting his fellow Muslims"—hold true for al-Baruni as well.[52] Their resemblance speaks of the world view of many of their generation, who, in campaigning for unity and reform, became cosmopolitan citizens of an Arab-Muslim world they perceived and defined as bonded by language, religion, and a quest for liberation from colonialism. It also points to the role of political exiles in sustaining the discourse of unity. Given al-Baruni's extensive network, he was no outlier in seeking a transnational framework for his Muslim identity, one defined by Arabism and replacing the now-defunct Ottoman one.

While al-Baruni managed to stay informed about regional events and to correspond with his network while residing in Oman, he often felt isolated there. His plans to reform and modernize the judicial and the economic systems did not go unchallenged, as he faced fierce opposition from conservative elements in the imamate, causing him much distress.[53] Moreover, Oman remained an isolated entity, lacking effective means of communications. The fact that it had opted not to get involved in regional affairs added to al-Baruni's sense of dissatisfaction. His horizon was broader than what the imamate could accommodate, and the intensity and frequency of his correspondence confirm his constant need to communicate with the outside world. Al-Baruni's acceptance of an employment offer from Sultan Saʿid bin Taymur in Muscat in 1938 points to his growing disenchantment with Oman. Perhaps the offer was an effort by the sultan, with whom al-Baruni had been on bad terms a few years back, to undermine the imamate. According to Sultan Saʿid's memo to the British consul in Muscat seeking approval of this appointment, al-Baruni had asked him for a job in 1935, but the sultan had turned him down.[54] Given al-Baruni's anticolonial past, the British had to evaluate the decision to hire this "adventurer of the 'notorious' type who for many years . . . before[,] during and after the Great War was a well known person in the Middle East."[55] However, as long as al-Baruni's role was confined to dealing with internal administrative matters, they were willing to approve.

While in Oman, al-Baruni and some other members of his family had contracted malaria, which necessitated frequent travel outside the country for treatment. King Faisal of Iraq granted them permission to come to Baghdad for treatment, and al-Baruni seems to have had greater opportunities to read newspapers
there and correspond with his contacts. On his first visit, in 1929, he was received
with much fanfare, being welcomed by King Faisal and Iraqi ulama, notables, and
dignitaries. He also saw his old friend al-Tha'alibi, who happened to be in Baghdad at the time.[56] It wasn't too long before the court in Iraq provided him with an
allowance and his son Ibrahim with a job at the palace.[57] The network of connection he had been a part of since the late Ottoman period facilitated this. After all,
decision making in Iraq at the time was in the hands of those who, like al-Baruni,
were either previous Ottoman officers and dignitaries or their relatives.[58]

Al-Baruni kept moving back and forth between Oman and Iraq, the only two
places where he was allowed to set foot, but it was increasingly mostly from Baghdad that he corresponded with friends and newspaper editors. Relentless, and desperate to leave Muscat, he wrote to the French foreign minister in September 1939
offering his services should Italy declare war on France and suggesting that he
should go to Tunis right away.[59] He hoped France would help liberate his home
country from the Italians and end his exile. The opportunity to return home finally
presented itself. On June 8, 1940, the Middle East Intelligence Centre in Cairo sent
a telegram to the British political resident in Muscat requesting on behalf of the
French general officer commanding North Africa that al-Baruni be asked if he was
willing to go to Algiers "as soon as possible to undertake certain work in connection with Libya."[60] He certainly would have relished that long-awaited opportunity.
But he had died on May 1, during a trip to Bombay in the company of Oman's
sultan, Sayyid Sa'id. Before he traveled, he had confided to his daughter that he
would try again to find his way into either Tunisia or Egypt.[61] He never got the
chance. The places that had provided him with the opportunities to enter the
realms of journalism, publishing, politics, and diplomacy and that were part of a
broader world he defined and defended as his own remained out of his reach.

CONCLUSION

Discussing his biography of Evelyn Baring, the first Lord Cromer, a British administrator in Egypt, Roger Owen notes how issues relating to globalization and imperialism "present themselves in a somewhat higgledy-piggledy fashion in the com-
pass of an individual life."[62] The life of Sulayman al-Baruni certainly illustrates
developments in these fields. His movements between different cities and centers
of learning, his adoption of a definition of Islam that sought Muslim unity, and his
publishing activities all shaped a career that defined him as a Muslim reformer, an
Ottoman pasha, a field commander, and an anticolonial leader. Lord Cromer was

a punch line for al-Baruni, epitomizing European imperialism's insult and threat to Islam, which only a united Muslim community could neutralize.[63]

Of all the phases of globalization in world history, the one in the late nineteenth and early twentieth centuries presented exceptional challenges to Muslim societies. It featured Western imperialism and colonialism of Muslim lands and undermined Muslim political sovereignty in many localities. But it also provided Muslims with tools that enabled them to resist, respond to, and maneuver within the new realities: improved means of travel and communication, such as the printing press. The challenges and the opportunities of this new world order greatly affected al-Baruni and his generation of Muslim intellectuals. As an institution of connectivity among them, the network was widely transformed; more frequent and faster interactions meant a greater ability to generate and execute responses to challenges. One such response was the Ibadi-Sunni attempt to form a united front against imperialism, born of and creating further opportunities for cross-sectarian and transnational encounters in cosmopolitan Arab cities—and beyond. Using globalization as a framework of analysis to understand such crucial developments at the end of the nineteenth century reveals new answers and sheds light on new dynamics. It allows us to highlight interactions in their multiple directions, map communications, trace the new ties and connections forged by more-globalized groups and individuals, and track the movement of ideas and their impacts on specific localities. It produces a richer, if not a more complete, picture, as it brings together multiple currents and captures the width and breadth of cross-regional and transnational interactions channeled through networks.

NOTES

Research for this project was made possible by grants from the Social Sciences and Humanities Research Council in Canada and from the Gerda Henkel Foundation in Germany.

1. Abi al-Yaqzan al-Hajj Ibrahim, *Sulayman al-Baruni Basha fi Atwar Hayatih,* 2 vols. (n.p., 1956), 1:169.

2. Miriam Cooke and Bruce B. Lawrence, preface to *Muslim Networks: From Hajj to Hip Hop,* ed. Cooke and Lawrence (Chapel Hill: University of North Carolina Press, 2005), xii.

3. Anthony Hopkins's characterization of the interwar period as a phase of "deglobalization," when "the closing of global possibilities after 1914 seems to have been very far-reaching," does not hold true. The presence of thriving transnational networks defies such a conclusion. See Hopkins, "The History of Globalization," in *Globalization in World History,* ed. Hopkins (London: Pimlico, 2002), 158–59; see also Amira Bennison, "Muslim Universalism and Western Globalization," in ibid., 92–93.

4. The only work in English on the life and career of al-Baruni is A. J. Peterson, "Arab Nationalism and the Idealist Politician: The Career of Sulayman al-Baruni (1870–1940)," in *Law, Personalities and Politics in the Middle East: Essays in Honor of Majid Khadduri,* ed. James Piscatori and George S. Harris (Boulder, CO: Westview, 1987), 124–39.

5. Cooke and Lawrence, *Muslim Networks,* 1.

6. Juan R. I. Cole, "Printing and Urban Islam in the Mediterranean World, 1890–1920," in *Modernity and Culture: From the Mediterranean to the Indian Ocean,* ed. Leila Fawaz and C. A. Bayly (New York: Columbia University Press, 2002), 344–64.

7. Saskia Sassen, ed., *Global Networks: Linked Cities* (New York: Routledge, 2002).

8. For an excellent account of Khariji history, see Najiya al-Warimi Bu ʿJila, *Al-Islam al-Khariji* (Beirut: Dar al-Taliʿa li-l-Nashr, 2006).

9. For more details on the tenets of Ibadism, see Valerie Hoffman, *The Essentials of Ibadi Islam* (Syracuse, NY: Syracuse University Press, 2012). The Ibadi scholar Amr Ennami also wrote a useful guide, "Studies in Ibadism" (PhD thesis, Cambridge University, 1971). However, it adopts the reformist approach of Ibrahim Atfiyyash, which disassociates Ibadism from Kharijism (see n. 14). It is also the case that studies on the history of Ibadism have focused on Oman more than North Africa. See, for instance, Adam Gaiser, *Muslims, Scholars, Soldiers: The Origin and Elaboration of the Ibadi Imamate Traditions* (Oxford: Oxford University Press, 2010); John C. Wilkinson, *Ibadism: Origins and Early Development in Oman* (Oxford: Oxford University Press, 2010).

10. Amal Ghazal, "Seeking Common Ground: Salafism and Islamic Reform in Modern Ibadi Thought," *Bulletin for the Royal Institute of Inter-faith Studies* 7, no. 1 (2005): 119–41.

11. Amal Ghazal, *Islamic Reform and Arab Nationalism: Expanding the Crescent from the Mediterranean to the Indian Ocean, 1880s–1930s* (New York: Routledge, 2010).

12. Ibrahim Atfiyyash, *Al-Diʿaya ila Sabil al-Muʾminin* (Cairo: Al-Matbaʿa al-Salafiyya, 1923).

13. Qasim ibn Saʿid al-Shammakhi, *Al-Qawl al-Matin fi al-Radd ʿala al-Mukhalifin* (Cairo: Matbaʿat Majallat al-Manar, 1906).

14. Ibrahim Atfiyyash, "Safha min al-Tarikh: Kayfa Imtazat al-Ibadiyya ʿan al-Khawarij," *Al-Zahra* 1, no. 3 (14 October 1924): 186–89.

15. Ibrahim, *Sulayman al-Baruni*, 1:40–41.

16. ʿAli al-Zaydi, *Al-Zaytuniyyun: Dawruhum fi al-Haraka al-Wataniyya, 1904–1945* (Sfax, Tunisia: Dar Noha, 2007).

17. James McDougall, *History and the Culture of Nationalism in Algeria* (Cambridge: Cambridge University Press, 2006), 36.

18. Arnold H. Green, *The Tunisian Ulama 1873–1915: Social Structure and Response to Ideological Currents* (Leiden, Netherlands: E. J. Brill, 1978), esp. pt. 2.

19. Ibrahim, *Sulayman al-Baruni*, 1:48.

20. Salih al-Khirfi, ʿAbd al-ʿAziz al-Thaʿalibi: min Atharih wa Akhbarih fi al-Mashriq wa-l-Maghrib (Beirut: Dar al-Gharb al-Islami, 1995).

21. Sulayman al-Baruni, *Diwan al-Baruni*, vol. 2 (Cairo: Al-Azhar al-Baruniyya, 1908), 40–41, 69–72.

22. Nur al-Din al-Salimi, *Tuhfat al-Aʿyan bi Sirat Ahl ʿUman*, vol. 2 (Al-Sib, Oman: Maktabat al-Imam Nur al-Din al-Salimi, 2000), 263.

23. Muhammad bin Yusuf Atfiyyash, *Izalat al-Iʿtirad ʿan Muhiqqi Al Ibad* (Oman: Wizarat al-Turath al-Qawmi wa-l-Thaqafa, 1982).

24. Ibrahim, *Sulayman al-Baruni*, 1:74.

25. Zaʿima Sulayman al-Baruni, *Safahat Khalida min al-Jihad* (Cairo: Matabiʿ al-Istiqlal al-Kubra, 1964), 12, 59–65.

26. Al-Baruni, *Diwan*, 21–32. Unless otherwise stated, all translations are mine.

27. 13 August 1318 (31 August 1902), Dahiliye Nezareti Mektubi Kalemi (DH.MKT) 575/44, Başbakanlık Osmanlı Arşivi (BOA), Istanbul.

28. Muhammad Atfiyyash, "Talab Itlaq Sarah al-Baruni bin Abd Alla," *Rasaʾil wa Ajwibat al-Qutb* (digital copy), Jamʿiyyat al-Shaykh Abi Ishaq Ibrahim Atfiyyash li Khidmat al-Turath, Ghardaia, Algeria.

29. Ibrahim, *Sulayman al-Baruni*, 1:83; al-Baruni, *Diwan*, 5, 120.

30. Zaʿima al-Baruni, *Safahat Khalida*, 8–30.

31. Ibn Bashir bin Humayyid al-Salimi, *Nahdat al-Aʿyan bi Hurriyyat ʿUman* (Beirut: Dar al-Jil, 1998), 92–93.

32. Zaima al-Baruni, *Safahat Khalida,* 13–16.

33. "Action Turque en Tripolitaine," 7 February 1920, no. 33, box 29/H/9, Archives nationales d'outre-mer (ANOM), Aix-en-Provence, France.

34. "Tripoli. Correspondence," 5 January 1923, no. 521, box 29/H/9, ANOM.

35. Ibrahim, *Sulayman al-Baruni,* 2:10.

36. Ibid., 1:185–191.

37. Letter from Slimane el Barouni, 8 December 1922, no. 7083, box 29/H/9, ANOM.

38. Le Ministre des Affaires Etrangers à M. le Gouverneur Général de l'Algérie, 15 January 1923, box 29/H/9, ANOM.

39. Ibrahim, *Sulayman al-Baruni,* 1:197–98, 204–6.

40. Ibid., 1:237–53.

41. Ibrahim, *Sulayman al-Baruni,* 2:44.

42. He also contributed to *Al-Rabita al-Arabiyya* (Tunisia), *Al-Liwa ʾ al-Tarabulsi* (Libya), and *Alif Ba* (Iraq).

43. For the central role of al-Khatib and his printing press in Salafi networks, see Amal N. Ghazal, "The Other Frontiers of Arab Nationalism: Ibadis, Berbers and the Arabist-Salafi Press in the Interwar Period," *International Journal of Middle East Studies* 42, no. 1 (2010): 105–22.

44. "Janib ʿAmir min Jawanib al-Qiyada," *Al-Fath* 551 (28 May 1937): 15; "Kitab min Sahib al-Saʿada Sulayman Basha al-Baruni," *Al-Fath* 532 (14 January 1937): 18. Those accusations were leveled mostly by Muhammad Fekini. See Angelo del Boca, *Mohamed Fekini and the Fight to Free Libya,* trans. Anthony Shugaar (New York: Palgrave Macmillan, 2011), 31–36. Al-Baruni's biographer Abu al-Yaqzan Ibrahim asked al-Baruni's daughter Zaʿima to answer them. Her refutations are in Ibrahim, *Sulayman al-Baruni,* 1:169–83.

45. Ibrahim, *Sulayman al-Baruni,* 2:154–59.

46. Sulayman al-Baruni to Hashil al-Maskari, 13 February 1929, private collection.

47. Muhammad Sadun Jubran, *Sulayman al-Baruni: Atharuh* (Libya: Al-Dar al-ʿArabiyya li-l-Kitab, 1991), 279–335.

48. Ibrahim, *Sulayman al-Baruni,* 2:126–77.

49. Ibid., 82–84.

50. William Cleveland, *Islam against the West: Shakib Arslan and the Campaign for Islamic Nationalism* (Austin: University of Texas Press, 1985), 128.

51. Sulayman Pasha al-Baruni, "Sulayman Pasha al-Baruni Yuʿlin al-Baraʾa min al-Amir Shakib Arslan," *Al-Umma* 4, no. 147 (21 December 1937): 1–2; no. 148 (28 December 1937): 1–2; no. 149 (4 January 1938): 1–2.

52. Cleveland, *Islam against the West,* 161–62.

53. Ibrahim, *Sulayman al-Baruni,* 2:32–33, 45–46.

54. "Suleman al-Baruni al-Nufusi," 19 October 1938, PZ 7014/38, HM's Political Agency and Consulate at Muscat, the National Archives (TNA), Kew, Richmond, U.K.

55. "Activism of Suleiman al-Baruni al-Nufusi," 17 November 1938, E 6895/6895/91, India Office, TNA.

56. Ibrahim, *Sulayman al-Baruni,* 2:98–99.

57. Ibid., 105–6.

58. In one of his letters to Ibrahim, al-Baruni explains that the decision to provide him with an allowance was due to the intercession of Mahmud Shawkat, the Ottoman minister of war between 1910 and 1912 and grand vizier in 1913, who knew al-Baruni well and used to praise him in front of the Iraqi prime minister Hikmat Sulayman, Shawkat's brother. Ibid., 112–13.

59. "Suleiman al Baruni al Nafusi," 19 September 1939, R/15/6/449, India Office, British Library.

60. Telegram from Middle Eastern Intelligence Center, Cairo, to political resident, Muscat, 8 June 1940, R/15/6/449, India Office, British Library.

61. Ibrahim, *Sulayman al-Baruni*, 2:243.

62. Roger Owen, "Using Present Day Notions of Imperialism, Globalization and Internationalism to Understand the Middle East's Late Nineteenth Century/Early Twentieth Century Past," *MIT Electronic Journal of Middle East Studies* 4 (2003): 8.

63. Za'ima al-Baruni, *Safahat Khalida*, 11–15.

3

"A Leading Muslim of Aden"

Personal Trajectories, Imperial Networks,
and the Construction of Community
in Colonial Aden

Scott S. Reese

INTRODUCTION

In a 1922 letter to the first assistant resident of Aden, the chief qadi of the settlement, Da'ud al-Battah, declared that Muhammad Yasin Khan, his friend and colleague on the city's Waqf Committee, was a learned and "leading Mohammedan of Aden."[1] A number of peculiarities surrounding this statement make it worthy of note. First, M. Y. Khan, while certainly learned, was not a member of the local ulama but a Bombay-trained lawyer and an active member of the Indian Civil Service. Second and even more intriguing, neither Khan nor al-Battah was from Aden. Al-Battah hailed from Zabid, a town in Yemen's interior known as a center of Sunni religious scholarship, while Khan was from the United Provinces in India and had lived in Aden for fewer than four years. Despite this, al-Battah had no qualms about claiming membership for both of them in the community of Aden Muslims. And in fact, through the 1920s, Khan played an increasingly important role in the day-to-day affairs of Aden's Muslim community, beyond the scope of his official duties. Rather than exceptional, declarations such as al-Battah's of being Adeni were commonplace among the Muslims who resided in the port even for brief periods and generally went unchallenged by their coreligionists.

This volume is devoted to the study of Muslim global networks in the Age of Steam and Print, a period brought about in large part by the advent of European empire building across Africa and Asia. In recent years a great deal has been written about the webs, nodes, and networks of the various European Indian Ocean empires. Most of these works have focused on the political, legal, or economic consequences of empire, with far less attention devoted to the realms of the personal or the social, let alone the spiritual.[2] The global connections among Muslims of this period constituted an important system of networks that frequently ran parallel to those created by empire. For many Muslims, interactions with imperial networks were incidental and intermittent (the Muslim students and pilgrims discussed in Amal Ghazal's and Eric Tagliacozzo's chapters 2 and 5, respectively, who traveled on European steamships to either further their educations in the lesson circles of Al-Azhar or fulfill religious obligations in Mecca). I do not wish to imply that such brushes with imperial networks were inconsequential, but in terms of shaping individual lives, interactions with fellow Muslims remained more important. For others, the intersection with imperial networks not only was more direct and long term but also brought them together with other individuals and their attendant religious proclivities in novel ways, resulting in the creation of new social realities. While many of the pieces in this collection rightly focus on broad geographic sweeps to understand the extent of Muslim networks in the nineteenth and twentieth centuries, this contribution focuses on a single locale to unpack the ramifications of global Muslim intellectual networks on the everyday lives of believers.

Using the British Settlement of Aden, this chapter examines the convergence of various—though not necessarily incompatible—individual religious trajectories brought together by the networks of the British imperial state. Through the careers of Muhammad Yasin Khan,[3] Qadi Da'ud, and others like them it explores how individuals from widely disparate backgrounds created a cohesive community using the one commonality at their disposal: their faith.[4] Specifically, it considers how Islamic institutions and spiritual ideas served as parameters for the creation of this community and the kinds of symbolic and cultural capital an individual needed to attain influence as a "leading Muslim" within the confines of imperial rule.

ADEN, EMPIRE, AND THE CONVERGENCE OF PERSONAL TRAJECTORIES

In a recent series of essays, Frederick Cooper challenged historians to reconsider and question many of our common assumptions about colonial milieus and examine empire as a space where "concepts were not only imposed but engaged and contested."[5] In particular, he argues, we spend so much effort constructing models of domination and hegemony that we frequently neglect large swaths of historical process, giving "insufficient weight to the ways in which colonized peoples sought ... to build lives in the crevices of colonial power, deflecting, appropriating, or reinterpreting the teachings and preachings thrust upon them."[6] He notes that, in effect, we systematically lose sight of the dialogues among the colonized, forgetting to ask how people put their thoughts together within the contexts of their own social and cultural traditions as well as those constructed and promoted by the colonial milieu. Cooper's argument is a clarion call for a deeper and more nuanced approach to colonial social history. However, his words are also an invitation to explore the construction of "place" within the imperial context.

Over the past several years, historians have begun to approach empire as a complex web of political and economic power.[7] This has been helpful in challenging the presumed hegemonic dominance of the imperial center by, in the words of David Lambert and Alan Lester, "enabl[ing] us to think about the inherent relationality of nodal points or 'centres' within an empire" and to undercut "simple metropole-binary divides."[8] This analytical framework is enormously useful in allowing us to approach empire from a perspective that avoids privileging the metropole over the colony, enabling us to envision empire as a dynamic process of multidirectional flows in which not only the metropole but also other colonies can have an impact on each colony, and vice versa. Until now, historians of Britain's Indian Ocean Empire have focused largely on the political, social, and ideological consequences of flows created by the state. While this work is important, in doing it they have largely ignored the networks created by colonized subjects that also cut across imperial space.[9]

As Thomas Metcalf and Sugata Bose have both demonstrated, in the absence of large white settler populations, only the mass migration of thousands of non-European—largely South Asian—soldiers, bureaucrats, merchants, and laborers made possible Britain's empire in the Indian Ocean. And, as Metcalf notes, "the practice of empire [around the Indian Ocean] was . . . shaped by structures of governance devised in British India," which left an indelible mark on many of the colonized peoples there, "creat[ing] a sense of . . . 'Indian' nationality" among local South Asians who participated in the imperial project.[10] Colonial India constituted a critical "subimperial" node which tied Britain's Indian Ocean domain together and played a crucial role in creating contemporary Indian national identity.[11]

While important works of synthesis that provide us with a compelling framework for conceptualizing the totality of Britain's Indian Ocean empire, Metcalf's and Bose's books leave us with a somewhat incomplete picture. Both focus largely on the Hindu and, to a lesser extend, Sikh experience of empire. They presume that Muslims, who constituted a significant proportion of the police, military, civil service, and even overseas merchant communities, fell into the same patterns as their Hindu, Jain, and Sikh colleagues. An initial examination of the evidence from Aden, however, suggests otherwise. Metcalf contends, for instance, that the overseas colonies outside South Asia were fertile ground for the growth of Indian nationalism in general and the Congress party in particular. Curiously, however, neither Congress, the Muslim League, nor even the Khilafat movement was ever able to gain any ground among the large South Asian community of Aden, which was largely, if not wholly, Muslim. The Congress party's one attempt to establish itself there received an apathetic response from local Indians, while the Khilafat movement was met with open derision by at least one prominent Muslim intellectual with close ties to

India.[12] Instead, the Muslim South Asians of Aden involved themselves far more closely in local issues concerning daily life in the settlement. Concern over the administration of pious endowments, saints' festivals, and the reform of local religious practice tended to dominate public debate, revealing a much greater preoccupation with real and immediate local problems than with any discussion of a distant and nebulous national consciousness. This is not to suggest that the larger religious and political networks that individuals belonged to were unimportant, nor that Metcalf's conclusions are incorrect. However, by exploring data for various parts of the empire and from differing perspectives (in this case those of Muslims), it is possible to provide a more nuanced picture. Even in a place as highly mobile as the busy port of Aden, attachment and identification with the local community could form as important an element of an individual's social existence as his or her affiliation with any larger social identity.

Despite recognition of the fact that the creation of the imperial web required the occupation and domination of new spaces, there is surprisingly little thought given to the creation of place within this context. Lambert and Lester, in their book *Colonial Lives across the British Empire*, argue that within the network concept of imperial space, "places are not so much bounded entities," but rather specific juxtapositions or constellations of multiple trajectories . . . of people, objects, texts and ideas."[13] In short, place emerges as a result of the convergence of various trajectories in space and time. If we are to gain any insight into the creation of communities within the web of empire, we need to look not simply at the legal, administrative, and economic apparatuses it created but, more importantly, at the lives of individuals and the social frameworks they created.

There were probably few spots in Britain's empire where as many intellectual and social trajectories intersected to shape a new community as at Aden.[14] When troops of the East India Company occupied the port in 1839, it was home to a modest population of no more than twelve hundred residents. This had grown to more than twelve thousand by the 1849 census, nineteen thousand by 1871, and nearly fifty thousand by 1939.[15] The overwhelming majority were Muslim; Jews formed the largest minority, always less than 10 percent of the whole, and there were never more than a few hundred Parsis, Hindus, and "native" Christians. This Muslim community was also one of the most ethnically and confessionally heterogeneous in the empire, including Arabs, Indians, and Somalis, who might be Sunnis, Shi'is, or Isma'ilis.

Aden's administration was no less eclectic than its population. While a select few Europeans always occupied the upper echelons of power, mainly non-Europeans, largely Indians and Arabs, staffed the vast bureaucracy of the station. In addition to gazetted and nongazetted officers of the Civil Service (who ranged from sanitation inspectors and patrolmen on the beat to inspectors of police and lower civil court judges), British administration depended on the local religious elite and other "respectable" citizens to oversee various bureaucratic and social needs of the community. Government-appointed qadis, for instance, oversaw the registration of marriages and divorces, while the *shams al-ʿulama* (literally the "sun of scholars" and always the leading member of the Aydarus family of sharif notables) was charged with mediating minor civil disputes and overseeing the running of the settlement's numerous cemeteries.

Probably the biggest social question facing this disparate body of believers through the nineteenth century and into the twentieth was who or what constituted an Adeni. The anthropologist Abdullah Bujra noted in an article from 1970 that this particularly preoccupied the enclave's elites.[16] But the issue is not only how the boundaries of community were delimited but also how elites—who were enormously transient—laid claim to the moral authority necessary to create such boundaries. While the elite Muslims of Aden had a multiplicity of personal trajectories, faith—and the institutions and ideals associated with it—provided a common template for the articulation of community and the exercise of power and authority within it.

ELITE TRAJECTORIES

By the early twentieth century, there existed two distinct—though intertwined—groups of elite Muslims in what was officially referred to as the Aden Settlement. One consisted of largely secular educated individuals who were either members of the imperial bureaucracy or had some tangential tie to it, such as being the children of bureaucrats. The other comprised traditionally educated religious scholars, merchants, and other notables whose connection to the state, and thus official authority, was far more tenuous. Rather than engaging in perpetual rivalry, however, these various elites of Aden frequently mixed in the same social and political circles.

Several factors may help account for the complex relationships we find among these elites. First, virtually none could be described as entrenched, or the beneficiaries of hereditary authority or power. Both secular and traditional elites (with one significant exception) can best be described as nouveau, with their traditions of social authority rarely extending further than a couple of generations into the past. Many influential bureaucrats, such as Yasin Khan—the focus of this chapter—had no connection with the city before their posting. Others, such as Khan's predecessor as registrar, Sayyid Rustom ʿAli, or members of the ubiquitous Luqman family, were born in the settlement but rose to prominence only via their relatively recent connections with the state. The service lists describe Rustom ʿAli, for instance, who was born in Aden in 1863, as an "Indian Mohammedan" who joined the residency in a "non-Gazetted" position in 1877 (at the age of fourteen)."[17] He rose to the senior post of registrar apparently by dint of his ambition rather than any kind of family legacy. Similarly, the rise of 'Ali Isma'il Luqman to the post of head residency interpreter at the end of World War I marked the ascent to local prominence of his family—whose members were important landlords, lawyers, and intellectuals starting in the 1920s—although they made rather shaky genealogical claims to a presence in the city dating to the seventeenth century.[18]

However, if imperial—for lack of a better word—elites could not lay claim to deep roots in the city or impressive intellectual legacies to sustain their social authority, neither could most of the so-called traditional elites. The Sharaf family, for instance, who maintained a monopoly over the qadiship of Shaykh 'Uthman (an important outlying suburb) from the late 1890s through the Second World War, were the descendants of a minor port officer rather than a family of 'alims, or trained religious scholars. The Makkawis—prominent landlords, merchants, and notables, plus the occasional religious scholar—owed their power, wealth, and social standing to their dubious past as fixers for the British administration and their uncanny ability to simply make problems go away. In fact, two of the settlement's most prominent religious leaders of the interwar period, Da'ud al-Battah, the qadi of Crater, and Shaykh Ahmad al-Abbadi, the recognized leader of the local Salafi movement, were outsiders, the former from Zabid and the latter from Ibb, both in Yemen. Although both were well educated in the Islamic sciences, neither seems to have been able to lay claim to a distinguished family or intellectual genealogy or any longstanding connection to Aden. The lone exception to the dearth of familial prestige was the shams al-'ulama' Sayyid 'Abdullah al-'Aydarus. Virtually alone among Aden's notables, he was convincingly able to trace his ancestry to precolonial Aden, via his ancestor Abu Bakr 'Aydarus (d. 1508), who also happened to be the port's most important wali, or saint. As a result of his genealogical and scholarly bona fides, the British administration recognized Sayyid 'Abdullah as the head, or *mansab*, of the local Muslim community. Somewhat ironically, however, he was also one of the most marginalized of Aden's elites.

While most of those in Aden with pretentions to social influence and authority might be described as neophytes, they could not be called parochial. Across the board, the notables of twentieth-century Aden were well traveled and well read. The registrar Rustom 'Ali, while mostly self-educated, owned a large library of both Western and Islamic law books. His successor, Yasin Khan, was a Bombay-trained lawyer with a penchant for quoting Alfred Tennyson who went on the hajj three times and traveled throughout the Hijaz.[19] Muhammad 'Ali Luqman, the most prominent member of the Luqman family, was similarly educated in Bombay but also worked for the Antonin Besse Company, in Berbera, in what is now Somalia, and maintained links with at least one Egyptian reformist newspaper, to which he contributed before founding his own newspaper dynasty in Aden in 1940.

Those on the opposite side of the coin were no less sophisticated, and many of the settlement's religious leaders were well educated and widely traveled. Ahmad al-Abbadi, the leader of the local Salafi movement, studied and traveled throughout Persia and South Asia before settling in Aden, while Ahmad al-Asnag, another prominent advocate of Salafism, was a self-made man (with a fishmonger father) who had traveled throughout the Horn of Africa, Egypt, and even Europe and wrote at least two books on the necessity of social reform and the virtues of Salafism.[20] Da'ud al-Battah, while seemingly less well traveled, appears in the colonial record as a well-read 'alim conversant with current intellectual trends in the *umma*.

The elite Muslims of Aden had a plethora of personal trajectories and ties to a variety of Islamic intellectual networks, but they all shared certain commonalities that might draw them together. In particular, education and official—sometimes quasi-official—positions pushed these individuals to the forefront of local society. Let us now turn to a detailed examination of some of the complex relationships that evolved among elements of these two groups in the 1920s as part of a reimaging of communal Muslim leadership in the age of high colonialism. In particular, I want to delve into the associations among the settlement's registrar, Yasin Khan; Qadi Da'ud al-Battah; and other notables as a window onto some of the ways in which personal trajectories could combine to create a local space.

REGISTRAR KHAN AND THE WAQF COMMITTEE

As a fresh law graduate from the United Provinces of Agra and Oudh, Yasin Khan arrived in Aden in 1918 to serve as a temporary extraordinary assistant resident. In 1919 he was named acting registrar, an appointment that was made permanent in 1920. He served for at least fifteen years in this position, which included a number of secondments as hajj officer in the mid-1920s. As registrar, Khan's primary duties involved adjudicating civil cases over property valued at—generally—less than five hundred rupees. However, he involved himself in several matters that concerned religious practice rather than civil wrongs. Early in his tenure a group of notables led by the shams al-'ulama' Sharif 'Abdullah 'Aydarus, with the support of the Aden qadi, Da'ud al-Battah, petitioned the resident for official recognition of a Waqf Committee to oversee the administration of properties within the settlement dedicated to the support of various mosques and shrines. Waqf, or pious endowment, is a practice dating to the earliest centuries of Islam, in which the revenue from a particular property—which might include agricultural land, shops, market stalls, or, as in this case, rental properties—is dedicated to the upkeep of a given institution such as a mosque, madrasa, or hospital.

The 1921 petition stated that the agents charged with overseeing the settlement's numerous waqf properties frequently embezzled the rents, and as a result, the mosques and the properties themselves were in a disgraceful state of repair. If steps were not taken, the mosques of Aden would soon "become a danger to the public and the public health." In an effort to remedy the situation, the letter said, "a number of leading citizens of Aden have met in [the] Shams al-'Ulama''s house and appointed a committee of 6 persons ... with [the] Shams al-Ulema [*sic*] as chairman to take delivery of these houses, to recover the rents [and] spend the same in the interests of the mosques, and generally to look after (preserve) the mosques and their interests."[21] The British administration declined to formally recognize the committee but acknowledged that such a group would undoubtedly improve the state of sacred sites in the settlement and permitted Registrar Khan to act, in "his private capacity," as an adviser to the group.[22]

In its first year of operation, the Waqf Committee encountered a number of problems, in the attempted resolution of which Khan played a pivotal role, becoming an ardent partisan of the so-called traditional elite—or, as we shall see, at least some of them. Not surprisingly, a number of waqf administrators were not pleased with the formation of the committee or its self-appointed charge. Soon after its creation, the committee began to serve notice to administrators that it would henceforth collect all waqf property rents. At least two of these agents refused to cooperate and raised formal objections. In April 1921, Ahmad 'Abdullah Khayyat protested the actions of the self-appointed committee to the first assistant resident, Bernard Reilly.[23] Khayyat stated that he had been "superintendent and collector of the incomes of certain wakfs in Aden" for a great many years. He carried out his duties "with all honesty and energy to the entire satisfaction of the judges and the last Kazi [qadi] Sayyid Muhammad bin Hasan al-Hazmi," who had appointed him, and the usurpation of his duties by the committee was both egregious and illegal. The committee chair, Sharif 'Abdullah, had said that "I must hand over my charge to him and he has instigated the tenants not to pay the rents to me as customary." This, Khayyat argued, was "contrary to all usage for I have not been guilty of any breach of trust or misconduct in [my administration] of the Wakfs."[24] 'Ali Ghalib Noman lodged a similar petition, seeking legal action against members of the committee for trespass when they began collecting rents from tenants of waqf properties administered by his father, Ghalib ibn Noman.[25]

Whether encouraged by the residency or on his own initiative, Khan stepped in as negotiator for and adviser to the Waqf Committee, assuring acceptance of its authority in principle over the settlement's waqf property. In a note to the first assistant resident dated September 20, 1921, Khan noted that he and the committee had overcome Khayyat and Noman's objections by agreeing to add them to the group. "All persons concerned," he wrote, "agree that the Wakf property should be placed in charge of the Wakf Committee and that Ahmad 'Abdullah Khayyat and Ghalib Noman should also be members of that Committee ... [and that] past accounts, so far as possible, will not be considered and that any dispute relating to the management of the Wakf property will be decided amicably by the members and that if any dispute arises it will be referred to the undersigned [M. Y. Khan] for [adjudication] in his private capacity. The matter is considered settled and every one promises that he shall abide by it and make no further petitions."[26]

The importance of Khan's role in this matter was twofold. First, from the point of view of the administration, his participation (in his "private capacity," of course) established the legitimacy of the committee and secured its right to collect rents from waqf property. Writing to the parties involved a few days later, FAR Reilly endorsed not only the supremacy of the committee over waqf property but also Khan's place as arbiter of any and all related disputes:

> With reference to the correspondence ending with your letter dated 8th August 1921, we write to inform you that Mr. Yasin Khan, Registrar, Court of the Resident, has informed us that the question regarding the management of *wakf* property in Aden has been amicably settled and that all persons concerned agree.
>
> 1. That wakf property should be placed in charge of the Wakf Committee.
> 2. That Ahmed Abdulla Khayat [*sic*] and Galib [*sic*] Noman should also be members of the Committee.
> 3. That past accounts will not, so far as possible, be considered.
> 4. That any dispute relating to the management of the wakf property will be decided amicably by the members.
> 5. That if any dispute arises, it will be referred to the Registrar, Court of the Resident, for opinion in his private capacity.
> 6. That the matter is considered settled and every one promises that he will abide by it and make no further petition.
>
> We are glad to hear of this and we trust that the wakf property will prosper under the management of the Wakf Committee as now constituted.[27]

This statement effectively recognized Khan as the Waqf Committee's most influential, if informal, member and made him (in the words of Qadi al-Battah) a "leading Mohammedan" of the settlement. He was a man to be courted.

Despite his obvious conflicts of interest, Khan was allowed to rule on petitions concerning the committee, which, needless to say, had a chilling affect on complaints—the second important effect of his appointment. Still not satisfied with the result of mediation, for instance, 'Ali Ghalib Noman once again sought to bring a case against the committee, in October 1921, for the return of his father's seized waqf properties. Khan dismissed the case summarily, noting that the suit had already been decided against Noman and that while he was sure to appeal, "no action [was] necessary on petitions that don't come under any rule of law." FAR Reilly anxiously agreed, writing on the following page, "As suggested by the Registrar no action need be taken in the matter."[28] It can hardly be seen as coincidental that no further cases were brought against the committee before the registrar for more than ten years.

One aim of those who founded the Waqf Committee was certainly to exert influence over an important local social institution that could serve to establish their claims of authority and the right to speak for the community as a whole. As we will see below, in taking control of the settlement's sacred endowments, at least some of the committee's members hoped to extend this authority to include most other sacred spaces in Aden (i.e., mosques and tombs), with the goal of making themselves the arbitrators of acceptable religious behavior, which could be used to define the community. The enthusiastic addition of Khan provided the committee with the bureaucratic weight to give their claims to authority real power. At the same time, Khan's officially sanctioned role on the committee gave him his own social capital and the ability to shape his adopted community.

While the committee was successful in gaining control over the settlement's religious endowments, all was not well within its ranks. In April 1922, Sayyid 'Abdullah al-Aydarus composed an impassioned letter to the first assistant resident denouncing the very committee he had helped to form. He accused certain members of attempting to expand their authority beyond the simple administration of the religious endowments to encompass virtually every aspect of public religious life. The sharif noted that he had initially given his support to the committee because many of the city's waqf properties had come under the control of "unsuitable persons who did not properly maintain their trusts." The committee had been formed at a meeting held in his own home and given a charge of one year. Unfortunately,

> after the aforesaid agreed upon period had expired, Muhammad 'Abd al-Qadir Makawi [sic] made 27 clauses, like a Law, which I did not consider to be suitable for the Mahomedan minds of Aden because it detracted [from] the respect [given to the Sufi brotherhoods called turuq] and gave all the power of authority in the Mosques and their employees and repairs of the Mosques and their Wakfs to his Uncle's son Saleh [bin] Abdulla Khalifa so that everything connected with reading prayers for the dead or addresses in the mosques could not take place except by permission of Saleh [bin] Abdulla Kahlifa [sic].[29]

Sharif 'Abdullah's complaint was not entirely disinterested, as his letter was accompanied by three petitions calling for the resident to recognize him as the leader of the Muslim community and the "chief" of all mosques and waqf property.[30]

Ultimately, al-Battah was identified as the leader of a number of confederates in this effort to take control of the town's public religious spaces—part, Aydarus implied, of their ideological agenda. Following the sayyid's preemptive complaint to the residency, however, al-Battah and his supporters were forced to abandon their plans and instead found themselves defending the committee they now largely controlled against charges of being a disruptive influence. Khan, who had already proved effective in assuring the Waqf Committee's authority over endowed properties, was quickly—and one could say cynically—pressed into service.

The registrar composed a letter regarding the legal position of the committee under both Islamic and British law that supported the actions of al-Battah and his followers. Unfortunately, that letter is apparently lost, but Qadi al-Battah refers to it in his denunciation of Sharif ʿAbdullah. From the text of this missive, it is evident that Khan, rather than being a mere pawn, exerted influence over the ideas and rhetoric that the Waqf Committee dissenters employed. The qadi wrote:

> With all due respect we beg to state that we are British Subjects and have, according to Mohamedan law as well as the laws of the British Government, certain rights which nobody can deprive us of (so long as we are under the protection of the British Government) by such threats as the occurrence of a breach of the peace. If this were possible nobody's rights would be safe and no court of justice can pressure them for him. The Mahomedan law and the British laws, the last of which is the Wakf Act of 1920, provide the necessary facilities for every Mahomedan to ask for an account and for all other particulars relating to wakfs from any trustee and to ask for his removal and the appointment of another trustee if necessary. Can Sayed Abdulla deprive any Mahomedan of this right by saying that a breach of the peace will take place if an account is demanded from him or if he is not allowed to preside over the Wakf Committee?[31]

In the end, neither side won a clear victory in this encounter.[32] Al-Battah and his allies were not able to exert control over the mosques, but Aydarus found himself quietly forced off the committee. However, the real importance of this incident lies in the correspondence concerning it and in Khan's apparent success in shifting the scope of the legal boundaries used to define the community. Unlike most correspondence from local ulama (Muslim scholars) prior to this, the qadi's letter did not invoke custom and mentioned Shariʿa only as a vague principal and only in concert with "British laws." Instead, it focused on the committee's right to exist under "the Wakf Act of 1920" and emphasized the rights under the law that were due to all British subjects.[33]

Al-Battah's adoption of such rhetoric was almost certainly opportunistic and should not be seen as a sudden, heartfelt recognition of the equality of British civil law and the holy Shariʿa. His letter does, however, indicate Khan's success in shifting an important communal boundary, as the law of the empire was now accepted as an important tool that could be brought to bear on the public religious lives of the community's members. Serving the Waqf Committee was not Khan's only encounter with religious authority during his tenure as resident. In 1925 he was again embroiled in a religious controversy. This time, however, he found himself at odds with his former ally Daʾud al-Battah.

THE INCIDENT ON KAMARAN ISLAND

The incident in question occurred on the island of Kamaran, which the British administered from Aden, and focused on a proposed extension to the local congregational mosque. Kamaran was an Ottoman possession until the end of the First World War, and its primary importance was as a quarantine station for pilgrims on their way to the hajj—a use that continued under the British (see chapter 5). As a result of this seasonal importance, it maintained a colonial presence much greater than its small population would have warranted otherwise and included a full-time European civil administrator, a sizable police contingent, a hospital, and a large administrative support staff.

In July 1924, a wealthy local merchant, Sayyid Muhyi al-Din Nur Ahmad, applied to the civil administrator for permission to extend the Friday mosque on the island. The CA consulted with the local qadi, who indicated that as long as the people of the community did not object, there was no obstacle to the plan. To cover his decision, the qadi also sent a letter to a certain Sayyid ʿAbd al-ʿAziz of Hodeidah seeking a fatwa, or legal opinion, on the matter, which was returned in the affirmative.[34] The mosque extension could go forward.

In mid-August, however, another wealthy merchant, Taher Rajab, returned to the island from the mainland and demanded that work cease. He carried three fatwas from ulama in Hodeidah declaring the work unlawful according to the Shariʿa. In a letter to FAR Reilly, the CA noted that before moving to the mainland, Rajab had served as the island's "nazir," and his family retained business interests on Kamaran. Locals viewed his opposition to the mosque extension as an effort to undercut the influence of Sayyid Muhyi al-Din, an up-and-coming rival. Work ground to a halt, and the CA called a meeting of the "leading inhabitants" to resolve the matter, but without a satisfactory result. So he decided to embark on a rather peculiar exercise in direct democracy. "I then suggested that a secret vote be taken by myself as to what was the true wish of the people, which I did yesterday, both parties agreeing to abide by the result. The question was: 'Do you wish the extension of the mosque on the northern side [?]' The responses were 43 yes, 107 no, and 18 'as the shariʿa orders.'" The CA further noted that "many did not express an opinion, and I think belong to the third class." He asked the first assistant resident to inquire among the learned of Aden "by whom should the expenses incurred by Sayyid Muhyi al-Din [for the work already done] be borne."[35]

The FAR sent the request to Khan for his opinion. The registrar in turn forwarded the case to Qadi Daʾud for the learned man's view. The judge responded by noting that the authorities were, in fact, asking the wrong question. Whether Sayyid Muhyi al-Din should be reimbursed was—as far as he was concerned—beside the point. The real issue, from the perspective of religious law, was whether the extension of the mosque was legal. The qadi stated uncategorically that those who opposed it—and claimed to provide a legal basis for their opposition—were in error. His opinion is worth quoting at length:

> On the subject of the permissibility of enlarging the Mosque situated at Kamaran about which there is a dispute among the Mohammedan inhabitants there, I inform you that ... the two written opinions contradict one another. One of them supports the permissibility and the other precludes it, hence the difference in its legality and illegality. ...

I have already received the contents of both opinions from Kamaran through one of the merchants of Aden, named Muhammad Awadth Moharez, and I have made my endorsement. . . . I quote from the fatwas of the learned Ibn Hajjar—

He was asked "Whether it is permissible to pull down and enlarge a Mosque?" He replied, saying, "Ibn Igal Al-Yamani permitted it, but the Asbaha disallowed it." Some commentators in the book "al-Wasit" [declared] that it was permissible provided there is a need for it and the Imam or his representatives supervises it. Such work has been done on the Mosques of Mecca and Medina on several occasions . . . and no one objected to such work.

As long as the intention of the person undertaking the work was to please God and to serve the interests of the people, and the mihrab (the niche in the wall that indicates the direction of prayer) and the minbar (the pulpit) were not pulled out of their proper alignments, there could be no objection to such a project. Da'ud concluded, "I concur with the learned men who gave permission for this [work] and I am of the opinion that it should not be prevented. No attention is to be paid to the majority of voters when there are no grounds for it."[36]

In his response, Khan began by dismissing the qadi's opinion. He remarked to Reilly that he had asked for the judge's opinion, but the reply was "irrelevant." The matter, as far as he was concerned, had "already been decided by votes against Muhyi al-Din. He was building the mosque for his own spiritual benefit and must bear the costs. A mosque is the property of God in the eye of the law and any money that is spent in extending or repairing it is an act of charity, and is not recoverable. If Muhyi al-Din had held the position of a trustee and spent money out of the trust funds in his hand, the position might have been different, but I presume this was not the case."[37]

In a striking fit of evenhandedness, Reilly forwarded both responses to Kamaran, as well as a third, joint opinion written by Da'ud and Sharif 'Abdullah al-'Aydarus that simply reiterated the qadi's original points. The dispute over the mosque continued on Kamaran for several months and largely ignored the opinions of both the qadi and the registrar. In the end the expansion project was abandoned, and Sayyid Muhyi al-Din was never reimbursed.

This incident sheds light on the complex relationship between Muslim bureaucrats and traditional religious elites in colonial Aden. As we have already seen, bureaucrats such as Khan, who were, for the most part, secularly educated, and more traditional ulama could work together to push a social agenda they found mutually agreeable, as in the case of the Waqf Committee. But this relationship was not without its cleavages. Khan believed that his education and his position entitled him to weigh in on religious matters and even critique the views of the traditional scholarly class. At the same time, as we see in the Kamaran mosque dispute, the ulama did not view this as a one-sided relationship. Friction between them and high-level bureaucrats, such as registrars, occurred throughout the period in question.[38] However, conflict was not necessarily axiomatic. The result was an almost continuous renegotiation of the boundaries of authority among Aden's Muslims, which was, of course, key to defining the community's moral limits. Such struggles invariably centered on Muslim ideals and institutions, with the various participants drawing on the broader intellectual networks to which they belonged. They also inevitably drew on the imperial context that formed the other important backdrop of their lives and ensured that their lives intersected with those of the people they fought with.

PERSONAL TRAJECTORIES, COMMUNITY BOUNDARIES

In her book *For Space,* Doreen Massey suggests that place can best be understood as the confluence of the trajectories of individuals.[39] I suggest that examining the discourses between individuals such as Khan and al-Battah helps us not only construct a history of place, by way of the trajectories that brought them together, but also understand how such trajectories helped shape the ideals these people held in common (or contested). Place is not a free-for-all, as Massey and Lambert and Lester are at pains to point out. "Trajectories," Lambert and Lester write, "both impose constraints on the material practices that humans adopt in place, and condition the imagination of place."[40] Hence it should come as little surprise that not only would Aden's public sphere be defined as inherently Islamic but any Muslim seeking to shape the community would have to do so through that rubric. The diversity of personal trajectories among the settlement's Muslims, however, meant that the boundaries and meanings of good standing in that community were constantly moving targets, subject to regular contestation.

The public careers of al-Battah and Khan provide an instructive window onto how the intersection of two individuals' trajectories—and their intellectual networks—could shape a local social context. With little in the way of an entrenched elite, Aden offered Khan and al-Battah far more opportunities for social and municipal prominence than their brief residences in the settlement might have afforded otherwise. Both, in fact, owed much of their influence in local circles to their official positions and ties to the administration. If their connections to official imperial networks endowed them with authority, it was the religious networks to which each belonged that caused them to take an interest in the moral fiber of the community and seek to effect change in a particular direction. While serving as functionaries of the state, both men were ideologically committed to the moral reform of Muslim society. Curiously, when the two worked in concert, they appeared as an almost unstoppable force. When opposing each other, they seemed to cancel out.

It would be easy to dismiss Khan as an ambitious imperial flunky anxious to lord his authority over the locals. However, there is a great deal of evidence to suggest that his interest arose from his religious convictions and was facilitated by the always fuzzy (if not nonexistent) lines between political, religious, and social authority in most Muslim societies. The registrar was a complex individual who was as much a pious Muslim as a skilled bureaucrat—a fact demonstrated by his making at least three hajjs during the 1920s. Twice (in 1923 and 1924) he was an official hajj officer, but his first experience, in 1921, was as a private individual using precious annual leave to undertake the trip. His official reports on the pilgrimage are suffused with both a paternalistic concern for what he regards as the superstition and ignorance of the average believer and the desire—indeed duty—to "fix" the faith through a combination of rationality and technical progress.[41] In this context, his involvement in various public religious issues can be read as the sign of a genuine desire to improve the lives of local believers through reforms that derived from his—what he viewed as—Enlightenment-informed principles (e.g., the bureaucratization of waqf and the introduction of limited democratic principles). Khan, it could be argued, wished to use his official position to improve the spiritual and social lives of his fellow believers. His thought and actions shared a great deal with what has come to be known as the Aligarh school of Islamic reform in India, which was associated with Sir Sayyid Ahmad Khan (no relation; 1817–98) and championed "scientific progress" as the remedy for Islam's nineteenth-century malaise.[42]

Because he was an ʿalim, al-Battah's interest in local moral affairs was hardly surprising. As with Khan, the qadi's activities outside the Waqf Committee reveal a good deal about his ideological leanings. Although little is known of his life before his arrival in Aden and appointment as qadi, various activities and associations of his within the settlement throughout the 1920s revealed his reformist leanings. During his involvement in the intrigues of the Waqf Committee, al-Battah was also prominent in a movement to ban various popular local practices considered of dubious morality. In particular, in the mid-1920s he joined forces with local Salafists in their efforts to outlaw the performance of various spirit possession ceremonies (known as *zar* and *tamburra*) and in an abortive attempt to prohibit or at least severely curtail various activities surrounding local saints' festivals known as *ziyarat* (pilgrimage). The strict scripturalist school of these reformers holds that only a return to the teachings and practices of "the pious ancestors" (*al-salif al-salih*) and the elimination of centuries of "unlawful innovations" (*bidaʿ*) rife among the faithful can revitalize the moral fiber of Muslim society. While al-Battah never declared himself an adherent of Salafism, his signature on several petitions supporting Salafist initiatives certainly points to sympathy with the school's aims and beliefs.[43]

As each had a clear concern for the moral well-being of their fellow believers, the trajectories of Khan and al-Battah, as well as other religious notables, naturally intersected. Their cooperation resulted in the reshaping of at least one communal norm, with the shift from private management by individuals to corporate communal control of waqf property, although al-Battah's larger goal of central control over all local religious institutions was frustrated. The use of Khan, however, caused other, unanticipated shifts in the boundaries of local practice. In defending their ill-fated scheme, al-Battah and his allies acknowledged that imperial law could be recognized as virtually equal to religious law. Almost certainly a ploy on the qadi's part, the citing of imperial law as a ruling norm of his society was a novel avenue for bolstering religious and communal authority, through subjecthood.

However, as we saw in the example of the incident on Kamaran, the effectiveness of Khan's involvement was hardly a foregone conclusion. While certain boundaries could be shifted, others could not. When Khan attempted to appropriate the right to interpret religious law, applying his Aligarh-inspired principles, the reaction was swift and unequivocal. To check the ambitious thrust of his sometime ally, al-Battah pushed back with all the weight of Islamic learning, including the legal opinions of a renowned jurist (Ibn Hajjar). While neither side seems to have prevailed in an official sense, Khan never again attempted to usurp purely religious authority.

Much of the recent research on Islamic reform in the nineteenth and twentieth centuries is increasingly transregional in scope, as illustrated by chapters 1, 2, and 12 (by Michael Laffan, Amal Ghazal, and Zvi Ben-Dor Benite, respectively). This work adds a great deal to our understanding of the interconnectedness of reformist discourses, which the development of regular steam travel and cheap lithographic print rendered more rapid and profound. More importantly, these efforts afford nuance to our understanding of these schools of thought themselves. Rather than forming rigid ideological camps of scriptural purists and westernizing modernizers, reformers, inspired by their personal contexts and scholarly influences, slid along a wide continuum of belief. Most of this research, however, focuses on the highest levels of discourse and remains firmly fixed on discussions among reformist intellectuals. It has devoted little space to examining the impact of intellectual networks on individual communities and the lives of ordinary believers.

Like other contributions to this volume—those by Ilham Khuri-Makdisi (chapter 4) and Ronit Ricci (chapter 9) in particular—this chapter focuses on the visible effects of transregional Muslim networks in the imperial period on a particular community. From the early 1900s through the 1930s, we find numerous examples of individuals in Aden calling for changes in ritual, belief, and conduct inspired by reformist discourses from across the community of believers. These included strict scriptural reformers (who could be termed Salafis), their opponents, and those we might call—for lack of a better term—religious modernizers, such as the adherents of the Aligarh school in India.[44] All of these ideological groups were connected to larger intellectual networks via the webs of steam and print that empire created. In the larger context of global Islamic reform, these various groups are generally viewed as at loggerheads. Within the confines of Aden, they frequently came together as an ever-shifting constellation of alliances and antagonisms, based partly on individual self-interest but also on coinciding beliefs, to shape the community at large.

The case of Yasin Khan and Da'ud al-Battah can be read as part of this much larger pattern of social and religious reform in the imperial context of the early twentieth century. These men's personal trajectories pointed them in divergent, though not wholly incompatible, directions. Khan was an urbane, dedicated civil servant who saw westernizing trends as the savior of Islam. Al-Battah was a traditionally trained religious scholar from a far more provincial background who found a more scripturalist school of reform appealing. When the networks of imperial service caused their paths to cross, ripples and shifts in the framework of public religiosity in Aden resulted. The imperial record has preserved an image of these currents that allows us—to paraphrase Frederick Cooper—to see at least part of the lives built in the communal crevices that the colonial moment created. Through the lives and actions of these individuals, we see how the global networks of the age coalesced into communities of everyday lives.

NOTES

1. Da'ud al-Battah and Wakf Committee to FAR [first assistant resident of Aden], April 1921, R/20/A/876, India Office Records (hereafter IOR), British Library, London.

2. Most notably Thomas Metcalf, *Imperial Connections: India in the Indian Ocean Arena, 1860–1920* (Berkley: University of California Press, 2007); Sugata Bose, *A Hundred Horizons: The Indian Ocean in the Age of Global Empire* (Cambridge, MA: Harvard University Press, 2007). Two important exceptions to the trend are Nile Green, *Bombay Islam: The Religious Economy of the West Indian Ocean, 1840–1914* (Cambridge: Cambridge University Press, 2011); Kerry Ward, *Networks of Empire: Forced Migration in the Dutch East India Company* (Cambridge: Cambridge University Press, 2009).

3. While appearing in official registers as Muhammad Yasin Khan or M. Y. Khan, the registrar is referred to simply as Yasin Khan in most official correspondence, and I will use this rendering of his name throughout this chapter.

4. It might be tempting to argue that their imperial subjecthood also united the Muslim residents of Aden. But while this may indeed have created a certain linkage between individuals such as al-Battah and Khan, who were both imperial civil servants, such a link should not necessarily be generalized to all of the settlement's inhabitants. Thousands of Somalis, Ethiopians, and Highland Yemenis were long-term residents but did not consider themselves subjects of the British Empire. That being the case, this article focuses on religion as a source of social cohesion.

5. Frederick Cooper, *Colonialism in Question: Theory, Knowledge, History* (Berkeley: University of California Press, 2005), 4.

6. Ibid., 16.

7. The most important of their works include Metcalf, *Imperial Connections;* Bose, *A Hundred Horizons;* Tony Ballantyne, "Rereading the Archive and Opening Up the Nation-State: Colonial Knowledge in South Asia (and Beyond)," in *After the Imperial Turn: Thinking with and through the Nation,* ed. Antoinette Burton (Durham, NC: Duke University Press, 2003).

8. David Lambert and Alan Lester, *Colonial Lives across the British Empire: Imperial Careering in the Long Nineteenth Century* (Cambridge: Cambridge University Press, 2006), 10.

9. Ibid., 12.

10. Metcalf, *Imperial Connections*, 2, 3. See also Bose, *A Hundred Horizons*.

11. Ibid., 6.

12. "Non Cooperation Movement," 1922, R/20/A/3035, and "Caliphate," 1923, R/20/A/3088, IOR.

13. Lambert and Lester, *Colonial Lives*, 13.

14. Others include places such as Zanzibar, Hong Kong, and Singapore.

15. In fact, these are likely conservative numbers, as they do not count the garrison—including camp followers—or the more transient populations such as day laborers and merchants or those who otherwise often actively sought not to be counted. Figures for the 1839 (R/20/E/5), 1849 (R/20/E/34), and 1871 (R/20/A/400) censuses can be found in the IOR. Figures for the 1931 census are from R.J. Gavin, *Aden under British Rule, 1839–1967* (London: C. Hurst, 1975), 445.

16. Abdullah S. Bujra, "Urban Elites and Colonialism: The Nationalist Elites of Aden and South Arabia," *Middle Eastern Studies* 6, no. 2 (1970): 189–211.

17. *The India Office List, 1907–37* eds. (Great Britain: Harris and Sons, 1907–37).

18. The origins of the Luqman family in Aden are cloudy at best. According to some sources the family published, they were a Sunni scholarly family from northern Yemen who were forced to flee Arabia for a time after running afoul of the Zaydi imam. After a brief sojourn in India they returned to Yemen and settled in Aden in the early seventeenth century. However, an interview that the political science scholar J. Leigh Douglas conducted with the family's most noted historian, Hamza Luqman, tells a different story. According to Hamza, "The Luqmans were originally from Hamdan in the north [of Yemen,] but because they were Isma'ilis they were persecuted by the Zaydi imams and forced to leave for India." They returned, according to Hamza, only in the late nineteenth century, and there are hints in the British archives that their conversion to Sunnism postdated this return. See Douglas, *The Free Yemeni Movement, 1935–1962* (Beirut: n.p., 1987), 72n12.

19. "Yasin Khan Report on the Pilgrimage," 1925, R/20/A/3122, IOR.

20. While important in their own right, these figures are not explored here in detail. For a discussion of al-Asnag and Muhammad ʿAli Luqman, see Scott S. Reese, "Salafi Transformations: Aden and the Changing Voices of Religious Reform in the Interwar Indian Ocean," *International Journal of Middle East Studies* 44 (2012): 71–92.

21. "Letter of the Waqf Committee to the First Assistant Resident, February 1921," R/20/A/876, IOR. In addition to Sharif ʿAbdullah al-Aydarus, the committee included Muhammad ʿAbd al-Qadir Makkawi, Sayyid Ahmad bin Taha al-Saffi, Ahmad bin Umar Bazara, Sharif Muhammad bin Hasan, Salih bin Abdullah Khalifa, and Saʾid bin Abdullah Khalifa.

22. Khan to Bernard Reilly, September 1921, EN 24, R/20/A/875, IOR.

23. We should note here that Reilly had a long and distinguished career in Aden, from before the First World War until 1940. He served as resident of the settlement and then governor when it became a Crown Colony in 1937.

24. Petition of Ahmad Abdullah Khayyat, 14 April 1921, R/20/A/876, IOR.

25. Petitions of Ali Ghalib Noman, 7 April and 16 July 1921, R/20/A/876, IOR.

26. M.Y. Khan to FAR [Reilly], 20 September 1921, R/20/A/876, IOR.

27. FAR [Reilly] to Wakf Committee, 30 September 1921, R/20/A/876, IOR.

28. Ali Ghalib Noman to FAR [Reilly], 20 October 1921, and appended notes dated 26 October 1921, R/20/A/876, IOR.

29. Sayyid ʿAbdullah al-Aydarus to FAR Reilly, 4 April 1922, R/20/A/876, IOR.

30. Each petition is worded more or less the same and contains well over one hundred signatures. The text of one reads simply, "WE the undersigned citizens of Aden do hereby declare that our President and Munsab [sic] is Shums al-Ulama Sayed Abdulla Aidross [sic] and our mosques and wakfs administrations are wanted by us to be under his charge and care. We do not want any one else except him therefore we are submitting this for your kind information." R/20/A/876, IOR.

31. Letter from Wakf Committee, n.d., R/20/A/876, IOR. "The Wakf Act of 1920" appears to be a reference to the Charitable and Religious Trusts Act of 1920, enacted by the British government with the aim of regulating all religious and charitable endowments in India. Its relevance in Aden derived from the fact that until 1937, when it became a Crown Colony, the settlement was under the authority of the Bombay Presidency.

32. Unfortunately, IOR file R/20/A/876 does not contain any information about this dispute's resolution. Based on later correspondence, it seems a compromise was reached.

33. Khan's hand can be discerned in this letter. In addition to having a certain lawyerly turn of phrase, it was submitted in both English and Arabic (usually petitions were submitted in Arabic, and the residency translator made a translation), and the English text uses the Persianized form of *Qadi, Cazee,* rather than the more usual *Kadi.* While there is no reason to doubt that al-Battah was the author, Khan's influence is unmistakable. Such claims to rights as British subjects were increasingly common throughout the empire in this period. See, for instance, Lynn Hollen Lees, "Being British in Malaya, 1890–1940," *Journal of British Studies* 48 (2009): 76–101.

34. Civil administrator, Kamaran Island, to FAR [Reilly], Aden, 22 August 1925, R/20/A/4216, IOR.

35. Ibid.

36. Qadhi Da'ud al-Battah to Registrar Mohamed Yaseen Khan, 3 October 1925, R/20/A/4216, IOR.

37. M. Y. Khan to B. Reilly, 9 October 1925, R/20/A/4216, IOR.

38. Khan's predecessor, Sayyid Rustom 'Ali, maintained a particularly contentious relationship with local ulama and lobbied successfully to curtail the power of the qadis during his long tenure.

39. Doreen B. Massey, *For Space* (London: SAGE, 2005).

40. Lambert and Lester, *Colonial Lives,* 14.

41. "Yasin Khan Report on the Pilgrimage," 1925, R/20/A/3122, IOR.

42. For an overview of the Aligarh school and Sayyid Ahmad Khan's teachings, see Peter Hardy, *The Muslims of British India* (Cambridge: Cambridge University Press, 1972), 94–104.

43. For a detailed discussion of scriptural reformists in Aden during this period, see Reese, "Salafi Transformations."

44. For a detailed discussion of the conflict between scripturalists and their opponents during this period, see ibid.

4

Fin-de-Siècle Egypt

A Nexus for Mediterranean and Global
Radical Networks

Ilham Khuri-Makdisi

INTRODUCTION

In the late nineteenth and early twentieth centuries, a number of radical leftist ideas began circulating among various segments of the populations of eastern Mediterranean cities, especially Cairo and Alexandria. These ideas, which may be described as selective adaptations of socialist and anarchist principles, included calls for social justice, workers' rights, mass secular education, and a general challenge to the existing social and political order at home and abroad. Such causes were almost never tackled independently or in isolation from larger issues. Rather, they were usually combined with more reformist and seemingly less radical demands, such as the establishment of a constitutional and representative government, freedom of speech, the curbing of religious and clerical authority, and an end to European political and economic encroachment. While many of these causes were deeply rooted in local matters and local institutions whose members wanted to change the status quo at home, people who self-consciously identified as socialists, anarchists, or radicals had an almost de facto internationalist and international outlook that made them hyperaware of and deeply interested in world events. These local groups were often connected—informationally, politically, and organizationally—to international and internationalist movements and organizations that sought to promote leftist ideas and implement leftist projects in various corners of the world.

What were the reasons behind the circulation, appeal, and implementation of a certain radical package of ideas and practices in Egypt in the late nineteenth and early twentieth centuries? How did this radicalism manifest itself, and what were its limits? How was radicalism—or leftism—understood and lived? To address these questions, this chapter examines two networks that articulated, explained, endorsed, or promoted leftist ideas. By *network,* I mean local and transnational institutions, organizations, and personal connections that established a system for the circulation of people, information, and ideas. The first network I will analyze consisted of Arabic-writing periodical owners and intellectuals, many of them Christian Syro-Lebanese, who played a crucial role in introducing the Arabic-reading public in Egypt and elsewhere to leftist ideas without necessarily endorsing them; the second network comprised predominantly Italian anarchists active in Egypt and beyond. While most of their members were non-Muslims, these networks nonetheless played a pivotal role in the articulation and dissemination of leftist ideas in a predominantly Muslim society, and Muslim individuals occasionally belonged to them. At the very least, partly because of the role these networks played, Muslim reformist thinkers and activists were aware of and interested in the debates on socialism and anarchism, to which they contributed. Thus, the two networks serve as a reminder that many Muslim networks and most Muslim societies at the time, certainly in Egypt and the Levant, did not operate in a sealed environment but rather were enmeshed in, interacted with, and were shaped by the presence, activism, and intellectual contributions of non-Muslims and Muslims alike.

EGYPT AT THE TURN OF THE CENTURY

The story of radicalism in the eastern Mediterranean and Egypt specifically is inextricably connected to globalization. Between 1870 and 1914, Egypt was integrated into the world economy, and its main cities, especially Cairo and Alexandria, and parts of its hinterland witnessed major changes resulting from this integration—a world phenomenon referred to as the late nineteenth-century wave of globalization.[1] Egyptian cities became well plugged into global information and communications networks, and news from all over the world reached them promptly, thanks to the telegraph, news agencies, a reliable postal system, and a plethora of periodicals.[2] The telegraph in particular "radically alter[ed] the way in which news was produced," leading to the media's "central role . . . in producing an experience of global simultaneity," as distant events intruded into everyday consciousness.[3] In 1865, the news agency Reuters opened its first non-European office, in Alexandria, where it had had claiming agents since 1861.[4] By 1910, the country had two telegraph systems: one belonging to the Eastern Telegraph Company, and another to the Egyptian government.[5] There were various postal systems and offices, linked to the different steamship lines that connected Alexandria and Port Said to many Mediterranean cities. Alexandria was one of the first ports of the eastern Mediterranean to be connected to such (competing) lines and their attached postal systems, as early as the 1830s.[6] By 1910, letters could be "dispatched to and received from Europe 5 times during the week at Alexandria, viz., Austrian and Italian, via Brindisi; Italian, via Naples; French, via Marseilles; Khedivial, via Constantinople; and British, via Brindisi and Port Said."[7] These ships ensured a speedy and regular delivery of mail and printed material. Periodicals formed a substantial share of this circulation: by 1909, newspapers published in or dispatched through Egypt constituted roughly a quarter of the packages that the Egyptian post sent overseas (which totaled twelve million), while periodicals and other printed matter accounted for half of the packages it received. These exchanges took place with Britain (27 percent of all exchanges), France (17 percent), and Italy and "Turkey" (10 percent).[8]

A transportation web developed—through extensive railway construction, the establishment of regular and frequent steamship lines, the completion of the Suez Canal in 1869, and accompanying large infrastructural projects such as port enlargements—allowing commodities, capital, and people (especially labor) to flock with ease and regularity to Egyptian cities from the rest of the Mediterranean and the world. The profound changes that these new links caused were similar to those happening throughout the rest of the world wherever global capital, transportation, and information flows were found. They triggered various forms of resistance and challenge to the capitalist world order, such as leftist thought and action; at the same time, it was precisely because of this integration into the capitalist world system that certain forms of contestation emerged.

Throughout the world, the changes that globalization brought forth partly shaped and made possible a global radical moment that marked the fin de siècle and manifested itself in the articulation and circulation of amalgams or matrices of leftist ideas and subversive social and political practices. In places as far afield as Buenos Aires, Alexandria, Baku, and Calcutta, there were talks, articles, pamphlets, plays, and songs discussing political and social reforms—advocating the eight-hour workday, the right of workers to strike, wealth redistribution, political representation, the abolition of private property or at least its redistribution among peasants, free mass education, and night schools for workers. A radical canon was being assembled; the names and ideas of the author and philosopher Leo Tolstoy (1828–1910) and the anarchist Mikhail Bakunin (1814–76) were on many people's lips. These discussions and themes were often—but certainly not always—accompanied by a critique of imperialism, if not a downright active resistance to it, and a call for the reform of religious institutions, when not an actual attack on them and their property. Despite this global dimension of leftist and radical ideas, local specificities, concerns, issues, methods of contestation, mechanisms, and vocabularies fundamentally shaped the multiple interpretations and manifestations of the left as they emerged throughout the world.

At the heart of the global radical culture that Egyptian cities helped produce and shape were two phenomena: translation and printing, of books but especially of periodicals. Translation, "a process which was central to globalization," was, as Timothy Harper succinctly put it, "rarely a search for pure meaning. It was an interactive process of borrowing. Translations of works . . . were unauthorized and not intended to be authoritative. Translators themselves became a vocal presence in the text; the aim was often 'translating the gist' and explicating the rest."[9] While the inequality of exchange and the power dynamics shaping translation choices is evident and should be taken seriously, the degree of cross-fertilization and complexity that marked the use and development of these ideas is outstanding. Some of the main anarchist theoreticians—Bakunin, Pyotr Kropotkin, Errico Malatesta—were translated (usually very selectively and loosely) into numerous languages. Or, more precisely, fragments of their thoughts were translated or summarized in the pages of periodicals—a point to which I shall return later. Similarly, Tolstoy and Maksim Gorky, among others, became bedside reading for radicals and aspiring radicals in the four corners of the world. The paths of translation were not necessarily linear and often involved multiple translations through various intermediary languages. Such is the case, for example, with some Arabic translations of Gorky's short stories that a Syrian who had emigrated to Brazil rendered from Portuguese, which were published in 1906 in São Paulo.[10]

COVERING AND ADAPTING THE LEFT: THE NAHDA AS GLOBAL INTELLECTUAL PRODUCTION

In Egypt and the Levant, the majority of the Arabic-reading audiences first became acquainted with the concepts of socialism and anarchism through articles that appeared as early as the late 1870s but became more frequent starting in the 1890s.[11] Many of these articles (such as "Rottenness of the Doctrine of the Socialists"[12]) appeared in the pages of Al-Muqtataf and Al-Hilal. Between 1890 and 1914, these two periodicals together published around fifty articles on socialism, anarchism, labor conflicts, workers, and related matters, culminating, in the last few months before the outbreak of the Great War, in three long, seminal articles on socialism, all unequivocally supporting it.[13] While both periodicals initially disapproved of socialism, by 1900 they were occasionally publishing articles by authors who were unabashedly sympathetic to socialists and painted graphic pictures of workers' exploitation, described the rich as being parasites "fed by workers . . . with their labor and sweat," and credited socialists with the "revolution of minds in Europe."[14] Such articles praised "moderate" socialism, whose aim was "to protect the oppressed from the oppressor," in no uncertain terms, along with the ideas and activities of specific European social-democratic, socialist, and anarchist figures.[15] In 1914, under the rubric of "Questions and Answers" (Bab al-Masa'il), Al-Muqtataf was unambivalent about socialism's benefits, going as far as to assert that "socialism is the reaping [istithmar] of the earth's goods in a better way than that which is occurring today, and their distribution to people with more justice than now. . . . [It is] people's sharing of goods in equal measure."[16]

What explains this growing interest in and sympathy for socialism? Throughout the world, socialism (or, more precisely, various interpretations of socialism and combinations of socialist and anarchist ideas) was increasingly popular in the first decade of the twentieth century, as reflected through the urns, in the pages of periodicals, and in the implementation of projects in places as far apart as the Philippines, Brazil, and Germany. In other words, socialism was altogether an unavoidable topic for any serious periodical claiming to be interested in social reform and worldly matters—as *Al-Muqtataf* and *Al-Hilal* staunchly declared themselves to be. At the same time, while this accounts for the relative frequency of articles covering socialism, other reasons, both local and global, help explain the increased sympathy toward socialism—and its actual endorsement by a growing number of intellectuals and publicists in the pages of the two periodicals.

One such reason pertained to the manner in which socialism had been progressively inserted into the dominant Arab-Ottoman intellectual framework of the time, the *nahda* (awakening, renaissance). A self-consciously intellectual articulation of the need for reform and its best possible manifestations by thinkers belonging to a variety of networks, groups, institutions, and intellectual traditions, the nahda was one facet of a larger reformist project called for and undertaken by local actors—rulers, administrators, and bureaucrats, as well as intellectuals—throughout the Ottoman Empire, especially in Syria and Egypt, in the late nineteenth century. This movement, which was both local and imperial, aimed to modernize states, institutions, and individuals to catch up with Europe and to defend Egypt and the Ottoman Empire against European hegemony.[17]

While various reformist groups emphasized and interpreted many aspects of reform differently, there were significant common concerns and interests among nahda thinkers that allowed for the formulation of a cohesive world view. Most central to this outlook was the conception of reform as a total project whose most important component was a social program that would rid society of various internal and external "diseases" threatening its cohesion. In place of their ailing society, reformers would build a strong social body (*al-hay'a al-ijtima'iyya*), a healthy organism in which various divisions, including those brought about by disparities of wealth, would be eliminated—or at least eroded. Nahda reformers progressively inserted socialism into this framework, and it is through this entry point that Arab reformers became interested in socialism and occasionally endorsed some of its tenets.

The indigenization of socialism allowed it to be inscribed into the nahda. What is particularly striking in *Al-Muqtataf, Al-Hilal,* and other Arabic periodicals that covered socialism is that regardless of whether the authors were supportive or critical of socialism, they articulated the topic through literary devices, tropes, and epistemic and ethical categories that were familiar and appealing to their readers. One tactic was to claim that socialism (and, in rare instances, anarchism) existed in prior epochs and in different geographical or "civilizational" spaces—in other words, to search for the roots or comparable manifestations of the ideology, especially in the Arab-Islamic past.[18] Another tactic was to use a genre familiar to readers, namely biography.[19] Indeed, many of the articles on socialism and anarchism that appeared in *Al-Muqtataf* and *Al-Hilal* between 1880 and 1914 focused on the biographies of great socialist and anarchist thinkers, such as Henri de Saint-Simon, Robert Owen, Élisée Reclus, and Pierre-Joseph Proudhon.[20] They typically gave a brief synopsis of the doctrines' most salient points, showed respect and admiration for these great figures, and steered clear of any deep ideological analysis. On a few occasions, each periodical devoted an entire issue to a European literary figure known for his radical positions—including Émile Zola[21] and Tolstoy.[22]

DOMESTICATING SOCIALISM: SNIPPETS AND BRICOLAGE

Socialism, and to a much lesser extent anarchism, was brought home through formal and substantive devices. Although the coordinates of socialism and anarchism changed over time, *Al-Muqtataf* and *Al-Hilal* consistently framed them within interconnected discourses and tropes (indeed, signifiers) with which their readers were familiar or becoming familiarized and which they were interested in, even obsessed with: civilization, natural science and natural law, progress, Darwinism, and modernity. The two periodicals, which proudly held on to their pretense of objectivity, thus demystified and reworked socialism, making it fit comfortably in the larger Weltanschauung of the nahda, which they were busy creating as well as reflecting.

Part of this process of familiarization and domestication entailed a selective and fluid understanding of what socialism and anarchism meant. The Arabic term used to translate *socialism* was not (relatively) fixed until the first decade of the twentieth century: in the 1880s and 1890s, *socialism* was mostly translated as *ishtirakiyya* (from the root *shrk*, which implies common participation), but it could also appear as *ijtima 'iyya* (social-ism, social, sociability). It was sometimes accompanied by the English or French term, in Latin characters or transliterated in Arabic characters.[23] The distinction between communism (*komunizm* or *ijtima 'iyya*)[24] and socialism was not always evident: the terms that designated them sometimes got switched or swapped; elsewhere, it is not clear from the descriptions and definitions of socialism itself which one of the two ideologies the authors were writing about. Similarly, in the 1880s and 1890s, anarchism and socialism were often written about in the same article, without necessarily a clear demarcation between the two. Furthermore, the fact that there were various brands of socialism introduced in the Arabic press in the early twentieth century—Fabianism and social democracy, as well as national differences among socialist parties—added to the conceptual fluidity. The terms that authors and translators used and the meanings they sought to convey depended on their personal trajectories, travels, and idiosyncratic interests.

Unsurprisingly, in most Arabic periodicals at the time, the bulk of articles on foreign topics—be it socialism or almost any news pertaining to the world beyond the Ottoman Empire—borrowed heavily from reports published in British, French, or American periodicals, which themselves often consisted of articles translated and summarized from other periodicals. Sometimes the Arab authors had read an article that inspired them or that they deemed important and beneficial, from which they extracted the core information, around which they built their article; other times they freely translated parts of an article. For instance, *Al-Muqtataf*'s editors and many of its contributors seem to have regularly read the *Review of Reviews* and the *Nineteenth Century,* two British periodicals (but, in the case of the former, with global ambitions and an American edition) that translated and published articles from various parts of the world.[25] The result was a certain cannibalization of the original articles and ideas and simultaneously a creative, utilitarian, and occasionally reductive appropriation of concepts, opinions, and news. In their haste to popularize and explain news and concepts, these periodicals might have diluted radical ideas, or perhaps is it more accurate to say that their authors were more interested in radical ideas and concepts that were less ideologically rigid than others.

This may explain why radicalism in Egypt, among other places, had certain omissions that might seem odd today, with some authors conspicuously missing or underrepresented. Most striking, from our modern perspective, is the relative absence of Karl Marx. While the *Communist Manifesto* was translated into a number of languages (including Armenian[26]) after Marx's death, it is unclear how many people actually read it or any of Marx's other works.[27] Only a few radicals and radical sympathizers active in the eastern Mediterranean mentioned Marx or commented on his work. And when some of them (such as Salama Musa and Farah Antun) did cite him, they did so quite briefly. In Antun's case, his constant and consistent misspelling of Marx's name (transliterated into Arabic as *Max*) suggests that he heard about Marx's theories before (or instead of) reading them.[28] The fact that they might overlook Marx or discuss him more than they read him was not unique to Egyptian radicals; the same was often true of radicals in many other parts of the world, including Europe.[29] Marx's absence did not necessarily mean that radicals were not familiar with his ideas; rather, other socialist authors were more popular (perhaps because they were more accessible) and deemed more worthy of being commented on and summarized. This included authors who had written commentaries on Marx or integrated some of his writings into their own and cannibalized or developed eclectic versions of his ideas—thus leading one historian of the European Left to conclude that "early socialist intellectuals acquired garbled versions of Marx."[30]

The fin de siècle thus witnessed a growing interest in and a mild endorsement of socialism by intellectuals both in Egypt and throughout the world. The progressive decline of laissez-faire economic thought in Britain from the 1880s onward had repercussions among intellectuals all over the world, both those whose regions had become part of the British Empire and those who simply read British economic periodicals and avidly followed discussions on the British economy.[31] Furthermore, support for socialism, anarchism, or some combination of both, while far from a sine qua non, was certainly not rare among non-European intellectuals and activists who had an anti-imperialist agenda—or who seriously questioned imperial projects. Moreover, the progressive popularity of socialism among intellectuals worldwide might have been linked to the worldwide wave of attacks launched by (or simply attributed to) anarchists in the 1890s. Indeed, socialism gained credit and legitimacy in certain milieus as a nonviolent alternative to anarchism, and one that advocated working within the system to change it. Equally significant in Egypt were the links among radicalism, the wave of global migrations, and the presence and activities of diasporic networks connecting the country to various parts of the world.

THE SYRIAN DIASPORA PRESS AND
THE MAKING OF A GLOBAL PUBLIC FORUM

Who exactly were the individuals who penned articles on radicalism and occasionally endorsed socialism, and why did they matter? They were part of a close-knit community and formed a new class of multilingual intellectuals—besides Arabic, most could read English and/or French—many of whom were trained in a handful of novel Beiruti institutions, most prominently the Syrian Protestant College (which in 1920 became the American University of Beirut). This class was equipped with its own symbolic and cultural capital, as well as relatively autonomous means of achieving authority and legitimacy. It was hence able and willing to challenge the authority of traditional bodies, namely state and religious institutions, as well as established elites, and it often did so through the investigation (and occasional promotion) of radical ideas and practices. Socialism was one of them.

Periodical production was more often than not the fruit of communal efforts, but Syrian migration brought it to a global level. This can be gauged from the articles published in the periodicals themselves—in Egypt, Syria, and North and South America—and from the correspondence of periodical editors, owners, contributors, and readers. A common reservoir of news and articles was available to Syrian periodical owners throughout the world, who would also send their own articles and copies of their periodicals to one another. It is striking how self-referential the authors and the works they produced and circulated were. In fact, the articles, subjects, and authors read and discussed by this intellectual class, Egyptian or Syrian, were surprisingly few, and highly intertextual. These periodicals took articles from one another (and from non-Arabic publications), cut and pasted, translated and plagiarized, creating a common public stock of news and texts. Examples abound of articles published and republished on different continents, including opinion pieces and reportage.[32]

This repertoire was created not only by article writers but also by readers around the world, usually immigrants who translated news items and articles they deemed interesting in Syrian, Egyptian, Brazilian, and American periodicals or forwarded these in their language of publication. Readers also played a central role in shaping the content of periodicals by sending in questions.[33] Significantly, many of *Al-Hilal*'s and *Al-Muqtataf*'s articles on socialism and anarchism were written in response to readers' questions: "What are the socialist and nihilist associations that are constantly mentioned in newspapers, and what are their origins?," two readers asked in 1897.[34] Several readers asked for *Al-Hilal*'s opinion on various radical ideologies a mere few years after it was founded, indicating just how authoritative it had become: "Do you consider the demands of socialists just, and is socialism beneficial to civilization? What is your opinion on this matter?"[35] "What is your opinion about the future of anarchists? Will states continue to let them be or annihilate them?"[36] Similarly, "a group of readers" keen to know *Al-Hilal*'s opinion of Tolstoy "commissioned" the above-mentioned piece on him.[37]

Many if not most of the questions addressed to *Al-Hilal* and *Al-Muqtataf* concerning socialism and anarchism came from Syrian readers in the Americas, especially the United States and Brazil, a country whose main cities had an active and visible anarcho-syndicalist movement in the late nineteenth and early twentieth centuries. From the 1890s, Brazil was a popular destination for Syrians, one hundred thousand of whom immigrated there between 1891 and 1916.[38] It was also the non-Arab country (or realm) with the highest number of Arabic periodicals.[39] From 1900, various Syrians in Brazil, especially São Paulo, who were exposed to socialist and anarcho-syndicalist ideas there occasionally showed interest in and even endorsed them. Some contributed articles on radical topics to *Al-Muqtataf* and *Al-Hilal*, while others penned and published what were probably the earliest Arabic translations of Tolstoy's and Gorky's works.[40] Accompanying and fanning this interest was the Syrian (Arabic) press in São Paulo, whose owners were constantly in touch with other Syrian intellectuals throughout Syria, Egypt, and North and South America. These periodicals also played a central role in promoting the ideas of two important radical thinkers, the Syro-Lebanese Amin al-Rihani and the Syrian Farah Antun, both of whom had deep Egyptian connections (especially Antun).[41]

The web of Syrian periodicals led to the emergence of a global public forum in which readers had access to information from multiple continents. Diasporic readers and writers in societies where socialism and other radical ideas were widely discussed and had many adherents prompted periodicals such as *Al-Muqtataf* and *Al-Hilal* to increase their coverage and endorsement of these ideologies. A large proportion of the articles produced by Syrian diasporic periodicals passed through these two, which functioned as key nodes and distribution hubs. They were also distributed and carefully read beyond the already wide expanse of Syrian diasporic communities: they were taken as important references in various corners of the Muslim world, in Zanzibar, South Asia, and beyond.[42]

RECENTERING EGYPT

While Brazil and North America occupied an important place in the forging of the Arabic corpus of radical concepts, articles, and authors, both the process and the result were intrinsically linked to Cairo and Alexandria. The nahda might have been a global production, but it was also an intensely local story. It was precisely because *Al-Muqtataf* and *Al-Hilal* were produced in Egypt that their editors and many of their core contributors took radical ideas seriously and engaged with them, even if they did not necessarily endorse them. Egyptian cities were the bases and convergence points of the main intellectual heavyweights of this global web, and of other intellectual networks. As previous discussed, the country's amenities and infrastructure allowed for the circulation of questions, articles, periodicals, books, and people from many continents: it had steamships, multiple and reliable postal systems, telegraph wires, news agencies, and a relatively free press. But Egypt was more than that: it was also the locus of an older and still vibrant infrastructure of intellectual production and dissemination, the enduring legacy of Cairo's unique historical place, with which newer knowledge-producing institutions intersected and overlapped. Cairo remained a major pole of attraction for Muslim intellectuals from around the world, who came to study at Al-Azhar University or wanted to attach themselves to or connect with some of the most important Muslim thinkers and institutions in the world.[43]

Many Egyptian and Egypt-based intellectuals (those who could read Arabic, anyway), as well as less illustrious and notable readers throughout the country, read *Al-Muqtataf* and *Al-Hilal*. Shibli Shumayyil, a doctor and socialist who penned many articles on socialism and related matters for a number of periodicals,[44] also discussed his ideas with Rashid Rida, the prominent Syrian Muslim reformer and founder of the influential *Al-Manar*,[45] and high-ranking Egyptian officials and public figures, such as Prince Muhammad ʿAli Halim and Ahmad Zaki Pasha.[46] Similarly, al-Rihani regularly sent his articles to Egyptian friends—including the poet Hafiz Ibrahim and the mufti Muhammad ʿAbduh—when he did not read out loud to them in Cairo.[47] Antun was also connected to a large intellectual circle in Egypt, including the nationalists, through his work at *Al-Liwaʾ* on his return to Cairo from the United States in 1909. Clearly, then, the supporters of radical and socialist ideas whose articles appeared in *Al-Muqtataf, Al-Hilal,* and elsewhere formed a socially permeable group with a certain intellectual weight.

Like *Al-Muqtataf* and *Al-Hilal, Al-Manar* had a wide readership throughout the Muslim world, and its owner's views on socialism and related issues softened over time. In a piece from 1899 titled "Islam and Progress" (*Al-Islam wa 'l-taraqqi*), Rida argued that Islam was egalitarian and that Europe would be forced to borrow Islamic principles, such as zakat (almsgiving), to counter the greatest of contemporary social ills, which was socialism.[48] To further stress his point, he referred to and reproduced an article by a Syrian Christian lawyer from Cairo, Niqula Yusef Debbane, that had appeared in *Al-Muqattam* (an explicitly pro-British periodical that *Al-Muqtataf*'s founders had started in 1889) and claimed that the East had established all sorts of useful remedies for injustice long before Europe, which was now trying to do so, and that zakat had preceded socialism.[49] In fact, Debbane's argument was even more ambitious: "Precise research shows that republican and socialist principles that are now disseminated/widespread in the West and that the West considers progress and civilization were present in the East from the very beginning."

Ten years later, however, when the prominent Beiruti Muslim reformer 'Abd al-Qadir Qabbani attacked Shumayyil for his views on evolution, which he had expressed in *Al-Hilal* and which, according to Qabbani, showed that Shumayyil was opposed to religion, Rida reproduced Qabbani's letter before unequivocally defending its target, arguing that nothing in evolution (*madhhab Darwin*) was inherently incompatible with Islam, which Shumayyil (himself of Christian background) had systematically claimed was the only social religion (*din ijtima'i*).[50] Rida called on Qabbani (and his readers) to thus focus his energies on defending Islam from superstition and those members of the clergy who promoted wrong interpretations of the faith, for they were far more dangerous than Darwin's theories. He even went so far as to assure Qabbani and his readers that "doctors and chemists, naturalists and astronomers, communists [?] and socialists [*al-ijtima'iyyin wa'l- ishtirakiyyin*], lawmakers and politicians, would all prefer Islam over any other religion, and would prefer making it the religion of civilization in this day and age."

In 1911, *Al-Manar* picked up on the dispute over socialism between Salama Musa and *Al-Muqtataf*'s editors. In his piece "Al-Din wa'l-Ilhad wa'l-Ishtirakiyya" (Religion, atheism, and socialism), Rida started off by republishing *Al-Muqtataf*'s response to Musa's letter-article that taunted (or at least provoked) the editors— and most likely their readership—by bringing to the fore and indicating a certain sympathy toward the atheism of socialists.[51] While *Al-Muqtataf*'s editors conceded that socialism had done tremendous good in denouncing injustice and other social ills, they emphasized that it was just one possible path of many toward civilization and reform. However, they attacked atheism in no uncertain terms: "Its imposition is an error scientifically and socially and . . . will lead to the greatest of harms to the human species." Rida's comments, however, pertained only to atheism; he argued that religion was the basis of civilization, since "moral evolution was the basis of material evolution," and he concurred with his teacher Muhammad ʿAbduh that all self-proclaimed atheists—or, more precisely, all those who professed no religion—whose thoughts and actions benefited themselves and others and were therefore praiseworthy had in fact been reared within a religious tradition, which had profoundly shaped them.

Thus, some of the major articles and debates about socialism and related issues by some of the most prominent Egyptian and Egypt-based thinkers were published and reproduced in influential periodicals. These included *Al-Manar*, which had a wide readership throughout the Muslim world and an owner who selectively added to the debate without necessarily endorsing or fully rejecting socialist principles.

EGYPT: A PHAROS FOR ITALIAN ANARCHISM IN THE EASTERN MEDITERRANEAN

Beyond the Arabic periodicals and Arab authors who were interested in socialism and radicalism, there was a much larger matrix of political activists in Cairo and Alexandria who also expressed an interest in the left, selectively combining elements of radical leftist ideas with their own or, more rarely, fully endorsing them. Among the networks of thinkers and activists who converged in the Egyptian cities were Egyptian nationalists challenging British rule; Muslim reformers from various parts of the Muslim world (including the Caucasus); Young Ottomans and Young Turk reformers and revolutionaries; Armenian socialists and nationalists; Russian leftists who had fled their country after the crackdown following the 1905 revolution; and (predominantly) Italian anarchists, the focus of the following pages. As we shall see, while this last network's main impact was on immigrant communities, it was not restricted to them.

Egypt occupied an important position on the map of the worldwide Italian anarchist movement. The Ottoman Empire harbored all kinds of European revolutionaries who had fled the repression that followed the 1848 revolutions at home. Beginning in the 1870s, Egypt, deemed more liberal than the rest of the empire, received a new wave of revolutionaries: anarchists—mostly but not exclusively Italian. By the end of the decade, anarchist activities in Egypt were noteworthy, and some of the most prominent anarchists worldwide had visited or were there: among them, suffice it to mention Amilcare Cipriani and Errico Malatesta, a figure of tremendous importance in the history of anarchism, both of whom later headed the Italian anarchist party established in 1891.[52] In fact, Italian anarchists, including

Malatesta, are said to have fought on the side of Ahmad 'Urabi in 1882 against British imperialism.[53] As the witch-hunts against them intensified in Europe in the 1890s, many anarchists, especially Italians, decided to exile themselves to Egypt—which had not ratified the international treaties allowing for the arrest and expulsion of anarchists. Alexandria became a center of Italian anarchist propaganda, receiving periodicals and distributing them to the rest of Egypt and the world.

Another major reason behind the choice of Alexandria as a hub for Italian anarchist activities was the presence of a significant Italian working class there starting in the 1880s or so. By the end of the nineteenth century, there were around 12,000 Italians in the city, which had a total population of 320,000. The overwhelming majority of them were workers, employed primarily in the construction industry, as carpenters, masons, stone carvers, and painters, as well as in crafts. Many others worked as cooks, servants, shopkeepers, wine distributors, shoemakers, and tailors, while women found jobs as seamstresses, servants, and nannies. A large proportion seem to have been seasonally employed or were in Egypt for a number of years before moving elsewhere (to other parts of North Africa, the Ottoman Empire, the Americas, or Italy). Most Italian workers lived in mixed neighborhoods; the anarchists' HQ and main activities were in one, Moharram Bey, a poor neighborhood "of Jewish, Arab and European workers at the city's periphery [where] despite the few villas with beautiful gardens sprinkled here and there . . . one can see the misery."[54]

Under the dynamic initiative of some key activists, such as Ugo Parrini, Pietro Vasai, and Joseph Rosenthal,[55] members of the Egyptian (and especially the Alexandrian) anarchist scene held meetings; founded clandestine printing presses to publish manifestos, pamphlets, and periodicals; started "circles for the study of 'the Social Question'"; turned their wineshops into meeting places with anarchist libraries; established a branch of the International Workers' Association and sent delegates to internationalist conferences; led public demonstrations with speeches and chants;[56] helped organize labor into Leagues of Resistance (units that supported them in standing up to their employers, striking, and negotiating); and assisted workers in disputes with their bosses.[57] Anarchists also played an important role in organizing strikes, going so far as to publish the names of strikebreakers in the pages of their periodicals. They also raised funds for workers' widows and sick workers' families and helped widows negotiate financial compensation from their husbands' employers.[58] Other activities included organizing emergency services at the neighborhood level, such as sanitation and health services. Alexandrian anarchists propagated, published, and distributed (sometimes plastering on city walls) some of Kropotkin's and Bakunin's writings, including the latter's *Letters on Patriotism,* and information on unionization and labor issues in Alexandrian factories and workshops.[59] Anarchists also organized events to mark certain famous causes, such as the Ferrer affair of 1909, and the anniversary of the Paris Commune.[60]

PLUGGING EGYPT INTO THE WORLDWIDE
ANARCHIST WEB

The Egyptian anarchists particularly focused on periodical production. Between 1877 and 1914, no fewer than seven anarchist periodicals appeared in Alexandria (and four in Cairo), including the bilingual *La Tribuna Libera/La Tribune Libre*, founded in 1901 by Vasai and Rosenthal.[61] *La Tribuna Libera*'s publication figure hovered around one thousand, of which six hundred copies were sent to Italy.[62] It published texts by Italian anarchists such as Malatesta and translations of Kropotkin, Bakunin, Reclus, and Tolstoy. It also included a "Local Matters" section, which discussed local anarchist initiatives, such as talks, meetings, and strikes. That such a large percentage of *La Tribuna Libera*'s issues—and those of other anarchist periodicals published in Alexandria—were sent abroad indicates just how global a project anarchism was and how important a node Alexandria was.[63] Like many anarchists at the turn of the century, the Italian anarchists in Alexandria functioned on two levels, the global and the local. In fact, it would be more accurate to say that theirs was a world in which the two were inextricably linked, cognitively, politically, and socially. One of Vasai, Parrini, and their companions' prime concerns was plugging Alexandria and Egypt even more firmly into the global (and specifically the Italian) network that constituted the world anarchist scene. It spanned various parts of the Mediterranean, Europe (particularly Italy), and the Americas, including Argentina, Uruguay, Brazil, and the United States.

Besides being distributed locally, the periodicals were sent abroad to fellow anarchists in Naples, Buenos Aires, and Paterson, New Jersey, among other destinations. Members of the Egyptian anarchist scene also contributed articles and "entries" on the condition of anarchism in Egypt to periodicals in the above-mentioned places and engaged in discussions in the pages of famous anarchist periodicals such as Jean Grave's *La Révolte*. They followed one another's news closely and with concern, worried about their companions' fates,[64] sent news about individual anarchists and their itineraries, raised funds internationally to support anarchist families,[65] subsidized anarchist periodicals in Italy and abroad, and passionately debated anarchist theories. The periodicals were central to the establishment and maintenance of this global community and sense of solidarity, a feeling that was also consolidated by the constant circulation and visits of members of this network, who carried fellow anarchists' letters, news, books, and periodicals. Thanks to their presence and activities, Alexandria became a pharos of Italian anarchism and a necessary stop on the anarchist grand tour. The city's anarchists invited their famous fellows to come and give talks and even convinced some to settle in Egypt, promoting it as a safe haven and a vibrant center for anarchism.[66] Anarchists from all walks of life passed through Alexandria, coming from or on their way to North Africa, Italy, Switzerland, and South or North America. Even those who were merely transiting for a couple of days would get in touch with their anarchist companions.

Perhaps most remarkably, Alexandria's anarchists were the motor behind the establishment, in 1901, of the Université Populaire Libre (UPL), which lasted more than a decade.[67] This project, unique in the eastern Mediterranean and the Middle East, offered free courses (mostly in Italian or French, although initially it did offer some courses in Arabic) and saw its mission as "extending literary and scientific education among the city's popular classes."[68] The UPL sought to educate the masses about social issues and social activism, enlightening them about social theory (it offered classes on Bakunin, for instance) and teaching them how to negotiate with their employers and even go on strike. It seems to have been well attended, with the first few classes holding on average fifty-five students.[69] Two years after it was founded, the university claimed that it had attracted fifteen thousand individuals (including eight hundred women), who, in the previous fifteen months, had attended courses, conferences, and artistic or literary evenings organized by the university.[70] Besides its courses, the UPL prided itself on its public reading room, which carried many books and subscribed to radical leftist, including anarchist, periodicals from France and Italy. While the university seems to have eventually slipped from the control of the anarchists and been run by bourgeois radicals, many of the ideas that its founders promoted continued to be taught in and disseminated through the evening classes.

THE VEXED QUESTION OF IMPACT

How can we assess the impact that the Italian anarchist network had on the Italian working classes in Alexandria and more generally on Alexandria workers as a whole and on Alexandrian and even Egyptian society? On one hand, one could argue that the constant surveillance to which the Italian community in Egypt was subjected and the ongoing reports on anarchist activities until roughly 1914 show that at least the Italian consulate took this network seriously, which might indicate that its propaganda work mattered and was dangerous. An Italian consular report estimated that there were sixty-six anarchists in Alexandria around 1900.[71] However, counting those who could be labeled sympathizers or novices would increase this figure fairly significantly. While the number of workers who attended anarchist meetings and joined their leagues was not massive, it was also not negligible, with various leagues having attendance and membership figures between eighty and two hundred. Occasionally, consular reports mention "a huge crowd" attending a talk given by one anarchist or another—such as Gori's 1904 series of lectures on "bread and liberty in workers' revolutions, which were very warmly received."[72]

Obviously, success and impact are relative, and different sources paint different pictures,[73] but a number of memoirs and other items suggest that anarchists were getting their message across, despite various hurdles, rivalries, and tensions. Although many anarchist periodicals were short-lived, there were quite a few of them, thus guaranteeing a constant flow of anarchist information and propaganda.[74] And many of the events the anarchists organized were quite visible: public demonstrations, distribution of manifestos, and strikes, some of which the Arabic and foreign-language press reported on. While the coverage these events received was not necessarily positive, it meant added visibility and free advertisement—especially when the periodicals translated and reproduced some of the manifestos. It was not only Italians who participated in such events: besides Russian and probably Austro-Hungarian Jews, we find the occasional Greeks and Armenians and (in the UPL) the rare Syrians.[75] Many of the propaganda talks were given in more than one language.[76] Furthermore, the UPL, which lasted until at least 1909, must have disseminated some of the anarchists' ideas to a fairly substantial segment of the population—if indeed fifteen thousand people had attended its lectures and other events in its first fifteen months. Given that the anarchists did so much of their propaganda work in informal, oral discussions and among nonelites, in wineshops or coffee shops, its impact is difficult to measure.

Various signs indicate that Italian anarchists in Egypt were reaching out to or otherwise having contact with locals, indigenous or immigrant: one of their activities was distributing, throughout the city, anarchist and socialist tracts in some combination of Italian, Greek, Arabic, Hebrew (or Judeo-Spanish), and French.[77] Records also indicate that the multiethnic and multilingual Cairene Typographers' League, which anarchists had heavily infiltrated, pledged its support to the unionization efforts of the League of Indigenous Typographers, which it considered serious about labor militancy.[78] Furthermore, the International Association of Cooperation for the Improvement of the Working Classes (Association Internationale de Coopération pour l'amélioration des classes ouvrières), whose political sympathies can be surmised from its name and which anarchists established in 1909 in Alexandria, counted both indigenous and nonindigenous locals among its members. The title of a new anarchist periodical, *Malesc . . . Bukra!* (No worries . . . tomorrow!), which supposedly appeared in March 1904 (although there seem to be no extant copies), suggests it was bilingual—most likely Arabic and Italian.[79] Less direct indices of collaboration, perhaps, were the numerous strikes, lockouts, and other instances of workers' militancy, including efforts to unionize, that took place in Egypt between roughly 1900 and 1914. Many of these initiatives came from workers from various ethnic communities planning together, with nonindigenous workers often playing a key role at the organizational level.

Hence we should cautiously reassess the verdict of Roberto D'Angiò, a local anarchist of the period, and the historian Leonardo Bettini that Italian anarchists had no impact on the indigenous Egyptian population.[80] In fact, and quite tellingly, the Egyptian Italian anarchist community appears to have split on the issue of including and reaching out to non-Italians (indigenous and otherwise). Vasai at least seems to have been favorable to collaborating with and doing propaganda work among non-Italian workers. He collaborated with Rosenthal, and one source indirectly suggests that one of the leagues he founded included indigenous Egyptians as well as Italian and other immigrant workers.[81]

ANARCHISM AMONG INDIGENOUS EGYPTIANS

In Egypt, if anarchist ideas were not confined to Italian workers, neither were they confined to workers *tout court.* According to Egyptian police reports, anarchism was a popular ideology among indigenous Egyptians around 1910, its principles increasingly familiar and appealing to a wide range of individuals and groups contesting the status quo, especially those engaged in anti-British and nationalist activities. One, Ibrahim al-Wardani, an ardent supporter of the Egyptian nationalist leader Mustafa Kamil who assassinated Prime Minister Butrus Pasha Ghali in February 1910, was said to have mixed, while studying in Lausanne, with Russian "revolutionaries and anarchists."[82] On his return to Egypt, Wardani played a prominent role in the labor syndicates and workers' night schools affiliated with the Egyptian Nationalist Party (Al-Hizb al-Watani). According to British sources, in these schools, Egyptian "lower classes . . . were taught revolutionary doctrines and systematised hatred of the occupying Power." Furthermore, the British claimed, Wardani had "on several occasions give[n] utterance to anarchist (not socialist) doctrines of an advanced tinge," and they concluded that "this makes his choice as organiser of labour syndicates and preparer of strikes the more significant of the recklessness of these leaders as to the means they are ready to employ for the furtherance of their projects, and emphasises their moral responsibility for any violence that may result."[83] Although Wardani vehemently denied the allegation that he was an anarchist, more likely than not anarchist principles colored his political thought and actions.

Not surprisingly, the assassination and Wardani's subsequent trial unleashed a wave of panic and triggered a witch-hunt and a full-fledged investigation of secret societies in Egypt. A special police bureau was established for the task, and it soon transpired that there were at least twenty-six such societies, many of them plotting political assassinations and other violent acts.[84] One was called the Society for the Encouragement of Free Education (Jam'iyyat al-Tashji' 'ala'l-Ta'lim al-Hurr).[85] It counted thirteen members, of whom about "half . . . were students at the government schools and the other half were employees and students at al-Azhar. . . . Words were sometimes uttered showing that the youths had anarchist tendencies [*anna lahum muyul fawdawiyya*]."[86]

Anarchism and anarchist ideas were gaining ground in Egypt and being synthesized with other radical movements, including nationalism, trade unionism, and Muslim reformism. If anarchism and nationalist liberation movements have been deemed incompatible in certain historical contexts, they seem to have occasionally had a symbiotic relationship in non–Western European settings around the turn of the century, which shaped both ideologies and movements.

CONCLUSIONS

The story of Italian anarchism in Alexandria sheds light on important features of the city and of the eastern Mediterranean generally. First, it shows that Alexandria—and perhaps to a similar extent Cairo—was very much integrated into global networks. Rather than having a history that was isolated from world trends, Alexandria was in fact a major player in globalization and radicalism at the end of the nineteenth and the beginning of the twentieth century. Its anarchist story is somewhat comparable to that of Rio de Janeiro or even Paterson, New Jersey, the major difference (a significant one) being that of scale. The presence and activities of the anarchist network in Alexandria, alongside the Syro-Lebanese one linking Egyptian cities to the eastern Mediterranean and to North and South America, underline the necessity of viewing the intellectual, social, and labor histories of the eastern Mediterranean in this period through a global lens. None of these histories can be fully understood without sketching the movements of intellectuals, workers, periodicals, and books beyond individual cities, states, or even regions and across seas and oceans. Egyptian cities were crossroads for all kinds of radical and reformist networks, both local and global, Muslim and non-Muslim, and provided them with opportunities to intersect, cross-pollinate, and learn from one another—and occasionally demarcate themselves more clearly.

NOTES

1. On the 1870–1920 wave of globalization, see Christopher A. Bayly, *The Birth of the Modern World, 1780–1914: Global Connections and Comparisons* (Oxford: Blackwell, 2004); Anthony G. Hopkins, ed., *Globalization in World History* (London: Pimlico, 2002); Roger Owen and Şevket Pamuk, *A History of Middle East Economies in the Twentieth Century* (Cambridge, MA: Harvard University Press, 1999), 4–5.

2. Alfred Cunningham, a British resident in Egypt with "some connection with public affairs," as he put it, described the State Telegraphs in Egypt, which fell under the Railway Administration, as providing a service that "is good and cheap." Cunningham, *To-day in Egypt: Its Administration, People and Politics* (London: Hurst and Blackett, 1912), 149. He was much less impressed by the postal system, though—a feeling not shared by the editor of *Handbook for Egypt and the Sudan*, who profusely praised its efficiency. H. R. Hall, ed., *Handbook for Egypt and Sudan* (London: Stanford, 1910), 11.

3. Esperança Bielsa, "The Pivotal Role of News Agencies in the Context of Globalization: A Historical Approach," *Global Networks* 8, no. 3 (2008): 348. Bielsa summarizes and paraphrases Anthony Giddens, *Modernity and Self-Identity* (Cambridge: Polity, 1991).

4. Bielsa, "Pivotal Role of News Agencies," 355.

5. Hall, *Handbook for Egypt and Sudan*, 12.

6. Marie-Françoise Berneron-Couvenhes, "French Mail Contracts with Private Steamship Companies, 1835–1914," *Business and Economic History Online*, vol. 2 (2004), www.thebhc.org/publications/BEHonline/2004/BerneronCouvenhes.pdf.

7. Hall, *Handbook for Egypt and Sudan*, 11.

8. "Egyptian Postal Administration: Annual Report for the Year 1909" (Alexandria: n.p., 1910), 9.

9. Timothy N. Harper, "Empire, Diaspora and the Languages of Globalism," in Hopkins, *Globalization in World History*, 154.

10. Ibrahim Shihadi Farah translated the first of these short stories, which had initially appeared in Russian in 1899.

11. E.g., "Ta'alim al-Nihilist," *Al-Muqtataf* 4 (1879): 289–92.

12. "Fasad madhab al-ishtirakiyyin," *Al-Muqtataf* 14 (March 1890): 361–64. Unless otherwise stated, all translations are mine.

13. For the list and a more comprehensive analysis of these articles, see Ilham Khuri-Makdisi, *The Eastern Mediterranean and the Making of Global Radicalism* (Berkeley: University of California Press, 2010), ch. 2.

14. E.g., Khalil Thabit, "Al-Ishtirakiyyun al-dimuqratiyyun," *Al-Muqtataf* 25 (August 1900): 146–51. Thabit was a regular contributor to *Al-Muqtataf.*

15. E.g., "Francisco Ferrer wa'l-ishtirakiyya fi Isbanya," *Al-Hilal*, 1 November 1909, 114–18. This article argues that the recent wave of protests in Spain served as a warning to the government that it should not neglect its duties toward the people.

16. "Bab al-Masa'il," *Al-Muqtataf* 44 (January 1914): 93–94.

17. People throughout the Ottoman Empire argued that reform had become urgent, due to the unequal and exploitative relationship between the East and the West. In Alain Roussillon's words, "La nécessité et l'urgence de la réforme [en Egypte] s'y sont d'emblée formulées et y ont été vécues dans le cadre d'une relation inégale avec l'Autre." Introduction to *Entre réforme sociale et mouvement national: identité et modernization en Egypte (1882–1962)*, ed. Roussillon (Cairo: CEDEJ, 1995), 13.

18. See, e.g., "Socialism and Nihilism" [in Arabic], *Al-Hilal*, 15 December 1897, 290–94. Here the author claims that socialism "accompanied humanity from its first civilization . . . from Elias of Chalcedon . . . to Plato's Republic . . . and the Asyneans [?], in pre-Christian Syria." As for anarchism, see "Al-Fawdawiyya fi'l-Islam," *Al-Hilal*, 1 October 1901, 7–8. Here the author (most likely Jirji Zaydan) argues that "anarchism did not appear in Islam in the same manifestation as in Europe, but it appeared, in a similar way to today's anarchism, in different manifestations."

19. For a comprehensive discussion of the role of biographies in *Al-Muqtataf*, see Nadia Farag, "*Al-Muqtataf* 1876–1900: A Study of the Influence of Victorian Thought on Modern Arabic Thought" (DPhil thesis, Oxford University, 1969), 167–68.

20. For a detailed Who's Who of socialism and anarchism, see "Al-Ishtirakiyyun wa'l-fawdawiyyun," *Al-Muqtataf* 18 (August 1894): 721–29. This article positively describes the life and work of Saint-Simon, Owen, Reclus, and Proudhon, as well as Charles Fourier, Louis Blanc, Ferdinand Lasalle, Karl Marx, Bakunin, and Kropotkin.

21. "Zola," *Al-Hilal*, 15 February 1897, 441. An article on the Dreyfus affair that appeared a year later evidently mentioned Zola and examined his role in it (*Al-Hilal*, 15 February 1898, 469). *Al-Hilal* also published and advertised (15 October 1903, 63) a book on Zola's writings by Esther Azhari Moyal (1873–1948), a Beiruti Jew who had settled in Cairo. On Moyal, see Lital Levy, "Partitioned Pasts: Arab Jewish Intellectuals and the Case of Esther Azhari Moyal (1873–1948)," in *The Making of the Arab Intellectual (1880–1960): Empire, Public Sphere, and the Colonial Coordinates of Selfhood*, ed. Dyala Hamzah (New York: Routledge, 2013), 128–63.

22. "Count Tolstoy" [in Arabic], *Al-Hilal*, 1 May 1901, 425–29. *Al-Hilal* was particularly interested in Tolstoy's theories on the social body's corruption by wealth and the consequent need for wealth redistribution. The Russian author was very much *en vogue* among radicals all over the world.

23. Malcolm Kerr, "Notes on the Background of Arab Socialist Thought," *Contemporary History* 3, no. 3 (1968): 145–59; Mourad Magdi Wahba, "The Meaning of *Ishtirakiyah*: Arab Perceptions of Socialism in the Nineteenth Century," *Alif: Journal of Comparative Poetics* 10 (1990): 42–55; Dagmar Glaß, *Der Muqtataf und seine Öffentlichkeit: Aufklärung, Räsonnement und Meinungsstreit in der frühen arabischen Zeitschriftenkommunikation* (Würzburg, Germany: Ergon Verlag, 2004), 557–58.

24. *Shuyu'iyya*, the term currently in use, was not used before World War I and, I suspect, not before the Russian Revolution.

25. See, for instance, "Al-Ta'lim fi'l-Yaban" (Education in Japan), *Al-Muqtataf*, August 1907, 609–16. This article was a translation of a speech given by the famous Japanese baron Kikuchi Dairoku, reproduced from the periodical the *Nineteenth Century*.

26. Geoff Eley, *Forging Democracy: The History of the Left in Europe, 1850–2000* (Oxford: Oxford University Press, 2002), 43.

27. Marcello Musto, "The Rediscovery of Karl Marx," *International Review of Social History* 52 (2007): 477–98.

28. See Farah Antun, "Al-din wa'l-'ilm wa'l-mal," *Al-Jami'a*, June 1903, 258. For Salama Musa, see his booklet *Al-Ishtirakiyya* (Cairo: Mu'assasat Musa li'l-Nashr wa'l-Tawzi', 1962 [2nd ed., 1913]). See also Sami Hanna and George Gardner, *Arab Socialism* (Leiden, Netherlands: Brill, 1969), 53–54.

29. See Benedict Anderson, *Under Three Flags: Anarchism and the Anti-colonial Imagination* (London: Verso, 2005), 29. Note also Geoff Eley's remark that only 4.3 percent of borrowings from workers' libraries in Germany were in the social sciences, versus more than 63 percent in fiction, and that "works by Marx and Engels . . . were mainly absent from the chosen reading" (*Forging Democracy*, 43).

30. Eley, *Forging Democracy*, 44. Eley also points out that "even if Marx's own writings were hard to get hold of, there were many commentaries about them—some three hundred titles in Italy alone from 1885 to 1895, or over two books a month on Marxism and socialism for a decade" (43–44).

31. On the decline of laissez-faire in Britain, see Walter L. Arnstein, *Britain Yesterday and Today: 1830 to the Present*, 6th ed. (Lexington, MA: D.C. Heath, 1992), 189–95.

32. Khuri-Makdisi, *Eastern Mediterranean*, 50.

33. *Al-Muqtataf* claimed to have covered the topic of political economy on hearing of its readers' interest in it: "We have spoken . . . to two famous men in Egypt, and have learned through them the readers' interest in this science." "Al-Ra's mal," *Al-Muqtataf* 11 (January 1887): 214.

34. "Socialism and Nihilism," 290–94. The question was from Salih Effendi Yusuf (Rawda, Syria) and Najib Effendi Bannut (Beirut).

35. "Socialists" [in Arabic], *Al-Hilal*, 1 October 1900, 20–21. The question was from Amin Effendi Qattit (São Paulo, Brazil).

36. "The Future of Anarchism" [in Arabic], *Al-Hilal*, 1 February 1902, 285. The question was from Ibrahim Effendi Shihadi Farah (São Paulo, Brazil).

37. "Count Tolstoy," 425–29.

38. Clark Knowlton, "The Social and Spatial Mobility of the Syrian and Lebanese Community in Sao Paulo, Brazil," in *The Lebanese in the World: A Century of Emigration*, ed. Albert Hourani and Nadim Shehadi (London: I.B. Tauris, 1993), 292.

39. If Filib di Tarrazi is to be trusted, then this figure was ninety-five by 1922. Many of these periodicals were short-lived, though. Tarrazi, *Tarikh al-Sihafa*, vol. 2 (Beirut: Dar Sadir, n.d), 493.

40. [Dr. Sa'id Abu Jamra], "Al-Fawdawiyyun fi'l-Islam: ta'ifat al-hashshashin," *Al-Hilal*, 1 November 1901, 83–86. See also n. 10.

41. On the coverage of radical ideas by some of these South American periodicals, see Khuri-Makdisi, *Eastern Mediterranean*, 51–54.

42. See Jeremy Prestholdt's ch. 10, especially his reference to Sultan Barghash of Zanzibar's interest in Egyptian newspapers and "his subscription to a variety of publications."

43. On Ibadi reformers and reformist networks that converged in Egypt around the turn of the nineteenth century, see Amal Ghazal's ch. 2. For Yemeni Salafi reformers who spent time in Egypt, see Scott Reese's ch. 3.

44. These included family-owned publications, such as his nephew Rashid's *Al-Basir* (founded in Alexandria, 1897).

45. On *Al-Manar*, see Dyala Hamzah, "From 'Ilm to Sihafa or the Politics of the Public Interest (Maslaha): Muhammad Rashid Rida and his Journal *Al-Manar* (1898–1935)," in Hamzah, *Making of the Arab Intellectual*, 90–127.

46. Shibli Shumayyil, *Hawadith wa khawatir: mudhakkirat al-duktur Shibli Shumayyil*, ed. As'ad Razzuq (Beirut: Dar al-Hamra', 1991), 255.

47. Amin al-Rihani, letter to Jamil Ma'luf, 15 May 1905, Cairo, reproduced in *Rasa'il 1896–1940*, ed. Albert al-Rihani (Beirut: Dar Rihani li'l-Tiba'a wa'l-Nashr, 1959), 57. For more on 'Abduh, see Zvi Ben-Dor Benite's ch. 12.

48. Rashid Rida, "Al-Islam wa'l-taraqqi," *Al-Manar* 1 (February 1899): 881–85.

49. Niqula Yusef Debbane, "Asbab inhitat al-Sharq (al-Hay'a al-ijtima'iyya al-sharqiyya)," *Al-Muqattam* 2989, reproduced in ibid.

50. Rashid Rida, "Al-Duktur Shibli Effendi Shumayyil," *Al-Manar* 12 (August 1909): 624–32.

51. Rashid Rida, "Al-Din wa'l-Ilhad wa'l-Ishtirakiyya," *Al-Manar* 13 (January 1911): 908–13. The *ishtirakiyyun* in question sound more like anarchists than socialists, since Musa reported that they carried a banner with the logo "Neither God nor Master."

52. Malatesta was a leading anarchist activist and thinker whose importance among anarchist circles throughout the world was tremendous. In addition to heading the Italian anarchist party at one point, he was elected secretary of the Anarchist International in 1907. For more information on his life and work, see Vernon Richards, *Errico Malatesta: His Life and Ideas* (London: Freedom, 1965); Max Nettlau, *A Short History of Anarchism* (London: Freedom, 1996); Jacques Droz, ed., *Dictionnaire biographique du mouvement ouvrier international* (Paris: Éditions ouvrières, 1990), s.v. "Malatesta, Errico"; Pier Carlo Masini, *Storia degli anarchici nell'epoca degli attentati* (Milano: Rizzoli editore, 1981).

53. It is not altogether clear whether this actually happened. The *Dizionario biografico degli anarchici Italiani*, though, is adamant about Malatesta's participation in this revolt, his arrest by the British, and his liberation in early 1883. Maurizio Antonioli, ed., *Dizionario biografico degli anarchici Italiani*, vol. 2 (Pisa: BSF, 2003–4), 59.

54. Enrico Pea, *Vita in Egitto* (Florence: Ponte alle Grazie, 1995), 169.

55. Rosenthal was one of the cofounders and directors of the bilingual newspaper *La Tribuna Libera/La Tribune Libre* and helped found the Egyptian Socialist Party in 1921. His identity remains something of a mystery; the archives of the Italian consulate in Egypt referred to him at times as an "Israelite and Austrian subject" and at other times as a "Russian." See, e.g., *segreto*, 5 [month illegible] 1901, Cairo, ref. 68 ("Miscellania"), Ambasciata al Cairo, Ministero degli Affari Esteri (MAE), Rome.

56. For instance, the public demonstration of March 1892 most likely organized by Parrini that took place in Moharram Bey. During this demonstration, one of Bakunin's manifestos was stuck on the walls of the city. See "Un Vecchio" (An old man) [I. U. Parrini], "L'Anarchismo in Egitto," *La Protesta umana* (San Francisco) 2, no. 36 (21 November 1903), reproduced in Leonardo Bettini, *Bibliografia dell'anarchismo: periodici e numeri unici anarchici in lingua italiana pubblicati all'estero, 1872–1971*, vol. 1 (Florence: Crescita politica editrice, 1976), 307.

57. See, for example, Italian Ministry of the Interior memo no. 94, 20 January 1903, folder 87 (1900–1904), Ambasciata d'Italia dal Cairo, MAE.

58. Confidential note no. 121, 10 May 1902, folder 87 (1900–1904), Ambasciata d'Italia dal Cairo, MAE.

59. Ibid.; *La Tribuna Libera/La Tribune Libre*, 20 October and 2 November 1901, among others, in "Stampa anarchica" file, folder 87 (1900–1904), Ambasciata d'Italia dal Cairo, MAE.

60. See *La Tribuna Libera/La Tribune Libre* issue written by Pietro Vasai in 1913; "18 marzo 1871–1909" (on the Paris Commune), *L'Idea: periodico di propaganda anarchico* (Cairo), 1 May 1909; both in "Stampa sovversiva" file, 17, folder 120 (1909–10), Ambasciata dal Cairo, MAE.

61. Bettini, *Bibliografia dell'anarchismo:* 81–88, on various periodicals; 281–88, on "points of reference for the history of Italian anarchism in Egypt;" 303–7, reproduction of "Un Vecchio" [I. U. Parrini], "L'Anarchismo in Egitto." Bettini's work relies extensively on material published in anarchist periodicals worldwide.

62. Confidential memo no. 156, 16 September 1901, Cairo, "Periodicals" file, folder 84, Ambasciata dal Cairo, MAE.

63. Davide Turcato, "Italian Anarchism as a Transnational Movement, 1885–1915," *International Review of Social History* 52 (2007): 407–44.

64. "Universita popolare libere in egitto/Universita popolare libera in Alessandria," folder 87 (1900–1904), Ambasciata dal Cairo (1904), MAE.

65. See, for example, *La Protesta Umana* 32, 22 October 1903, which appealed to anarchists in San Francisco to send money to the parents of someone named Angelilio, since he was incapacitated (possibly arrested) in Alexandria and his parents, who were in Italy, were in dire straits.

66. One anarchist star invited to Alexandria was Pietro Gori (who also spent many years in Argentina, where he played a central role in the establishment of the country's first labor federation, in 1901). See Ruth Thompson, "Argentine Syndicalism: Reformism before Revolution," in *Revolutionary Syndicalism: An International Perspective,* ed. Marcel Van der Linden and Wayne Thorpe (Aldershot, U.K.: Scolar, 1990), 169.

67. Khuri-Makdisi, *Eastern Mediterranean,* 120–26; Anthony Gorman, "Anarchists in Education: The Free Popular University in Egypt (1901)," *Middle Eastern Studies* 41, no. 3 (2005): 303–20.

68. Université Populaire Libre d'Alexandrie (UPL), *Revue des Cours et Conférences,* 1902–3 ed. (Alexandria: Librairie L. Schuler, 1903), 295.

69. *Le Lotus* 3 (June 1901): 130–38, quoted in Robert Ilbert, *Alexandrie 1830–1930: histoire d'une communauté citadine* (Cairo: Institut Français d'Archéologie Orientale, Bibliothèque d'étude 112/1, 1996), 683.

70. UPL, *Revue des Cours et Conférences,* 302. By another estimate, female participation was around 10 percent of the total. See L. A. Balboni, *Gli Italiani nella civiltà egiziana del secolo XIX* (Alexandria: n.p., 1906), 89–90.

71. "Affare: Scioperi e questioni relative leghe operaie" (1902), folder 88 (1904), Ambasciata dal Cairo, MAE.

72. Ministero dell'interno direzione gen. della PS Gabinetto 4680, 11 March 1904, Rome, folder 86, Ambasciata dal Cairo (1904), MAE.

73. For example, Italian consular reports from 1902 suggested (perhaps as wishful thinking) that there was no need to worry too much about the "study groups" that Vasai and others were establishing, which, like previous attempts, were doomed to fail. Various documents in "Circolo di studi sociali al Cairo" and "Circoli ed associazioni anarchiche" files, ref. 68 (1903), folder 86, Ambasciata dal Cairo, MAE.

74. At least one, *L'Idea,* which was to be distributed for free, was expected to have a publication figure of two thousand—nonnegligible for the period and for Egypt. "Questionario," 15 August 1909, Cairo, folder 120 (1909–10), Ambasciata dal Cairo, MAE.

75. To give one example among many, in March 1894 a Greek man published an anarchist pamphlet in Cairo celebrating the anniversary of the Paris Commune of 1871 and enjoining, "Unite, o oppressed workers . . . and long live the social revolution and anarchism." He was arrested and taken to court. See "Manshur fawdawi ʾaqim," *Al-Hilal,* 1 April 1894, 475.

76. Note no. 359, 12 July 1909, Cairo, folder 120 (1909–10), Ambasciata dal Cairo, MAE. The text reads, "Réunion des adhérents de l'Association internationale de coopération pour l'amélioration des

classes ouvrières: 'Y assistaient 100 ouvriers environ—des discours ont été prononcés dans différentes langues, par le socialiste Grando Facio, et les anarchistes Nicolas Dumas et Salamon Goldenberg.'"

77. Ilham Khuri-Makdisi, "Levantine Trajectories: The Formulation and Dissemination of Radical Ideas in and between Beirut, Cairo and Alexandria, 1860–1914" (PhD dissertation, Harvard University, 2004), 326–27.

78. Confidential note no. 861, 23 January 1911, Cairo, "Stampa sovversiva" folder, 17, folder 120 (1909–10), Ambasciata dal Cairo, MAE.

79. "1899 processo in Alessandria d'Egitto contro diversi anarchici," document included in Ministero dell'interno direzione gen. della PS Gabinetto 4680, 11 March 1904.

80. For a summary of their arguments, see Khuri-Makdisi, *Eastern Mediterranean,* 128–29.

81. Confidential note no. 137, 25 March 1903, Cairo, "Affare: Scioperi e questioni relative leghe operaie" (1902), folder 88 (1904), Ambasciata dal Cairo, MAE.

82. Crime case no. 140, 'Abdin police precinct, 1910, quoted in Malak Badrawi, *Political Violence in Egypt, 1910–1924: Secret Societies, Plots and Assassinations* (Richmond, U.K.: Curzon, 2000), 46. See also Mr. Cheetham to Sir Edward Grey, 30 June 1911, Kitchener Papers, PRO 30/57/36, the National Archives (hereafter TNA; formerly Public Record Office), Kew, Richmond, U.K., reproduced in Anita L. P. Burdett, ed., *Arab Dissident Movements, 1905–1955,* vol. 1, *1905–1920* (n.p.: Archive Editions, 1996), 135–44, esp. 139.

83. Memorandum by Dr. Nolan on the Wardani case, enclosure 2, no. 82, 154, in Gorst to Grey, confidential, 6 May 1910, Cairo, "Further Correspondence Respecting the Affairs of Egypt and the Sudan, 1910," no. 66, 138, Foreign Office Records, FO 407/175, pt. 72, TNA.

84. Gorst to Grey, confidential, 6 May 1910, 169. Although many of these plots turned out to be hoaxes, Badrawi argues that the degree to which they were taken seriously reflects the state's profound insecurity vis-à-vis subversive movements, especially anarchism, and the popularity of their ideas (*Political Violence in Egypt,* 83–84).

85. According to a 1911 British Foreign Office report, the president of this society was a tailor, Ahmad Ibrahim al-Sarrawy. The report states that "on a perquisition made at the house of the secretary [Ismail Farag, a lawyer's clerk], papers were seized which showed that he had been, since 1909, member of a secret society of anarchists, which had in view the assassination of the editor of *Al-Mu'ayyad,* who was at the time on open war with the Nationalists." The report classifies the organization's goal as "ostensibly the collection of money for Sheikh Shawish's scheme of national education." Mr. Cheetham to Sir Edward Grey, 30 June 1911, reproduced in Burdett, *Arab Dissident Movements,* 139.

86. Badrawi, *Political Violence in Egypt,* 84. Badrawi adds that the expression *lahum muyul fawdawiyya* became popular in police reports after the Wardani case (106n30).

PART TWO

Contagions and Commodities

5

Hajj in the Time of Cholera

Pilgrim Ships and Contagion from Southeast Asia to the Red Sea

Eric Tagliacozzo

INTRODUCTION

David Arnold has pointed out that disease was an important yardstick in how Europeans conceptualized the rest of the world during the past several hundred years.[1] This was particularly so as the industrial age wore on and definite links started to be established between sanitation and public health in the metropolitan capitals of the West.[2] Yet as Myron Echenberg has shown to such devastating effect in his recent book *Plague Ports,* the industrialization of steam shipping, increased transoceanic travel, and global commerce went hand in hand to facilitate the spread of pathogens on a theretofore unparalleled scale.[3] Technology enabled virulent microbes to spread much quicker than previously. Europeans may have seen the non-West as filthy, diseased, and dangerous. But in the very act of conquering the rest of the world with state-of-the-art technologies, they also laid some of the preconditions necessary for a number of diseases to spiral out of control. This was true in the German Pacific, where colonials both fought and spread disease in a number of isolated island chains, such as the Carolines, the Marianas, and the Marshalls.[4] It was also true in the Philippines, where the Americans attempted at the start of the twentieth century to lay a new sanitary order (mostly against the spread of cholera), with only mixed success.[5] In the distant Belgian Congo and even in the jewel in the crown of Britain's global empire, India, cholera spun out of control on a number of occasions throughout the nineteenth century.[6] The French dealt with the spread of smallpox, cholera, typhus, and plague on an almost equally broad basis as the British, giving employment to generations of French medical professionals from Algeria all the way to Indochina.[7]

This chapter examines the nexus between the hajj and health, particularly through the lens of cholera (and other diseases) that traveled on the steamships that made the pilgrimage to Mecca possible from places such as Southeast Asia. This was truly a medical mountain to climb. Hajjis made these journeys by ship during the colonial period in vast numbers (by the thousands in the mid-nineteenth century and by the tens of thousands around the fin de siècle), and the prospect of contagion traveling on the wings of the hajj became one of the great health issues of the late nineteenth and early twentieth centuries. The chapter analyzes this state of affairs by providing a brief background on both cholera and the structures that were put in place to try to control it, before narrowing the field of vision to the Red Sea region and asking how a regime was enacted to deal with the disease as it spread every year on the myriad ships that pulled into Jeddah. Subsequent sections examine how Dutch and British Southeast Asia mirrored the Middle Eastern theater of disease control in varied and either effective or ineffective ways, respectively. The fight against cholera on the hajj became a global phenomenon, with the center of action remaining the Red Sea and important tendrils of prophylaxis stretching all the way to small villages in distant Muslim lands, such as parts of India and Southeast Asia. Yet this fight also became very much a European crusade, as the disease was terrifying in its outcomes and acknowledged as all too penetrative to Western societies as well. For this reason a huge period literature on the subject is available in French, Dutch, Italian, and English, as the European powers sought to manage the hajj on the grounds of global epidemiological survival and a host of related concerns.

CHOLERA AND THE ROAD TO GLOBAL RUIN

There are perhaps few worse ways to die than through contracting cholera. Period journals and correspondence preserved in the Wellcome Institute of Medicine in London and the Academy of Medical Sciences in New York City make this abundantly clear.[8] The disease moves with astonishing swiftness: a healthy human being can contract cholera and be dead less than a day later. The primary symptom is a loss of the body's fluids: extreme diarrhea is accompanied by small white particles floating in the victim's stool, which are parts of the intestinal lining that have peeled off the afflicted body. Once the diarrhea starts, vomiting is never far behind, and the subject loses at an alarming rate the body water that makes up 60 percent of the substance of all human beings. The body begins to cramp from the loss of water; eventually patients turn blue and sallow, the eyes sinking farther and farther into the skull yet at the same time protruding because the body itself is shrinking so quickly. Eyewitness descriptions of people with cholera are horrific. Left untreated, close to 50 per cent of cholera's victims succumb to the disease. It is usually contracted by drinking the bacterium cholera vibrio in unclean water, almost

always as a result of feces appearing in a public water supply. The German physician Robert Koch discovered this fact in 1883, but by that time cholera had already
ravaged large swaths of the world for more than half a century. It was first noticed
in 1817 when it spread from the Gangetic Plain in India, appearing wherever Indians were sent to perform manual labor as coolies. The pilgrimage to Mecca by sea
was almost tailor-made for cholera to thrive and spread: the disease found in the
nineteenth-century hajj the perfect vehicle to survive and imprint its misery on
millions of human beings, all of them in perilous close contact in the holds of
slow-moving ships.[9]

In 1821, cholera was found in Arabia for the first time, and it likely came to the
Arabian Peninsula from India via the Persian Gulf. Ten years later it was in the
Hijaz, and after that date cholera became a mainstay on the pilgrimage routes, with
the sea a particularly dangerous conduit because of the poor sanitation and close
proximity of pilgrims on crowded vessels. The 1831 epidemic in the Hijaz killed
twenty thousand people, and subsequent epidemics came to the region of the holy
cities in 1841, 1847, 1851, 1856–57, and 1859. Cholera entered Europe during the
middle decades of the nineteenth century too, though it likely came not through
the Middle East but rather over the Eurasian steppe, from Russia and eventually
into Germany. However, the 1865 epidemic in the Hijaz was so powerful and did
such damage not only in Europe but all the way west to the United States that the
hajj became a matter of international concern and huge scrutiny. Fumigant devices,
new disinfection techniques, and the distillation of water on a mass scale were all
experimented with in a short time frame to try to combat the disease.[10] Yet cholera
continued to plague the pilgrimage routes to Mecca, and there were further outbreaks in 1883, 1889, 1891, and 1893. The epidemic of 1893 was colossal in scale and
in the impression it left on horrified European observers. Afterward international
arrangements to try to deal with the disease were rushed forward, when bickering
and mistrust between the emerging European powers had been the rule before.[11]
And not just cholera but also smallpox, malaria, dengue fever, and amoebic dysentery were in grim evidence during the annual months of the hajj, ensuring that the
pilgrimage and disease were manifestly equated in the consciousness of the West.[12]

The most obvious physical result of this history of infection and misery over
several decades was the establishment of quarantine stations at several points in
and around the Red Sea and the holy cities. Some were erected for land caravans,
but the more important ones (from a numerical point of view, considering the
steady stream of pilgrims who passed through them) were on either side of the
Red Sea waterway. The single most important station was on the barren, tiny island
of Kamaran, not far off the Yemeni coast.[13] Kamaran became the central locus for
trying to combat the cholera and other diseases attendant on maritime hajj traffic.
It was particularly important for Southeast Asians, as almost all pilgrims from "the
lands beneath the wind" came on ships that passed through Kamaran. The bare

spit of land had an embarkation jetty, a disinfection station, buildings for administration services, a bacteriological laboratory, campsites for pilgrims to stay in their thousands while they awaited cleansing, a cholera hospital, and a few small villages of fisherfolk who scraped a living from smuggling, pearling, or fishing in the blazing heat of the Tihama.[14] Pilgrims had to stay in Kamaran for anywhere between ten and fifteen days while the colonial or Ottoman authorities contented themselves that anyone sick with one of the more serious communicable diseases could be isolated (and hopefully cured, though many people who were sick enough after the long voyage from Southeast Asia never made it off the island alive). All pilgrims had to pay dues for the sanitary processes that were enforced on Kamaran, but the island had no banking facilities, so the procedure was cumbersome and rather inefficient.[15] In addition to this, there was constant wrangling among the various governmental powers and Muslim interests in the Red Sea region as to who was to control Kamaran, its operations, and its revenues, a fact that receives almost as much ink in the period sources as the care of the countless pilgrims for whom the station was constructed.[16] This was the reality of the hajj: pilgrimage, politics, disease, and revenue were all part of the same sprawling system.

Kamaran and the other quarantine stations in the Red Sea were set up as part of the larger rubric developed by the sanitary conventions, a series of large-scale international meetings held to deal primarily with the threat of cholera (they also debated other contagious diseases that were judged to be dangerous). The first of these meetings was held at Constantinople in 1866, and it became known simply as the cholera conference, because that pandemic was in fact the one on everyone's minds. Subsequent meetings were held every few years, in Dresden (in 1883), in Venice (in 1892), and in Paris (in 1894), the last of these coming about so soon after the Italian meeting because of the devastations wrought by cholera during the 1893 hajj, as previously mentioned.[17] Correspondence in the Wellcome Collection shows how frightened contemporary observers were of the spread of cholera—hard-won facts about the disease and enduring superstitions existed side by side in an uneasy mix.[18] A British surgeon commented that in the last great epidemic of the disease prior to his writing (in the mid-1880s), some 88 percent of victims had died—and these were British soldiers in India, who had been "placed under the best possible conditions—conditions it would be impossible to equal in any civil community."[19] Yet despite the international character of these meetings, the epicenter of scholarship, debate, and eventual collective action on the emerging sanitary regime became Paris, where the majority of the most-detailed reports were written and assembled. For this reason the list of important period studies on cholera, containment, and the operation of the sanitary system in the Hijaz is preserved in the Bibliothèque Nationale in Paris, which became an unofficial archive of sorts of how late nineteenth-century humans tried to deal with this truly frightening disease.[20]

The substance of the sanitary regimes may have been epidemiological, but the mechanics of policy and enforcement were always going to be political in an era of rapidly expanding and aggressive imperial states. Some of this political maneuvering was between Europeans themselves, who saw the Middle East (and the Red Sea waterway in particular, especially after Suez opened in 1869) as part of the great game of international politics. Therefore the British kept German designs in the region under close scrutiny, for example, in and around the First World War, and London did it all it could to support King Hussein, whom it saw as a valuable ally.[21] This kind of international politicking around the hajj also occurred during the Second World War, when the British competed with the Japanese in Southeast Asia to assure the millions of local Muslims under their respective jurisdictions in the region that the hajj would be allowed, with Japanese news broadcasts in English on this subject particularly interesting in their form and content.[22] Shipping statistics throughout the first several decades of the twentieth century paid close attention to how many pilgrimage vessels came to the Hijaz from each European colony as well, with the British, French, and Dutch all tabulating the numbers to keep an eye on their neighbors' movements.[23] Yet there was also a sense of playing the politics of the hajj vis-à-vis the Muslim world, as the European powers tried to show increasingly "restive" Muslim populations (both in the Middle East and in places like Southeast Asia) that the West had their best interests at heart. The emplacement of Muslim pilgrimage officers (who sometimes doubled as medical personnel) by each of the European powers in Jeddah in the 1920s was part of this general trend, although there were reasons besides politics why these moves made good sense.[24] Yet as a rule, politics was never far from the medical situation of the hajj in the Hijaz, and this continued from the late nineteenth into the early twentieth century.

These are all bird's-eye, systemic visions of the pilgrimage and health maintenance in the age of cholera; it would be wrong to finish this section without a glance at how these matters operated at ground level. For this we can hope for no better source than the memoirs of doctors who were attendant on the hajj in the Red Sea, either as medical professionals in situ or as members of epidemiological study tours, often under the patronage of the sanitary conventions.[25] Of the spread of these examples perhaps none is as useful a social and epidemiological document as Dr. Marcelin Carbonell's *Relation Médicale d'un Voyage de Transport de Pèlerins Musulmans au Hedjaz, 1907–1908* (Medical account of a journey transporting Muslim pilgrims to the Hijaz, 1907–1908).[26] Carbonell saw the hajj up close as a doctor in the Hijaz in the first decade of the twentieth century: his memoir contains horrendous descriptions of the overcrowding, dirty conditions, disease, and suffering of the ethnically mixed choleric populations of Arabia during that time. The disease was on the road to being mapped and understood as a plague to humanity, but the abilities of both the local Muslim governments and the

European powers were not yet developed enough to eradicate cholera as a ghostly presence hovering over the global pilgrimage. Carbonell's account stands out as a scientific and moral document in a prevailing landscape of despair as humans dealt with the affliction during the fin de siècle.

One gets a sense in reading through its pages that a corner was being turned in efforts against the disease. This does not mean that ignorance and superstition of cholera as a danger to the hajj (and to Europe, ultimately) had disappeared: far from it. In the decades on either side of 1900 there were still plenty of misconceptions about the best way to tackle the nightmare of plagues such as this one.[27] But there was a growing sense that the problem could be examined, both in the laboratory and out in the field among the believers, and that the disease could be halted. Carbonell's descriptions of pilgrims embarking on the ship *Nivernais* in Sinope on the Black Sea coast of Ottoman Turkey and his subsequent accounts of Constantinople and Smyrna en route to Arabia show the development of an infrastructure to deal with cholera. He mapped out the quarantine station at El Tor too, showing the spatial alignment of the camp and how it was evolving to deal with thousands of pilgrims from the Mediterranean and beyond. And his descriptions of Jeddah—in all of its terrifying complexity—as a place where people met and exchanged ideas, sickness, and perceptions of one another, all at the same time, is unusual for its candor and sensitivity, both against European airs of superiority and toward the suffering of Muslim pilgrims. There is an optimism to the account, even in the midst of the horrors described; perhaps things might one day get better. This would not happen quickly, but by the end of the colonial period in the mid-twentieth century, cholera was a far less threatening problem than it had been for a century previously, even if the disease had not yet disappeared from the face of the earth.

THE DUTCH CONNECTION: THE INDIES
TO THE DESERT

Large numbers of the pilgrims who sailed into the Red Sea came from the Dutch East Indies, so knowledge and cognizance of the health situation in the Hijaz was a matter of yearly concern in Indonesia, despite these islands being half a world away from Arabia. We have little knowledge of how Indies populations (and indeed Southeast Asians as a whole) dealt with cholera before the advent of colonial record keeping. The *Koloniaal Verslag* (Colonial report) that was published in the Indies each year makes careful mention that chiefs of residencies were responsible for letting indigenes within their administrative orbits know the state of cholera in Mecca. This information included the charges for sanitary control in the Red Sea, as well as the possibility in certain years that Indies pilgrims would not be allowed in the Hijaz at all.[28] From the documents preserved in the Arsip Nasional Malaysia (National Archives of Malaysia) in Jakarta we can get a sense of how

matters functioned at an even lower level, within each residency: in 1875, for example, in Japara (Java), cholera statistics were kept for each village, and locals made
decisions on whether to go on hajj partially based on the rumors they heard about
health conditions in Arabia.[29] A few years later in Besoeki, the number of pilgrims
dropped off, apparently because of the fear of cholera, which was now prevalent in
the Hijaz, the resident said.[30] Sixty-two pilgrims left Besoeki for Arabia in 1882, but
in 1883, the year of the resident's writing, only twenty-six decided to go. The local
legal edifice in the Indies for dealing with this cycle of disease and transport eventually legislated careful laws requiring all hajj aspirants to be inoculated against
cholera, typhus, and bacillary dysentery before they left the Indies.[31] These rules
were often ignored, however, and enforcement was not uniform.

Yet by the late 1930s there was a steady transport of medical officers from the
Indies to the Red Sea, including one Javanese named Manjoedin, a civil servant
first class at the Batavia Central Laboratory who was sent to Kamaran to look after
Dutch interests there.[32] He set sail on the Rotterdamsche Lloyd ship *Kota Baroe* on
August 9, 1939, though we have little notion of what befell him after this trip and his
arrival in the Hijaz. Concurrent events of global importance relegated the passage
of this Muslim medic to a mere footnote in history: by this time the British and the
Dutch were consolidating their operations on the island, as the Second World War
was on the horizon and they were making an all-out effort to save on costs.

Health practices in the Indies were one thing; regulating such affairs on the
long voyages across the Indian Ocean was quite another. The huge, rusting steamships that crawled across the surface of the sea with pilgrims cramped together
inside were the incubation chambers, as it were, for the worst of the infections. For
this reason strict care was paid to a number of their details that might affect the
health of their passengers. Doctors were put aboard the pilgrim ships, and by
Indies law these men needed certain qualifications and experiences.[33] The decks of
the steamships were to be made of wood, iron, or steel, and the upper decks needed
to be covered so as to ensure that pilgrims were not overexposed to the ferocious
sun.[34] Adequate provisions also had to be reckoned for the whole voyage, not just
the roughly three weeks that it took to get across the ocean but also the ten to
fourteen days that pilgrims could expect to be in quarantine, where they also
needed to eat and drink. Canned foods such as sardines and salmon were favored,
as were dry goods such as biscuits, which did not go off in the heat of the Red Sea,
and Australian meats that were cooked at over 100 degrees centigrade (212 degrees
Fahrenheit) in chlorocalcium baths.[35] Certain allocations were reckoned by weight
per person: one and a half ounces of meat per man for five days, sixty-five kilo-
grams (143 pounds) of rice per one hundred men for the whole trip, and fifty kilo-
grams (110 pounds) of sugar per one hundred men per journey.[36] Medicines down
to individual dosages and chemical minutiae of prophylaxis and drug treatments
were also legislated, so that trained medical personnel on board could deal with

outbreaks of infection quickly and efficiently.[37] Finally, a yellow shipboard flag was instituted as an immediate sign for caution. It meant that cholera or some other virulent, contagious sickness was on board—and that everyone should maintain a strict distance, on pain of the spread of the disease.[38]

When Dutch ships from the Indies finally pulled into Kamaran, most of their pilgrims were exhausted. They had been out at sea for weeks by this time, living in close quarters and mostly at the mercy of the elements (and one another). While every care was taken to protect the passengers against epidemic, quite often the ships would pull into port with a number of sick people on board. The Dutch consul at Jeddah spent time at Kamaran during the pilgrimage seasons, and he made careful notes of the ships coming in, one by one, from the huge expanse of the Indian Ocean. Just one of these reports, from January 1938, gives an idea of the kind of reportage desired of this official. The *Clytoneus* arrived from Singapore on January 1: we know its tonnage; the number of passengers, subdivided by gender and age (there were 680 in total); the number of sick on board; and the nature and outcomes of their sicknesses. The *El Amin,* a much smaller ship, arrived the next day from Aden, and the *Buitenzorg* arrived on January 4 from Batavia, with several deaths reported.[39] The Dutch military kept track of a number of these kinds of statistics: like colonial armed forces elsewhere at this time, they took a keen interest in finding out the routes of contagion across the seaways as the world became a much smaller place in the space of a few decades.[40]

British records on shipping were at least as complete as those of the Dutch. A British report from nearly a half century earlier lays out in exquisite detail the provenances, national flags, and tonnages of pilgrim vessels that pulled into Kamaran in 1891. Whereas in previous decades far fewer ships had made the journey, predominantly by sail and usually over a period of many months, by 1891 steamships from all over the Indian Ocean were entering this quarantine port. The ships were British, Dutch, French, Portuguese, and Zanzibari; their tonnages ranged from a few hundred to several thousand tons. They came from everywhere: Surabaya, Batavia, Calcutta, Bombay, Muscat, and Zanzibar, to name just a few places.[41]

The entire system of Kamaran, including its health procedures for pilgrims, became public knowledge and an issue debated in print, with a number of authors (writing primarily in Dutch, French, and English) giving windows onto how this vast medical apparatus stretched its radials of surveillance, maintenance, and care across the oceans.[42] Yet it is only by reading the detailed autobiographical accounts of some of the travelers, such as the Indies regent of Bandung, Raden Adipati Aria Wiranatakoesoma, that we get a more human sense of Kamaran's scope and operations. The raden's account, published in 1924, gives a rare firsthand glimpse of the pilgrimage through the eyes of an Indonesian hajji who was at the same time schooled in Western forms of discourse and narrative. He chronicles in careful detail the voyage by sea, its dangers and annoyances (including seasickness), and the tedium of the quarantine station, where all vessels were obliged to moor. His account also describes, in glowing tones, the mosques and palaces of Arabia, as well as the arid plain of the desert, a landscape that was totally new to him. The raden found the desert's topography almost as awe-inspiring as the Muslim shrines he had imagined from afar; this was an alien world in almost all ways to a man who had lived his whole life in the tropics. He finished the narrative of his travels through the region with a melancholic description of two Indies children who had died en route to Mecca and been buried in Jeddah, only a few miles from the destination they had traveled so far to see.[43]

Jeddah became the most important stopping point for the Dutch Indies pilgrims to organize themselves before they disappeared into the interior: it was a crucial way station for the hajj, for both arriving and leaving, especially from a medical point of view. Because of this fact the Dutch spent a fair bit of time trying to decide who would be their medical representatives there—these appointments were important, which officials from many levels of government seem to have understood. In the early 1930s, for example, a Dr. Hartmann was mooted for the Dutch medical post in Jeddah, but some of the deciding civil servants who debated candidates for the post felt that he did not have enough experience, despite his several years of medical service on the SS *Tapanoeli* and the SS *Niewkerk*.[44] The portfolio was a large one, and the responsibilities, given the seriousness of cholera in particular, were huge: during the month of Ramadan in 1933 more than five hundred patients passed through the Dutch clinic in the city, many of them sick with a number of debilitating diseases.[45] The Dutch medical facility was only one among four there: Jeddah also had an Arab station, a Russian station, and an English station, the last staffed with a Muslim British Indian doctor.[46] The Dutch establishment had somewhere between sixty and one hundred beds, depending on whose letters we can believe, but its care was limited: for food, the afflicted received only small quantities of bread and milk from the Dutch and had to rely on their families for anything else.[47] However, the Dutch clinic had a drug dispensary, which gave out medicines not only to Dutch subjects but to a number of poor Arabs as well.

From Jeddah, the East Indies pilgrims would wind their way into the desert and toward Mecca, Medina, and the other holy sites that make up the religious stations of the hajj. The Dutch consul in Jeddah knew that his facility was the last one where the pilgrims under his charge could expect to receive any real standard of care, as the medical stations in the interior were less modern. Because of religious prohibitions, Middle Eastern Muslim doctors staffed these facilities as a rule: the dispensary in Medina had an Egyptian doctor, for example, an Ottoman Turk staffed the one in Yambo, and Syrian doctors ran the three dispensaries in Mecca.[48] These stations were mostly off-limits to nonbelievers, so we have little information on them, especially compared to what is known about the daily operations of Kamaran and El Tor, which were part of larger colonial circuits.

In a report from November 1936, a Dutch vice-consul in Jeddah told the minister for foreign affairs in The Hague the kinds of diseases he was treating as the hajj season progressed; he had just seen more than one hundred patients, who had a variety of ailments ranging across the spectrum of disease (malaria, influenza, amoebic dysentery, gonorrhea, rheumatic disease, lymph disease, laryngitis, acute bronchitis, bronchopneumonia, bronchial asthma, dental disorders, diarrhea, menstrual problems, and abscesses).[49] He pointed out to his superiors that a number of hajjis were now using automobiles to cover the large distances across the desert to places such as Medina, though the majority still went by foot and were more in want of his help. He tried to provide for their immediate needs, he explained, but also gave them things that they would likely require for the journey once they were out of his reach.[50] In this we can see something of the confluence of philanthropy and epidemiological self-interest in the Western regimes now firmly ensconced in the Hijaz as they attempted to regulate the massive flood of pilgrims, on whose continuing health so much had come to depend.

THE BRITISH CONNECTION: THE MALAY PENINSULA TO THE HOLY CITIES

Health maintenance on the hajj from British colonial Southeast Asia mirrored the Dutch regime in many ways. Brenda Yeoh has shown how disease control and the erection of a sanitary port in Singapore were priorities for the British there. In this they were always ahead of the Dutch, who had a far larger and more unruly colony to administer in the region.[51] By the 1880s, bills of health were being issued to pilgrim ships sailing from Singapore's harbor, and it is clear that part of the reason for this move was London's worried eye on Mecca, where plague had been reported in the years before.[52] Singapore was expressly tasked to ensure that these ships were cholera-free, though the applicable regulations were nowhere near foolproof at this date.[53] Corruption and avarice conspired to make this the case, the British consul at Jeddah reported in an exasperated letter to his administrative superiors in Asia that expressly singled out certain shipping companies for their negligence in allowing too many pilgrims on board in Singapore.[54]

Many peasants in British Southeast Asia avoided inpatient care in Westerner-run hospitals when possible and preferred exposure to disease (often brought to the desas by pilgrims returning from the hajj) to undergoing inoculations and prophylaxis.[55] In 1899, an entire company of British troops with fixed bayonets even stormed a Malay village because its peasantry refused to allow a diseased body (and the corpse's house) to be fumigated and burned.[56] Disease was seen as a normal part of life in many of the *desas,* and something that God regulated, even if human intervention could be salutary. Besides, few indigenes trusted the motives of the Christian colonizers, especially when they came bearing needles. William

Roff has also commented on the fact that the British in Southeast Asia "bore the burden" of the hajj only because they felt they had to, and there was a concerted sense in local colonial circles that the entire exercise was much more trouble than it was worth, from both political and public health points of view—something the natives would have picked up on.[57] The British High Commission in Malaya seems to have carried these attitudes and practices into the twentieth century, the high colonial era, continuing to see the health of pilgrims as a millstone of sorts around the necks of the colony's overlords.[58] Administering a global empire required coordination and sacrifices, however, and the British realized that the same mastery of the sea lanes that conferred primus inter pares status on them as colonizers also made them vulnerable from an epidemiological point of view.

Once ships left British Southeast Asia and reached the high seas, they faced many of the same issues as the Dutch ships that paralleled them across the Indian Ocean. Overcrowding was the serial killer of the vessels: a handwritten letter from the British consul in Jeddah to the Foreign Office in London describes how captains turning a blind eye to legal capacity could net themselves small fortunes. (Only one hundred extra hajjis would easily pay off any fine if the captain was caught overcrowding his ship—and many weren't—and since many of these vessels were several hundred souls over capacity, it's clear that serious profits were on offer.)[59] The British colonial administration in Singapore also fought a long battle with the steamship companies, particularly the Alfred Holt line, to ensure that qualified doctors were on board every ship, as the doctors' salaries and any enforcement against overcrowding cut into the companies' profits.[60] Legislation laying out what the ships needed to do to be deemed ready for pilgrim traffic got more and more stringent every year, as a series of acts published in the *Straits Settlements Government Gazette* makes clear. As with the Dutch ships, everything was meticulously detailed, from the number of passengers and the amount of space each was to have to provisions for food and water and search procedures and fines.[61] Yet the imperfect understanding of how cholera and other infectious diseases spread made following (and enforcing) the regulations difficult, even as a fuller cognizance of containment regimes developed and was instituted in various ports along the international seaways.[62] Fighting cholera even on British ships, the best vessels in the world, took time: it was not a zero-sum outcome that was achieved in a day.

At Kamaran, there were more ships flying British flags than those of any other nation on earth. Many of these were from British Southeast Asia, reflected in the fact that signs posted on the island often included Javanese or Malay, and many Indies pilgrims chose to make their journeys via Penang or Singapore in British-owned bottoms.[63] The report of the civil administrator of Kamaran in 1939 even specified diseases that were particularly common among the "Malay races" coming to the island: paralysis, furunculosis, bronchopneumonia, and gangrene, in addition to the more common epidemic sicknesses.[64] Occasionally, vessels from

British Southeast Asia were put into detention in Kamaran for longer than was normally the case, if pathogens that might endanger the hajj were suspected to be on board.[65] Yet the flow of ships from the Straits Settlements and the Malay Peninsula was fairly relentless, and the sanitary board on Kamaran made large sums of money off their taxes, which were well integrated into the pilgrimage regime by the early twentieth century.[66] In the fin de siècle, the laws and acts enforcing the cordon sanitaire before the holy cities even stretched into gendered terms, with regulations spelling out how female passengers were to be searched, since many women were hidden away from the public by the older male members of their families.[67] Fewer and fewer stones were left unturned by the colonial authorities. In the years before the outbreak of the Second World War, the dues paid at Kamaran by Malayan pilgrims ended up totaling a very large amount, a sum that seems all the greater considering from how far away these Straits dollars had come. There were few competitors who could rival this Southeast Asian combination of cash and religiosity.[68]

The British in Singapore and Malaya, like the Dutch in Southeast Asia, kept a close eye on disease in Jeddah vis-à-vis the health of their hajjis, noting how many were in formal medical care there and what ailments they had.[69] Straits correspondence is full of discussions between colonial officials about the health situation in that port. In years of plague or cholera, word of local epidemics and their progress spread back to Southeast Asia quickly, through both official and unofficial channels.[70] Pilgrims who died in Jeddah had to be buried and their affairs arranged; one of the most important issues that might stem from this situation (which did not occur infrequently) was family members' wishing to get a refund on the hajji's return ticket, which was often a lot of money. Only in the 1920s were procedures set up to amend shortcomings in this system; from then, half the cost of the deceased's unused ticket could be sent as a bank draft to their family.[71] The confluence of health and financial concerns became more and more important, especially in the First and Second World Wars, when the imperial powers— particularly Britain—took extra steps to try to win over the hearts and minds of Southeast Asian pilgrims through programs such as these.[72] Jeddah became the clearing port, therefore, for both epidemiological matters and the attendant administrative issues, which needed to be dealt with together. The coffin industry and gravestone makers had a part in this story, as did the many levels of bureaucrats who insured that the remains of hajjis—bodily or pecuniary—ended up where they were supposed to go. Indeed, the progress of hajjis' death markers across the Indian Ocean is one of the earliest tracks of these transoceanic movements, well before the high colonial era.[73]

The last step of this pilgrimage is the holy cities, and here too the authorities in British Southeast Asia kept watch on what was going on, despite the fact that nonbelievers are not allowed into Mecca or Medina's core. Singapore knew when there was cholera in Mecca, not just in Jeddah or Kamaran—reports circulated back and forth with the Foreign Office in London at such times, as they did for other outposts of the British Empire.[74] Right after the end of hostilities in the First World War, the British began to prepare detailed reports on diseases circulating in the holy sites, with separate folders on cholera (and the application of quarantine measures), plague (including the progress made on destroying sources of infection), typhus (again on the eradication of sources, which included lice and vermin on people, in dwellings, and even on railways), and epidemic influenza, which had become a new nightmare with the pandemic of 1918.[75] Similarly, when the Second World War ended, energies could again be spared for disease control on the hajj, and the West commissioned reports on protecting Mecca and Medina by land quarantine and air quarantine (the quarantine on the older and more populous sea route via Jeddah was still observed).[76] The British high commissioner in Kuala Lumpur and the British consul in Jeddah discussed how to reduce the amount of time that Malay pilgrims might spend in the Hijaz, partially for political reasons but also very much as an epidemiological precaution after the particularly grim death toll of the hajj of 1951.[77] The colonial focus on the confluence of health and the hajj stretched even into the age of decolonization, therefore, when the old issue faced a new world of independent Muslim states, whose policies had been decided for them for decades by imperial powers.

CONCLUSION

Vivian Nutton has remarked that diseases are often ascribed to individual countries or races as a kind of disgrace (e.g., the "English sweat," the "Danish disease" (scurvy), the *morbus hungaricus,* the plica polonica).[78] One of the reasons that cholera is so interesting—and why it was so dangerous in the eyes of late nineteenth- and early twentieth-century humans—is that it was not identifiable with any particular group: it killed anyone it came into contact with, regardless of ethnicity or class. Cholera may have had its origins in India, but the pilgrimage routes to and from Mecca were some of the main arteries that spread the disease. Though Western and Muslim societies at the time had different concepts of what contagion might be, they agreed that the most important task was stopping cholera before it spiraled out of control and massacred entire civilizations.[79] Theories of how infection worked gradually progressed in Europe in the middle decades of the 1800s, and by the second half of the century, cholera was being used as a tool for social and economic analysis, propagating a number of reasonably correct conclusions about how uncleanliness and physical proximity conspired to get people sick.[80] The medical pluralities that existed in places such as the Ottoman world of this time (in that case, many nations having a medical presence in the same narrow strip of the Red Sea) made it difficult to enforce sanitary regimes, however, so

European governments increasingly took it upon themselves to guarantee the overall health of the hajj on a large, systemwide basis.[81] They accomplished this very slowly, however, with the difficulties of politics, nascent epidemiology, and enforcement militating against the saving of many thousands of lives. Cholera for many decades was an inescapable component of the Muslim pilgrimage, in other words; many people, both Muslim and Western, were fatalistic about this, and the graves of members of both groups still litter the Hijaz as testament to this fact.

The transmission of cholera along the transoceanic pilgrimage routes in the late nineteenth and early twentieth centuries effectively rendered the hajj a dangerous, often fatal, institution, not only to members of the *umma*—the community of Muslim believers—who practiced its rites but also to Westerners. Because of this, the maintenance of public health measures as part of the global pilgrimage became a matter of pressing concern to the expanding imperial powers and never more so than after years of particularly serious epidemic, such as 1831, 1865, and 1893. These three dates, roughly every thirty years across the breadth of the nineteenth century, reminded all parties involved in the hajj how serious the consequences of inaction could be, and attempts were increasingly made to ameliorate the situation. The various colonial empires passed legislation to try to rationalize shipping and to maintain clean and adequate water supplies on board the vessels, as well as a modicum of space for each pilgrim. Sanitary conventions were also held on a grand scale, giving rise to large public documents (and even larger reams of correspondence) about how to control the hajj's epidemiological radials. Finally, authorities even commandeered land for quarantine stations, which were set up at semiregular intervals, wherever caravans (of animals, ships, or other vehicles) might pass into the Red Sea region and disgorge thousands upon thousands of pilgrims toward the religious cities of the Hijaz. Stations such as Kamaran became emblematic of the age's possibilities: bacteriological laboratories, docking complexes, and limed-in grave sites appeared within a few hundred meters of one another, and the ships in port flew the flags of many nations. In some ways this confluence best suggests the nature of the medical mountain that was there to climb, as the healthy, the sick, and the dead passed along the same roads on their ways to and from the cities of the Prophet.

NOTES

1. David Arnold, "Disease, Medicine and Empire," in *Imperial Medicine and Indigenous Societies*, ed. Arnold (Manchester: Manchester University Press, 1988), 7.

2. Jean-Pierre Goubert, *The Conquest of Water: The Advent of Health in the Industrial Age* (Princeton, NJ: Princeton University Press, 1989), 58–67.

3. Myron Echenberg, *Plague Ports: The Global Bubonic Plague of 1906* (New York: New York University Press, 2007). For a review that puts this book into context with the rest of the Indian Ocean world, see Eric Tagliacozzo, "Underneath the Indian Ocean: A Review Essay," *Journal of Asian Studies* 67, no. 3 (2008): 1–8.

4. Wolfgang Eckart, "Medicine and German Colonial Expansion in the Pacific: The Caroline, Mariana and Marshall Islands," in *Disease, Medicine and Empire*, ed. Roy Macleod and Milton Lewis (London: Routledge, 1988), 81, 89, 91.

5. Reynaldo Ileto, "Cholera and the Origins of the American Sanitary Order in the Philippines," in Arnold, *Imperial Medicine*, 131.

6. Maryinez Lyons, "Sleeping Sickness, Colonial Medicine and Imperialism: Some Connections in the Belgian Congo," in Macleod and Lewis, *Disease, Medicine and Empire*, 247; I. J. Catanach, "Plague and the Tensions of Empire: India, 1896–1918," in Arnold, *Imperial Medicine and Indigenous Societies*, 149.

7. Anne Marcovich, "French Colonial Medicine and Colonial Rule: Algeria and Indochina," in Macleod and Milton, *Disease, Medicine and Empire*, 105, 109.

8. The Wellcome Institute of Medicine Collection (hereafter Wellcome Collection) is particularly important for getting a sense of the genealogy of cholera in nineteenth-century science; the materials here, particularly the correspondence, are second to none. Anyone desiring to see how conceptions of cholera grew and changed during this period must stop in London to peruse these papers.

9. The dozens upon dozens of period journal articles preserved in the New York Academy of Medicine's library are useful in getting a sense of how cholera was appraised at the high point of the epidemic period. Some of the more important ones are S. W. Johnson, "Cholera and the Meccan Pilgrimage," *British Medical Journal* 1 (1890): 1218–19; A. Proust, "Le choléra de la Mer Rouge en 1890," *Bulletino Academica de Medica* 3S, no. 25 (1891): 421–45; E. Rossi, "Il Hedjaz, il Pelligrinaggio e il cholera," *Giornale de Societa Italiana* 4 (1882): 549–78; R. Bowman, "Cholera in Turkish Arabia," *British Medical Journal* 1 (1890): 1031–32; anonymous, "Cholera, the Haj and the Hadjaz Railway," *Lancet* 2 (1908): 1377.

10. C. Izzedine, *Le Choléra et l'hygiène à la Mecque* (Paris: n.p., 1909), 30–36.

11. D. Oslchanjetzki, "Souvenirs de l'épidémie de choléra au Hedjaz en 1893," in F. Duguet, *Le pèlerinage de La Mecque au Point de Vue Religieux, Social et Sanitaire* (Paris: Les Éditions Reider, 1932), 297.

12. Izzedine, *Le Choléra et l'hygiène*, 9–11.

13. For an interesting history of this station, see Nigel Groom, "The Island of Two Moons: Kamaran 1954," *British-Yemeni Society Journal* 10 (2002): 29–37. See ch. 3 for more on Kamaran.

14. "Rapport de la Commission des Lazarets Presente Au Conseil Superieur de Sante le 23/24 Aout 1896, Plan General des Lazarets de Camaran et Abou-Saad (Mer-Rouge) avec Planches," following p. 15, fiche #155, 1.2.4 Medische Aangelegenheden, Djeddah Archives, Algemeen Rijksarchief (National Archives of the Netherlands; hereafter ARA), the Hague.

15. Colonial secretary, Singapore, to Government of India Department of Education, Health and Lands, 26 January 1928, #1202, in IOR/L/E/7/1513/File 4070, India Office Records (hereafter IOR), British Library, London.

16. Inter-departmental Pilgrimage Quarantine Committee, 25 July 1922, E7501/113/91, in IOR/L/E/7/1908/File 7376, IOR.

17. For the details on these conferences, see William R. Roff, *Sanitation and Security: The Imperial Powers and the Nineteenth Century Hajj*, Arabian Studies 6 (London: Middle East Centre, University of Cambridge, 1982).

18. Sir William Gull to Sir Joseph Fayrer, 1885, in RAMC/571/Box 126, Letter from Sir William Gull to Sir Joseph Fayrer on the Causes of Cholera (1885), Wellcome Collection.

19. Surgeon-Major Hamilton, *Cholera: Its Endemic Area and Epidemic Progression* (Dublin: John Falconer Printers, 1885), 20. There is a copy in RAMC/474/47 Box 87: Parkes Pamphlet Collection, Wellcome Collection.

20. The list of useful period studies in the Paris collections of the National Library is very long. Two of the more important sources are E. A. Buez, "Le Pèlerinage de la Mecque," *Gazette Hebdomadaire de Médecine et de Chirurgie* 2, no. 10 (1873): 633–34 (on shipping between the Hijaz and Penang and Batavia); M. le Catelan, "Choléra au Hedjaz en 1890: Prophylaxie Sanitaire dans la Mer Rouge," *Recueil des Travaux*

du Comité Consultatif d'Hygiène Publique de France et des Actes Officiels de l'Administration sanitaire 21 (1891): 830–42. See especially 839, which shows the spread of cholera along the Asian sea routes, including Formosa, the Philippines, Tonkin, Annam, Cochinchina, Java, Sumatra, Siam, and Burma.

21. See "Peace Conference (1919)" folder, Foreign Office (hereafter FO) file 608/101/17, the National Archives (hereafter TNA; formerly Public Record Office), Kew, Richmond, U.K.: "Minutes of a Conference on the Pilgrimage," FO, 18 March 1919; cypher telegram #616 "Very Urgent," FO to General Allenby, Cairo, 18 May 1919; telegram #710, FO to General Allenby, Cairo, 6 June 1919; "Note on the Present Situation with Regards to Kameran," by S. Buchanan, medical officer and minister of health, to chairman of the Hedjaz Quarantine Committee, 8 June 1919.

22. Netherlands Embassy to M. E. Dening, FO, 27 May 1943, #1710, in "Hajj of Muslims from Japanese-Controlled Lands (1943)," FO 371/35929, TNA. The Japanese proclamation, in English, reads: "Tokyo reports in English to the world, April 7, Singapore: Assurance by the chief of the Military Administration that efforts are being made for resumption of the pilgrimages by Mohammedans to Mecca has evoked an expression of loyalty to Japan from the Mohammedan Religious Conference which closed yesterday. The conference represented 10,000,000 followers of Islam. Mohammedans all over the world are said by observers to have hailed the assurance of provision of ships for the Mecca pilgrimages despite pressure of war on shipping space. This further evidence of Japan's solicitude for the millions of Mohammedans under its protection has smashed malicious Anglo–United States propaganda that Japan is intolerant of religion."

23. See, for example, the shipping statistic documents (in FO 195/2320 and FO 195/2350, both from 1907–10) reproduced in A. de Rush, ed., *Records of the Hajj: The Pilgrimage to Mecca,* vol. 3 (Cambridge: Cambridge Archive Editions, 1993), 341–69.

24. Government of India, Foreign and Political Department, to U.K. consul, Jeddah, 25 January 1926, #482E, in "Kamaran: Establishment of Pilgrimage Officer," 1926, IOR/R/20/A/4121, IOR.

25. Just a few of the studies that I have found helpful in this respect are B. Schnepp, *Le Pèlerinage de La Mecque* (Paris: n.p., 1865); P. Remlinger, *Police Sanitaire: Les Conditions Sanitaires du Pèlerinage Musulman* (Paris: n.p., 1908); Duguet, *Le Pèlerinage de La Mecque;* L. Couvy, *Le Choléra et le Pèlerinage Musulman au Hedjaz* (Paris: n.p., 1934).

26. Marcelin Carbonell, *Relation Médicale d'un Voyage de Transport de Pèlerins Musulmans au Hedjaz, 1907–1908* (Aix-en-Provence: Publications de l'Université de Provence, 2001 [reprint]).

27. For example, anonymous, "Travaux Originaux: Epidemiologie," *Gazette Hebdomadaire de Médecine et de Chirurgie* 38 (19 September 1873): 604; anonymous, "Sociétés Savantes: Académie des Sciences," *Gazette Hebdomadaire de Médecine et de Chirurgie* 46 (14 November 1873): 734.

28. *Koloniaal Verslagen* (1872), 98, and (1875), 122.

29. Japara #59, in "K. 18 Japara, #59. Tahun 1875. Aankomende brieven (Vendu kantoor; Bedevaart; ziekte rapport; politiezaken), January–April 1875," 30, Arsip Nasional Republik Indonesia (National Archives of Indonesia; henceforth ANRI), Jakarta.

30. "Algemeen Verslag over het Jaar 1883, Residentie Besoeki," in "K. 23 Besuki, #78 (Nomor lama 9/14), 1883. B.b. Uitbreiding van het Mohamedanisme toe –en afname van het aantal bedevaartgangers," ANRI.

31. *Bijblad* 44114 (1885): 376–77; 10236 (1922): 387–88; 11780 (1928): 605.

32. Chief of health, Kamaran, to Batavia Central Laboratory, 31 October 1937, and "Uitreksel van het Register der Besluiten van het Hoefd van den Dienst der Volksgezondheid," Batavia, 26 July 1939, #24724, fiche #164, 1.2.4 Medische Aangelegenheden, Djeddah Archives, ARA.

33. *Bijblad* 11018 (1926): 362.

34. *Staatsblad* 557 (1912): 3; 507 (1937): 3.

35. Inspector for Netherlands East Indies to captains of pilgrim ships of the Rotterdamsche Lloyd, 30 January 1922, fiche #156, 1.2.4 Medische Aangelegenheden, Djeddah Archives, ARA; "Verduurzaamde Levensmiddelen," *Indische Militair Tijdschrift* 1 (1896): 482–90.

36. "Regeling Betreffende Extra Voeding Pelgrims," fiche #156, 1.2.4 Medische Aangelegenheden, Djeddah Archives, ARA.

37. *Staatsblad* 597 (1923): 4–5.

38. *Staatsblad* 208 (1911): 1–2.

39. Maandrapport, Dutch consul in Jeddah, Kamaran, January–February 1938, fiche #157, 1.2.4 Medische Aangelegenheden, Djeddah Archives, ARA.

40. P. Adriani, "De Bedevaart naar Arabie en de Verspreiding der Epidemische Ziekten," *Nederlandse Militair Geneeskundige Archief* 23 (1899): 7, 156, 245.

41. "Report on the Quarantine Station at Camaran for the Year 1891," in FO 195/1730, TNA.

42. J. Eisenberger, "Indie en de Bedevaart naar Mekka" (PhD dissertation, Leiden University, Netherlands, 1928), 103–11.

43. G. A. van Bovene, ed., *Mijn Reis Naar Mekka: Naar het Dagboek van het Regent van Bandoeng Raden Adipati Aria Wiranata Koesoma* (Bandung, Indonesia: N. V. Mij. Vorkink, 1924), 38.

44. Dutch consul, Jeddah, to directors, Nederlandsch Handels Maatschappij (Amsterdam), 16 September 1932, and Dutch consul, Jeddah, to minister of foreign affairs, 20 January 1933, #84, fiche #161, 1.2.4 Medische Aangelegenheden, Djeddah Archives, ARA.

45. Medical Service of the Dutch Consulate, Mecca, to Dutch Consulate, Jedda, 31 December 1933, #5, fiche #158, 1.2.4 Medische Aangelegenheden, Djeddah Archives, ARA.

46. Medical Service of the Dutch Consulate, Mecca, to Dutch Consulate, Jedda, 15 December 1933, fiche #158, 1.2.4 Medische Aangelegenheden, Djeddah Archives, ARA.

47. Dutch consul to minister of foreign affairs, 5 January 1934, #33, fiche #163, 1.2.4 Medische Aangelegenheden, Djeddah Archives, ARA.

48. Ibid.

49. Vice-consul, Dutch Consulate, Jeddah, to minister of foreign affairs, 11 November 1936, #896, fiche #159, 1.2.4 Medische Aangelegenheden, Djeddah Archives, ARA.

50. Vice-consul, Dutch Consulate, Jeddah, to minister of foreign affairs, 2 February 1936, #93, fiche #159, 1.2.4 Medische Aangelegenheden, Djeddah Archives, ARA.

51. Brenda Yeoh, *Contesting Space in Colonial Singapore: Power Relations and the Urban Built Environment* (Oxford: Oxford University Press, 1996), esp. 85–93, 119–35.

52. CO 273, 142/12072, 8 January 1886. Because the volume of correspondence in the series is so large and its full citation would take up far too much space, in this section I provide only rubrics for the U.K. National Archives Colonial Office (henceforth CO) 273 series, which subsequent researchers can easily consult.

53. CO 273, 53/11250, 14 October 1871.

54. U.K. consul, Jeddah, to secretary of government, Bombay, 30 April 1875 (FO 78/2418), in de Rush, *Records of the Hajj*, 7.

55. John M. Gullick, *Malay Society in the Late Nineteenth Century: The Beginnings of Change* (Singapore: Oxford University Press, 1987), 259.

56. *Malay Mail*, 23 March 1899. An incident along these lines also happened in Parit Buntar, Perak, Malaysia.

57. Roff, *Sanitation and Security*, pages before table 1.

58. High Commission, #1305/1928, Arkib Negara Malaysia (National Archives of Malaysia; henceforth ARNEG), Kuala Lumpur.

59. U.K. consul, Jeddah, to FO, London, 20 August 1875 (FO 78/2418), in de Rush, *Records of the Hajj*, 7.

60. CO 273/396/28656, 22 July 1913; CO 273/402/26309, 30 July 1913; CO 273/408/35816, 19 September 1914; CO 273/418/34307, 9 September 1914; CO 273/418/38345, 5 October 1914.

61. *Straits Settlements Government Gazette* 1867, no. 31, 1868, no. 12, 1890, no. 7.

62. Clippings of revisions to "Notations on Diseases, Manual of Medicine," in MS. 1495/5, box 32, Wellcome Collection. For cholera on the seaways, see "Extract from Law #3 Dated 9 February 1918,

Issued by the Minister of the Interior and Published in the *Journal Officiel* #12, Dated 11 February 1918," in RAMC/1756/5/1, box 354: "Rules for Containment of Cholera, Port Said (1923)," Wellcome Collection.

63. "Note from Col. E. Wilkinson to the Committee," 15 December 1919, in FO 608/275/1, "Peace Conference (1919)," TNA.

64. Report of the civil administrator and director, Kamaran Quarantine Station, 1939, in CO 323/1699/14, "Health and Sanitary (1939–40)."

65. See, for example, CO 273/355/18927, 5 June 1909.

66. CO 273/256/11913, 24 March 1900; CO 273/264/4246, 7 February 1900; CO 273/264/13611, 2 May 1900.

67. *Straits Settlements Government Gazette* 1897, no. 16, clause 34: "Medical inspection of women." As far as possible, female officers were to inspect female pilgrims.

68. High Commission, #187/1936, ARNEG.

69. CO 273/501/50389, 16 September 1920; CO 273/505/37352, 27 July 1920.

70. See, e.g., CO 273/232/12204, 8 July 1897; CO 273/232/12416, 9 July 1897; CO 273/232/13471, 21 July 1897; CO 273/232/13559, 23 July 1897.

71. "Report on the Pilgrimage of 1923," Eastern Confidential E 25/11/91, in IOR/R/20/A/4347, file 44/1, IOR.

72. Confidential memo from W. H. Lee-Warner to U.K. consul, Batavia, 11 October 1918, #6115 (Prop. 21/18), in "Sanitary and Destitute Pilgrims, 1920–23," T161/1086, TNA.

73. Elizabeth Lambourne, "From Cambay to Samudera-Pasai and Gresik: The Export of Gujarati Grave Memorials to Sumatra and Java in the Fifteenth Century CE," *Indonesia and the Malay World* 31 (2003): 221–89.

74. For two examples, see CO 273/209/11948, 9 July 1895; CO 273/491/21684, 5 April 1919.

75. "Report by the Delegate of Great Britain on the Autumn Session of the Committee of the Office International d'Hygiène Publique, Paris 1919," in "Peace Conference (1919)" (FO 608/275/1), TNA.

76. E.g., "Report of Dr. N. I. Corkill on the Jeddah Quarantine and Certain Related Matters as Seen during the 1948 Mecca Pilgrimage, 25 November 1948," in "Anti-cholera Certificate: Report and Correspondence, 1937–55" (MH 55/1888), TNA.

77. U.K. Embassy, Jeddah, to high commissioner, Federation of Malay, 17 January 1952, #1784/3/52, in "Arrangements of Pilgrimages to Mecca from Southeast Asia (1952–53)," CO 1022/409, TNA.

78. Vivian Nutton, "The Contact between Civilizations," in *The Great Maritime Discoveries and World Health*, ed. Mario Gomes Marques and John Cule (Lisbon: Escola Nacional Saúde Pública, Ordem dos Médicos, 1991), 77.

79. For the Greco-Roman and classical Muslim world views as bases for later thought on disease, see Saul Jarcho, *The Concept of Contagion in Medicine, Literature, and Religion* (Malabar, Florida: Krieger Publishing, 2000), 1–20, 21–26.

80. J. K. Crellin, "The Dawn of Germ Theory: Particles, Infection and Biology," in *Medicine and Science in the 1860s*, ed. Frederick N. L. Poynter (London: Wellcome Institute, 1968), 61–66; Charles Rosenberg, *Explaining Epidemics and Other Studies in the History of Medicine* (Cambridge: Cambridge University Press, 1992), 109.

81. Yaron Perry and Efraim Lev, *Modern Medicine in the Holy Land: Pioneering British Medical Services in Late Ottoman Palestine* (London: Tauris Academic Studies, 2007); Bridie Andrews and Mary P. Sutphen, introduction to *Medicine and Colonial Identity*, ed. Sutphen and Andrews (London: Routledge, 2003), 5.

6

Trafficking in Evil?

The Global Arms Trade and the Politics of Disorder

Robert Crews

INTRODUCTION

Between the 1850s and 1930s, the territory stretching from the Euphrates to the Indus formed the epicenter of a commodity revolution whose effects are still felt throughout the region. The technologies of printing, telegraphy, the steamship, the railroad, photography, and cartography facilitated the emergence of new ways of imagining time and space, unleashing global flows of goods, people, and ideas. Beginning in the 1860s, however, innovations in the manufacture of a single commodity—guns—played a disproportionate role in ushering in a new era of politics. Modern firearms served as both instruments of European colonial expansion and indigenous state-building programs. But trade in these objects quickly escaped colonial and state controls. Various actors appropriated these commodities for their own political projects and integrated them into new patterns of circulation. This chapter reveals how an illicit traffic in small arms gave rise to networks of manufacturers, merchants, smugglers, insurgents, and revolutionaries that crossed imperial, national, and regional boundaries. The trade in modern arms established novel linkages among distant communities and made possible new kinds of commerce and politics throughout this space.

Authorities anxiously tied the new weapons to a surge in brigandage, crime, unrest, and, from 1905, political terror, as militants, bandits, and rebels tapped into these global flows to challenge existing state orders. In 1907, a British survey condemned the trade as "at least as great a public evil as the slave trade," arguing that "in the Middle East, ... besides intensifying anarchy and bloodshed in Central Arabia and in some of the smaller states, it has weakened the authority of the

Persian and Turkish Governments and threatens in the end to produce widespread and incurable disorder."[1] Once imagined by colonial authorities as a sign of European dominance, guns became synonymous with disorder in the early twentieth century, a condition that local elites sought to tame in constructing more powerful—and often more violent—states to govern disarmed populations.

"ROUGH AND CLUMSY ARMS"

In the early modern period, consumers in the region extending from the Ottoman borderlands to the Indo-Afghan frontier were connected to numerous markets of arms, including those of local production. Yet the volume of this trade, the quality of its weapons, and the density of the networks that sustained it were all of a different character from what emerged later. From the early nineteenth century, Iranian consumers imported firearms and other manufactured goods from Russia, from "cutlery of all descriptions, glassware, looking glasses, stationery, broad cload and cashmeres" to "spirits, gold lace, and gold thread, furs of all descriptions . . . and chintzes, velvet, clocks, watches, guns and pistols, oil, iron, brass, steel, lead and sea horse teeth."[2] But guns did not yet circulate in vast quantities. A survey of household inventories in Istanbul from 1800 suggests that daggers, swords, and knives were still far more common than rifles or other firearms.[3] In 1838, a British visitor to Kabul's bazaars found "pistols and muskets" from Russia. Imported via Bukhara (now in Uzbekistan), these were "generally small, neat, and of a good fashion, but are not much used." Only "the chiefs" and "other great men" purchased the "superior kind," while "the common soldiers, who cannot afford to buy them, use the rough and clumsy arms manufactured in Cabool." Flints (used to fire flintlock guns) were in "considerable demand" and were imported from Russia and especially India, though they were also being produced "in this country of late."[4]

Iranian towns formed critical nodes in the manufacture and distribution of assorted weapons. In 1801, John Malcolm, an East India Company official, reported that Shiraz was the center of this production. Its "chief manufactures," he wrote, were "guns, pistols, swords and other military arms, glassware, sheep and lambskin for caps, articles of gold and silver, enameled work and coarse cloths, all of which are exported to other parts of the Empire."[5] In the 1820s, artisans conscripted into government workshops at Tabriz and Tehran cast guns and made gunpowder under the direction of British masters.[6] The Iranian city of Mashhad was another hub of manufacture. As far away as Kandahar one could find "Mashadi double barrelled guns, pistols, and swords." Kazakhs north of the Caspian Sea could not get "sabres, guns, rifles, pistols, gunpowder and shot, [or] percussion caps [cylinders used to ignite a powder charge]" from the Russians but did manage to procure "a few bad rifles . . . from Persia with matchlocks."[7] In 1831 the Burgess brothers imported rifles and pistols from Britain to Tabriz, while in the 1840s French weapons arrived in Iranian bazaars.[8] The traveler Jakob Polak observed that in the 1850s, locally made copies of rifles and pistols based on "European models" were "very close to the originals, including even the factory trademarks."[9] Still, in 1857 a Prussian visitor in Iran, Otto Blau, encountered swords and blades from Khorasan, Daghestan, Bukhara, and Herat, where, he noted, a colony of artisans had settled from Damascus. Isfahan and Mashhad were renowned for knife blades that, along with saber blades, went "yearly in a vast quantity to Turkey, Kurdistan, the Caucasus and Russia." These remained in demand in more distant borderlands—among the "independent Kurds" and "Circassian mountaineers"—even if they no longer satisfied domestic consumers.[10] From 1855, the peasantry and tribes of the eastern Mediterranean acquired from Belgium and elsewhere inexpensive shotguns and muskets, which they used to press their political demands against local notables.[11]

Elites seeking luxury goods and officials responsible for supplying the military also looked abroad for arms. Blau praised the Iranians' taste for weapons, remarking that they were careful and attentive consumers at the stores in Istanbul. In the 1840s, they paid forty tomans for English hunting rifles at Tabriz but later balked when cruder French versions appeared for ten to twelve tomans. In the early 1850s, American missionaries apparently brought Colt revolvers to Tabriz, but local consumers were skeptical about their quality.[12] The reputation of European guns only recovered, Blau reported, during the Crimean War (1853–56), when the arms depots of Istanbul overflowed with weapons that intermediaries redirected to Iranian markets, where buyers snatched up hunting rifles, shotguns, pistols, and Colt and Adams revolvers. Most came from Europe, though some muzzle-loading pistols and rifles arrived from Russia. Blau concluded that demand would have been far greater had percussion caps and other essentials for long-term use of the guns been available. As a result, he noted, "many Persians, Kurds and Turks are in possession of quite beautiful and perfectly useful weapons, but these must be left unused because it is in only a few of the larger cities, which often are many days' travel away, that stocks of these indispensible items are available." Thus locals were never more grateful, Blau observed, than when foreign travelers gave them "percussion caps, bullets, and powder."[13] In 1870 a Russian visitor to Tabriz encountered a strong preference for English weapons, pointing out that buyers carefully sought them out over French and Belgian copies, which were suspected to be inferior. Despite the proximity of the border and the large quantity of Russian goods already in Tabriz, local tastes made the prospect of Russian arms sales look hopeless.[14]

TOOLS OF EMPIRE?

Long governed by "gunpowder empires" that marshaled new technologies in the formation and maintenance of imperial polities in the sixteenth and seventeenth centuries, societies from the Balkans through the Indian subcontinent had lengthy experience with a variety of weapons. Guns imported from Europe circulated from at least the fifteenth century, and domestic manufacture has persisted into the present. But from the 1860s, mass production of industrially made firearms such as breech-loading rifles marked a shift. Spurred by advances during the American Civil War, Winchester, Colt, Providence Tool, and other American firms sold more than one and a half million rifles between 1865 and 1870.[15] They offered more efficient, and lethal, alternatives to the often unwieldy and unreliable smoothbore, muzzle-loading muskets and short guns then in circulation. The technique of rifling, creating grooves in the barrel that made bullets spin, allowed shooters to fire with far greater precision, and metallic cartridges made firing more secure and predictable, even in inclement weather. The Martini-Henry rifle, which the British Army adopted in 1871, and similar models could hit targets at more than one thousand yards. Between 1869 and 1879, the Ottomans bought more than one million of these weapons, along with half a billion cartridges.[16] In the 1880s several armies added magazine rifles and machine guns to their arsenals. By the turn of the century, according to a British description of the arms trade in the Persian Gulf, consumers of guns had become so discerning that they would purchase only breech-loading rifles: the older muzzle-loaders "had ceased to be saleable in either Arabia or Persia."[17]

Arms exports were almost completely in the hands of private companies in the United States, Great Britain, Germany, France, Belgium, and Austria-Hungary. Seeking markets around the globe, governments supported exports and used arms sales to gain influence.[18] In turn, manufacturers looked for state backing, even though the intermediaries who facilitated the trade frequently operated beyond government scrutiny. Political and economic motives were intertwined: private adventurers—such as the Britons who ran guns to Circassians in the North Caucasus for use against the Russians—sought imperial glory as well as fortune.[19] Although European firms and large states dominated the trade and crafted international agreements to manage it, the explosion in arms production in the industrial era gave rise to a global market that eluded regulation. This was a murky world of clandestine activities that knitted together manufacturers, traders, and consumers along intersecting maritime and land routes.

The arms traffic depended on a variety of agents, though the identities of the smugglers and most of their dealings remain opaque. Muslims, Christians, and Hindus, they included Belgian gunmakers, French traders, Zanzibari commercial agents, British steamship company employees, Indian merchants, Afghan nomads, Arab tribal leaders, Armenian revolutionaries, and Iranian officials, royalists, and racketeers. From Birmingham, England, to the villages of the Kohat Pass on the Indo-Afghan frontier and from Tbilisi in the Caucasus to Muscat and Bandar 'Abbas in Persia, these producers, traders, and consumers of guns formed adaptive circuits. In East Africa, the arms trade flourished in Ethiopia and Djibouti. Via steamship and sail, crucial entrepôts in the Persian Gulf and the Gulf of Oman connected these markets with Europe and the greater Middle East. To the north, the Caucasus-Iran frontier formed a land bridge for Russian and European arms manufacturers. Gun traders and consumers constantly devised new routes and strategies over land and sea to confound Ottoman, Qajar, and Afghan officials and circumvent the main agents of interdiction, colonial British and Russian authorities.

Although manufacturers and states played essential roles in production and regulation, consumers were hardly passive recipients in this commodity chain. Numerous sources attest to the discriminating tastes of buyers, who brought their own estimations of aesthetics and utility to the market. Like the consumers of other commodities throughout the region, gun traders worked with a variety of suppliers but developed clear preferences for particular brands, even among firearms of the same vintage. Producers and traders, in turn, were compelled to adapt to these shifting demands, making gun buyers key participants in this global exchange.[20]

The consumers of firearms in Qajar Iran, the Ottoman Empire, British India, and elsewhere not only shaped this traffic by making choices about their purchases but also frequently engaged in production themselves. Like lithographic printing and other industrial technologies, modern gun making was readily domesticated by aspiring state builders from Cairo to Tehran and Kabul. Nile Green's observation about lithography applies to gun making as well: "The spread of industrialization was not only a matter of quashing traditional production methods outside Europe, but also in some cases a matter of the 'bottom up' adaptation of machines and methods to suit older indigenous markets and their local suppliers."[21] From the 1820s, Egyptian and Qajar elites studied the manufacture of firearms in Europe and Russia and developed the means, aided by foreign technical expertise, to produce their own.[22] In Iran, Muhammad Shah (r. 1834–48) invested in the production of guns and gunpowder for Qajar forces. In 1850 the government established a factory in Tehran capable of producing one thousand rifles per month, and others for making gunpowder and percussion caps followed.[23] Linked to mines in Gilan and Mazandaran, industrial workshops domesticated imported gun designs, alongside samovars, printed books, and other commodities.[24] In the North Caucasus in the 1840s and 1850s, the Muslim rebel Shamil created factories that produced gunpowder and cannon to equip his forces against the tsarist Russian army. By 1860, Egyptian forces had eighty thousand rifled muskets, most of which were modeled on a French design and produced at a factory in Cairo.[25] Similarly, in Chinese Central Asia in the 1870s, Yaqub Beg not only received arms from the British and Ottomans but also established workshops for converting thousands of older weapons and making rifles, powder, and cartridges. An Afghan émigré to Yaqub Beg's state established a cannon foundry in Kashgar. By 1875, according to one Russian report, six thousand of Yaqub Beg's soldiers possessed breech-loading rifles, and his arms factory produced "sixteen rifles a week."[26] In Afghanistan, indigenous manufacture was the chief industrial priority of the ruler, ʿAbd al-Rahman Khan (r. 1880–1901), whose official biography boasted that he had mastered the art of rifle making as a boy and had "made [two] entirely from start to finish without help from any one." Under his direction, the Afghans constructed ten or more breech-loading rifles a day, as well as artillery pieces and "Maxim, Gardiner, and Gatling guns."[27] Appropriating European and American designs was not limited to states, however. Artisans everywhere managed to turn out reliable reproductions of the latest imported models, often with the counterfeit brand plates attached. Consumption bred new kinds of diffusion, and indigenous production created yet another node on the arms circuit.

The diffusion of guns complicated state efforts to extend and maintain control. Frequently portrayed as tools of empire that gave European states crucial advantages over societies with less sophisticated weapons, firearms have figured in heated debates about the relationship between guns and violence, especially in the United States.[28] Looking beyond the distinctive American context and its politicized debates about guns and personal rights, the connection between the diffusion of arms and particular kinds of violent collective action emerges more clearly. State-building elites in numerous contexts recognized the dangers posed by small arms, especially in the hands of young and desperate men. As early as 1607 an Ottoman decree complained that the firearm (tüfeng) had become "available to people of evil intention" and that its spread was "the main source of the disorders and banditry in the empire."[29] Rulers took great care to regulate the circulation of firearms, to deprive subjects of the means to resist their authority. At the same time, guns tended to be symbols of prestige and aristocratic distinction. Royal courts incorporated firearms into the hunt in the sixteenth and seventeenth centuries, while Ottoman law denied non-Muslims the right to bear arms. In most locales, only a "pistol gentry," to adopt the phrase of one contemporary Egyptian observer, enjoyed the privilege of legally carrying such a weapon.[30]

In the nineteenth century, policing of borders and regulation of trade increasingly focused on managing the diffusion of guns, while internal policing concentrated on disarming populations. A time of rapid technological change, the period stretching from the 1880s to the 1920s was also one in which states broadened their attempts to monopolize the means of violence within their territories and to count, immobilize, and disarm populations, especially in sensitive borderlands, where emerging state boundaries became crucial symbols of territorial sovereignty. Nonetheless, policing and profit gave impetus to the emergence of new entrepreneurial circuits that crossed ethnic, religious, and political boundaries. The underground weapons trade evolved out of this state-building matrix and its confrontation with smuggling and transborder mobility.

The proliferation of sophisticated and relatively inexpensive arms had complex and heterogeneous political effects. This traffic shifted the balance in contests over authority and access to wealth. In many borderlands, the redistribution of power enabled by the trade in firearms also served as a check on European expansion. In East Africa, the Ethiopian Empire succeeded in procuring sufficient arms to acquire new territory and fend off an Italian army; in South Africa, the Boers inflicted heavy losses on British forces.[31] Assorted groups connected to the diffusion of guns gained new leverage against centralizing states and rival political and social groups. At the same time, this traffic led to profound shifts in the articulation of authority in local communities. On the Indo-Afghan frontier, for instance, it contributed to the militarization of the authority of the mullahs. "Religious militancy," Sana Haroon concludes, "was as much fashioned by this illegal arms trade as it was by ideology, agnatic rivalry and the Pakhtun [i.e., Pathan] code of honour."[32] But these transformations were not driven by new technology alone. Like other commodities, guns took on new meanings in particular cultural contexts, even as these networks tied local communities to global commodity flows.

DEADLY COMMODITIES

In the second half of the nineteenth century, imperial Russian and British competition in Eurasian borderlands intensified demand for the new industrial weapons throughout the region, and the great powers responded with measures to curb the emerging traffic. In the Caucasus, the tsarist army had just defeated Shamil, whose forces had been well equipped with captured weapons and those produced by local artisans such as Muhammad al-Hidali from the village of Kudali, who had managed by 1859 to replicate the latest revolver technology.[33] In expanding into Central Asia, tsarist authorities worried already in the 1870s that modern British weapons were reaching Turkmen communities around the Caspian and beyond.[34] In 1876, an official writing about the Tekke Turkmen warned that "it was already rare for the Tekkes who arrive here not to have one or even two English repeaters." Summing up the anxiety of colonial authorities generally, he deplored the prospect that they would not enjoy their technological advantage forever: "That which we can achieve now without a shot will with time hardly be managed without significant sacrifices."[35] With the demarcation of the Russo-Persian border in 1881, Turkmen continued to migrate across the boundary, and tsarist border guards sought to regulate the commodities that crossed with them. The authorities permitted weapons for personal use but remained on the alert for larger caches of weapons, along with contraband such as sugar, tea, narcotics, and manufactured goods.[36] Seeking to cut off the smuggling of arms from the Caucasus, in 1883 they warned Shi'a pilgrims to Mashhad to apply for documents before carrying guns.[37]

British officials also targeted this trade. The Indian Arms Act of 1878 mandated licenses for anyone bearing arms or engaging in imports or exports; however, it did not apply in its entirety until later decades in some districts along the Indo-Afghan frontier, where locals were permitted to carry personal arms without licenses.[38] During the Second Anglo-Afghan War, of 1878–80, the discovery of European-made percussion caps in the possession of Afghan soldiers suggested that the Afghans had forged ties with international dealers, though the extent of these contacts was not yet clear. Farther to the west, anxieties about the spread of insecurity gripped Tehran, which was also under pressure from London to restrict the entry of arms at the port of Bushehr on the Persian Gulf. In 1881, the Qajar government formally recognized the political threat posed by an increased circulation of guns and designated the import of arms a monopoly of the shah. As with other commodities, however, interdiction efforts increased profitability. In the 1880s, partial repression combined with growing demand to expand the trade across these vast frontiers.

Flowing through multiple legal jurisdictions and across porous borders, the global traffic in guns drew on varied resources and operated in a shadowy world where no single and unambiguous law applied. Just as states pursued commercial and political rivalries and presented conflicting arguments about the morality of their participation in the arms trade, traders maintained differing views about this commerce. The Iranian merchant and memoirist Hajj Mohammad-Taqi Jourabchi recalled how, in the early 1870s, his father highlighted the moral danger of engaging in ammunition sales and pushed one relative to give up the trade and become a goldsmith instead.[39] But many more expressed no such reservations about morality or politics. Indeed, there was a spike in the trade in 1883, when British firms began to introduce firearms to Bushehr. Despite the threat that cheap, modern arms posed to British hegemony, these rifles, colonial authorities conceded, were "made in England, the exporting firms were British, the ships that carried the arms were British, and the firms that handled the trade in Persia were British."[40]

The diffusion of these weapons had wide-ranging effects. In Iran, they supplanted many locally made guns. In 1886, Tehran was still home to more than a hundred gunsmiths (*tofangsaz*), mostly Christians and Jews.[41] Yet a local chronicle tells the story of decline and the reorientation of the geography of domestic arms production. In 1891, Mirza Hoseyn Khan Tahvildar's *Geography of Isfahan* lamented the fate of the old-style artisans. Tahvildar praised the work of a notable master named Hoseyn, who was "better than the old renowned Russian masters" and whose "special guns" were "famous." Tahvildar noted the presence of "many other masters in Isfahan" but added that most ended up "in the Tehran workshops now, because of lack of work here." Most practitioners of an even more specialized trade, gun-hammer smiths, had long abandoned Isfahan for Tehran or had left for "Khorasan, Kurdestan, Fars and other places."[42]

Along the Indo-Afghan frontier, by contrast, gunsmiths were more successful in retaining a share of local markets, though this was not because they were isolated from the global flow of commodities. In 1879, British visitors to Kandahar were startled to learn that with the exception of "some stamped silk handkerchiefs from Bokhara" and local kabobs and bread, "everything else seemed to come from Bombay or Birmingham."[43] You could still find three shops in Kandahar that made guns, though, plus eight more that made gunstocks and one run by a "gunlock-smith."[44] Meanwhile in Peshawar, metalworkers continued to produce "pistols, daggers, knives and swords." As one British official observed, the city resembled "all the large towns between Delhi and Cabul" in that it also sustained an arms trade that the British had "not yet entirely closed."[45] Nevertheless, by the early 1880s, colonial authorities acknowledged that curbs on firearms, together with the arrival of new commodities, had begun to transform local livelihoods: "By the introduction of the Arms Act [of 1878] the manufacturers of arms and gunpowder have to some extent been deprived of their occupations. From the introduction of foreign cotton and cloth goods also, the trade of the weaver class has suffered, and that of the blacksmith for a similar reason. The number of wandering beggars is great, [and] it is possible it has been increased by including the Talib-ul-ilm [religious students]."[46]

Nonetheless, the artisans of Dera Ghazi Khan maintained a reputation for producing guns and related items. These included the leather belts "worn throughout the Derajat division, with neatly made powder flasks, bullet cases, flint and steel pouches," and bullet belts "with rows of bamboo tubes neatly wrought with embroidery, like those worn by the Kurds," a style adopted by communities from the frontiers of Anatolia to Central Asia.[47]

Like local manufacturers, suppliers adapted to colonial efforts to suppress the illicit traffic in arms. Intended to abolish the slave trade, the Brussels Conference of 1890 established a zone where the sale of firearms, which had been exchanged for slaves and had generally facilitated that trade, would be prohibited. As a result, arms merchants in Zanzibar shifted their base north to Muscat, where the sultan's commercial agreements with the Europeans and Americans created a new haven for the weapons trade. The rise of Muscat's arms business was linked in turn to a brief decline in the highly globalized commodity that Matthew Hopper's chapter 8 examines: dried fruit. When the export of Arabian dates to the United States fell sharply, Indian merchants in Muscat sought a new market. Drawing on their ties to Zanzibari intermediaries, European firms, and Afghan traders, merchants such as Muhammad Fadl, Ratansi Purshottam, Damodar Dharamsi, and Gopalji Walji traded arms before the arrival of European traders. They swiftly pivoted from satisfying the American taste for dates to meeting the demand on the Indo-Afghan frontier for arms and ammunition.[48] Diverse middlemen moved these weapons in steamers, dhows, and other craft to ports along the Gulfs of Persia and Oman, forcing Tehran to issue another ban in 1891.

Yet the trade continued to grow. Muscat remained a haven for free trade in a stunning array of arms and ammunition, among other goods. In this competitive climate, governments pursued "national interests" in promoting arms exports while seeking to keep these weapons out of their colonial possessions and dependencies. In the 1890s, British observers agreed that the trade was "chiefly in the hands of Messrs. Joyce and Kynoch," who were British subjects. Arms also came from Belgium, Germany, and France, the last of which had opted out of many of the provisions of the Brussels Conference and continued its arms trading operations in East Africa as well.[49] Arms thus passed from Zanzibar to Muscat and then on to the Persian Gulf via intermediaries such as the Iranian Armenian firm led by A. and T. J. Malcolm and a "Parsi and English house," Fracis, Times and Company.[50] In some cases, European firms shipped firearms directly: at Karachi in late 1890 the British intercepted a shipment of 420 Enfields rifles sent from Austria-Hungary and intended for Gwadar. Other deliveries went straight to Bahrain or Kuwait, where middlemen transported them to buyers in other Ottoman regions. Most of these firearms (60 percent) were thought to end up in Iran, with the remainder flowing to the "Turkish possessions in the Gulf" (25 percent) and "non-Turkish Arabia" (15 percent). At the turn of the century, trading houses based in France (M. Goguyer) and the Russian Empire (Kevorkoff and Co. at Odessa) also set up operations in Muscat.[51] By one estimate, in 1897, firms operating throughout the Persian Gulf region imported arms valued at nine hundred thousand dollars from Britain and one hundred thousand dollars from France. Middlemen then smuggled them into ports along the Persian Gulf coast for distribution inland among Arab, Qajar, and Afghan tribes.[52] In the same year, the key port of Bushehr received shipments of at least thirty thousand rifles, with nearby Shiraz emerging as a "distributing centre" in the Qajar interior, allowing groups such as "the Kashkai tribe and the Tangistanis ... [to be] excellently armed." The payment of bribes to customs officials was an essential step in these transactions, making the trade "a semi-clandestine activity."[53]

While colonial surveillance mapped ever-expanding networks, in 1895 British forces on the North-West Frontier faced Pathan tribes with "arms of precision" capable of inflicting grave casualties. In 1897–98, punitive expeditions against uprisings there yielded evidence of connections, on the one hand, between India and the frontier and, on the other, between this region and Muscat. Most of the breech-loading rifles could be traced back to British subsidies to frontier tribes and theft from the Indian army and local levies.[54] Yet authorities made a critical discovery in February 1898, when

> twenty packets of Martini-Henry ammunition were found in the house of a headman of Pasni in British Makran, and, in the same month, three Pathans in possession of a Martini-Henry carbine were arrested at Ormarah in the same district; the offenders in the second case proved to be Powindas [nomadic merchants] of the Dera Ismail Khan District in the North-West Frontier Province of India, who, after making a pilgrimage to Baghdad, had purchased twenty rifles at Muscat and, in attempting to carry them upcountry, had been robbed of all but one by Nausherwanis of Kolwa.[55]

For London, definitive proof linking the Gulf trade to the frontier came in November 1898, when a British political officer bought a Martini-Henry rifle from a Ghilzai trader in Kurram. Stamped "Fracis, Times and Company, 27 Leadenhall Street, London," the gun launched a renewed effort to eradicate the trade. In 1901, revolvers and ammunition with similar stamps turned up in Waziristan, while Martini-Henry rifles appeared in Mashhad, where they had been transported via a caravan of three hundred camels from Bandar 'Abbas by a British subject, Ghulam Khan.[56] Stolen rifles continued to find their way to the Indian frontier, where indigenous gunsmiths also ramped up production. "Of 1,497 rifles surrendered in 1897–98," one British Army source observed of the arms of the Afridi tribesmen, "245 were classed as 'stolen' (i.e., stolen complete), 130 as 'foreign' (of which 87 were from Kabul, 77 being Sniders), and 1,122 as 'made up.'"[57] Meanwhile, from the north, Russian officials tracked bands of tsarist subjects along the border east of the Caspian, including Turkmen and others, who smuggled firearms and other articles into Iran in exchange for sizable quantities of tea and opium.[58]

Citing the threat to "the peace of our Indian frontier from the wholesale armament of our frontier tribes," London deployed the empire's navy, police, and courts to track and suppress the trade.[59] However, the great variety of actors and routes, together with the volume of arms and profits, presented a daunting challenge. In February 1905, the British political agent at Muscat tracked the arrival of cases of arms and ammunition from Manchester, Marseilles, and elsewhere.[60] In May, the Russian steamer *Rostoff* brought seventy-five cases of arms and ammunition from Djibouti—along with Muslim pilgrims from Jeddah—and then passed on to Basra; in September the Russian *Trouver* brought another ten cases.[61] In January 1906, a Belgian arrived from Djibouti to set up an arms firm, assisted by Armenians formerly employed by M. Kevorkoff & Co.[62] A German firm, Robert Wönckhaus and Company, which had followed the trade from Zanzibar, and a French enterprise run by the Goguyer family appear to have been the largest European dealers at Muscat. But they were joined by local and regional players—including Jews, Parsis, Hindus, Christians, and Muslims—who, like the Indian merchant Ratansi Purshottam, pushed European suppliers to tailor their designs to customers' specifications.[63] A British report from 1910 identified a "syndicate" at the nearby Iranian port of Lingah comprising "Messrs. R. Wonckhaus & Co.'s Agents[,] . . . Haji Abdul Rahman Kazim, Agent of the Russian Steam Navigation Company[,] . . . [and] Abdullah bin Hasan Giladari, a naturalised British Indian subject."[64] Moreover, in addition to the sultan, other regional officials derived income from the trade. In 1908, British authorities received a report from Bushehr that "74 revolvers were landed from the S.S. *Sicilia* for Mirza Hussein, the German Consulate Munshi [secretary]; they were brought ashore by him and others in the pilot boat. They are selling in the bazaar for 15 tomans (£3) each. The Hamal Bashi complains bitterly that the entire subordinate Customs staff is . . . corrupt . . . and accuses Sheikh

Ibrahim, under whose direction the Customs watchmen are, of countenancing the smuggling."[65]

Customs and port officials around the Gulf abetted the circulation of arms. Meanwhile, to European rivals, the extensive British commercial and political presence in the region suggested London's complicity as well. St. Petersburg viewed the trade as a central piece of a grand British scheme to destabilize Iran and the Arab provinces of the Ottoman Empire.[66] For their part, the British suspected that Russians had supplied the Berdan rifles found among the Turkmen of northeastern Iran, to provoke a "crisis" for the Qajar authorities and allow Russia to annex more territory after declaring it "impossible any longer to tolerate the dangerous disorders on her frontier."[67]

Relying on Pathan informants and other sources, British officials learned that traders moved in large, well-armed caravans of up to eighty people and some two hundred camels, capable of carrying several thousand rifles and hundreds of thousands of rounds of ammunition.[68] Passing from India and Afghanistan through eastern Iran to the Gulf, these caravans traveled seasonally, delivering wool, pistachios, and other commodities to southern ports. Iranian travelers also collected detailed reports on the transborder movements of smaller groups of Afghan smugglers who sold weapons and arms along the Afghan-Iranian frontier, and their identities seem to have been widely known among local circles of merchants and notables.[69] Sometimes they coordinated their activities with Baluch communities, disguising themselves as Baluch or Arabs. Afghan traders maintained an impressive network of intermediaries in Muscat and throughout the Gulf who aided in the timing of their secretive missions and offered critical intelligence as policing intensified in the first decade of the twentieth century.

Afghan smugglers also improvised a maritime route. From India, they boarded steamers, often identifying themselves as religious pilgrims, to arrange future exchanges, though such missions were more vulnerable to British interdiction. In January 1908, for example, some fifty Afghans on the *Bulimba* were turned away from Muscat.[70] But they were permitted at Bandar 'Abbas, where a party of more than one hundred Afghans arrived on the *Kasara*.[71] Twenty-three of them landed two days later on the same ship at Bahrain. There they fell under suspicion of "being connected with the arms trade" and were "placed in open arrest (with roll-calls three times a day) in a mosque close to the Political Agency," and their money was confiscated "as security for their good behaviour" until they left.[72] Other Afghans and Baluch sailed by dhow in small groups from Makran.[73] In Muscat they joined buyers flocking to the shops of Ali bin Moosa, Baijeot & Co., and Goguyer & Co.[74]

When the time for the delivery of arms purchases arrived, a network of informants maintained watch along the coast of Iranian Baluchistan for Royal Navy ships. In 1907, rifles landed there at the rate of roughly two hundred per week, according to British estimates. Communities around ports and landing sites were fully integrated in the trade: pearl divers stood at the ready, to the dismay of British captains, to retrieve confiscated arms that they ordered thrown overboard, fearing that guns handed over to Qajar officials would end up in the bazaars. Even bakers who prepared bread for British ships were said to tip off gunrunners.[75] In returning to Afghanistan via routes leading to Herat or Kandahar, some arms dealers appear to have received the protection of the authorities. Others faced prosecution and confiscations.[76] Yet, against this risk, a gun brought from Bushehr might triple or quadruple in value by the time it arrived in Ghazni or Dera Ismail Khan via the tribesmen who purchased the weapons in Kabul either with cash or with payments "credited in Peshawar, and bills of exchange obtained on Hindu bankers of Kabul."[77] One British observer calculated that in the early twentieth century, the cost of a magazine rifle would be fifty rupees on the Afghan-Iranian border but would rise to five hundred rupees in Kabul and eight hundred rupees by the time it reached the Kohat Pass on the Indo-Afghan frontier.[78]

While the British struggled to cut off the supply of arms to the Iranian interior and India, London sold or gave vast quantities of weapons to the governments in Tehran and Kabul and contributed smaller amounts to tribal militias along the North-West Frontier.[79] Aided by British subsidies, the Afghan government also built up infrastructure for industrial weapons production. The workshops of Kabul turned out Martini-Henrys and Snider rifles and cartridges by the thousands—a development that inspired pride in visitors such as the Bukharan merchant Mirza Siraj al-Din Hakim, who wondered at the "progress" displayed by the "small Afghan state" that "needs nothing from anyone."[80] Across the frontier, in Bajaur, Dir, and Waziristan, where artisans had traditionally produced their own weapons, including guns, powder, and bullets, workshops turned to reproducing the modern European models.[81] In village workshops in the Kohat Pass, Punjabi gunsmiths stamped locally produced rifles with "Enfield," though one British visitor hastened to add that these markings were often misspelled.[82] Similarly, at Kerind in the Iranian province of Kermanshah, a British agent came across four gunsmiths who produced annually about one hundred "exceedingly good Martini rifles at about Tomans 20 (Rs. 45) a-piece and will copy anything."[83]

These multiple production sites, which extended in the early twentieth century from villages in the Kohat Pass to Tiflis, Tabriz, Baku, and elsewhere, meant that smuggling via the Gulf or the Caucasus was not the only path that firearms followed in circulating throughout this space. Traffickers targeted factories and armories in India and Russia alike.[84] In the late 1880s, police in Peshawar discovered a smuggling ring specializing in stolen guns and ammunition that linked a Pathan in a village in Bajaur and various Afghans to a blacksmith and gun repairer, Hajji Sham al-Din, in Bombay. Concealed in bales of cotton, the contraband eventually made its way to the frontier and then to the interior of Afghanistan.[85] Moreover, troops in the frontier region were particularly prone to having their weapons go missing. The military was forced to introduce more and more regulations to keep guns, as well as spare parts and even spent shell casings, out of local markets.[86] Shiʻa pilgrims from Russia brought stolen guns purchased at the Nizhnii Novgorod fair and at markets in the Caucasus to Ottoman Iraq. Procured from tsarist armories, revolvers sold for up to fifty rubles and rifles for up to eighty-five rubles, and buyers in Iraq were apparently willing to pay up to 170 rubles for a coveted Mosin rifle.[87] The distinction between "state" and "private" ownership of firearms was thus constantly in flux.

Army deserters were yet another link between government suppliers and the illicit flow of arms. Under Nasir al-Din Shah (r. 1848–96), the Qajar army remained a poorly supplied (and irregularly paid) composite of various kinds of forces, including irregular units under the control of local notables. Equipped with modern rifles, tribal forces outgunned the poorly supplied army, and frequent desertion, looting, and riots—even among troops charged with the defense of Tehran—resulted in the transfer of arms to civilians.[88] Janet Klein has shown what happened to the arms that Ottoman authorities distributed among Kurdish cavalry regiments along the eastern frontier: "Hamidiye tribesmen employed them on occasion to attack the government's forces when they saw fit, and others sold them to the very Armenians they were supposed to be fighting."[89] Afghan soldiers commonly abandoned their posts, or worse: in 1890 a soldier named Ibrahim Shah—thought to be a hashish addict, like many of his comrades—turned his gun on the emir at Mazar-i Sharif. Luckily for the emir, the shooter missed, and the government banned the use of hashish by its soldiers.[90] The distribution of arms among Afghan irregulars and reserves was an even riskier proposition. In 1897, the government responded to a rebellion and fear of invasion by training villagers in the use of arms and distributing guns and uniforms. This program proved short-lived, however, due to concern that these reserves, once armed and trained, would turn the weapons on one another.[91]

REVOLUTIONARY ARMS

This crisis in the Afghan army paled in comparison to the waves of revolutionary unrest that swept through Russia and Iran beginning in 1905. Along the periphery of both states, the availability of large quantities of modern arms, including Maxim guns, bombs, rifles, and handguns, permitted insurgents to wrest power from central authorities. As Mansour Bonakdarian has shown in the case of Iran's constitutional revolution, activists embraced these new weapons as means to forge a modern society and as symbols of national heroism and masculinity.[92] Linking these two societies and their politics, the Caucasus served as a conduit not only of arms but of fighters.

Decades of labor migration, intellectual exchange, and trade had forged transnational connections that provided the infrastructure for the movement of weapons and militants who simultaneously launched challenges to the tsarist, Ottoman, and Qajar orders. In 1891 the Armenian Dashnaktsutiun party had established an arms factory in Tabriz that employed workers from the Tula arms factory in Russia and produced arms for the revolutionary struggle in the Ottoman Empire.[93] Factories and prisons alike served as points of contact for activists belonging to different factions and ethnic communities. For example, Meshedi Muhammad Sadiq Khan Cherendabi was born in Tabriz but migrated to the Caucasus as a young man. He eventually landed in prison, where, like others, he established ties to a multiethnic underworld. During the revolution Cherendabi returned to Tabriz. He brought weapons and bombs, then raided the government citadel for guns, which he distributed among the mujahideen.[94] Armenians counted among their ranks gunsmiths such as Samson (Stepan Tadeosian), whose activities included overseeing armories run by the Dashnaktsutiun party and coordinating Armenians in the Russia Empire and Iran.[95] In Tabriz, Georgian and Armenian Social Democrats delivered fighters and bombs to the mujahideen and established a bomb-making "laboratory."[96] Expertise in producing explosives and replicating other weapons circulated widely. In November 1906 the Iranian authorities discovered the first locally produced bombs in Kermanshah. A presumed bomb maker accidentally blew himself up in his home, and the authorities identified a blacksmith as the maker of seventeen more bombs.[97] Similarly, Isfahan underwent a resurgence as a gun-making hub. Local artisans copied European models, adding to the vast arsenal of the Bakhtiyari tribe whose arms played a central role in the course of the revolution.[98] Flamboyantly adopting the new weapons as a form of revolutionary dress, militants strapped cartridge belts across their chests. Like the bandoliers that their contemporaries in revolutionary Mexico wore, these implements demonstrated their wearers' martial valor and manly devotion to the cause, especially when coupled with an iconic pose reproduced in mass-produced photographs of leading personalities and their armed retinues.[99]

As more of the Iranian population took up arms during the revolutionary period, violent acts ranging from banditry and raiding to assassinations and personal assaults heightened insecurity throughout the country. The spread of anarchic conditions and gun violence in turn sharpened the authorities' focus on the movement of arms. In Astarabad, Husaynquli Maqsudlu wrote detailed reports about the local arms traffic in his capacity as a British news writer. Focusing on Turkmen efforts to acquire weapons, he compiled frequent accounts of smuggling and arms sales, as well as murders and robberies. The news writer even recorded accidents linked to firearms, relating the case of a girl who pointed a gun at a woman in jest and accidentally shot and killed her.[100] The British and the Russians were not the only observers concerned with such violence, however. Merchants such as Hajj Mohammad-Taqi Jourabchi avoided the illicit trade in weapons. Accused by rival traders from Rasht and Enzeli of arming Armenian insurgents in

1905, he denied involvement and asserted in his memoirs that his family had never been tied to the trade.[101] For their part, Iranian revolutionaries confronted the challenge of restoring public order. They even struggled to impose discipline on their own militias. Enlisting young children in military drills with toy guns was one tactic.[102] In Afghanistan the emir had long disarmed specific groups who stood in the way of the expansion of his state, and he made submission and loyalty preconditions of the legal possession of arms.[103] In 1906 and again in 1910–11, Iranian constitutionalist forces went further. They improvised laws strictly regulating the bearing of arms and initiated campaigns to disarm the populace at large.[104] Their efforts failed to curb the widespread availability of cheap firearms, but these initiatives established a guide for subsequent state interventions concentrating on disarming Iran's restive society. Similarly, when the British landed an expedition at Makran in 1910–11, they disrupted the flow of arms to the Indo-Afghan frontier while demonstrating to regional elites the possibility of making forcible disarmament the cornerstone of modernist state building.

Such attempts at removing guns from circulation enjoyed limited success, and the borderlands linking the Ottoman, Russian, Afghan, and Qajar states remained heavily saturated with weapons. In addition to tribal raiding and competition among regional strongmen, intercommunal violence fueled demand for arms. At the same time, gun manufacturers continued to target the region. As an American report of 1910 observed, the eastern Ottoman Empire was "a good market for revolvers and shotguns." The "majority of all classes," it noted, "carry revolvers of one kind or another, the higher public official, banker, and business man, the middle-class employees, and particularly the carriage and Arabic, Turkish, and Kurdish camel drivers and muleteers who travel the country districts."[105] Smuggling operations carried on across the region's land and maritime borders, extending as far west as Beirut, where, a British official complained, "revolverism" had taken hold and "shots are continually heard all over the place day and night."[106] In northern Iran, occupying armies continually replenished local supplies. After the First World War, as these soldiers made their way home, they traded Russian rifles and ammunition for cognac and cash.[107] The victory of Afghan forces over the British in 1919 established their country's independence. Yet it did not end Kabul's quest for foreign weapons, which expanded in the 1920s and 1930s despite British attempts to suppress Afghan deals with German and Italian suppliers.[108] Restive borderland communities too continued to seek firearms, and Indian revolutionaries and Soviet intelligence dreamed of igniting revolution in India by arming the tribes.[109] In Iran, the state-building project of Reza Shah (r. 1925–41) realized the constitutionalists' aspiration of a more powerful state with the capacity to establish a monopoly on the use of firearms. However, it frequently faced dogged resistance and was forced to draw on the traditional practice of arming loyal tribes against hostile ones.[110] In Afghanistan, King Amanullah (r. 1919–29) confronted a similar dilemma. He had armed his state with more modern weapons and expanded its reach. In 1929, however, he desperately resorted to distributing guns to the residents of Kabul to defend against insurgents who had been supplied from the state's armories.[111]

CONCLUSIONS

From Kabul to Tabriz and Baghdad, gun violence in the early twentieth century was never solely the product of local struggles. From the late nineteenth century, consumers were tied to a variety of global commodity chains, including those that brought arms from as far away as the factories of Birmingham to the bazaars of the Indo-Afghan frontier. The illicit arms trade gave rise to dynamic circuits that transcended regions and social groups that scholars have tended to treat in isolation: it intertwined the fates of European industrial gunmakers with Zanzibaris, Muscatis, Bakhtiyaris, and Pathans and tied Armenian revolutionaries to artisans in Baku and Kerman. The technologies that produced the modern rifle, revolver, and machine gun were born in the United States and Europe. But blacksmiths and gunmakers readily domesticated them in villages and towns from the Caucasus to the Indus. Deploying the weapons for diverse social and political ends and pushing sellers to accommodate their preferences, local actors also refashioned these symbols of Western superiority into emblems of nationalist authority, wearing the new rifle cartridges as badges of masculine honor and revolutionary prowess. Facilitated by tribal smugglers and European shipping magnates alike, the illicit circulation of such arms proved impossible to suppress, not only because colonial interdiction guaranteed profits for various participants but also because consumption bred domestic production and increased demand in the form of arms races that gripped antagonistic groups in mountain valleys and town quarters throughout this space. In the first two decades of the twentieth century, the disorders that colonial and monarchical regimes in this region feared were among the complex effects of local integration into global circuits. Technological innovation and entrepreneurship bred new interconnections—and novel forms of lethal opposition.

NOTES

1. John G. Lorimer, *Gazetteer of the Persian Gulf, Oman and Central Arabia*, vol. 5 (Calcutta, 1908 and 1915; repr., Oxford: Archive Editions, 1986), 2586–87.

2. John Malcolm, "Industry and Foreign Trade, 1800," in *The Economic History of Iran, 1800–1914*, ed. Charles Issawi (Chicago: University of Chicago Press, 1971), 264.

3. M. Şükrü Hanioğlu, *A Brief History of the Late Ottoman Empire* (Princeton, NJ: Princeton University Press, 2008), 29–32.

4. *Report on the Trade and Resources of the Countries on the North-western Boundary of British India* (Lahore: Government Press, 1862), appendix, ii, v. On local weapon production, see E.S.

Mendel'son, *Remeslennoe proizvodstvo i torgovlia v Afganistane (XIX–nachalo XX v.)* (Tashkent: Izdatel'stvo "FAN" Uzbekskoi SSR, 1983), 73–75, 93.

5. Malcolm, "Industry and Foreign Trade," 262.

6. N.A. Kuznetsova, "Guild Organization, Early Nineteenth Century," in Issawi, *Economic History of Iran*, 287.

7. *Report on the Trade and Resources*, appendix, xlviii, xxii; H.B. Lumsden, *Mission to Kandahar* (Calcutta: C.B. Lewis, Baptist Mission Press, 1860), appendix, 160.

8. N.G. Kukanova, ed., *Russko-iranskaia torgovlia 30–50-e gody XIX veka: sbornik dokumentov* (Moscow: Glavnaia redaktsiia Vostochnoi literatury, 1984), 35; L. Berezin, "Foreign Firms in Tabriz, 1830s," in Issawi, *Economic History of Iran*, 106; Willem Floor, *Labor and Industry in Iran, 1850–1941* (Washington DC: Mage, 2009), 11–15.

9. Jakob Polak, "Handicrafts, 1850s," in Issawi, *Economic History of Iran*, 273.

10. Otto Blau, *Commerzielle Zustände Persiens* (Berlin: Hofbuchdruckerei, 1858), 116. Unless otherwise stated, all translations are mine.

11. Marwan R. Buheiry, "The Peasant Revolt of 1858 in Mount Lebanon: Rising Expectations, Economic Malaise, and the Incentive to Arm," in *The Formation and Perception of the Modern Arab World: Studies by Marwan R. Buheiry,* ed. Lawrence I. Conrad (Princeton, NJ: Darwin, 1989), 499–511.

12. Blau, *Commerzielle Zustände Persiens*, 137–38. See also the account of East Africans' preferences regarding imported weapons in Jeremy Prestholdt, *Domesticating the World: African Consumerism and the Genealogies of Globalization* (Berkeley: University of California Press, 2008), 65.

13. Blau, *Commerzielle Zustände Persiens*, 137–138.

14. F. Bakulin, "Ocherk vneshnei torgovli Azerbaidzhana za 1870–71 g.," *Vostochnyi sbornik*, vol. 1 (St. Petersburg: Tipografiia Ministerstva Putei Soobshcheniia, 1877), 236–37.

15. Jonathan A. Grant, *Rulers, Guns, and Money: The Global Arms Trade in the Age of Imperialism* (Cambridge, MA: Harvard University Press, 2007), 15.

16. Ibid., 36.

17. Lorimer, *Gazetteer,* 2559.

18. Grant, *Rulers, Guns, and Money,* 15–64. See also Emrys Chew, *Arming the Periphery: The Arms Trade in the Indian Ocean during the Age of Global Empire* (Houndmills, Basingstoke, Hampshire: Palgrave, 2012).

19. Charles King, "Imagining Circassia: David Urquhart and the Making of North Caucasus Nationalism," *Russian Review* 66, no. 2 (2007): 238–55.

20. On the critical role of consumers more broadly, see Prestholdt, *Domesticating the World.* On the Indian Ocean trade, see Chew, *Arming the Periphery.*

21. Nile Green, "Stones from Bavaria: Iranian Lithography in Its Global Contexts," *Iranian Studies* 43, no. 3 (2010): 313.

22. John Dunn, "Egypt's Nineteenth-Century Armaments Industry," in *Girding for Battle: The Arms Trade in a Global Perspective, 1815–1940,* ed. Donald J. Stoker and Jonathan A. Grant (Westport, CT: Praeger, 2003), 1–23.

23. Floor, *Labor and Industry in Iran,* 13; Muhammad Ali Jamalzadeh, quoted in Issawi, *Economic History of Iran,* 308–9.

24. Feridun Adamiyat, quoted in Issawi, *Economic History of Iran,* 294–95; Mohammad Ali Kazembeyki, *Society, Politics and Economics in Mazandaran, Iran, 1848–1914* (London: RoutledgeCurzon, 2003), 78–86; Green, "Stones from Bavaria."

25. Dunn, "Egypt's Nineteenth-Century Armaments Industry," 6.

26. A.N. Kuropatkin, *Kashgaria: Eastern or Chinese Turkestan,* trans. Walter E. Gowan (Calcutta: Thacker, Spink, 1882), 188–95.

27. Mir Munshi Sultan Mahomed Khan, ed., *The Life of Abdur Rahman Amir of Afghanistan,* 2 vols. (London: John Murray, 1900), 2:29–30. See also Hasan Kawun Kakar, *Government and Society in*

Afghanistan: The Reign of Amir ʿAbd al-Rahman Khan (Austin: University of Texas Press, 1979), 193–98; Grant, *Rulers, Guns, and Money,* 15–36.

28. Daniel R. Headrick, *The Tools of Empire: Technology and European Imperialism in the Nineteenth Century* (New York: Oxford University Press, 1981); Randolph Roth, "Guns, Gun Culture, and Homicide: The Relationship between Firearms, the Uses of Firearms, and Interpersonal Violence," *William and Mary Quarterly* 59, no. 1 (2002): 223–40; Eric Monkkoken, "Homicide: Explaining America's Exceptionalism," *American Historical Review* 111, no. 1 (2006): 76–94.

29. Quoted in Halil Inalcik, "The Socio-political Effects of the Diffusion of Fire-Arms in the Middle East," in *War, Technology and Society in the Middle East,* ed. V. J. Parry and M. E. Yapp (London: Oxford University Press, 1975), 197. See also Rudi Matthee, "Firearms," *Encyclopaedia Iranica,* online edition, 15 December 1999, www.iranica.com/articles/firearms-i-history.

30. Yusef Hekekyan, quoted in Dunn, "Egypt's Nineteenth-Century Armaments Industry," 5. See also Lisa Golombek, "A Safavid Bottle with Matchlock Hunt in the Royal Ontario Museum," in *New Perspectives on Safavid Iran: Empire and Society,* ed. Colin P. Mitchell (London: Routledge, 2011), 123–49.

31. Philip D. Curtin, *The World and the West: The European Challenge and the Overseas Response in the Age of Empire* (Cambridge: Cambridge University Press, 2000), 27–32.

32. Sana Haroon, *Frontier of Faith: Islam in the Indo-Afghan Borderland* (New York: Columbia University Press, 2007), 88. When mullahs commanding tribal retinues raided foes, they placed a premium on seizing ammunition.

33. Clemens P. Sidorko, *Dschihad im Kaukasus: Antikolonialer Widerstand der Dagestaner und Tschetschenen gegen das Zarenreich (18. Jahrhundert bis 1859)* (Wiesbaden, Germany: Reichert Verlag, 2007), 349–51. See also Thomas M. Barrett, "Crossing Boundaries: The Trading Frontiers of the Terek Cossacks," in *Russia's Orient: Imperial Borderlands and Peoples, 1700–1917,* ed. Daniel R. Brower and Edward J. Lazzerini (Bloomington: Indiana University Press, 1997), 227–48.

34. On firearms in Central Asia, see Shir Muhammad Mirab Munis and Muhammad Riza Mirab Agahi, *Firdaws al-iqbal: History of Khorezm,* trans. and ed. Yuri Bregel (Leiden, Netherlands: Brill, 1999), 584–86.

35. A. Il'iasov, ed., *Prisoedinenie Turkmenii k Rossii (sbornik arkhivnykh dokumentov)* (Ashkhabad: Izdatel'stvo Akademii Nauk Turkmenskoi SSR, 1960), 227–28.

36. B.-R. Logashova, *Turkmeny Irana (istoriko-etnograficheskoe issledovanie)* (Moscow: Nauka, 1976), 111–12.

37. A. M. Dondukov-Korsakov to K. E. Argiropulo, op. 528a, d. 1283, ll. 2–2 ob, f. Missiia v Persii, Arkhiv vneshnei politiki Rossiiskoi imperii (hereafter AVPRI), Moscow.

38. Indian Arms Act, 1878 (Simla, India: Government Central Printing Office, 1892); R. Hughes-Buller, ed., *Baluchistan District Gazetteer Series,* 8 vols. (Ajmer, India: Scottish Mission Industries, 1907), 5:215.

39. *Khatirat-i Hajj Muhammad Taqi Jurabchi: Vaqayiʿ-i Tabriz va Rasht 1324–30 Qamari,* ed. ʿAli Qaysari (Tehran: Nashr-i Tarikh-i Iran, A.H. 1386 [2008]), 71.

40. Lovat Fraser, "Gun-Running in the Persian Gulf," in *Proceedings of the Central Asian Society* (Guildford: Billings and Sons, 1911), 4–5; see also Mansureh Ettehadieh, "The Arms Trade in the Persian Gulf, 1880–1898," in *Proceedings of the Second European Conference of Iranian Studies,* ed. Bert G. Fragner et al. (Rome: Istituto Italiano per il Medio ed Estremo Oriente, 1995), 177–84.

41. Willem Floor, *Guilds, Merchants and Ulama in Nineteenth-Century Iran* (Washington DC: Mage, 2009), 114, 117.

42. Mirza Mohammad Hoseyn Khan Tahvildar, *Joghrafiya-yi Isfahan,* ed. M. Setudeh (Tehran: Daneshgah, A.H. 1341 [1962]), reproduced in ibid., 182–83.

43. Augustus Le Messurier, *Kandahar in 1879* (London: W. H. Allen, 1880), 78.

44. Ludwig W. Adamec, ed., *Historical and Political Gazetteer of Afghanistan,* 6 vols. (Graz, Austria: Akademische Druck-u. Verlagsanstalt, 1980), 5:246.

45. *Gazetteer of the Dera Ghazi Khan District, 1883* (n.p., 1883), 218.

46. Ibid., 214.

47. Ibid., 215; *Gazetteer of the Dera Ismail Khan District, 1883–1884* (Lahore: Arya, 1884; repr., Lahore, Pakistan: Sang-e-Meel Publications, 2002), 141.

48. Calvin H. Allen, "Sayyids, Shets and Sultāns: Politics and Trade in Masqat under the Al Bū Saʿīd, 1785–1914" (PhD dissertation, University of Washington, 1978), 158–62.

49. Lorimer, *Gazetteer*, 2559; Grant, *Rulers, Guns, and Money*, 58.

50. Lorimer, *Gazetteer*, 2557.

51. Ibid., 2560–66. On the trade through Bahrain, see James Onley, *The Arabian Frontier of the British Raj: Merchants, Rulers, and the British in the Nineteenth-Century Gulf* (Oxford: Oxford University Press, 2007), 195–200.

52. Fraser, "Gun-Running," 6.

53. Lorimer, *Gazetteer*, 2558–59; Ettehadieh, "The Arms Trade," 178.

54. T. R. Moreman, "The Arms Trade and the North-West Frontier Pathan Tribes, 1890–1914," *Journal of Imperial and Commonwealth History* 22, no. 2 (1994): 187–216.

55. Lorimer, *Gazetteer*, 2572.

56. Lorimer, *Gazetteer*, 2574–75; R. M. Burrell, ed., *Iran Political Diaries 1881–1965*, 14 vols. (Oxford: Archive Editions, 1997), 2:22.

57. William Henry Paget, ed., *Frontier and Overseas Expeditions from India*, 6 vols. (Simla, India: Government Monotype Press, 1908), 2:2.

58. Moreman, "The Arms Trade," 201–4; report from Russian consul general at Mashhad to the Russian Ministry of Foreign Affairs (n.d.), Russian agent at Daragez-Kalat to the Russian consul general in Mashhad (10 November 1901), Russian Mission in Tehran to Russian consul general in Mashhad (6 November 1902), and subsequent correspondence, f. 263, op. 775, d. 190, ll. 11–15, 61 ob., 164–76, AVPRI.

59. Sir Henry McMahon, the agent to the governor of Baluchistan, quoted in R. M. Burrell, "Arms and Afghans in Makran: An Episode in Anglo-Persian Relations, 1905–1912," *Bulletin of the School of Oriental and African Studies* 49, no. 1 (1986): 16; see also Arnold Keppel, *Gun-Running and the Indian North-West Frontier* (London: John Murray, 1911), xi.

60. *Political Diaries of the Persian Gulf*, 20 vols. (Farnham Common, England: Archive Editions, 1990), 1:28–29.

61. Ibid., 91, 172.

62. Ibid., 273.

63. Ibid., 3:550; Allen, "Sayyids, Shets and Sultāns," 163–65.

64. *Political Diaries of the Persian Gulf*, 4:273.

65. Ibid., 3:51.

66. I. P. Senchenko, *Persidskii zaliv: vzgliad skvoz' stoletie* (Moscow: Mezhdunarodnye otnosheniia, 1991), 80–81.

67. Burrell, *Iran Political Diaries*, 1:46.

68. Burrell, "Arms and Afghans," 8–24; Lorimer, *Gazetteer*, 2583; "Monthly Summary of Events in Persia," 21 June 1906, Foreign Office Records, FO 416/28, the National Archives (hereafter TNA), Kew, Richmond, U.K.

69. See, for example, Muhammad ʿAli Sadid al-Saltanah, *Safarnamah-i Sadid al-Saltanah: al-Tadqiq fi Sayr al-Tariq* (Tehran: Bihnashr, A.H. 1362 [1983]), 623–25.

70. *Political Diaries of the Persian Gulf*, 3:21, 31–32, 40–41, 66.

71. Ibid., 48.

72. Ibid., 49–50.

73. Ibid., 355.

74. Ibid., 459, 550.

75. Burrell, "Arms and Afghans"; Lorimer, *Gazetteer,* 2583.

76. Lorimer, *Gazetteer,* 2583–85; *Kandahar Newsletters,* 10 vols., 2nd ed. (Quetta, Pakistan: Directorate of Archives Department, 1990), 3:156.

77. *Final Report on Afghanistan by Fakir Saiyid Iftikhar-ud-din, British Agent at Kabul* (Simlar, India: Government Monotype Press, 1910), 59, L/MIL/17/14/15/1, India Office Records (hereafter IOR), British Library, London.

78. C. M. Enriquez, *The Pathan Borderland: A Consecutive Account of the Country and People on and beyond the Indian Frontier from Chitral to Dera Ismail Khan,* 2nd ed. (Calcutta: Thacker, Spink, 1921), 92.

79. On the Qajar import and transport of weapons, see Murtaza Nura'i, ed., *Asnad-i Karguzari-i Bushihr* (Tehran: Mu'assasah-i Mutala'at-i Tarikh-i Mu'asir-i Iran va Bunyad-i Iranshinasi-i Shu'bah-i Ustan-i Bushihr, A.H. 1385 [2006]), 9, 50; on Afghan imports, see Kakar, *Government and Society in Afghanistan,* 102–3.

80. Mîrzâ Sirâdj Ad-Dîn Hakîm, *Souvenirs de voyage pour les gens de Boukhara,* trans. Stéphane Dudoignon (Arles, France: Actes Sud, 1999), 223. See also Shah Mahmoud Hanifi, *Connecting Histories in Afghanistan: Market Relations and State Formation on a Colonial Frontier* (Stanford, CA: Stanford University Press, 2011), 115–20; Vartan Gregorian, *The Emergence of Modern Afghanistan: Politics of Reform and Modernization, 1880–1946* (Stanford, CA: Stanford University Press, 1969), 143.

81. L. Temirkhanov, *Vostochnye pushtuny v novoe vremia* (Moscow: Nauka, 1984), 11.

82. Enriquez, *Pathan Borderland,* 91–92. In the early twentieth century, gun manufacturing appears to have shifted from Kohat District to the Afridi villages of the Kohat Pass, including Darra Adam Khel, which later achieved notoriety as the center of artisanal gun manufacturing in the region. See *Frontier and Overseas Expeditions from India,* 2; General Staff, India, *Military Report on the Kohat District,* 3rd ed. (Simla: Government of India Press, 1928). Already well known by the 1960s and 1970s, Darra Adam Khel started to produce heavy weapons alongside Kalashnikovs, mines, and rocket launchers during the anti-Soviet jihad in the 1980s. See Aamer Ahmed Khan, "Pakistan's Flourishing Arms Bazaar," BBC News, 21 June 2006, http://news.bbc.co.uk/2/hi/5066860.stm.

83. *Political Diaries of the Persian Gulf,* 1:351.

84. Telegrams from Graf Crenneville to Vienna, 24–25 July 1909, PA XXXVIII/314, "Tiflis [Tbilisi] 1899," Haus-, Hof- und Staatsarchiv, Vienna.

85. *A Biographical Sketch of Sardar Mir Abdul Ali, Khan Bahadur, Head of the Detective Police, Bombay, with an Account of Interesting Criminal Cases* (Bombay: Bombay Gazette Steam Printing Works, 1896), 214–217; *Report on the Police Administration in the Punjab for the Year 1896* (Lahore: Civil and Military Gazette Press, 1897), 22.

86. Moreman, "The Arms Trade," 199–204.

87. Senchenko, *Persidskii zaliv,* 81.

88. A. Reza Sheikholeslami, *The Structure of Central Authority in Qajar Iran, 1871–1896* (Atlanta: Scholars Press, 1997), 173–85; Reza Ra'iss Tousi, "The Persian Army, 1880–1907," *Middle Eastern Studies* 24, no. 2 (1988): 206–29.

89. Janet Klein, *The Margins of Empire: Kurdish Militias in the Ottoman Tribal Zone* (Stanford, CA: Stanford University Press, 2011), 39, 213.

90. Kakar, *Government and Society in Afghanistan,* 101.

91. Ibid., 112.

92. Mansour Bonakdarian, "A World Born through the Chamber of a Revolver: Revolutionary Violence, Culture, and Modernity in Iran, 1906–1911," *Comparative Studies of South Asia, Africa and the Middle East* 25, no. 2 (2005): 318–40.

93. Houri Berberian, *Armenians and the Iranian Constitutional Revolution of 1905–1911: "The Love for Freedom Has No Fatherland"* (Boulder, CO: Westview, 2001), 49–50.

94. Samad Sardari Niya, *Mashahir-i Azarbayjan* (Tabriz, Iran: Zoughi, A.H. 1370 [1991]), 118. See also 'Abd al-Husayn Nava'i, *Dawlat-ha-yi Iran: Az Aghaz-i Mashrutiyat ta Ultimatum* (Tehran: Babak,

2535 [1976]), 84; Iraj Afshar and Muhammad Rasul Daryagasht, eds., *Mukhabarat-i Astarabad: Guzar-ish-ha-yi Husaynquli Maqsudlu Vakil al-Dawlah* (Tehran: Nashr-i Tarikh-i Iran, A.H. 1363 [1984]), 160; telegram from Alexander V. Miller to Russian envoy in Tehran, 19 July 1911, Tabriz, box 14, Russia, Legatsiia (Hesse, Germany) Records, Hoover Institution Archives, Stanford, CA; M. N. Pokrovskii, ed., *Mezhdunarodnye otnosheniia v epokhu imperializm: dokumenty iz arkhivov tsarskogo i vremennogo pravitel'stv 1878–1917*, 2nd ser., 20 vols. (Moscow: Gosudarstvennoe izdatel'stvo politicheskoi literatury, 1938), vol. 18, pt. 2, 234.

    95. Berberian, *Armenians*, 129.

    96. V. Tria, *Kavkazskie sotsial'-demokraty v persidskoi revoliutsii* (Paris: Izdanie Tsentral'nogo Organa R.S.-D.R.P. "Sotsial'-demokrat," 1910); Nava'i, *Dawlat-ha-i Iran*, 85; Berberian, *Armenians*, 54.

    97. *Political Diaries of the Persian Gulf*, 1:533.

    98. Arash Khazeni, "The Bakhtiyari Tribes in the Iranian Constitutional Revolution," *Comparative Studies of South Asia, Africa and the Middle East* 25, no. 2 (2005): 377–98.

    99. See the photographs in Nava'i, *Dawlat-ha-i Iran*; Berberian, *Armenians*, xvi. On photography, see Bonakdarian, "A World," 337–40.

    100. Afshar and Daryagasht, *Mukhabarat-i Astarabad*, 28, 135, 137, 149, 247. More accidents accompanied the increased circulation of firearms, for example at Muscat, where in 1907 an Iranian customer "fired a revolver and wounded a Baluch in the shop of Ali bin Moosa the arms seller." *Political Diaries of the Persian Gulf*, 2:387.

    101. *Khatirat-i Hajj Muhammad Taqi Jurabchi*, 27–28.

    102. Bonakdarian, "A World," 336–37.

    103. See, for example, Fayz Muhammad Katib, *Siraj al-Tavarikh* (Tehran: Mu'assasah-i Tahqiqat va Intisharat-i Balkh, A.H. 1372 [1993/94]), 656–58.

    104. Bonakdarian, "A World," 325–27; Mansoureh Ettehadieh (Nezam-Mafie), "Crime, Security, and Insecurity: Socio-political Conditions of Iran, 1875–1924," in *War and Peace in Qajar Persia*, ed. Roxane Farmanfarmaian (London: Routledge, 2008), 174–82.

    105. *Monthly Consular and Trade Reports, June 1910*, pt. 2, no. 357 (Washington DC: Government Printing Office, 1910), 29.

    106. Consul-General Cumberbatch to Sir G. Lowther, 12 April 1909, FO 424/219, TNA. See also Cem Emrence, *Remapping the Ottoman Middle East: Modernity, Imperial Bureaucracy, and the Islamic State* (London: I. B. Tauris, 2012), 75–99.

    107. Russian vice-consul to Baku, 23 January 1913, Ardabil, f. 15, op. 1 d. 375, l. 8, Georgian State Historical Archive (Sakartvelos sakhelmtsipo saistorio arkivi), Tbilisi; Viktor Shklovsky, *A Sentimental Journey: Memoirs, 1917–1922*, trans. Richard Sheldon (Champaign, IL: Dalkey Archive, 2004), 110.

    108. "Afghanistan: Arms Traffic," L/P&S/10/984, IOR.

    109. Iu. N. Tikhonov, "Bor'ba sovetskoi diplomatii za 'afganskii koridor' v zonu pushtunskikh plemen v 1919–1921 gg. (po arkhivnym materialam)," in *Afganistan i bezopasnost' Tsentral'noi Azii*, ed. A. A. Kniazev, 4 vols. (Bishkek: Ilim, 2005), 2:32–51.

    110. See, for example, "Persia: Annual Report, 1929," FO 416/113, TNA; Stephanie Cronin, "Reinterpreting Modern Iran: Tribe and State in the Twentieth Century," *Iranian Studies* 42, no. 3 (2009): 357–88.

    111. *Kabul under Siege: Fayz Muhammad's Account of the 1929 Uprising*, trans. and ed. Robert McChesney (Princeton, NJ: Markus Wiener, 1999), 36–39.

FIGURE 1. The French steamboat *Carthage* arriving at Tunis, 1910–15. From the collection of the authors.

FIGURE 2. Pilgrims making the hajj aboard the steamship *Tireno,* 1915. From the collection of the authors.

FIGURE 3. Train station, Ismailiyya, Egypt, n.d. From the collection of the authors.

FIGURE 4. Train station, Zabadani, present-day Syria, 1916 (?). From the collection of the authors.

FIGURE 5. By the early twentieth century, telegraph lines and underwater cables stretched from Morocco . . .

FIGURE 6. . . . to Aden and beyond. Both images from the collection of the authors.

SIDI-ABD-EL AZIZ EL HADJ Marabout du Ksar Charef-Djelfa . Il invoqua Dieu qui lui envoya

IFRIT ce génie ou DJENN cheval ailé qui l'emportat dans une nuit à la Mecque

FIGURE 7. Newspapers found their widest audience in coffee shops, where they were read aloud. Istanbul, n.d. From the collection of the authors.

FIGURE 8. Pilgrims visiting the tomb of the sixteenth-century Sufi saint Sidi ʿAbd al-Aziz al-Hajj in Marrakech, Morocco, could purchase printed cards such as this one (from 1929) to commemorate the occasion. From the collection of the authors.

FIGURE 9. Mosque for Indian Muslims in Delhi, 1920s.
From the collection of the authors.

FIGURE 10. Mosque for Indian Muslims in Saigon,
1910. From the collection of the authors.

FIGURE 11. Mecca-bound caravan crossing the Suez Canal, 1902. From the collection of the authors.

FIGURE 12. The Ottomans originally built this quarantine station on Kamaran Island, Yemen (pictured here circa 1910), for pilgrims en route to Mecca. From the collection of the authors.

FIGURE 13. Persian Turkmen posing with their British-made Martini-Henry rifles, introduced in 1871. From the collection of the authors.

FIGURE 14. Ottoman ladies, *à la mode,* promenading in Istanbul, n.d. From the collection of the authors.

FIGURE 15. Switch in hand, an Egyptian teacher instructs his charges, 1905. From the collection of the authors.

FIGURE 16. Persian schoolchildren participate in celebrations commemorating the second anniversary of the 1905 constitutional revolution. From the collection of the authors.

FIGURE 17. Casablanca: Moroccan workers loading barges, 1912. From the collection of the authors.

FIGURE 18. Casablanca: European workers heading home, 1927. From the collection of the authors.

FIGURE 19. An American date factor on the Shatt al-Arab, Iraq, n.d. From the collection of the authors.

FIGURE 20. A German visitor poses with Malay boys at a banana plantation in Sumatra, n.d. From the collection of the authors.

7

The Creation of Iranian Music in the Age of Steam and Print, circa 1880–1914

Ann E. Lucas

INTRODUCTION

In October 2009, the United Nations Educational, Scientific and Cultural Organization inscribed the Iranian musical form known as the *radif* on its Representative List of the Intangible Cultural Heritage of Humanity. The concept of the radif encompasses a collection of around two to three hundred melodies that form the basis of improvised performance of what Iranians have consistently identified as their traditional music (*musiqi-i sonati-i irani* or *musiqi-i asili-i irani*).[1] Contemporary Iranian musicians who use the radif claim that this collection of melodies is the ultimate result of music making that has been going on for hundreds if not thousands of years in a context perpetually defined by Iranian cultural parameters. Indeed, as part of UNESCO's list, the radif is conceived as a premodern tradition through the identification of its need for preservation in the context of modernity, which threatens its existence. Thus, UNESCO's selection of the radif endorses the notion long held by Iranian musicians and never denied by music scholars that the radif is a form of cultural heritage (*miras-i farangi*) that exemplifies the continuity of Iran's long and glorious history.

In reality, the radif has always embodied a distinct contradiction. Musicians claim it as a demonstration of Iran's ongoing cultural continuity and unity. Yet the radif emerged rather abruptly in the mid-to-late nineteenth century, as a unique form used by musicians involved in private Qajar court entertainment.[2] Additionally, all the historical evidence clearly indicates that the music making of Persian speakers was largely inseparable from the music making of Arabic and Turkic speakers before the rise of the radif. Under these circumstances, there is no evidence that any of the melodies of the radif go back any further than the nineteenth century. Thus, while Iran claims a thousand-year history of cultural development, the core of its musical heritage is grounded in the first period of globalization during the modern era.

This situation raises questions about how the novel practices of an isolated court music tradition came to represent an entire nation's cultural essence. Certainly the temporal location of the music is no accident. As both a localized phenomenon and a universal of human experience, music spoke to emerging global expectations for national culture at the turn of the twentieth century even as these expectations affected change in music, which now needed to represent the local in a globalizing context. Yet modern Iran encompassed a variety of indigenous peoples with distinct musical aesthetics, leaving open the question of why the radif tradition was consistently singled out as representing all Iranians of the modern era and all Persian speakers going back to prehistoric times.[3] Yet the radif's position as a cultural heritage of Iran is intimately tied to its particular place in Qajar society during the first period of globalization, where music was well positioned to be affected early and often by certain structural shifts in the social construction of music and of musicians fostered by changes in economy and technology. These changes allowed for Qajar music to be imagined as having collective ownership among Qajar subjects. I further argue that the structural phenomenon of the radif arose as a function of the newly emerging nation-state of Iran, which needed a historic musical existence and a collective music repertoire to legitimate its claims to a united, perennial cultural existence.

In light of these perspectives, this chapter looks at several overlapping categories of activity that demonstrate changes that needed to take place in order for the radif to be conceived, justified, and executed as it has been for more than a century. The chapter first provides background on this music tradition and the tradition of court music in the Persian-speaking world. The next section examines how the rise of an upper-class Iranian citizenry in the mid-to-late nineteenth century fostered independent performance opportunities for Qajar musicians outside the court. These included public performances given on the musicians' terms for the benefit of all people as well as opportunities to teach and perform in private settings for anyone who could pay. The new performance spaces gave Qajar court musicians a new economic basis for subsistence as well as exposure to nationalist ideas and the ability to act on these ideas. The chapter goes on to discuss the new phenomena of touring and recording for foreign music companies, which brought Qajar court music to Europe and provided a basis for it to be heard by anyone via the technology of the gramophone. For Iranians, buying, selling, and marketing gramophone recordings started right at the turn of the century and created the possibility for many different people from many different walks of life to hear and thus relate to the same music at the same time. On this basis, the radif of Qajar court musicians could be perceived as shared by Qajar subjects in different parts of Qajar territory where notions of the nation of Iran were being propagated, even before the rise of radio in the 1930s.

Next, the chapter considers how both new technology and new social mobility fed into the creation of informal educational institutions and new pedagogical techniques for radif musicians which ensured that a large repertoire of melodies could be accurately learned and passed on in ways that would have been unthinkable if not impossible a century earlier. The developments in radif education before World War I fed into formally established conservatory education later in the twentieth century and remain central aspects of the tradition today. Finally, the conclusion examines how the concept of the radif depends on the unity of the Iranian nation and the modern cultural demand for music to reflect national unity: ideas that had no relevance for premodern music in the region but conversely had great relevance in the development of an Iranian nation during the Qajar constitutional period, of 1906–11. Modern technology further facilitated the sharing of this music with other parts of the world, as "Persian music," which allowed the radif tradition to be defined as culturally central to Iran within a global context. Overall, we will see that the radif aided in creating cultural viability for the nation of Iran in ways that were both contingent and dependent on changes that occurred in the Age of Steam and Print.

THE RADIF, COURT MUSIC, AND THE RISE OF MODERNITY IN THE MIDDLE EAST

The use of the music form currently called the radif predates its title by several decades. Its earliest documentation, from the 1880s, lists seven sets of melodies, with each set labeled as a "system" (*dastgah*) that was the basis for performance. In performance, musicians would take one of these systems and improvise on its melodies in a fairly set order, while also performing some melodies without substantial improvisation.[4] The melodies of the radif range in size and form from short motifs to longer multisectional pieces. Historically, only some of these melodies were improvised on extensively in performance, while others were only slightly embellished and others were played without improvisation. Many of these melodies lack a strong rhythmic pulse, and music scholars describe them as unmetered, though they may be metered according to poetic structure.[5] Melodies with a strong pulse that a drum could accompany were most often conceived as structured compositions, and musicians composed new melodies based on their structures.[6]

Musicians who carried this tradition into the late twentieth century have indicated that it traces back to the Qajar court musician Mirza ʿAbdullah (1843–1918). However, historical writings also point to the brother of Mirza ʿAbdullah, Husayn Qoli (1854–1916), and the ruler Nasir al-Din Shah's head of court musicians,

Muhammad Sadeq Khan (fl. 1850), as some of the earliest figures in the tradition. Qajar officials who were involved early on include the minister Mehdi Qoli Hedayat (c. 1864–56) and the physician Makhbar al-Saltaneh (fl. 1888). These professional and amateur musicians were significant figures in the tradition long before Mirza 'Abdullah became regarded as the sole legitimate source of the radif. Additionally, several of the earliest *tasnif*—a song form created with melodic structures of the radif—were composed by women of the Qajar court, including the court musician Sultan Khanom (fl. 1850) and the princess Taj al-Saltaneh (1883–1936).[7]

Historically, music was largely dependent on dynastic patronage in the Persian-speaking world, even before the rise of Islam. After its rise, however, court patronage expanded to Arab and Turkic dynasties, and there is ample evidence that professional musicians under Islamic rule in the Middle East and North Africa were largely dependent on royal patronage in the centuries preceding and including the nineteenth.[8] The Qajar dynasty, like others, employed musicians for its own entertainment, and some of its courtiers took up music as a courtly pastime that further served as personal entertainment. Yet the music these musicians—professional and amateur—played was unlike that of the past. Balancing this novelty with the need to demonstrate its lineage in earlier tradition, Qajar writings describe the radif as new and different from past musical practices even as they attempt to cast it as part of past court music practices. Yet the new music created in the Qajar court highlights the new world from which it emerged as a tradition, a world where court patronage was dying at the same time that new performance and teaching venues were being born. It was in this new world of globalization and nationalization that the radif emerged and thrived.

THE SOCIAL REORGANIZATION OF QAJAR COURT MUSICIANS INTO IRANIAN MUSICIANS

Radif musicians from the early twentieth century reported that toward the end of the nineteenth century a talented Qajar court musician called Darvish Khan (Gholam Husayn Darvish; 1872–1926) fled the service of his patron, Prince Malek Mansour Mirza Sho'a' al-Saltaneh (1880–1920).[9] According to oral tradition, he fled because the prince threatened to cut off his hands as punishment for performing at a party for a group of people outside his assigned royal entourage. Writing in the 1950s, the music historian Ruhullah Khaleqi further indicated that Darvish Khan was not satisfied with the living he made at court and found that he could earn extra money by performing for other people around Tehran.[10] In the end, he obtained sanctuary from his patron in the British Embassy, which eventually won his safe release from Qajar service.

Though this story draws on oral tradition for its details, it provides general insight into the position of all Qajar court musicians at the moment when the radif emerged as their dominant musical framework, at the turn of the century. They were starting to realize that they were not treated well and perhaps deserved better than what they were getting from the Qajars. At the very least, they deserved as much financial support as they were willing to pursue as both court musicians and independent entrepreneurs. Past episodes of Persian royalty killing musicians suggest that the prince's reaction to Darvish Khan's actions would not have been unusual at other points in history.[11] Historically, the only time a musician left a court was to find another one to work in after a royal patron had been deposed. However, now musicians had leverage against the royal patronage system. In the mid-to late nineteenth century, they gradually gained more opportunities to perform for pay on a consistent basis outside the court, so they did not necessarily need the Qajars' patronage to survive. Additionally, the influence inside Iran of foreign powers such as Great Britain was making the historic patronage system more difficult to enforce. Because musicians in Europe had predominately been free agents since the beginning of the nineteenth century, European powers had many reasons to view the Qajar patronage system as antiquated and unnecessary.[12]

At the same time that court musicians were moving out of the court, Qajar nobles and officials were being drawn into new social circles that reached beyond the court. As the nineteenth century ended and the twentieth century began, some of these newly social officials were the very people preaching the new ideas of constitutionalism and the rule of law, even as their musicians sought to gain greater respect from—and even equality with—their Qajar patrons. And, in fact, playing music in the style of the court became a popular pastime for a certain number of Qajar officials, who began to treat Qajar musicians as equals and colleagues in the pursuit of musical knowledge.[13] The effects of the exodus and ensuing equality of Qajar musicians and nobles had its strongest representation in the chapter of the Anjuman-i Ukhuvvat, the Society of Brotherhood, founded in Tehran in 1899 and led by Zahir al-Dowleh. It appears that many of the most prized musicians of the Qajar court at the turn of the century participated in this society and played at some of its meetings.[14] Yet the Society of Brotherhood's presence in Tehran grew out of the Thursday-night Sufi gatherings held by Safi 'Ali Shah (d. 1899), of the Ni'matullahi order, which many Qajar officials and even some princes attended.

In the past, music scholars have largely viewed the Anjuman-i Ukhuvvat in terms of the ancient roots of Sufism. Indeed, Safi 'Ali Shah was a religious figure with a following that spread across Qajar and Indian territory. I argue, however, that Zahir al-Dowleh turned the Anjuman-i Ukhuvvat in Tehran into a civic organization that demonstrated political ideology, not unlike the explicitly political secret societies of the period.[15] Zahir al-Dowleh was a Qajar official who decided first to become a mystic and then to push an agenda of social unity and equality. Indeed, the Anjuman-i Ukhuvvat's slate of pro-constitutional activities is well documented.[16] Even in private settings and nonpolitical events, however, democratic ideology defined this society, or *anjuman*. Under Zahir al-Dowleh, the group brought together Qajar royalty and officials with their musician servants in a setting of equality and shared respect. Within the Anjuman-i Ukhuvvat, musicians gained status for being equal with their Qajar employers and sharing their knowledge with people who would have simply listened to them a century earlier.

The anjuman took this message of equality beyond its members by staging public performances that shared the private music of the Qajar court with all, using it for the greater good. Members of the Anjuman-i Ukhuvvat famously produced and performed the first privately organized public concert featuring Qajar radif musicians.[17] This concert was held in a park in northern Tehran as part of the Anjuman-i Ukhuvvat's inaugural celebration of the birth of the first Shi'a imam, 'Ali. The society charged thirty tomans per ticket for those who could pay and allowed those who could not to attend for free.[18] Although the concert was presented as an apolitical event, it had strong political implications for Qajar music. Music that the dynasty had strictly controlled—and confined to the court—was now being given to the people willfully and openly. The music and the musicians no longer belonged to the court exclusively or even primarily: they were now the possession of society at large.

A song that the poet Sheyda (1843–1906) composed for this inaugural event enshrined the dedication of the Anjuman-i Ukhuvvat and its radif musicians to societal unity and equality. As a tasnif, it was composed to accent an improvised performance derived from the radif and thus testifies to the use of the radif in the concert:

> It is the birth of the beloved prophet of God [i.e., 'Ali]
> From this beauteous manifestation is the celebration of the poor
> My manner is such that the gathering stands up
> Together in sincerity, the sultan and the mendicant
>
> Oh how sincere!
> On how faithful!
> Oh a king!
> Oh how pleasant!
> Oh a mendicant![19]

The Anjuman-i Ukhuvvat went on to produce two more large public concerts besides their yearly celebration of 'Ali. One was a charity concert, given in Tehran's Majlis chamber, for victims of fire in the city. They also did another charity concert, for the victims of the 1909 bazaar fire in Tehran. Like the anjuman's annual concert for 'Ali, these used the music and the musicians of the Qajar court for the betterment of all society. Certainly performing in the meeting place of the newly established Constitutional Assembly demonstrates a strong pro-constitutional feeling among the musicians of the anjuman. But the introduction of charity performances also demonstrates a strong interest in using music for the benefit of society's disenfranchised rather than strictly as the dynasty dictated. Charity and civic events became significant aspects of radif performance as the twentieth century progressed. Additional performances like these in the early twentieth century include a concert in Tehran in 1925 to raise money to restore the tomb of the "national" poet Firdawsi (d. 1020) and one in 1927 to inaugurate the new city hall in Resht. Designed for all to hear, these types of large public performance were part of the initial development of new spaces for music in Qajar territory.

Another phenomenon that emerged at the end of the nineteenth century was musical performance in private homes, in settings often referred to as garden parties. Both written and oral histories indicate that Qajar court musicians played for private gatherings in the homes of people outside the court.[20] The Anjuman-i Ukhuvvat also had private salons where music was played, and musicians describe such salons occurring in private homes throughout Tehran and Isfahan as a matter of common practice at the turn of the century. While it is difficult to know the details of these gatherings, eyewitness accounts suggest that when Qajar court musicians performed in private homes, they were shown great respect: crowds listened to them in silence and watched intently as they performed. There are also indications that these private concerts could be politically charged. At such gatherings, the constitutional-period poet 'Aref Qazvini (1880–1933) sang tasnif songs he wrote for radif performance. His poetry is famous for its nationalist and populist tone, and his tasnif texts were often highly political, nationalist and anti-Qajar. For example, one stanza praised the newly constructed history of Iran even as it criticized the country's leaders:

> The temporary government, what does it do? Who do you listen to?
> The house of Jamshid is conquered by a foreign face.
> The palace and the royal court went to the wind and dirt.
> Silence comes from Bisitun, because the palace is destroyed . . .
> Where are the leaders of Iran, the heroes of Iran?
> What happened that not even one brave individual remained from the warriors of
>   Iran?[21]

Beyond 'Aref's tasnif, there are other indications that political discourse was common at these private gatherings. The nationalist work *Rastakhiz-i Shahr-i Yaran-i Iran* (The resurrection of the citadel of the memory of Iran) by the journalist and poet Mirzadeh 'Eshqi (1893–1924) was first performed at a garden party in Isfahan on the cusp of World War I, its text accompanied by both Western music and radif.[22] 'Eshqi's piece presents Iran as a once-great nation that has fallen into disrepair, using imagery not unlike that employed by 'Aref in his songs. Indeed, these garden parties brought musicians into contact with many political forces of the constitutional period. There are also indications that through such intimate concert performances, the first and greatest teacher of radif, the Qajar court musician Mirza ʿAbdullah, had contact with the Babi movement.[23]

In this way, Qajar court musicians moved out of the court and into socially and politically significant circles, where they enjoyed the respect of the Qajar elite and revolutionary forces. This also appears to have fostered a greater demand for professional musicians throughout the urban population. In the early twentieth century it was more and more common for people to have professional musicians at their weddings and holiday parties. The hosts of these parties would not have been able to afford such a luxury in the past. Indeed, they still could not afford to have Qajar court musicians. Thus the demand increased for musicians who could entertain anyone in the general population for a reasonable fee. Under these circumstances, there was heavy stratification between the Qajar musicians and their protégés, who were referred to as masters (ostadan; singular: asatid), and the professional musicians with no connection to the court, who came to be called motreban.

Before the twentieth century, in the Persian language motreb meant a musician or performer, with connotations that ranged from neutral to positive. Every musician at court would have been considered a motreb, with no offense intended or taken. But now the word had a new meaning: a common musician who played primarily for dancing at weddings and parties, without any of the extensive radif training or high society experienced by the asatid. These Qajar musicians had become esteemed people whom audiences listened to in silence as if they were dignitaries giving a speech whose every word was important. The motreb were not listened to in silence, a sign that they were not as respected, but they nevertheless benefited from the demand for music that the asatid created in wider society.

MUSIC FOR IRAN TO SHARE: THE RISE OF COMMERCIAL RECORDING

What we see in musicians' circumstances thus far is that, during the first period of globalization, new types of public and private space emerged that redefined musicians' socioeconomic positions and thus music's place in society. In this context, Qajar court musicians could share their music with more people from diverse backgrounds, bringing them into contact with revolutionary and nationalist sentiments of the wider population. This also created more demand for musicians in new sectors of the population, which led to more people training to be professional musicians. Yet this proliferation of musicians seems to have generated more cachet and exclusivity for those who knew the radif and practiced it in association with the now prestigious musical lineage of the Qajar court. But this was only the beginning of Qajar court musicians' exposure to the outside world and of music's move toward commoditization in both the local and the global marketplaces. In the mid-to-late nineteenth century, recording companies from Europe began conducting expeditions all over the Middle East, Central Asia, and India. The purpose was to record music that could be mass-produced on disc for the gramophone, then sold along with the gramophone to indigenous populations.

Qajar court musicians and nobles who enjoyed playing music were recorded on several occasions before World War I for discs that were marketed to the Qajar public. The first was in 1906/7, when Gramophone and Typewriter Ltd. came to Tehran and requested specific permission from the ruler Muzaffar al-Din Shah to record his musicians. These initial recordings mostly feature court musicians and a handful of their students, including members of Iran's emerging intelligentsia and various people affiliated with the court.[24] Thus, the courtier 'Ali Khan Nayeb al-Saltaneh features on the 1906/7 recording alongside many musicians who could have been heard only in the court just a few years prior. This recording is also the first to feature Husayn Taherzadeh (1852–1955), a singer who was not affiliated with the court but who came to Tehran and studied with court musicians as a private citizen. He was a renowned singer in the radif tradition, and these recordings only served to increase his stature in society. The 1906/7 recording also shows some overlap between the radif musicians who performed for private court entertainment and those who played music used for official Qajar representation outside the court, including the tafizieh singer Husayn Taz'ieh-Khan Shahi and the musician Qoli Khan Yavar, who played clarinet and coronet for the Qajars' newly established European-style military band.

The next major recording sessions for radif musicians occurred around 1909, when a small group of court musicians and their protégés undertook a tour outside Qajar territory that included the cities of Baku, Istanbul, Vienna, Paris, and London. In the last two, their live performances were billed as "Persian Concert Parties," whose purpose was to pay for the musicians' overland travel to and from London, where Gramophone and Typewriter Ltd. recorded them for commercial release.[25] The recordings made on this tour feature some of the musicians previously recorded in Tehran and some new names, including Habibullah Khan (1886–1969), a student of Aqa Husayn Qoli who became known for his work with the radif on the piano, and Asrollah Isfahani (d. 1950), a musician from Isfahan who played the nay (a reed flute) and also came to Tehran to learn the radif tradition from Qajar court musicians as a private citizen.

The tour was undertaken because of the political unrest in Tehran, which was threatening to compromise Gramophone's recording operations. In response to this situation, the company also moved its offices to Tbilisi shortly after the 1906/7 recording sessions and handed over distribution in Tehran to local entrepreneurs. These new local distributors pushed Gramophone to make more recordings of Qajar court music, outside the country. After the tour ended, recording sessions took place in Tbilisi, one in 1912 and at least one more around 1915. In addition to when the sessions took place, it is unclear who recorded in Tbilisi. This is partially due to disruptions in pressing and marketing caused by World War I but also to the fact that many radif musicians went to the Caucasus to perform for parties and could have been recorded anytime between 1912 and 1915. In any case, the recordings feature singing by the Qajar noble Iqbal al-Saltanehand 'Abdullah Khan Davami (1899–1980), another singer who came to Tehran as a private citizen to study the radif tradition with Qajar court musicians. While Asrollah Isfahani is credited with expanding the radif tradition to include the nay, Davami is credited with doing much to standardize the radif for voice.

The recordings of Qajar musicians from 1906/7, 1909, 1912, and 1915 were all pressed as one-sided discs, though the 1915 recordings never made it to market, because they were pressed in Germany and the outbreak of World War I prevented them from being shipped to Tehran for distribution in Iran. Though Gramophone tried selling radif recordings from specialized storefronts, their local distributors found more success at the bazaar.[26] These recordings remained in circulation for quite some time, thanks to the inability to produce more recordings that began with the onset of World War I. Not until 1926, more than a decade after the last one, would any new recordings of radif musicians be pressed.

The advent of music recording in Qajar Iran changed the entire dynamic between Qajar musicians and their audiences. Their music could now be in places where they were not. The unity and cohesion of Qajar music and musicians was no longer a question of live performance or even shared space: it was now out there in the ether, creating the appearance of an objective musical reality shared by many people beyond the court and even beyond the city of Tehran.

The touring that accompanied the recording further presented the radif tradition on a global stage. No court music of the Persian-speaking world had ever been heard so far from dynastic quarters, yet now musicians had the socioeconomic ability to travel and present their music to foreign audiences. The Persian Concert Party took Qajar court musicians and their students to Europe and positioned them as carrying the tradition of an entire nation to various other nations. Yet these touring musicians also reached out to Persian-speaking peoples beyond direct Qajar control. In Tbilisi, Baku, and Istanbul, they performed to Persian-speaking people, who thus shared in a musical experience of other Persian speakers. All of this affirmed the unity of an Iranian cultural existence even as it affirmed the right of radif musicians to claim their musical practices for all of Iran.

ENSURING THE RADIF'S EFFICACY AS IRANIAN MUSIC THROUGH MODERN PEDAGOGY

While the music industry for the radif was just getting off the ground before World War I, both audio recording and the development of new social spaces were facilitating the construction of a modern pedagogical approach to teaching the radif.

This modern emphasis on pedagogy created systematic means for the large amount of melodic material within the radif to be passed on to others over time. It also ensured a general accuracy in the reiteration of the radif by new generations of musicians. Students of Qajar court musicians who were still alive in the mid-to late twentieth century consistently spoke of learning the radif tradition in the context of attending a school. Thus, there was a school of Darvish Khan, a school of Mirza 'Abdullah, a school of Mirza Husayn Qoli, and so on. While these schools did not exist in a physical sense, they appear to have been clearly defined social institutions with hierarchies of learning and teaching established by the namesake Qajar court musician.[27] Perhaps the clearest evidence of the institutional hierarchy within these schools was the Golden Hatchet (*Tabarzin-i Tala 'i*), an award given to the most accomplished students of Darvish Khan. It was a physical pin that these musicians received once they entered the most advanced stage of their education.[28] This type of official award and recognition of status demonstrates the rather formal structure found in these informal schools, which maintained stability through teaching and learning the radif according to a set perception of seniority within the tradition.

The ability to record also affected how musicians learned music. The relatively high social standing of radif musicians gave them access to wax cylinder recording technology, which facilitated easy home recording even as discs replaced wax cylinders in the marketplace. Though any number of radif musicians had access to this technology, the singer Taherzadeh (1820–1955) became famous for his meticulous use of the gramophone and wax cylinders to record and rerecord his voice to teach himself how to improve his singing.[29] In this way wax cylinder recording opened up new pedagogical possibilities for radif musicians, as it allowed them to hear themselves in an objective setting and learn from this experience over and over again.

The advent of new print technologies also impacted the pedagogy of radif musicians. In the late nineteenth and early twentieth centuries, several Qajar officials—including a minister, an army officer, and a French teacher at Tehran's European-staffed technical school Dar al-Funun—used various forms of notation to record what the Qajar musicians were playing. Mehdi Qoli Hedayat (1863–1955), 'Ali Naqi Vaziri (1887–1980), and Alfred Jean-Baptiste Lemaire (1842–1907) were thus the first people to write down the radif, though Lemaire's partial rendering is the only version that survives. In 1914, the first book about this music, *Buhur al-Alhan* (The meters of melodies), was published in Bombay. Its author was a visitor to the Qajar court in Tehran in the 1880s, a poet from Shiraz known as Forsat al-Dowleh. He became fascinated with the interest surrounding the music at court and thus added a description of it to the book he was already writing about music and poetic meter.

Buhur al-Alhan was the first publication to fully list radif melodies, organized into seven distinct sets, largely as music scholars still find them. In it, Forsat further describes some aspects of performing using the sets of melodies that match late twentieth-century interpretations of the tradition. He consistently depicts this Qajar court tradition as new (*jadid, tazeh*), distinct from past music traditions. Forsat's book also says that being able to write down music will transform how students learn this tradition at some later date. And this is exactly what happened. For while the advent of World War I put many publication and recording projects for the radif on hold, afterward they proliferated to become fundamental aspects of radif pedagogy by the 1930s.

What we see in all of this pedagogical writing and recording is that both audio and written forms were beginning to provide a basis for music to be learned and remembered on an absolute basis, while the proliferation of an educational mentality within the tradition further assured a secure form of high-quality transmission. Melodies in the radif could be recorded in multiple mediums and thus remembered by many people in an absolute manner, unlike before. Because both mediums were designed for mass production and distribution, people hundreds of miles away from Qajar musicians could learn and accurately render the melodies of the radif. Such a feat was historically unimaginable, yet the radif came to depend on these structures and technologies as the twentieth century progressed. Indeed, the informal early schools of the radif promoted a sharing mentality that ran counter to the culture of court music, which was an esoteric and even secretive pursuit until the middle of the nineteenth century.[30] Thus it was only in the early 1900s that Qajar court music gained enough exposure and esteem in wider society to make it something that should be shared as a communal property of Iranians.

CONCLUSIONS

The social and economic changes in Qajar Iran at the turn of the twentieth century brought court musicians into the broader population and positioned them to produce music that could be shared among the population in ways that created the appearance of a national tradition. Even as this was happening, Qajar musicians were some of the first people to be exposed to notions of national sovereignty for the Iranian people and the technology to foster it. Indeed, Qajar court musicians cultivated the radif to create an iconic musical repertoire for the nation and affirm its cultural vitality in both past and present. The opening up of public space for musical performance, the rising economy of private and recorded performance, and systematized and recorded pedagogy turned Qajar court music into Iranian national music, thus creating the demand for a demonstrably national tradition. Indeed, the radif could not still exist without these key socioeconomic changes, nor could it have had any wider cultural efficacy without the technological and cultural changes. All of these requirements were characteristics of the Age of Steam and Print.

What we have seen is that traditional Iranian music is a function of the modern era rather than the evolutionary remnants of ancient Persia. By shifting the focus of analysis to socioeconomic structure and its relationship to musical macrostructure, the modernity of this tradition becomes clear. Moreover, the social power of music is revealed. Musicians of the Middle East and Central Asia did not sit idly by when globalization first swept the region. Quite the contrary: they were some of the first people to respond and precipitate the changes that needed to be made for indigenous people to maintain a central role in their socioeconomic and cultural existence in the modern age. In light of this, the modernity of the radif is something that both musicians and music scholars should embrace as a positive demonstration of music's power and musicians' agency even in the most turbulent times.

NOTES

1. For studies of the radif, see Nur ʿAli Borumand and Jean During, *Radif-i Tar va Setar Mirza ʿAbdullah* (Tehran: Chapkhaneh-i Soroush, 1995); Bruno Nettl, *The Radif of Persian Music: Studies of Structure and Cultural Context in the Classical Music of Iran* (Urbana-Champaign, IL: Elephant and Cat, 1992); Ella Zonis, *Classical Persian Music: An Introduction* (Cambridge, MA: Harvard University Press, 1973).

2. The Azeri music system referred to as *mugham* has many of the same structural features as the radif and is also tied to the Qajar court. While the radif emerged in the court of the Qajar capital Tehran, mugham emerged in the court of the Qajar crown prince in Tabriz.

3. Works that make this claim include Hooman Asadi, "Az Maqam ta Dastgah," *Mahoor Music Quarterly* 11 (2001): 59–75; Taqi Binesh and Dariush Safvat, "Introduction to the *Risala dar Musiqi* of Miʾmar ʿAli bin Muhammad known as Banaʿi," in *Risala dar Musiqi,* ed. Nasrallah Purjavadi (Tehran: Markaz-i Nashr Danishgahi, 1989), 10–15; Margaret Caton, *The Classical Tasnif: A Genre of Persian Vocal Music* (PhD dissertation, University of California, Los Angeles, 1983), 35; Jean During, Zia Mirabdolbaghi, and Dariush Safvat, *The Art of Persian Music* (Washington DC: Mage, 1991), 31, 35, 231; Hassan Mashun, *Tarikh-i Musiqi-yi Iran* (Tehran: Farhang-i Nashr-i Naw, 2001), 571.

4. Later, certain subsets of melodies from the original seven systems were designated as independent sets, although musicians have disagreed on how many of these smaller structures existed (and continue to exist) independent of the original seven. These smaller structures are referred to as either *naghmeh* or *avaz.* Much of the disagreement about them concerns the dastgah named *shür,* from which the majority derive. Some musicians have taken more avaz from shür than have other musicians, though there is evidence that most musicians have recognized three since the 1930s, with an optional fourth and fifth avaz being designated in shür later on. For the history of avaz, see ʿAli Naqi Vaziri, *Taʿlimāt-i mūsīqī* (Berlin, Kāviānī, 1923); Vaziri, *Mūsīqī-i nazarī* (Tehran: Tuluʿ Alāʿddowlih, A.H. 1313 [1934]); Maryam Danayi Borumand, *Arziabi-ye asar va araʿ-e Sadeq Hedayat* (Tehran: n.p., 1995); Jean During, "*Radif. Intégrale de la musique savante persane*" review, *Cahiers de musiques traditionnelles* 8 (1995): 265–69; Dariush Talaʿi, *Traditional Persian Art Music: The Radif of Mirza Abdollah* (Costa Mesa, CA: Mazda, 2000).

5. Genʾichi Tsuge, "Rhythmic Aspects of the Avaz in Persian Music," *Ethnomusicology* 14, no. 2 (1970): 205–27.

6. These precomposed instrumental pieces include one called the *pish-daramad,* usually performed by a group of instrumentalists in a meter that approximates a moderate 2/4. While there are no pish-daramad in the radif, material from the various melodies of a given dastgah may be used to

compose the pish-daramad. Another compositional form associated with the dastgahs is *chahar midrab*: an instrumental piece for a solo instrument in a fast 2/4. Some chahar midrab are in the radif, while others are precomposed pieces that are based on the basic format of those melodies. Historically, a performance based on a dastgah ended with a *reng*: an instrumental dance piece performed in a meter that approximates 6/8. Like chahar midrab, a reng may be a melody from the radif or a precomposed piece based on such a musical form. Performances of traditional Iranian music also feature at least one *tasnif*: a precomposed song that is composed separate from the radif and performed by the full ensemble, including percussion instruments that do not typically accompany melodies from the radif.

7. Sultan Khanom was initially the personal musician of Malek Jahan Khanom, the mother of Nasir al-Din Shah (1831–96). According to the memoirs of Mehdi Qoli Hedayat, Sultan Khanom eventually married into the Qajar family and thus ended her servitude as a musician for the court. *Khaterat va Khatarat* (Tehran: Rangin, 1950/51), 2.

8. Some of the best evidence of this reality comes from the movement of musicians from one royal patron to another. One well-documented case of this type can be seen in the life of ʿAbd al-Qader Maraghi (d. c. 1435), a musician who was initially patronized by Jalayirid rulers, first Sultan Husayn I (r. 1374–82) and then Sultan Ahmad (r. 1383–1410), before moving to the Timurid court, where he was patronized briefly by Khalil Sultan (r. 1404–9) and then by Shah Rukh (r. 1409–47). A music treatise writer known under the pen name Banaʾi (fl. 1482) followed a similar path. He served the Timurids in Herat before defecting to White Sheep territory when it seemed that all of the Timurid lands would fall to the Turkmen. He reversed his defection when the White Sheep Turkmen Empire dissolved on the death of his patron, Amir Yakub (r. 1478–90). This kind of mobility appears to have continued in the sixteenth and seventeenth centuries. A descendant of ʿAbd al-Qader Maraghi carried on as a musician in the early Ottoman court. While it seems that some Timurid musicians joined the Safavid court, some Safavid musicians also defected to the Ottoman court. See ʿAbd-al-Qādir Ibn-Gaibī Marāgī, *Gāmiʿ al-alhān*, ed. Taqi Binesh (Tehran: Muʾassasa-i Mutāliʿāt wa Tahqīqāt-i Farhangī, A.H. 1366 [1987]); ʿAlī Ibn-Muhammad Miʿmār and Daryūs Safwat, *Risāla dar musīqī*, ed. Binesh (Tehran: Markaz-i Nasr-i Dānisgāhī, 1989).

9. Shoʿaʿ al-Saltaneh was the second son of Muzaffar al-Din Shah Qajar (1853–1907), whose first son, Muhammad ʿAli Shah (1872–1925), briefly ruled (1907–9) after him.

10. Ruhullah Khaleqi, *Sargozasht-i Musiqi-i Iran* (Tehran: Safi ʿAli Shah, 1954), 302–5.

11. While it is difficult to know how often royal patrons had their musicians intentionally maimed, there are indications that this type of violence was often a real possibility. In the music section of *Durrat al-Taj li-Ghirrat al-Dibaj*, Qutb al-Din al-Shirazi (c. 1236–1311) reports that Miran Shah killed his musicians en masse. In his "The Musical Codex of Amir Khan Gorji" (PhD dissertation, University of California, Los Angeles, 2005), on music in the Safavid court, Amir Hosein Pourjavady reports several instances of Safavid heirs killing off one another's musicians as part of their court intrigue.

12. The career of Wolfgang Amadeus Mozart (1756–91) is a well-documented example of how musicians gradually shifted from relying on royal and church patronage to operating as free agents. This started in the eighteenth century, leaving European musicians with little to no royal patronage by the late nineteenth century.

13. Qajar nobles who performed music alongside court musicians include Montezam al-Hokma, Hassam al-Saltaneh, Fakam al-Saltaneh, Yahiʾi Khan Qavam al-Dowleh, and ʿAʾlam al-Saltaneh.

14. Khaleqi, *Sargozasht*, 82–90.

15. Some scholars argue that there was also Freemason influence in these organizations. See, e.g., Mahmud Katiraʾi, *Feramasoneri dar Iran az Aghaz ta Tashkil-i Luzh-i Bidari Iran* (Tehran: Iqbal, 1968).

16. On the role of the Anjuman-i Ukhuvvat in Iran's Constitutional Revolution, see Iraj Afshar and Zahir al-Dowleh, *Khaterat va Asnad-i Zahir al-Dowleh* (Tehran: Kitabha-i Jibbi, 1972); ʿA. Anwar, "Anjoman-e Okowwat," in *Encyclopaedia Iranica*, online edition, www.iranicaonline.org/articles/anjoman-e-okowwat, accessed 14 March 2010; Ibrahim Safaʾi, *Rahbaran-i Mashruteh*, vol. 1 (Tehran, 1962).

17. Previously, the Qajar government had sponsored various public performances of military music and ta 'zieh plays, at which it is probable the radif was played However, this representation of Qajar music was directly controlled by the government, whose subjects heard it only at the discretion of the court.

18. The celebration came to be repeated every year as part of the Anjuman-i Ukhuvvat's devotion to 'Ali. In addition to the concert, the first celebration included a movie and a meal served to all attendees.

19. *Divan-i 'Aref Qazvini* (Tehran: Mu'assaseh-i Intishirat-i Negah, 2002), 343. This is a reprint of *Divan-i Mirza 'Abu al-Qasem 'Aref Qazvini* (Berlin: Chapkhaneh-i Mashreqi, 1924). Unless otherwise stated, all translations are mine.

20. Khaleqi, *Sargozasht,* 78–80, 151–55, 81–83, 280–86; Mashun, *Tarikh,* 562–65, 74–75.

21. *Divan-i 'Aref Qazvini,* 343.

22. Ruhullah Khaleqi wrote of attending this garden party with his parents when he was a child (*Sargozasht,* 78–80).

23. In an interview with the ethnomusicologist Margaret Caton in 1976, General Shuaullah Ala'i reported seeing Mirza 'Abdullah at a Babi gathering around the time that Baha'ism was emerging. 'Abd al-Baha wrote several letters to Mirza 'Abdullah, who did not likely possess the literacy to read them. See Caton, "Baha'i Influences on Mirza Abdullah, Qajar Court Musician and Master of the Radif," in *Studies in Babi and Baha'i History,* ed. Juan R. Cole and Moonjan Momen (Los Angeles: Kalimat, 1984), 30–64.

24. Sassan Sepanta, *Tarikh-i Tahul-i Zabt-i Musiqi dar Iran* (Tehran: Mu'assaseh-i Farangi-i Honar-i Mahur, 1998), 122–30.

25. Michael S. Kinnear, *The Gramophone Company's Persian Recordings, 1899 to 1934: A Complete Numerical Catalogue, by Matrix Serials, of Persian Recordings Made from 1899 to 1934 by the Gramophone Company, Ltd., Together with a Supplement of Recordings Made by Columbia Gramophone Company, Ltd., from 1928 to 1934* (Heidelberg, Australia: Bajakhana, 2000), 9–11. According to Khaleqi, the concert in Istanbul was not a profit-making event for the musicians but a charity concert to raise money for a Persian school in the city (*Sargozasht,* 134).

26. Kinnear, *Gramophone Company's Persian Recordings,* 6–7.

27. Indeed, different versions of the radif exist because these court musicians practiced it differently and thus passed it on differently within their schools.

28. Shapur Bihruzi, *Chehreh-ha-i Musiqi-i Iran* (Tehran: Shirkat-i Kitab-i Sara, 1988), 105–13.

29. Sepanta, *Tarikh,* 81–82.

30. Khaleqi, *Sargozasht,* 114; Mashun, *Tarikh,* 567.

8

The Globalization of Dried Fruit

Transformations in the Eastern Arabian Economy, 1860s–1920s

Matthew S. Hopper

INTRODUCTION

The *Glide,* an American bark, sailed into Muscat's harbor on September 15, 1862, to obtain a precious payload. The ship had left Salem, Massachusetts, six months earlier and stopped first at Zanzibar and Aden to load coffee, ivory, hides, gum copal, beeswax, and chili peppers. But its most valuable cargo was to be loaded at Muscat. The *Glide* was the property of John Bertram, Salem's most successful merchant. It had been built the previous year specifically for the Indian Ocean trade, and this was its second voyage to Muscat. Charles Benson, the ship's steward and the only African American member of the crew, carefully observed as it was loaded over four weeks in Muscat and recorded his impressions in his diary. The first ten days in harbor consisted mainly of formalities: a local merchant named Musa came aboard on the first day, bringing gifts of mutton, eggs, greens, and milk. In the following days two Indian merchants, Mr. Ludda and Mr. Bumagee, paid formal visits to the captain, John McMullan, who repaid their visits on shore several times until the terms of sale were reached. On the tenth day, lighters began to pull up alongside the *Glide* to load their prized cargo: heavy bags of soft, sticky dates. Workers hired from shore toiled for hours storing the palm frond bags in the hold while the *Glide*'s crew unloaded stone ballast into the harbor. For twenty more days, workers loaded hundreds of bags of dates, 2,060 in all, in intense heat. Temperatures ranged from 92 to 100 degrees Fahrenheit in the shade, and "very thick" swarms of hornets harassed the workers (they "sing severe," Benson noted, and wounded ten or twenty men a day). All of this was endured for the profits the dates would bring on arrival in the United States. In the final days before departure, the Muscat merchants threw a party featuring a troop of African dancers and drummers aboard the *Glide* for the crew. At sunset, Musa brought Persian rugs and chairs aboard and festooned the deck with lanterns, colorful flags, and an American ensign, and Indian and Arab merchants came aboard for a performance that lasted until nearly four in the morning. On the final day, Mr. Ludda and Mr. Bumagee came aboard and gave parting gifts to the captain and the officers. Musa and his brothers stayed aboard all night and gave presents to the crew. After a month's stay in the harbor, the transactions were complete; the *Glide* sailed for Salem with more than two hundred tons of dates.[1]

Benson and the crew of the *Glide* were agents in a vibrant trade between the United States and eastern Arabia that lasted for more than a century. The growing global trade networks of the late nineteenth and early twentieth centuries and the accompanying increase in speed of transportation and communication—in a word, globalization—helped transform Arabia's formerly regional markets into truly global markets. In the Age of Steam and Print, the eastern Arabian date industry, which fed local and regional diets for centuries, took on global dimensions, serving faraway ports in Southeast Asia, Europe, and North America. The American market in particular was increasingly important in the nineteenth century. The United States eventually became the region's best foreign customer, importing nearly eighty million pounds of dates a year by 1925. Arabian date exports helped fuel an economic boom in the Persian Gulf, increasing opportunities for consumption and demand for slave labor. But the same forces that helped create Arabia's global markets also helped destroy them. As expanding global trade networks grew, so did competition. Globalization created new rivals, including the United States. The U.S. Department of Agriculture used the same faster communication and transportation networks that built the date trade to send plant explorers around the world to find new crops suitable for propagation in the United States. The country then changed from date consumer to date producer, ending its century-long trade relationship with Muscat, Basra, and Baghdad as Southern California created a date industry of its own. As chapters 6, by Robert Crews, and 7, by Ann E. Lucas, demonstrate, global networks of transportation and communication challenged state and colonial authorities just as they transformed communities: guns and phonographic records circulated as commodities at unprecedented rates using new technologies and global connections. This chapter argues that even a humble commodity (for there could hardly be anything more humdrum than dried fruit) can illustrate the far-reaching social and economic effects of expanding global trade networks during this early period of globalization.

THE UNITED STATES AND THE GLOBALIZATION
OF ARABIAN DATES

Dates were the first Gulf commodity to be drawn into the expanding global markets of the nineteenth century. They may not be the most obvious example of a cash crop, since most were consumed locally or exported to India. However, date growers from Muscat to Basra shared experiences similar to those of producers of silk and tobacco in Anatolia, grain in Iraq, olives in Tunisia, oranges in Palestine, and cotton in Egypt and Sudan.[2] In the Gulf, as in many parts of the Middle East and around the world, the expanding global economy absorbed and augmented a trade that already existed on a regional level. In the largest date-producing areas of the Gulf—Basra, Al-Hasa (the east coast of today's Saudi Arabia), and Oman— date exports provided the basis for extensive regional trade and facilitated the importation of staples such as rice from India. In the eighteenth century, ships from Muscat exported tons of locally produced dates from the Ottoman *sanjaq* of Basra (a subdivision of the Baghdad vilayet) each September and brought home coffee from Yemen and other goods in exchange. Basra dates found their largest outlet in India, which annually exported an estimated thirty lakhs (one lakh is one hundred thousand) of rupees' worth of cotton piece goods, rice, indigo, sugar, and metals to Basra in exchange.[3] Oman too carried on an extensive trade in dates with India, largely in exchange for rice. Muscat trade statistics of date exports and rice imports between 1874 and 1904 are mirror images on a graph—they rose and fell in tandem.[4] Every part of Oman has rice as the base for its local cuisine, although no part of the country can produce it in any quantity. Omanis have long depended on India for this staple.

By one estimate, the world possessed some ninety million date palms at the start of the twentieth century. More than half of these were in the countries touching the Arabian Gulf, with an estimated thirty million palms in Iraq alone. Oman's share of the world's date palms was relatively small, estimated at around four million, with most on the Batinah Coast.[5] Yet it was Oman that contributed the most to the creation of global markets for dates in the nineteenth century, particularly the lucrative United States one. American ships carrying cotton cloth from Massachusetts mills visited Zanzibar and Arabian ports annually beginning in the first years of the nineteenth century and within a few decades were the leading foreign traders in the region.[6] Following the seasonal monsoon winds of the western Indian Ocean, American ships visited Arabia to exchange cotton cloth, piece goods, and specie for coffee, hides, and dates.[7] Muscat was the center for Arabian date exports, and Oman was home to particularly hardy varieties that could survive lengthy sea voyages and ripened earlier than most others, on account of Oman's southern latitude and intense summer heat. The fardh variety ripened in August, which allowed American ships enough time to load at Muscat, trade at Zanzibar, catch the monsoon winds, and make the hundred-day journey home in time for the winter holidays. The arrival of Arabian dates in New York before Thanksgiving became an American tradition.[8] By 1871, the pressed fardhs that American merchants preferred were selling at thirty dollars a bag in Muscat, which was exporting fifteen thousand bags annually.[9]

Although fardhs were not highly regarded in Arabia, Americans loved the sweet, sticky variety, and grocers stocked and sold millions of pounds annually as a holiday confection. They would use an ice pick to chisel off portions of blocks of sticky dates and sell them by the pound. The first American export company in Muscat, W. J. Towell Company, was established in 1866 specifically for shipping Omani fardhs.[10] With the arrival of steamships in the mid-nineteenth century and the opening of the Suez Canal in 1869, the voyage from the Gulf to New York was cut to sixty days, and merchants began to add varieties of dates from Basra to their annual imports of fardhs from Muscat. By 1885, Americans imported more than ten million pounds of dates annually, valued at nearly four hundred thousand dollars.[11] A British observer in Oman noted that it was "from the labors of the date cultivator that the country derives most of such wealth as it has."[12]

It is unclear when the first shipment of dates arrived in the United States, but it must have been early in the republic's history. The brig *Fairy* brought a shipment of "Arabian dates" to New York and Baltimore in 1818, which was advertised in newspapers in Charleston, South Carolina; Georgetown, District of Columbia; and New York.[13] If that early shipment of dates was America's first, it would be a fitting testament to the changing world of the nineteenth century: the *Fairy* was a slave ship refitted for the Indian Ocean trade, and its captain later sailed the founding group of African American settlers to Liberia. Packages of Arabian dates may well have arrived in smaller loads at American ports earlier than 1818 as ships returned from Aden and Mocha with loads of coffee. The celebrated trade between Salem and Zanzibar began essentially as a by-product of the coffee trade with Yemen. The brig *Ann* was the first Salem ship to visit Zanzibar, in 1826—it had come for coffee, but its captain found Mocha short of provisions and went to Zanzibar to engage in some coasting trade.[14] In the decades that followed, Salem vessels made a habit of using the Indian Ocean's regular monsoon winds to visit both Zanzibar and Arabia, gathering the best of both markets and selling Massachusetts cottons in each.

In the 1850s, several American ships visited Muscat each year by way of Zanzibar and Aden and brought back enormous loads of dates. Atkins Hamerton, the British consul at Muscat, listed eleven such ships in Muscat's harbor in 1851 and 1852, nearly all of them from Salem—the *Cherokee, Sophurnia, Tom Corwin, Lucia Maria, Iosco, Arthur Pickering, Lewis, Sacramento, Elizabeth Hall, Emily Wilder,* and *Said bin Sultan* (three of these visited twice in two years). Some of these ships brought large shipments of American cloth from Salem mills (*Lucia Maria* sold 200 bales of cloth in Muscat in 1850 and 110 in 1851; *Arthur Pickering* sold 114 bales in 1850 and 369 in 1851). Hamerton observed that Americans carried on a massive business in dates at Muscat, paying "from 20 to 25 dollars the Bahar [a nineteenth-century Arabian weight] of 1800 lbs . . . which yields, if they are of the proper sort and reach America in good condition, 100 percent profit." The vessels, he estimated, each carried away between fifteen hundred and four thousand bags of dates on average, but since they were simply purchased in the open market and not taxed he could not conclude any specific amounts.[15] The logbooks of American ships confirm Hamerton's estimates: the bark *Warren White* of New York left Muscat's harbor on January 29, 1853, with fifteen hundred bags of dates, the ship's primary cargo.[16] Hamerton explained that American ships typically purchased wool with cash at Gwadar or Karachi, then sold cloth or sugar and paid for dates with cash at Muscat before proceeding (sometimes via Bombay) to Zanzibar to fill up with more cargo and returning to the United States.[17] A later British consul at Zanzibar, Christopher P. Rigby, lamented in 1860 that American merchants were "acquiring a monopoly of the carrying trade of coffee and grains from Aden, of dates, hides, etc. from Muscat, and of wool and hides from Mekran."[18]

American trade with Arabia boomed in the 1850s and 1860s, with dates and coffee at the fore. The Salem bark *Elizabeth Hall* was one of many Americans ships engaged in this lively trade. The then-sixteen-year-old Lawrence Peirson Ward kept an unusually careful diary on his first voyage from Salem to Arabia, aboard this ship in 1851, and his account demonstrates how central dates were to this trade. According to Ward's diary, the *Elizabeth Hall* left Salem on March 26, 1851, and arrived in Zanzibar fourteen weeks later, on June 30. It stayed there for ten days as the crew unloaded a thousand kegs of gunpowder and several hundred bales of cotton cloth and took on firewood and lumber for Arabian markets. As Robert Crews's chapter 6 demonstrates, gunpowder and guns remained profitable commodities in the western Indian Ocean into the early twentieth century. The *Elizabeth Hall* sailed for Aden on July 9, arriving July 23. In Aden it unloaded tobacco, sugar, and cloth and took in stone ballast before sailing for Mocha on August 12. On arrival at Mocha on August 18, the crew unloaded more cotton cloth and "Zanzibar poles" (mangrove wood), and the ship took on two thousand dollars in cash, several hundred bags of coffee, and sheep and goat hides. Sailing from Mocha on September 6 by way of Aden, it arrived in Muscat on October 12, then discharged stone ballast and took on bales of merino wool and more than eight hundred frails (of two hundred pounds each, or eighty tons total) of dates, most of the ship's cargo, in just three days, from November 3 to 5. The ship sailed from Muscat on November 8 and arrived back in Zanzibar on November 28, where it loaded a few hundred bags of gum copal and cloves, then left on December 5 for Salem, where it arrived three months later.[19] The voyage from Salem to Zanzibar by sail across the Atlantic typically took eighty to one hundred days in each direction. Because most ships stayed nearly a month in each of several ports in Arabia and East Africa, round-trip voyages to the Indian Ocean typically took eleven to thirteen months, and longer voyages were not uncommon.

Dates served a dual purpose, as both ballast and commodity. Heavy sacks of the fruit replaced stone ballast in the holds of Indian Ocean trading vessels on their return to the United States. The importance of dates as a commodity is evident not only from the sheer volume the American ships carried but also from the lengths that were gone to in order to procure them. A journal that young Salem sailor, William H. Townsend, kept aboard the bark *Imaum* (named after the ruler of Muscat and Zanzibar) in 1858–59 makes this point clear. The *Imaum* left Salem on February 12 and arrived in Zanzibar on April 28, 1858. There the crew unloaded gunpowder, cotton cloth, soap, and copper wire and took on oranges and wood for Aden (rumors that they could make a 400 percent profit on the oranges inspired the master to buy up ten thousand). The ship left Zanzibar on May 11 and arrived seventeen days later in Aden, where the crew unloaded oranges and poles in expectation of buying coffee. When the coffee crop turned out to be too expensive, they took on stone ballast instead and returned to Zanzibar, departing on June 12 and arriving on July 11. After making repairs and restocking with provisions, the *Imaum* left Zanzibar on July 20 and returned to Aden on August 1. Two weeks later the desired coffee finally came in, and the crew loaded several hundred bags, in addition to several thousand hides, before sailing for Muscat on September 2. Despite its already considerable payload, the *Imaum*'s captain would not consider returning to the States without an additional month's journey to obtain dates from Muscat. The ship arrived in Muscat on September 12, where the crew spent several days unloading stone ballast with the help of six African men from shore and building stowage for the dates in the hold belowdecks. It then took on hundreds of bags of dates—the bulk of its cargo—in addition to hides and provisions before heading out to sea on September 22. On October 27 the *Imaum* was back in Zanzibar's harbor, where it took on ivory, chili peppers, gum copal, and cloves before sailing for home on November 5. When the ship arrived in Boston on January 31, it had been at sea for eleven and a half months.[20]

By the 1860s, business was brisk enough for Bertram to send an agent to stay in Muscat and help facilitate his part in the date trade. William Hollingsworth Hathorne negotiated for the best prices possible and sent regular intelligence to Bertram about what their rival buyers from New York and Boston were shipping and how much they paid. His letters reveal that American buyers did not dictate the terms of exchange but had to compete with buyers for markets at Calcutta, Mocha, and Singapore. Nor did Americans have a monopoly on information. Sellers in Muscat were in communication with other date-producing regions, and a bad harvest elsewhere could drive up prices for their crop, as happened in 1866, when Hathorne wrote to Bertram, "The reason why the Dates are so high is because the crop in Bussora has failed and the dows that always went there, have come to Muscat this year for their cargoes." As a result, Hathorne explained, Arab buyers from Yemen had recently outbid him: "The day before yesterday I tried to break down the price of the Dates by refusing to buy any more at $42.50 [per bahar] but it was 'no go.' The Mocha men bought them all at that price." A New York merchant also arranged to have an American agent buy for him in Muscat: Captain Upton of the *Hellespont*, a rival of Bertram's *Glide*, bought several thousand frails of dates for the *Hellespont* and the *Ella Virginia* in 1866 (although the latter never returned home, instead wrecking off the coast of Mozambique).[21]

Globalization provided new avenues for trade, but old patterns endured. When the Suez Canal opened in 1869, steamers cut the voyage from New York to Muscat by a third, but large sailing vessels such as the Salem barks continued to make the annual voyage to Muscat to bring back tons of dates. Bertram's *Glide* made thirty voyages to the Indian Ocean before 1887, when it wrecked off the coast of Madagascar.[22] Bertram commissioned several other ships for the Indian Ocean trade, the most famous of which was his *Taria Topan*, built in 1870 and named for a leading Indian merchant of Muscat and Zanzibar, one of the region's most successful creditors. The double-decked, 631-ton bark made twenty-six voyages to the Indian Ocean before being sold 1893, and a replica of its cabin is preserved as a dining hall on the roof of the Hawthorne Hotel in Salem today. With its three masts and capacious hold, the *Taria Topan* could bring back exceptionally large loads very quickly (it broke the existing time record on its maiden voyage to Zanzibar—sixty-eight days from Salem around the Cape) and almost always ran the same itinerary, Zanzibar-Aden-Muscat, usually in about nine months. When the ship completed its third journey, in 1873, the *Boston Journal* reported that "she brings one of the most valuable cargoes ever received here from Arabia, consisting of ivory, ebony, dates, gum copal, etc. Among the leading items of her cargo are 6035 frails [six hundred tons] of dates, 1600 bags of cloves, and 3539 blocks of ebony."[23]

New forms of communication also sped the expansion of markets for Arabian dates. The Indian Mutiny of 1857–58 underscored London's need for a direct telegraphic cable to India. The British Government of India's newly created Indo-European Telegraph Department oversaw the completion of cables linking London to Bombay by way of Suez and Aden and to Calcutta by way of Karachi and Tehran. By 1860, a telegraph cable linked Muscat to Aden and Karachi, although it suffered from outages and had to be replaced. More-reliable communications were available by the 1870s.[24] By the 1890s, merchants in the United States could communicate by telegraph with buyers in date-producing centers such as Muscat and Basra. Telegraphic cipher guides had translations for several date-related code words, including:

Amidst   Frails Arabian Black Dates
Amnesty   Boxes Persian Dates
Amorist   Skin Frails Golden Dates
Amorous   Boxes Bassorah Dates[25]

Dates continued to grow in popularity well into the twentieth century. American date imports increased from an average of ten to twenty million pounds annually between 1893 and 1903 to an average of twenty to thirty million pounds between 1903 and 1913. They then soared from thirty-two million pounds in 1920 to fifty-three million pounds in 1922, and peaked at nearly seventy-nine million pounds in 1925.[26]

In the later nineteenth century, New York importers built relationships with Indian merchants in Mutrah, the terminus of Omani caravan routes, to arrange date exports each autumn. Mutrah, only one cove (Riyam) and some rocky outcrops north of Muscat, was the domestic trade center of Oman, home to large Sindhi and Gujarati merchant families and the primary port for dhow exports to India, East Africa, South Arabia, and the Persian Gulf. Muscat, with its superior protected harbor for larger, square-rigged sailing ships and later steamships, dominated trade with the West. Small seacraft connected Mutrah and Muscat, keeping the two nearly adjacent walled port cities in constant communication. Merchants at Mutrah received orders from New York syndicates by post and later telegraph and then arranged purchases from producers. Some large landowners resided in Mutrah, having purchased date farms or acquired them as collateral for loans, so some shipments could be arranged locally. Others had to be arranged in the areas of production.[27] Merchants preferred to arrange the purchase when producers were in greatest need of cash, while the fruit was on the tree and well before the harvest.[28] In describing the annual harvest, Paul Popenoe, who visited Muscat and the Semail Valley of Oman in 1912, explained that once September 1 arrived, "the whole of Oman is affected" and the operation "takes place on a large scale." Growers were responsible for delivery to Mutrah, at a cost of about six dollars for every *bihar*, about eighteen hundred pounds. Popenoe estimated that in 1911, growers received only one to one and a half cents per pound, or one and a half to two dollars for the fruit of each tree.[29]

In the 1860s, in place of traditional woven palm frond bags for shipments to the West, date packers in the Gulf began using wooden boxes in which tea and dry goods had been imported. This switch greatly improved the appeal and profitability of Gulf dates. Under the old system, many were lost or damaged when the bags that held them were removed, and parts of the fruit had been notoriously dirty. Just before the turn of the century, Count Albert Asfar, who oversaw packing for an American firm in Basra and later owned his own firm, introduced the seventy-pound standard wooden box, which was specially imported from Scandinavia. This transition made date packing a truly global affair. By the early twentieth century, New York agents routinely shipped prefabricated pieces (called shooks) of wooden crates from Scandinavia to be assembled at Muscat and Basra in advance of each date season. Each date-importing syndicate had its logo on its boxes, to distinguish them from its competitors'. Hills Brothers used *A1* on one side and a crown on the opposite side, for example, while Asfar and Company used *A. & Co.* Carpenters nailed the boxes together at the packing sites, or godowns, where seasonally hired date packers filled the boxes. In Oman, camel caravans brought harvested dates to Mutrah in palm frond sacks. In Iraq, small local craft brought dates to Basra in palm frond baskets.[30]

In the contemporary world of mass-manufactured sweets, it is difficult to comprehend the popularity in the nineteenth century of sticky dried fruit imported from Arabia. However, one must recall that processed candies manufactured on a massive scale were virtually unknown before Milton Hershey marketed his first chocolate bars in 1900.[31] In the United States, dates were considered a confectionary delicacy well into the twentieth century. They were a popular ingredient in cooked desserts as well as ordinary meals. One 1923 cookbook includes forty-two recipes for dates, including stuffed dates, date custard pie, date corn bread, date and celery salad, date corn muffins, date mush, mocha date icing, date tea cakes, rich date muffins, date fruitcake, date soufflé with custard sauce, date sponge with lemon sauce, date cream pie, Old English date pie, date cream filling, date scones, date and nut bread, date marmalade, Newport date ice cream, and bacon and date sandwiches.[32]

BASRA AND THE GLOBAL DATE TRADE

The Omani fardh remained the most popular date variety imported into the United States throughout the nineteenth century and consistently sold at a higher price than all other pressed varieties well into the twentieth century. Paul Popenoe, a date expert from West India Gardens in Altadena, California, who visited the Gulf in the early twentieth century, attributed the popularity of the fardh in America over its Iraqi competition to the fact that it was the only variety imported to the United States "which can be bought in fairly presentable condition." He explained: "Its tough, firm flesh allows it to come on the table intact, while the superior Halawi and Khadhrawi of Busreh have been so squeezed out of shape by the heavy feet of the Arab packer that they do not look presentable, no matter how good their flavor may be."[33] In Los Angeles in November 1895, Newberry's grocery store sold "New Fard Dates" (from Muscat) for fifteen cents a pound and "New Golden Dates" (from Iraq) for ten cents per pound. In February 1917, Ralphs Grocery Company sold "Fancy Fard Dates" at nineteen cents per pound in its four Los Angeles locations while offering "Golden Dates" (Iraqi varieties) for thirty-five cents for two pounds.[34]

Yet in volume, Iraqi dates surpassed the Omani fardhs well before the turn of the century. Basra date exports roughly doubled with the opening of the Suez Canal, jumping from £67,000 worth in 1868 to £126,000 worth in 1869.[35] Although Omani fardhs had whetted America's appetite for dates, Iraqi produce increasingly satisfied it. By 1911, fardhs accounted for only 3,882,008 pounds (roughly 13 percent) of the 29,504,592 pounds of dates imported into the United States, although this still represented a quarter of the value of date imports. Five years earlier fardhs had accounted for roughly 27 percent of the value of American date imports.[36] By 1929, 83 percent of the dates imported into the United States came from Iraq.[37]

By 1860, New York had surpassed Salem in imports from the Indian Ocean to the United States, and its port had established its dominance of American imports, clearing more than all other major American ports combined.[38] The fruit docks of Brooklyn came to handle nearly all of the date imports, along with most of the other fruit imported into the United States. In the 1880s, steamers brought five hundred boxes of dates at a time to Brooklyn, each box weighing fifty pounds. Sailing barks were a rare sight by the mid-1880s but still occasionally docked in Brooklyn with shipments of up to six thousand frails (weighing two hundred pounds each) of dates. In 1885, the United States imported ten million pounds of dates, "mostly from Bussorah [Basra] and Muscat."[39]

In the 1870s, Basra date exports soared. At the start of the decade, several foreign steam navigation companies facilitated the movement of freight down the Tigris and the Euphrates to Basra. Gray Dawes & Co., Lynch Bros., D. Sassoon & Co., the Oman-Ottoman Co., and the Euphrates and Tigris Steam Navigation Co. competed for shipping between Baghdad and Basra and for export routes to Bombay, Karachi, and London. A deal in 1878 against the backdrop of the heightened traffic on the Tigris during the Russo-Turkish War of 1877–78 created a powerful partnership of most of the big European companies, merging the capital of major players such as Edwyn Dawes, Thomas Lynch, and William Mackinnon and dramatically increasing trade volume in the region. The biggest beneficiary was the date industry. Gray Mackenzie & Co. shipped 6,718 tons of dates from Basra in 1879, which increased to 11,868 tons in 1882.[40] Americans imported a growing proportion of Basra dates to supplement their Muscat dates, but initially the trade with Basra ran via British steamers, by way of London. The American trade nevertheless contributed to the growing wealth of Basra, which in the 1870s was visible to visitors such as Major R. M. Smith, the director of Persian Telegraphs, who wrote:

> Anyone acquainted with Bussorah only a few years ago could not fail to be struck with its altered and improved appearance. Instead of the unbroken line of Palm Groves which concealed the Town at some distance behind them and the river on which nothing but a few Buggalows [large trading dhows] were to be seen, the bank now presents an imposing line of substantial European-looking houses, offices and godowns, while the river itself is alive with boats and barges going to and from the steamers whence the rattle of the steam winch is heard incessantly. The general bustle and movement are in striking contrast with the still monotony of former years.[41]

One of the concerns that established new offices in Basra was the Hills Brothers Company of New York, which became the largest importer of dates into the United States. It had developed from a small fruit enterprise founded by John Hills in 1871.

Originally an importer of "green" (fresh) fruit, citrus, and grapes, Hills was forced to specialize in dried fruit by the 1890s because of the growth of domestic fruit production in Florida and California. In 1893, he and his brother William joined forces and founded the Hills Brothers Company (unrelated to the later coffee company of the same name), with a small warehouse in Brooklyn. As its date imports from the Gulf increased, the company decided to send Vice-President Frank H. White to Iraq to establish a branch office in Basra, to end its reliance on London companies there. In the last years of the nineteenth century, the first steamers filled with fresh dates sailed direct to the Hills Brothers warehouse in Brooklyn, allowing the company to operate autonomously of London. In 1900, Hills Brothers opened a distribution office in Chicago to facilitate the marketing of produce to the Midwest.[42] In 1902, the Hills Brothers agent in Basra was H. P. Chalk, who lived there with his wife. The company owned a riverfront building, which it called Beit Hills, from which it oversaw its operations, including its own date farm. It worked through a buyer named Hajji Abdulla Negem, whom it annually entrusted with ten thousand dollars in gold coins to procure dates for shipments to New York.[43]

John Hills served as the company president until his death in 1902, after which a family feud resulted in L. R. Eastman, his son-in-law, taking the helm and William Hills leaving to start a competing firm in February 1905.[44] Both the Hills Brothers Company and the William Hills Jr. Company decided to focus on packaged goods instead of bulk goods to maximize profits. Both sent waxed cardboard packing material in bulk to the Gulf, where the boxes were assembled and filled with dates, generally in one- and two-pound packages. William Hills built a partnership with the Mutrah merchant Ratansi Purshotum and carried on a brisk business in Muscat dates. By 1910, Hills Brothers had decided to brand its Basra dates with the word *Dromedary* and a trademark camel on each box and embarked on an aggressive advertising campaign to market the name as a symbol of consistent quality and cleanliness. That year, the company spent sixteen thousand dollars in marketing and sold twelve thousand cases of dates. Before long, the investment paid off.[45] In 1934, Hills Brothers accounted for fourteen million of the forty-nine million pounds of Basra dates imported into the United States, leading to its being charged in a federal antitrust suit in 1939.[46]

By the 1890s, American business with Basra was so extensive that merchants launched several steamers annually to sail directly to New York loaded exclusively with Basra dates. Beginning in 1899, shipping companies competed in an annual date race from Basra to New York to land the first shipment of "golden dates" for the holiday season.[47] Once dates were harvested and packed in Basra, competing ships—usually German and British steamers—were quickly loaded and sent the 9,981 miles to New York, stopping over in Muscat to pick up a selection of fardhs. Readers could follow their progress through wire reports in local papers, and fanfare heralded the arrival of the first ship. The winner of the date race received recognition, a monetary prize, and a bonus for the importing company, as the first shipments of dates sold at higher prices than subsequent ones. The bonus by the 1930s averaged about $1.75 per ton.[48]

This race grew faster and more competitive. In 1907, the steamship *Gulistan* lost to the *Umzumbie* by twenty-four hours. In 1912, Captain Charles Bliault and the *Turkistan* (owned by F. C. Strick & Co. of Swansea) won the race, beating out the *Stanhope* and earning $120,000 for the consignees of the dates.[49] In the 1920s, competition had increased to the extent that for thirty-first annual race, in 1930, Hills Brothers abandoned its three-time champion charter, the *Shahristan,* in favor of a brand-new oil burner, the *Gorjistan* (also owned by F. C. Strick & Co.), which broke all previous records, completing the Basra–New York journey in twenty-six days, beating its rival, the *Montauban,* and delivering a five-thousand-ton shipment of dates worth one and a half million dollars. The voyage was historic because it marked the first time a date ship had delivered its cargo fewer than forty days after the fruit was picked off the tree. Ten years earlier, the voyage took forty-two days, but by 1927 this had been cut to thirty-one. When a date ship arrived in the dockyards in Brooklyn, hundreds of longshoremen worked day and night to unload the cargo. In 1930 and 1932, more than two hundred stevedores unloaded the winning cargoes and filled trainloads of eighty cars with dates for the Midwest.[50]

DATES AND LABOR

The dramatic growth of the date export industry in the Gulf sharply influenced labor demands. Date trees must be planted, tended, and irrigated and their crops harvested, transported, and packed before dates can reach their global markets. In both Oman and Iraq, date packers in the chief port cities were usually women. By the first decade of the twentieth century, dates were packed by hand, one by one in neat rows and even layers inside each wooden box, sometimes with a sheet of wax paper between the layers. Then a board was placed on top of the dates and someone would stand on the box, pressing the dates together. Since the dates were arranged neatly in rows (thirteen or fourteen per layer in Basra, depending on the variety), they could easily be split into smaller portions for resale once they arrived at their destinations. In New York, date importers staffed warehouses where employees repacked date shipments into smaller containers.[51] In Oman, date packing was one of the few available forms of wage labor, and women eagerly crowded the Mutrah godowns to earn cash. Calvin Allen has suggested that this work "benefited many more people [in Oman] than any previous mercantile activity," and for part of its duration it was the only form of wage labor in the country.[52] The packing season ran from mid-August to early December—about one hundred days— and an experienced female employee could earn more than sixty Maria Theresa dollars (worth about sixty American silver dollars) in that period. Carpenters who assembled the wooden boxes earned from MT$75 to MT$125 in the same amount of time in 1912.[53]

The primary area of nineteenth-century date expansion in Oman was Batinah, the 150-mile stretch of coast on the Gulf of Oman north of Muscat beginning around Seeb and continuing north of Sohar. Consequently, Batinah became home to one of the largest populations of enslaved Africans in the Gulf. As the area of densest vegetation in eastern Arabia, Batinah had a bigger population and more agricultural production than any other part of the Persian Gulf south of Iraq. But it differed from the other date-producing areas in the region in that it required intense human effort to irrigate the palms. Most date production in Oman uses the *falaj* system of irrigation: gravity-flow channels of hand-crafted cement (*saruj*) convey water from natural springs in the Hajar Mountains in the Oman Ophiolite.[54] Although it has some of the richest soil in Oman, Batinah receives no consistent flow of water from the inland mountains and relies entirely on groundwater from wells for irrigation.[55] Batinah farmers employed the *zijrah* (or *zaygra*), the elevated well system used throughout the Arabian Peninsula and in Mesopotamia. A crossbar on a massive wooden framework usually constructed of palm trunks held a rotating pulley wheel called a *manjur,* around which ran a rope with a leather bag tied to one end and the yoke of a bull (or in rare cases a mule) to the other. As the bull was guided down a ramp up to fifty feet long with a low point three to ten feet deep, the rope pulled the bag out of the well. The bag emptied automatically when it reached its apex—the moment when the bull reached the nadir of the ramp, at which point it was escorted back to the top to repeat the process. The water thus lifted from twenty feet below the surface poured into cement-coated holding tanks that drained into irrigation channels, *aflaj,* and watered several acres of date palms. This labor-intensive process relied on one male worker, called a *bidar,* to water approximately every hundred trees. The work frequently fell on the shoulders of enslaved Africans.

An American date expert who visited in 1927 estimated that there were at least fifteen thousand wells of this kind operating in Batinah alone.[56] Bertram Thomas, who worked as the wazir (minister) of finance under Sultan Taimur bin Faisal in Oman between 1925 and 1930 and visited Batinah on a number of occasions, estimated that there were "tens of thousands of oxen daily" working these waterwheels in 1929.[57] "The cacophony from many wells operating at one time is really not unmusical," he wrote. "The effect is that of a weird assortment of stringed instruments, the cellos seeming always to delight in drowning the violas and fiddles, and the ensemble is a sort of tuning up of an orchestra. . . . 'Oil the wretched thing,' says a European impatient of its creaking and whining, but the owner has another view, for every well has a different note and he, from the far end of his garden, may thus know whether all goes well with his own."[58] V. H. W. Dowson of the Agricultural Directorate of Mesopotamia echoed Thomas: "Throughout the Batinah is heard the plaintive shrieking of the pullies. To a suggestion that the axils [*sic*] might be oiled, the reply comes that the noisy wheel was better, *Ahzain*."[59] Thomas added that apprehended runaway slaves were often punished with long hours in chains working in irrigation: "The metallic chink of ankle-chains, heard, perhaps, from the bull-pit of a well within the date grove, is an indication of some such ill-fated escapade."[60]

In addition to irrigation, Batinah date plantations required constant maintenance. Date palm pollination; the removal of offshoots (suckers), dead branches, and extra date bunches; the assurance of stock cleanliness; and—when the fruit was ripe—the enormous task of harvesting all had to be done by hand. In addition, in the shade of the date palms, farmers grew alfalfa (lucerne) and other animal feed in addition to vegetables for domestic consumption. Large parties of workers were required to boil the maseybili and khameyzi dates, common in Batinah and popular in India, in large copper cauldrons and dry them in the sun, turning them frequently.[61] The dates also needed to be packed or pressed and conveyed overland or by sea to ports of export. Palm frond bags to hold them had to be woven, and once they were ready for export, the dates had to be loaded onto boats, conveyed to their destination, and unloaded. Enslaved Africans, particularly men and boys. performed much of this work.

In the late nineteenth century, slave traders increasingly exported young boys from East Africa for work in the date and pearl industries. By the 1870s, the ratio of male to female slaves among captured slave dhows on the Arabian coast reversed previous trends, shifting overwhelmingly in favor of young males. In 1872 the HMS *Vulture* captured a large slave dhow off the coast of Ras Al-Hadd at the entrance to the Gulf of Oman. It was carrying 169 captives from Pemba to Sur and Batinah; 124 were male and 45 were female, and the majority were children.[62] The HMS *Philomel* captured a dhow in 1884 that had seventy-seven men, fourteen women, fifty-one boys, and twelve girls aboard.[63] In November 1885 the HMS *Osprey* captured a forty-two-ton dhow near Ras Madraka in Oman bound from Ngao in East Africa to Sur with forty-nine male and twenty-four female slaves (eight men, twelve women, forty-one boys, and twelve girls).[64] In fact, in the last quarter of the nineteenth century, it is virtually impossible to find evidence of any dhow captured off the Arabian coast carrying more female than male captives from East Africa.

With its requirement of extra labor for date production, Batinah was the primary destination of slaves in the late nineteenth and early twentieth centuries and home to the largest population in Oman of Africans and their descendants.[65] In 1885, S. B. Miles noted that in contrast to the interior behind Sur, where demand for slaves was limited, in Batinah slaves were "in high request," and consequently most slaves eventually landed there.[66] It thus makes sense that the dhow captured by the HMS *Philomel* was en route to Al Khadra (near Suwaiq) on the Batinah coast.[67] In 1930, the British consul at Muscat remarked that "apart from the Batinah Coast, the method of irrigation does not demand slave labour."[68] Western observers continued to describe the region as the center of the slave trade as late as 1930.[69]

From the second half of the nineteenth century through the early 1920s, Batinah absorbed the vast majority of enslaved Africans sent to eastern Arabia.[70]
Because of its high demand for agricultural labor, Batinah became what historians
of Atlantic slavery have called a "seasoning ground"—a zone for socializing, or
"seasoning," captive people. The newly enslaved had to be made to accept their
new positions and to learn the language and submit to the will of their masters to
be valuable as slaves.[71] The testimonies of enslaved Africans who received manumission certificates at British consulates and agencies in the Gulf between 1907
and 1940 almost universally describe a period of at least three years in Batinah
prior to being sold elsewhere in the Gulf.[72] For young African boys, who made up
a considerable percentage of those imported in the late nineteenth century, the
period between arrival in and exit from Batinah was often enough time to mature
to the age of a beginning pearl diver (early teens).

THE DECLINE OF THE GLOBAL DATE EXPORT
INDUSTRY

Just as quickly as globalization created vibrant export industries in the Gulf, it
ushered in their demise. The Gulf's two leading industries—dates and pearls—col-
lapsed in tandem in the late 1920s, both victims of competition from more-devel-
oped countries, the United States and Japan, which used technology to mimic and
exceed the Gulf's production. The Gulf's key date market in North America dwin-
dled as soon as the United States developed a date industry of its own in California. Likewise, Japanese cultured pearls brought an end to global demand for natural pearls from the Gulf.

In 1890 the USDA imported sixty-eight young palms, mostly seedlings, and
distributed them among experimental stations in Yuma, Arizona; Las Cruces,
New Mexico; and four locations in California. In 1905 a USDA plant explorer
named Thomas Kearney brought offshoots of varieties from Algeria and Tunisia.[73]
Three years earlier, David Fairchild, another agricultural explorer for the USDA
Bureau of Plant Industry, visited the Gulf to acquire the best offshoots for propagation in California. He traveled to Muscat in February 1902 in a steamer full of Shiʿa
pilgrims on their way to Karbala. Once there, he arranged for the American consul
to secure offshoots of fardhs from the Semail Valley and send them to Bombay,
where Fairchild picked them up and shipped them to California.[74] He then visited
Bahrain, where he had some offshoots of the khalasa date from Al Hufuf in Al-
Hasa (now in Saudi Arabia) sent to Bombay as well. At Basra, he collected samples
of several date palms, including the popular halawi variety. He subsequently
steamed up the Tigris to Baghdad, where he collected samples of dates from the
largest growers around the city, then packed the offshoots in mud-filled burlap
sacks, boxed them, and transported them on a nine-week voyage to Washington.

More than three decades later, Fairchild was pleased to report that several of the varieties he had brought from the Gulf were being grown around Mecca in the Coachella Valley in California.[75]

After extensive study, the USDA determined that the best soil and climate for date production in the United States were in the Salton Basin in California. Then, in 1905, water from the Colorado River, which was being diverted to the Imperial Valley for irrigation, broke through its canal system and rushed into the Salton Basin. Before it was finally restored, the Colorado flowed into the basin for two years, forming Salton Sea, now a permanent feature of the California landscape. This accidental flooding created the perfect environment for growing date palms.[76] These were all important steps, but the beginning of the end for Gulf date exports to the United States came in 1912. That was when a horticulturalist named Paul Popenoe, who had a stake in a farm at Thermal, near the Salton Sea, visited the Gulf, purchased offshoots of the most desirable varieties, and brought back nine thousand young palm trees, including those that grew fardhs.[77]

PAUL POPENOE AND THE END OF THE GULF'S AMERICAN DATE MARKET

Years before he became known as the leading proponent of eugenics in the United States, Paul Popenoe was a date farmer. He ultimately edited the *Journal of Heredity*, headed the Human Betterment Foundation, and advocated publicly for the sterilization of individuals with physical and mental handicaps. But he discovered his interest in heredity while propagating dates in a desert in Southern California. Popenoe also unintentionally became one of the main reasons why the Gulf date export market to the United States declined sharply in the 1920s. He traveled to the Gulf ostensibly on behalf of his father's horticulture business, West India Gardens of Altadena, but he also carried letters of introduction from the USDA and had a standing job offer from the agency's Bureau of Plant Propagation. Popenoe had visited Algeria and brought back North African varieties of date palms for his father's experimental farm in the Coachella Valley. After some initial success with these, he went to the source of the American imports to bring back the varieties that were already popular in the United States. His voyage to Arabia in 1912–13 demonstrates how the technologies that made possible the expansion of global markets could also lead to their downfall. Popenoe used steamships, telegraphs, river freighters, international lines of credit, and a network of American diplomats, merchants, and missionaries to successfully negotiate a foreign business environment and bring back the key to creating California's date industry.

The twenty-five-year-old horticulturalist arrived in Muscat on October 21, 1912, aboard the SS *Kasara* from Karachi in the company of his younger brother Wilson. In their letters home, both professed amazement at what "a fine clean little town"

Muscat was, with its vibrant market, population of thirty to forty thousand, and twin refurbished Portuguese forts overlooking the harbor with cannon on display and watchmen calling out the all clear at regular intervals between the towers. The weather was much like what the men were accustomed to in Southern California: "decidedly comfortable." Wilson likened the city to Avalon on Catalina Island and marveled that the sultan had electric lights and a telephone in his palace and that the town had a functioning hospital. The British consulate's tennis court was busy with sailors from the five British gunboats in the harbor, who also found cheap entertainment provided by boys who would dive from rocks for pennies.[78] The Popenoes found ten Europeans in residence in Muscat. Among them was Homer Brett, the American consul, a gentleman from Mississippi whom Paul reckoned was about fifty years old, who made all of their local arrangements. In response to an inquiry from Paul earlier in the year and the USDA's letter of introduction, Brett secured the sultan's permission for Paul to travel into the Semail Valley. The sultan, Faisal bin Turki, also offered to provide camels, letters of introduction to seven allied shaykhs in the area, and an armed escort.[79]

Popenoe interpreted the sultan's gesture as one of mutual benefit: "He likes to send out an occasional party under his protection that possesses some importance, just to show the upcountry chiefs that he still has friends."[80] In fact, the sultan's authority in the interior of Oman was considerably weak, and raids from rival shaykhs occasionally threatened even his control over the city of Muscat. But if sponsoring an American explorer's trip into the country's richest date-producing region for the purpose of creating a rival market in California was the sultan's idea of a self-strengthening measure, the plan backfired. Popenoe's journey to the Semail Valley met two ambushes, and the sultan was obliged to send a force of thirty-five hundred men the following month to avenge these insults.[81] Then, of course, Popenoe made things much worse, by bringing Muscat's prized commodity to California and undercutting a major portion of Oman's economy.

After paying a visit to Dr. Wells Thoms, the American missionary doctor at the Mutrah hospital, Popenoe and Brett journeyed along the coast to the Semail Valley, which they then followed seventy miles into the interior, traveling in the mornings and evenings to avoid the heat of the day and staying with the sultan's cousins and allies along the way. Altogether they were gone about a week. Popenoe found almost forty varieties of dates growing in the valley, although he estimated that roughly two-thirds of the palms under cultivation were the fardh variety, a testament to the importance of the American market. He noted that the fort overlooking the valley was armed with ten cannon (one of which worked) and a garrison of fourteen guards. The working cannon fired a shot each night at 9 P.M., when the gates closed. Popenoe had been studying Arabic for about a year and had visited date-producing parts of North Africa, so he could hold his own in discussions about dates, but Brett knew no Arabic and, according to Popenoe, had "absolutely no knowledge of Arab ways" even though he had been in Muscat for a year. The two Americans were almost entirely dependent on their translator and guide. Popenoe wore a pith helmet.[82]

When they returned to Muscat, Popenoe set about arranging to buy and ship five hundred offshoots, including two hundred of the popular fardh variety and one hundred of the khalasa variety, widely held to be the best in Arabia and native to Al Hufuf but grown in limited quantities in the Semail Valley. He doubted whether he could manage to get any more than fifty offshoots of the latter, since the British government had just bought up two hundred and sent them to Zanzibar. On Brett's recommendation, he commissioned a local merchant named Muhammad Fazel, whom Brett considered "the honestest man in Masqat [Muscat]," to secure, pack, and prepare the offshoots for export. Popenoe then left Muscat and headed to Basra on a passenger steamer.[83]

He arrived to find the city bustling with activity. The date-packing season was in high gear, and the whole Shatt al Arab north of Mohammerah (now Khorramshahr) was crammed with "innumerable" date-packing sheds and workers loading piles of boxes onto lighters. Popenoe found the harbor full of at least "a dozen big ocean steamers" and "any number of smaller craft, making it look much busier than lots of big ports I have seen."[84] His first order of business was to meet with H. P. Chalk, the manager of the Hills Brothers Company's operations at Basra, to whom Fairchild of the USDA had written to request aid for Popenoe. Fairchild had visited Basra in 1904 in his capacity as a USDA agricultural explorer and had relied on Chalk to secure a few offshoots of Basra varieties, which he sent to the USDA research station in Yuma. Fairchild took care to acknowledge Chalk in a piece he wrote for *National Geographic,* which could not have pleased Chalk's employers in New York.[85] Chalk realized that helping Popenoe could jeopardize his career. The creation of a rival date production center was the last thing Hills Brothers could have wanted. Chalk evidently hoped to drag his feet long enough that Popenoe would leave in frustration, but Popenoe was determined. "Every day he says, 'tomorrow,'" Popenoe complained. "He is a pin-headed Britisher who has got the idea that we are going to ruin his business by competition, he is too lazy to improve his own scandalously slack methods by which he might hold his own with us, so he is down on us."[86] Popenoe recalled their first meeting:

> When I met him he exclaimed, "So you are one of the men who is going to take the bread out of our mouths, are you?" "On the contrary," I replied. "We Californians are going to make you richer by increasing your sales." Then I went on to point out how ridiculously small the total consumption of dates in America was at present, how it was certain to jump as the public became acquainted with fresh, clean, attractive dates, and how, as California would be unable to supply more than a fraction of the demand for many years to come, the public would buy Busreh [Basra] dates because they could not get the California product. "Dates of some kind they must and will

have," I concluded, "and the demand is going to grow twice as fast as the supply that either you or we can turn out."[87]

However disingenuous, Popenoe nevertheless managed to secure offshoots of the most popular Basra varieties: khadhrawi, barhi, halawi. Chalk eventually gave in to his requests and introduced him to a prominent date grower in Basra named Yusef bin Ahmed.[88] Despite Chalk's efforts to the contrary, the Hills Brothers Company was an essential part of Popenoe's success in Basra. It ultimately agreed to a contract to secure date offshoots from Basra, for a commission of 450 rupees plus expenses.[89] But Popenoe never would have succeeded without a global support network, and in particular the help of American missionaries in the Gulf. The Reformed Church in America (RCA, of Dutch Reformed heritage) had established a series of mission hospitals in the Gulf through its Arabian Mission. The Cantine, Bennett, and Van Vlack families, the RCA missionaries who ran the hospitals at the time, took pity on the Popenoe brothers, who were attempting to maintain their vegetarian diet while living in an international guesthouse. The missionaries allowed them to stay in the mission house and to pay only the lowest possible rates for their room and board. Then when Paul came down with typhoid fever and suffered for several weeks from high fevers and delirium, the missionary doctors nursed him back to health.[90]

Once he was well again, Popenoe took advantage of the regular boat service on the Tigris River to travel north to Baghdad aboard the *Julnar*, one of three steamers operated by the Euphrates and Tigris Steam Navigation Co., a British company, whose business Ottoman regulations limited to privilege the rival Turkish company, Jaafer Co. (To get around these restrictions, the *Julnar* carried a large barge on each side to treble its capacity.)[91] At Baghdad, Popenoe settled into the British club and hired a young mixed-race assistant, Nasuri bin Anton Al-Baghdadi, from his hotel in Basra to accompany him as he met important date growers of the region. His first appointments were with Hajji ʿAbd al-Rahman and Mullah Naji al-Hajj.[92] Popenoe's main business partner in Baghdad was a merchant named Seyd Rawf, whose full name is unfortunately not preserved in Popenoe's records but who likely secured more than two thousand offshoots. Another of his most important connections in the city was a Kurdish shaykh named Bashaga ibn Sagakia, whom he contracted to procure five hundred offshoots from Bedra and transship to Al Kut. (The contract lists Popenoe as "Paul ibn Bobno.")[93] According to Popenoe, the shayk had been driven out of Persia by a quarrel and had immigrated to Baghdad with most of his community, who assembled Popenoe's order. Popenoe was surprised to learn that these workers were unpaid. After an inquiry, he reported:

> The sheikh and his tribesmen formed a sort of feudal community in Baghdad: he provided them with what money they needed for the necessities of life, and in return they worked for him on the various porterage and packing jobs that he had under-

taken. All the money from the contracts went to him, and they worked at his bidding. . . . The chief handled an immense amount of business with two or three hundred men always at his call. . . . That such a system of feudal organization could be extended into the modern business world was rather startling.[94]

Popenoe sent Wilson to Basra to oversee the packing of the date palms from that city and from Muscat while he wrapped up his sales in Baghdad and steamed down the Tigris by way of Al Kut to pick up his order of offshoots from Bashaga.[95] Wilson arrived in Basra to find the packing well under way, although not to his satisfaction. He thought that it was "a mighty good thing I came down here, with particular emphasis on the mighty." A Hills Brothers employee named Tomlinson had turned the packing of the palms over to a subcontractor, who was not using sufficient burlap to protect the offshoots for their journey to the United States. "I tell you the way that nigger was doing the job actually made me sick," Wilson wrote, explaining that he tore open the packaging of all of the palms and made the worker repack them under his supervision. The Basra offshoots were complemented by the arrival of the ones from Muscat and about four hundred khalasa offshoots from Al Hufuf, procured by an American missionary at Bahrain.[96] After several hours in customs and haggling with the laborers who loaded the palms on the ship, the Popenoes finally left Basra aboard the SS *Mokta* (Strick Line) on February 24 and arrived in London on April 17 by way of Suez. From London, the offshoots traveled to New York, where they were inspected, then transshipped to Galveston and sent by rail in refrigerator cars to Thermal. The total shipment amounted to more than nine thousand palms.

When the trees procured from the Gulf and from North Africa reached maturity a decade later, California began to replace the former as America's primary source of dates. An Australian visitor in 1914 calculated that two hundred thousand palms had been planted in the Coachella Valley.[97] With an additional injection of cash from the Gillette Company in the 1920s and a flurry of speculation among Southern California landowners (to the detriment of foreign imports), the California date industry took off. For the Gulf, this meant the loss of its largest export market.

In the years that followed, Popenoe's investment paid big dividends. California's date industry grew exponentially and replaced the dates imported to the fruit docks of Brooklyn from Basra and Muscat. Popenoe's offshoots helped ensure that California farmers had a sufficient supply of young date palms to create successful farms. As it turns out, his timing was perfect. World War I eliminated any chance of importing additional offshoots from the Middle East for several years. By the late 1920s, California dates were being harvested and brought immediately to markets around the country. Date importations to the United States fell sharply after 1925. Popenoe, Fairchild, and others like them had used the tools of global trade to undercut a major world market.

CONCLUSIONS

The forces of globalization that helped create global markets for Arabian commodities also helped destroy them. Steamships, telegraphs, global lines of credit, and networks of merchants, missionaries, and diplomats facilitated the global trade in Arabian dates. But agents from industrialized states used those same tools just as easily against Arab producers, creating rival production centers. The steamers that raced to Brooklyn from Basra each holiday season fed appetites created by sailing barks such as the *Glide* and the *Imaum*, which had brought dates to the United States decades earlier. The date trade with the United States, although initially minor and focused on Salem, grew into a major sector of the Gulf economy. The collapse of this export market in the wake of domestic competition coincided with the collapse of the region's pearl export market around the same time as Japanese cultured pearls, like California dates, undercut a major portion of Gulf exports and had disastrous consequences for the preoil Gulf economy. Thus, the circulation of luxuries as well as more-humble commodities, such as dried fruit, can help us understand the far-reaching effects of the expanding global economy of the late nineteenth and early twentieth centuries and the power of early forms of globalization in the Age of Steam and Print.

NOTES

1. "Journal of Charles A. Benson, Barque *Glide* 1862–63," Charles Benson Papers (MSS 15), Peabody Essex Museum (hereafter PEM), Salem, MA. See also George Granville Putman, *Salem Vessels and Their Voyages: A History of the "George," "Glide," "Taria Topan" and "St. Paul," in Trade with Calcutta, East Coast of Africa, Madagascar and the Philippine Islands* (Salem, MA: Essex Institute, 1924), 62–105; Edward S. Atwood, "Memorial of John Bertram," *Historical Collections of the Essex Institute* 21, no. 4–6 (April–June 1884): 81–96; Michael Sokolow, *Charles Benson: Mariner of Color in the Age of Sail* (Amherst: University of Massachusetts Press, 2003).

2. Victoria Bernal, "Cotton and Colonial Order in Sudan: A Social History, with Emphasis on the Gezira Scheme," in *Cotton, Colonialism, and Social History in Sub-Saharan Africa,* ed. Allen Isaacman and Richard Roberts (Portsmouth, NH: Heinemann, 1995), 96–118; Charles Issawi, "Middle East Economic Development, 1815–1914: The General and the Specific," in *The Modern Middle East,* ed. Albert Hourani, Philip S. Khoury, and Mary C. Wilson (Berkeley: University of California Press, 1993); José Morilla Critz, Alan L. Olmstead and Paul W. Rhode, "'Horn of Plenty': The Globalization of Mediterranean Horticulture and the Economic Development of Southern Europe, 1880–1930," *Journal of Economic History* 59, no. 2 (June 1999): 316–52; Roger Owen, *Cotton and the Egyptian Economy, 1820–1914: A Study in Trade and Development* (Oxford: Clarendon, 1969); Owen, *The Middle East in the World Economy, 1800–1914* (London: I. B. Tauris, 1993).

3. J. B. Kelly, *Britain and the Persian Gulf, 1795–1880* (Oxford: Clarendon, 1968), 36–37. For a regional perspective see Edward Alpers, "The Western Indian Ocean as a Regional Food Network in the Nineteenth Century," in *East Africa and the Indian Ocean,* ed. Alpers (Princeton, NJ: Markus Wiener, 2007), 23–38.

4. *The Persian Gulf Administration Reports, 1873–1947,* 11 vols. (Gerrards Cross, U.K.: Archive Editions, 1986).

5. Paul Popenoe, "The Distribution of the Date Palm," *Geographical Review* 16, no. 1 (1926): 117–21.

6. Erik Gilbert, *Dhows and the Colonial Economy of Zanzibar, 1860–1970* (Athens: Ohio University Press, 2004), 33–36; Norman Robert Bennett, *New England Merchants in Africa: A History through Documents, 1802 to 1865* (Boston: Boston University Press, 1965); Abdul Sheriff, *Slaves, Spices, and Ivory in Zanzibar: Integration of an East African Commercial Empire into the World Economy, 1770–1873* (London: James Currey, 1987); Jeremy Prestholdt, "On the Global Repercussions of East African Consumerism," *American Historical Review* 109, no. 3 (2004): 755–82.

7. Reda Bhacker, *Trade and Empire in Muscat and Zanzibar: Roots of British Domination* (New York: Routledge, 1992), 109–13, 136–37.

8. Calvin H. Allen, "Sayyids, Shets and Sultāns: Politics and Trade in Masqat under the Al Bū Saʿīd, 1785–1914" (PhD dissertation, University of Washington, 1978), 140–56.

9. *Administration Report of the Political Agency Muscat for the Year 1871–72*, R/15/6/5, India Office Records (hereafter IOR), British Library, London.

10. Allen, "Sayyids, Shets and Sultāns," 140–53.

11. Oscar Willoughby Riggs, "The Fruit-Ships at New York," *Frank Leslie's Popular Monthly* 21, no. 5 (May 1886): 599.

12. Bertram Thomas, *Alarms and Excursions in Arabia* (Indianapolis: Bobbs-Merrill, 1931), 142.

13. *Charleston (SC) City Gazette*, 7 November 1818; *Georgetown (DC) National Messenger*, 16 December 1818; *New York Evening Post*, 14 September 1818; *New York Daily Advertiser*, 10 October 1918.

14. Putnam, *Salem Vessels*, 62–63.

15. Atkins Hamerton to Malet, 26 August 1852, box AA 3/11, Zanzibar National Archives (hereafter ZNA). Each bale of cloth had twenty-five pieces of thirty-one yards.

16. "Journal Kept on Board the Bark *Warren White* of New York, Benjamin Creamer Master for a Transatlantic Trading Voyage. Carried Cargo of Dates" (Log 325), *Warren White* (Bark) Journal 1852–53, G. W. Blunt White Library, Mystic Seaport Museum, Mystic, CT.

17. Atkins Hamerton to Malet, secretary to the Government of India, 30 June 1853, AA 3/11, ZNA.

18. C. P. Rigby to W. M. Coghlan, 15 October 1860, AA 3/19, ZNA.

19. "Journal of Lawrence Peirson Ward Kept aboard the Bark *Elizabeth Hall* 1851–52" (LOG 1851E2 Elizabeth Hall, Bark), PEM.

20. "Journal Kept by William H. Townsend on Board the Bark *Imaum* of Salem, Mass., Stanford Perkins Master, 1858–59" (Log 579), G. W. Blunt White Library, Mystic Seaport Museum.

21. W. H. Hathorne to John Bertram, 20 October and 4 November 1866, John Bertram Papers (MSS 104), folder 5, box 5, PEM.

22. Putnam, *Salem Vessels*, 103.

23. *Boston Journal*, quoted in ibid., 108.

24. Dwayne Roy Winseck and Robert M. Pike, *Communication and Empire: Media, Markets, and Globalization, 1860–1930* (Durham, NC: Duke University Press, 2007), 1–42.

25. Joseph H. Wilson, *United States Telegraphic Cipher Adapted to the Use of Dealers in Fruit and Produce and Merchandise Brokers* (New York: Charles H. Parsons, 1893), 12.

26. United States Department of Agriculture, *Yearbook of the United States Department of Agriculture*, 1893–1935 eds. (Washington DC: Government Printing Office, 1894–1936).

27. Allen, "Sayyids, Shets and Sultāns," 140–56; Mark Speece, "Aspects of Economic Dualism in Oman, 1830–1930," *International Journal of Middle East Studies*, 21, no. 4 (1989): 495–515.

28. Paul Popenoe, "The Home of the Fardh Date," *Monthly Bulletin of the State Commission of Horticulture* 3, no. 1 (January 1914): 11.

29. Paul Popenoe, *Date Growing in the Old World and the New* (Altadena, CA: West India Gardens, 1913), 232–34; Popenoe, "Home of the Fardh Date," 11.

30. V. H. W. Dowson and A. Aten, *Dates Handling, Processing and Packing* (Rome: Food and Agricultural Organization of the United Nations, 1962), 261–62; Dowson, *Dates and Date Cultivation of the*

'Iraq, pt. I, *The Cultivation of the Date Palm on the Shat Al 'Arab* (Cambridge: Agricultural Directorate of Mesopotamia, 1921), 43–57.

31. Michael D'Antonio, *Hershey: Milton S. Hershey's Extraordinary Life of Wealth, Empire, and Utopian Dreams* (New York: Simon and Schuster, 2006), 106–26. Per capita candy consumption in the United States jumped from thirteen pounds in 1932 to nineteen pounds in 1941. See Gideon Hadary, "The Candy-Consumer—How Much Will He Buy in the Postwar Period?," *Journal of Business of the University of Chicago* 18, no. 2 (1945), 96–100.

32. Hills Brothers Company, *One Hundred Delights* (New York: Moore, 1923), 5–13.

33. Popenoe, *Date Growing*, 233.

34. *Los Angeles Times,* 16 February 1917.

35. Owen, *The Middle East in the World Economy,* 182.

36. Popenoe, *Date Growing,* 233; United States Department of Agriculture, *Yearbook of the United States Department of Agriculture, 1912* (Washington DC: Government Printing Office, 1913).

37. United States Department of Agriculture, *Yearbook of the United States Department of Agriculture, 1930* (Washington DC: Government Printing Office, 1930), 958.

38. Robert Greenhalgh Albion, *The Rise of New York Port, 1815–1860* (New York: Charles Schribner's Sons, 1939).

39. Riggs, "The Fruit-Ships at New York," 599–609.

40. J. Forbes Munro, *Maritime Enterprise and Empire: Sir William Mackinnon and His Business Network, 1823–1893* (Woodbridge, U.K.: Boydell, 2003), 178.

41. Major R. M. Smith to Major Bateman Champion, 1 June 1878, Foreign Office 60/414, the National Archives (hereafter TNA; formerly Public Record Office), Kew, Richmond, U.K., cited in ibid.

42. *The Story of a Pantry Shelf: An Outline History of Grocery Specialties* (New York: Butterick, 1925), 130–32.

43. David G. Fairchild, *The World Was My Garden: Travels of a Plant Explorer* (New York: Charles Scribner's Sons, 1938), 235–36.

44. William Hills to Ratansi Purshotum, 27 October 1905, Ratansi Purshotum Papers, private collection; *Story of a Pantry Shelf,* 133.

45. *Story of a Pantry Shelf,* 133–36.

46. "Hills Brothers Co., (et al.) v. F.T.C," in *Federal Trade Commission Decisions: Findings, Orders, and Stipulations,* vol. 31, *June 1, 1940, to November 30, 1940* (Washington DC: Government Printing Office, 1941), 931–42.

47. David G. Fairchild, *Persian Gulf Dates and their Introduction into America,* USDA Bureau of Plant Industry Bulletin no. 54 (Washington DC: Government Printing Office, 1903), 24.

48. "Nostalgic Note," *Time,* 8 December 1941.

49. "Turkistan Wins Date Race," *New York Times,* 10 November 1912, 6.

50. "Date-Laden Ships Racing from Iraq," *New York Times,* 3 October 1930, 55; "First Dates Arrive in Record Crossing," *New York Times,* 15 October 1932, 33.

51. Dowson and Aten, *Dates Handling,* 262.

52. Allen, "Sayyids, Shets and Sultāns," 155.

53. Ibid., 151–55.

54. J. C. Wilkinson, *Water and Tribal Settlement in South-East Arabia: A Study of the Aflaj of Oman* (Oxford: Clarendon, 1977), 28–32, 36–47.

55. Ibid., 47–51; Charles C. Graf, "The Batinah Hydrologic Area," in Sultanate of Oman, Public Authority for Water Resources, *The Hydrology of the Sultanate of Oman: A Preliminary Assessment,* PAWR 83–1 (Muscat: Public Authority for Water Resources, 1983), 28–43; Robert Dale, "The Water Resources of Oman" (report for TetraTech International), c. 1980, James H. Critchfield Papers, private collection.

56. "Report of Mr. Dawson, American Manager of the Iraq Date Company, Following a Visit to the Batina in 1927," R/15/1/460, IOR. For an excellent discussion of the social and cultural aspects of the

zaygra and the manjur in Oman, see Mandana E. Limbert, "The Senses of Water in an Omani Town," *Social Text* 19, no. 3 (2001): 35–55.

57. "The Word of Sultan Saʿid bin Taimur, Sultan of Muscat and Oman, about the History of the Financial Position of the Sultanate in the Past and the Hopes for the Future, after the Export of Oil, January 1968," reprinted in Whitehead Consulting Group, *Sultanate of Oman Economic Survey, 1972* (Windsor, U.K.: Harold Whitehead and Partners, 1972), appendix 2.

58. Thomas, *Alarms and Excursions*, 125–26, 142.

59. "Report of Mr. Dawson," R/15/1/460.

60. Thomas, *Alarms and Excursions*, 238.

61. Administration Report of the Political Agency, Muscat, for the Year 1876–77, 79–82, CDR ND1/H, Centre for Documentation and Research, Abu Dhabi, United Arab Emirates.

62. Senior naval officer in Persian Gulf (and commander HMS *Vulture*) to Rear Admiral Arthur Cumming, commander in chief, East Indies, 10 September 1872, ADM 1/6230, TNA; Lt. C. M. Gilbert-Cooper, "Capture of a Slave Dhow: Or the Vulture and Its Prey," n.d., BGY/G/5, Lt. C. M. Gilbert-Cooper Papers, National Maritime Museum, London.

63. Commander HMS *Philomel* to commander in chief, East Indies, 15 October 1884, ADM 1/6714, TNA.

64. Herbert W. Dowding, commander HMS *Osprey*, to Rear Admiral Frederick W. Richards, commander in chief, East Indies, 19 September 1885, ADM 1/6758, TNA.

65. Secretary of the Government of Bombay to political resident, Persian Gulf, 31 October 1889, R/15/1/200, IOR; Maj. Saddler, "Report on Visit to Sur," April 1895, no. 5–11, quoted in J. A. Saldanha, *Précis of Maskat Affairs, 1892–1905* (L/PS/20/C245, IOR), pt. I, 53: "Few [slaves] seem to be sent inland to the Sharkeyyeh and Jaalan, as owing to the system of irrigation in those parts, there is not the same demand for labor on the date plantations as there is in the Batinah, where the date trees have to be watered from wells."

66. S. B. Miles to E. C. Ross, 7 December 1885, L/PS/20/C246, IOR.

67. Miles to Ross, 31 October 1884, L/PS/20/C246, IOR.

68. Political agent, Muscat, to political resident, Persian Gulf, 21 January 1930, R/15/1/230, IOR.

69. PRPG [political resident, Persian Gulf] to foreign secretary to the Government of India, New Delhi, 18 March 1930, R/15/1/230, IOR.

70. G. P. Murphy, PA [political agent] Muscat, to PRPG, n.d. (no. 69 of 1929), R/15/1/225, IOR.

71. Claude Meillassoux, *The Anthropology of Slavery: The Womb of Iron and Gold* (London: Athlone, 1991), 99–116; Patrick Manning, *Slavery and African Life: Occidental, Oriental, and African Slave Trades* (New York: Cambridge University Press, 1990), 114–15.

72. For a discussion of these manumission testimonies, see Jerzy Zdanowski, "The Manumission Movement in the Gulf in the First Half of the Twentieth Century," *Middle Eastern Studies* 47, no. 6 (2011): 863–83; Hideaki Suzuki, "Some Observations on the Quantitative Analysis of Slavery and the Slave Trade in the Persian Gulf and the Gulf of Oman, 1906–1950," paper presented at that "Enslavement, Bondage and the Environment in the Indian Ocean World" international conference, Indian Ocean World Centre, McGill University, Montreal, 28–30 April 2011.

73. Roy Nixon, "First Dates Imported 78 Years Ago," in *Coachella Valley's Golden Years: The Early History of the Coachella Valley County Water District and Stories about the Discovery and Development of This Section of the Colorado Desert*, ed. Ole Nordland (Coachella, CA: Coachella Valley County Water District, 1968), 50–51; Thomas H. Kearney, *Date Varieties and Date Culture in Tunis*, U.S. Department of Agriculture Bureau of Plant Industry Bulletin no. 92 (Washington DC: Government Printing Office, 1906).

74. Fairchild, *Persian Gulf Dates*.

75. Ibid., *The World Was My Garden*, 226–44.

76. Nixon, "First Dates," 50–51.

77. Popenoe, *Date Growing*, xiv, 64, 92, 256.

78. Paul Popenoe to F. O. Popenoe, 21 October 1912, and Wilson Popenoe to F. O. Popenoe, 29 October 1912, folder 2, box 2, Paul Popenoe Papers (hereafter PPP), American Heritage Center, University of Wyoming, Cheyenne; Paul B. Popenoe, "With the Natives of Maskat," *Los Angeles Times,* 14 December 1912.

79. Homer Brett to Paul Popenoe, 8 October 1912, folder 2, box 2, PPP.

80. Paul Popenoe to F. O. Popenoe, 29 October 1912, folder 2, box 2, PPP.

81. Homer Brett to Paul Popenoe, 12 January 1913, folder 3, box 2, PPP.

82. Paul Popenoe to F. O. Popenoe, 29 October 1912.

83. Paul Popenoe to F. O. Popenoe, 3 November 1912, folder 2, box 2, PPP.

84. Wilson Popenoe to F. O. Popenoe, 8 November 1912, and Paul Popenoe to F. O. Popenoe, 9 November 1912, folder 2, box 2, PPP.

85. David Fairchild, "Travels in Arabia and along the Persian Gulf," *National Geographic* 15, no. 4 (April 1904): 139–51.

86. Paul Popenoe to F. O. Popenoe, 18 November 1912, folder 2, box 2, PPP.

87. Paul Popenoe, "Competition in Dates: Oriental Countries Have Heard of the New Industry in California," *Coachella Valley News,* 23 February 1913.

88. Wilson Popenoe to F. O. Popenoe, 22 November 1912, folder 2, box 2, PPP.

89. Contract between A. G. Tomlinson and Paul Popenoe, 16 December 1912, folder 2, box 2, PPP.

90. Paul Popenoe to F. O. Popenoe, 14 December 1912, folder 2, box 2, PPP.

91. Paul Popenoe to F. O. Popenoe, 1 January 1913, folder 3, box 2, PPP.

92. Paul Popenoe to F. O. Popenoe, 15 January 1913, folder 3, box 2, PPP.

93. Agreement between Peshaga ibn Sagakia and Paul Popenoe, 25 January 1913, folder 3, box 2, PPP.

94. Paul Popenoe, "To Baghdad for Date Palms" (unpublished manuscript), 1913, folder 3, box 174, PPP.

95. Paul Popenoe to F. O. Popenoe, 19 February 1913, folder 3, box 2, PPP.

96. Wilson Popenoe to F. O. Popenoe, 13 February 1913, folder 3, box 2, PPP.

97. W. M. Carne, "Notes on Date Culture in America with Some Consideration of Its Possibilities in New South Wales," *Agricultural Gazette of New South Wales,* 2 September 1914, 805.

PART THREE

Nodes and Routes

9
___

Remembering Java's Islamization

A View from Sri Lanka

Ronit Ricci

INTRODUCTION

Let us imagine a group of people sitting together and listening to a narrative being recounted aloud. They are assembled in a Sri Lankan home in Colombo's Slave Island or Kandy's Kampong Pensen during the final years of the nineteenth century. The reciter is reading from a Malay manuscript written in Arabic script, and the story he is telling his audience—titled "Hikayat Tuan Gusti"—relates the early Islamization of Java. Members of a minuscule Muslim-Malay minority living in Buddhist- and Sinhala-majority British-ruled Ceylon, those gathered around the manuscript epitomized the intertwined histories of colonized and colonizer across the Indian Ocean region, including the journeys and dislocations those histories entailed. In the following pages, I explore the significance of this seemingly unlikely scene of literary activity and consider how and why memories of a Javanese conversion to Islam were sustained in Sri Lanka through an ongoing engagement with such narratives. I suggest that this engagement represents a reaching back toward an earlier era of globalization, during which Islamic civilization was spreading to places ever farther from its site of emergence, including Southeast Asia. I also propose that although that earlier period predated the telegraph, the steamship, nationalism, and other emblems of modernity now associated with globalization, it too was marked by diverse interactions among peoples, places, and texts, by a contraction of space, and by multiple forms of mobility. Reading the "Hikayat Tuan Gusti" in the late nineteenth century was, in part, about imagining an earlier global age while living through another in the present.

The theme of mobility—of individuals, beliefs, symbols, and practices—is central to the account of the "Hikayat." This focus on movement, coupled with the emphasis on religious conversion, highlights relationships and contacts that go beyond Sri Lanka's shores and link its small Malay community to distant places, times past, and a global community of Muslims. Thinking about these connections—in particular their spatial and temporal dimensions as represented both within the story and at the scene of its retelling—is instructive for what it reveals about networks, community, and memory. Especially significant are the memories of Islam's earlier expansion, which, in the colonial world of the late nineteenth century, may well have been tinged with nostalgia and frustration at the current state of Muslim affairs. The emphasis of the "Hikayat" on mobility and travel echoes the Malay community's ties to this global, transregional past and evokes the far-reaching networks—of literature, trade, and proselytization—that shaped the community's distant history.

Several elements of this particular history will be discussed below. More broadly, the Sri Lankan Malays were part of the complex picture of Islam's long-standing presence in the Indian Ocean region, where trade, travel, and Sufi brotherhoods have been central to Islam's dissemination and expansion and where prominent Muslim communities lay claim to Arab descent.[1] In the Indonesian-Malay lands from which the Sri Lankan community's ancestors came, historical evidence points to a slow and gradual Islamization, by which the religion was established in northern Sumatra by the late thirteenth century, in Northeast Malaya, Brunei, and parts of Java in the fourteenth century, in Malacca and additional areas of the Malay Peninsula in the fifteenth century, and in most of the coastal areas of East and Central Java, but not yet its western region or interior, by the sixteenth century.[2] In South India, just across the Gulf of Mannar from Sri Lanka, archaeological evidence suggests an Islamic presence rooted in Arab trade along the Coromandel Coast since the eighth century C.E., whereas the Malabar Coast lay along Arab trade routes since pre-Islamic times.[3] Sri Lanka, also known to the Arabs prior to the advent of Islam, has long been associated with the important pilgrimage site of Adam's Peak, where, according to early Arab traditions, Adam was believed to have fallen from Paradise to earth. The Sumatran, Javanese, Coromandel, Malabar, and Sri Lankan coasts, among others, were part of the Indian Ocean's commercial networks, where towns that functioned as important trade hubs and ports developed into major centers of Islamic learning and culture.[4]

Literature was an important component of Islamic cultural production. Literary engagement—including the circulation of stories; the adoption of literary genres, idioms, and ideas; and the employment of the Arabic script to write their languages—connected Muslims from diverse regions of South and Southeast Asia, producing and sustaining a sense of shared narratives, shared knowledge, and a common past. Thinking about the broad contours of the Sri Lankan Malays' literary culture, and about the "Hikayat Tuan Gusti" in particular, can contribute to our understanding of the interconnectedness of Asian Muslim societies. It also allows us to see how one such society reflected on its past and its present in a period of intensifying global contacts and flows, with such reflections—focusing as they did on a prior globalized epoch—hinting at the diverse ways in which the notion of being globally connected has been understood, expressed, and lived.

I begin by introducing the idea of literary networks. These have served, along with the oft-discussed networks of trade, travel, and Sufi brotherhoods, to connect Muslims of diverse regions and cultures. I then briefly discuss the history of the Malays of Sri Lanka, a community that was deeply invested in literary production and networks. The next section explores the way the "Hikayat Tuan Gusti" represents and remembers this community's conversion to Islam. Finally, I consider what it meant to imagine a pre–print and steam globalized past that continued to exert its influence on those engaged in a globalized present, one marked by reading newspapers, serving in the British police, and educating children in modern schools.

LITERARY NETWORKS

South and Southeast Asia have been, and remain, crucially important to Islamic civilization's circuits and networks, linguistic and cultural diversity, and intellectual and literary output. They are also home to the world's majority of Muslims. A better understanding of the nature of contact, exchange, and transmission among and within these regions offers insight on the broad contours of Islamic history and its local manifestations. Different kinds of networks, often intertwined, traversed these regions, forging connections between and among individuals and communities. To the networks of travel, trade, and Sufi brotherhoods, mentioned above and often presented in the scholarship as the paths by which Islam spread and flourished in these regions, I propose adding the literary networks: these connected Muslims across boundaries of space and culture and helped introduce and sustain a complex web of prior texts and new interpretations crucial to the establishment of both local and global Islamic identities.[5] The literary networks I consider in this chapter comprised many shared works—including stories, poems, genealogies, histories, and treatises on a broad range of topics, written in Arabic and a range of vernaculars—as well as the readers, listeners, authors, translators, and scribes who created the texts, translated and transmitted them, and engaged with them in various ways, thus facilitating the networks, enhancing their reach and significance. Beyond particular texts and individuals, thinking about literary networks means exploring the multilayered histories of contact, selection, interpretation, and serendipity that shaped these transregional networks as we have come to know them.

Many literary works circulating among Muslims were told and retold in local languages that were profoundly influenced and shaped by the influx of Arabic, defined broadly as the bearer of new stories, ideas, beliefs, scripts, and linguistic and literary forms. To a large extent, Muslims across these linguistically and culturally diverse regions shared such inscribed texts, as well as oral sources, poetics, and genres. The written works included biographies of the Prophet Muhammad and the many prophets who preceded him, histories of Islam's early battles in Arabia, theological treatises, poetry, and works on jurisprudence and grammar. These contributed to a common repository of images, memories, and meaning that fostered a consciousness of belonging to a translocal community. The two-way connections many literary works had—both to the larger Islamic world and to local communities—made them dynamic sites of interaction, contestation, and negotiation of boundaries. Competing agendas, as for example between creative and standardizing impulses, often played out in their pages.

That Muslim communities across South and Southeast Asia shared many literary works was a product of the mobility and travels of traders, teachers, and explorers who facilitated the transmission and circulation of written texts, oral knowledge, and the performative traditions that enacted stories and conveyed guidance. As Sheldon Pollock has written, "Literary representations can conceptually organize space, and the dissemination of literary texts can turn that space into a lived reality, as much as space and lived realities condition conceptual organization and dissemination."[6] In its various forms, Islamic literature thus produced a shared space through its circulation.

With that space was created a sociotextual or, more pertinently here, a religio-textual community. This was the community for which literature is produced, in which it circulates and which derives a portion of its self-understanding from hearing, reading, performing, reproducing, and circulating particular texts. Because of Islam's universal message and the presence of Muslims in many world regions, the Islamic space and communities that circulating texts produced in South and Southeast Asia were by definition both local and global. Written in languages such as Tamil and Javanese, these works certainly addressed local and circumscribed audiences. But their content, their reliance on Arabic terminology and genres, and their perspectives on topics from cosmology to mysticism were common across languages, such that they also inspired much wider, cross-cultural and global affiliations. And in addition to producing literature in local languages, diverse communities in South and Southeast Asia had long-standing traditions of writing in Arabic, a vehicle of expression with a cosmopolitan status. The study of Islamic literary cultures thus casts light on how literary dissemination, translation, and adaptation gave rise to a form of religious globalization.

When striving to understand the interconnectedness of Asian Muslim societies, as reflected in circulating stories, literary genres, idioms, and ideas that produced and nurtured a sense of shared narratives and history, there is perhaps no better case to explore than that of the Sri Lankan Malays—a community of Southeast Asian descent living in South Asia.[7] This is also the case when considering how literary networks continued to sustain transregional memories and affiliations into the twentieth century. The Sri Lankan Malays' history, and notably their rich literary output, offers insights on the questions of literary transmission and circulation, networks, and Islamization as remembered and imagined across these regions.

THE SRI LANKAN MALAYS: A BRIEF HISTORY

The history of the present Malay community in Sri Lanka goes back to the middle of the seventeenth century, following the establishment of Dutch rule in the island in 1656.[8] The ancestors of today's community came from diverse backgrounds: many were of Javanese or East Indonesian ancestry, sent to Sri Lanka as political exiles or convicts, servants in various capacities, or soldiers in colonial armies, both Dutch and, at a later stage, British.[9]

A portion of the political exiles were members of ruling families in their home countries. For example, the Javanese ruler Amangkurat III of Kartasura was exiled along with his retinue in 1708, while the king of Gowa was exiled in 1767. Also exiled during the eighteenth century were, among others, the prince of Bantam, the crown prince of Tidore, and the king of Kupang.[10] Another important figure whom the Dutch exiled—even earlier, in 1684—was Shaykh Yusuf of Makassar, a leader, religious scholar, and "saint" from Sulawesi.[11] Such prominent figures had followers who joined them in exile and often also a local following in Sri Lanka.

Some members of the community eventually returned to their places of origin, as was the case when Prince Natakusuma and several other members of the Yogyakarta *kraton* (palace or court) were sent back to Java in 1758 following a request by Mangkubumi (later Sultan Hamengkubuwana I).[12] Many, however, stayed, married, and lived out their lives in Sri Lanka, whether they had a choice or no alternative: among the former were Malay soldiers who refused a 1799 call from the Dutch authorities in Java to "repatriate" after the colony transferred to British hands;[13] among the latter was Siti Hapipa, the widow of the exiled sultan of Gowa (r. 1753–67), whose 1807 letter to the governor-general of the Dutch East Indies in Batavia testifies to great hardship. In it she begs the Dutch administrator to free her from the burden of her deceased husband's debt and in exchange offers to return to Batavia and be at his service.[14]

The largest subgroup of the early Malay population in Sri Lanka was the Malay soldiers who served in the Dutch army, taking part in attacks on Portuguese fortifications in Sri Lanka and the Malabar Coast and in the expeditions against the king of Kandy.[15] After the British took control of Sri Lanka in 1796, and throughout the nineteenth century, many Malays joined the military regiments that they established, serving the new colonial power. The British army's willingness to incorporate them was due in no small measure to British admiration for their military abilities and bravery in opposing the British, as well as the constant need of the British to police the island. In 1873 the Ceylon Rifle Regiment, in which several generations of Malay men had served, was disbanded. The history of the regiment has been explored in depth elsewhere and is beyond the scope of this chapter.[16] What is pertinent to my inquiry, however, is the quite remarkable relationship between life in the regiment and Malay literary culture: members of the regiment copied classical Malay works and wrote their own stories and poems, especially in the form of *syair;*[17] the literature's principal promoters and audiences were related, in one way or another, to the regiment; members of the regiment conducted compulsory lessons for Malay children, instructing them in Malay written in the Gundul script and ensuring that the literature remained intelligible to the next generation;[18] and soldiers who traveled to Malaya on assignment served as a bridge between the community in Sri Lanka and the large Malay centers to the east by guaranteeing a two-way movement of ideas, religious texts, and people between them. Evidence of this multifaceted investment in Malay literary culture is the fact that most Malay manuscripts collected by local scholars in Sri Lanka to date are in the possession of the soldiers' descendants.[19] Some texts, including the "Hikayat Tuan Gusti" (see below), explicitly acknowledge their scribes' status as regiment retirees.

Sri Lankan Malay manuscripts, written and copied throughout the early twentieth century, have survived in archives and private collections. They include many poetic works, early histories of Islam depicting episodes from the Prophet Muhammad's life, literary narratives written in the *hikayat* (tale) genre, and theological treatises. The majority of these works are known from across the Malay world, but certain poems and stories appear to be the products of local creativity.[20] In the mid-to-late nineteenth century, print materials were increasingly entering into circulation among the Sri Lankan Malays, in the form of books and newspapers, both local and from Southeast Asia, especially British Malaya and Singapore. A central figure driving this development was Baba Ounus Saldin (1832–1906) a community leader, editor, literary figure, and pioneer of lithographic printing in Sri Lanka. His press published books and booklets in Malay, Arabic, and Arbu-Tamil, and during the last decades of the century he published three newspapers, including what is considered the world's first Malay newspaper, the *Alamat Langkapuri.*[21]

There is no doubt that these developments gradually transformed the dissemination of information, the nature of the public sphere, and the landscape of reading practices, through what Ian Proudfoot has termed "the silencing of texts," and they were certainly in the background of the story I am telling.[22] However, in this chapter I focus on a textual example of the older tradition, because if we are to consider representations of religious experiences and events, the rootedness of their memory in an earlier globalized era, and the narration of such memories in the Sri Lankan Malay community at the turn of the twentieth century, it is to that literary tradition that we must turn. Among such remembered experiences, the embracing of Islam is perhaps the most momentous.[23]

REMEMBERING CONVERSION TO ISLAM

Countless texts (as well as oral and performative traditions) in many South and Southeast Asian languages narrate conversion to Islam. Such accounts, despite their diversity, often share a great deal. For example, many emphasize the powers and charisma of individuals who carried the new religion from afar, thus high-lighting the tropes of travel and mobility; prominently feature miracles such as feeding the hungry and curing the sick; and often evoke dreams, with rulers waking to find themselves circumcised, conversing in Arabic, or still in awe after a personal encounter with the Prophet.[24]

The 1897 "Hikayat Tuan Gusti," from Sri Lanka, testifies to the persistence of such circulating conversion narratives across South and Southeast Asia. Written in Arabic-script Malay (Gundul) on South Asian soil, not far from the site where, according to Arab traditions, Adam fell from the heavens to earth, the "Hikayat" uses the biography of Sunan Giri, one of the nine Javanese saints (Javanese: *wali sanga*), to tell the story of the island's Islamization.[25] In all of these attributes—site of writing, language, script, and content—the "Hikayat" attests to complex and pro-tracted transmission and circulation patterns that are representative of the work-ings of the Islamic literary networks mentioned above. Such patterns gave rise to interconnected images and echoes of earlier conversions, the loci of religious and cultural transformations of great magnitude that continue to reverberate.

The genealogy of the "Hikayat" is unknown, nor can we be certain about when and how it arrived in Sri Lanka, where its only known copies are, in the form of handwritten manuscripts.[26] Some of its elements are similar to those in Javanese tellings of Sunan Giri's biography.[27] However, no Javanese manuscripts have been found in Sri Lanka to date. Interestingly, narrative of the "Hikayat" is not traceable to any other known Malay literary work from Southeast Asia.[28] This is unusual, as the majority of Malay works written in Sri Lanka are well known in the wider Malay world and can be found in private and public libraries in Indonesia, Malay-sia, Singapore, and Brunei, as well as the United Kingdom and the Netherlands. Besides the "Hikayat," I have been able to locate only a single Malay telling of Sunan Giri's biography, an interlinear translation from Javanese.[29] Whether the "Hikayat" manuscript exemplar is a copy or a translation of an older text, perhaps brought to Sri Lanka in the early eighteenth century by Javanese exiles, or whether it was introduced there in later years, its existence and its content are suggestive of an ongoing circulation of conversion narratives in South and Southeast Asia and of the susceptibility of such narratives to contemporary and differentiated reinterpretation. The "Hikayat" may have been told initially in oral form and then put into writing, offering a particular perspective on the wali (saint) stories and conversion, reimagining conversion on Java to suit local circumstances, and indicating both a transregional connection to the archipelago and a relevance to the local community in Sri Lanka. Although not widely recounted in Malay, the story of the "Hikayat" is, as mentioned, well known in the Javanese tradition, the biography of one of the nine saints who are said to have converted Java to Islam. There is a multitude of versions of these popular stories, in which the prominence of one wali or another is very much region-specific. These stories have many commonalities, as already noted, including the saints arriving from afar, performing miracles, tending to the needy, and accommodating local culture.

The "Hikayat" may well represent the farthest limits of the circulation in manuscript form of the wali tales. It portrays Sunan Giri (designated by the honorific Javanese titles *radèn* and *gusti* and the Malay *tuan* throughout) as the son of the Arabian shaykh Muhiddin. The shaykh, by virtue of his powers of intercession, averted a calamity that was about to befall the kingdom of Palembang (on the island of Sumatra) and in return was given the king's daughter in marriage. He later returned to his land, and the princess, who had converted to Islam but stayed in her country, died in childbirth. Palembang's king feared his infant grandson, whose face glowed like the full moon, and put him in a basket on the river (a motif familiar from the biblical story of Moses and the Javanese chronicles of the Prophet's uncle Ménak Amir Hamzah), but a wealthy merchant woman found and raised the boy. He grew into a man who exhibited many of the characteristics typical of the walis and other Muslim saints: traveling widely, interceding on behalf of the needy, performing miracles, marrying a princess, and propagating Islam.

The portrayal of Sunan Giri as the son of Shaykh Muhiddin is suggestive. The "original" Muhiddin (Arabic: Muhyi al-Din, "reviver of religion") was of course Ibn al-'Arabi, (1165–1240), a celebrated mystic, philosopher, and prolific author, but the epithet is also widely associated with the greatest of all Muslim saints, 'Abd al-Qadir al-Jilani (1077–1166). Although several of the saints are said to have had foreign (most notably, Arab) fathers or ancestors, the intimate connection in this telling between Sunan Giri and a figure of such supreme importance in Muslim history and culture is striking. As a descendant of Shaykh Muhyi al-Din (himself a great preacher of Islam), Sunan Giri had a genealogy that stretched back to the Prophet Muhammad. The appearance of this motif in a Sri Lankan manuscript may reflect its Javanese source. Biographies of the shaykh circulated in Central Java and were (and are) especially popular in the western part of the island.[30] The portrayal of Sunan Giri as Shaykh Muhiddin's son may also be attributed to close contacts between the Malay and Tamil Muslim communities in Sri Lanka, as the shaykh had been a central focus of devotion among Tamil Muslims in South India and Sri Lanka and the subject of a wide array of Tamil literary works since the seventeenth century.[31] According to localized hagiographical traditions, he traveled to places such as Tamil Nadu, Sri Lanka, and Java during his many years of wandering and asceticism before returning to Baghdad at the age of forty, in which case he could have fathered Sunan Giri along the way.

IMAGES OF CONVERSION

The "Hikayat Tuan Gusti" stresses several conversion elements repeatedly while remaining silent on others. It consistently upholds the erection of mosques, prayer (both communal and individual), the recital of the *shahada* (the profession of faith), and the complete shunning of idolatry (Malay: *berhala*). The narrative highlights the last in particular when it opens with an idol worshipped by the Palembang king falling to the ground and shattering, signifying approaching doom for nonbelievers. Throughout the "Hikayat," Sunan Giri and his representatives remind different communities that they encounter to refrain from resorting to idolatry. This may reflect the author's concerns in late nineteenth-century Buddhist-majority Sri Lanka, projected on an earlier, imagined Java. The story also emphasizes belief in and devotion to the Prophet, as well as the adoption of a new name on conversion. For example, when the Palembang princess Dewi Aranadani converts before marrying the shaykh, she is given the name Siti Jini.

War, violence, and threats toward those who refuse to convert are significant in this telling. This tendency distinguishes the "Hikayat" from many (although by no means all) Javanese wali narratives, which tend to stress accommodation and peaceful means in the conversion process. For instance, when the great infidel king of Kartasuru (likely Kartasura in central Java) sends a messenger to demand that Sunan Giri pay him tribute, the messenger is told to convert but refuses, only to be humiliated and sent home. The king is furious, gathers many allies and a large army, and charges at Giri. The sunan calls on God for help, and a great swarm of bees appears, attacking the enemy. After the king is killed, Sunan Giri announces that any caught opponent should be bound but not put to death unless he refuses to accept Islam. The people of Kartasuru joyfully agree to convert and return to their land along with two hundred tutors, leaders, and muezzins from Giri who will teach them the five pillars of Islam, including the profession of faith, and how to build mosques. The "Hikayat" contains several episodes portraying an acceptance of Islam after military defeat and under circumstances of significant threat.

Anxiety about the possibility of a reversal of faith—of converts reverting to old ways—is palpable in the "Hikayat." In several instances, Sunan Giri or his confidant Sunan Panji remind audiences of those who had converted under his influence (spiritual or military) not to go back on their commitment. For example, after being defeated by Sunan Giri, the king of 'Alenggar embraces Islam. His subjects follow his path, and he instructs them to limit or eliminate their idol worship, build a mosque, and recite the shahada and daily prayers, after which they are pronounced to be "perfected in the faith" (Malay: *sempurna beriman*). Then,

> one Friday all people gathered at the mosque along with the gurus, leaders, and king. They convened at the mosque and prayed and read the sermon. Then Sunan Panji spoke to those attending the Friday prayer, saying, "Listen, all of you: old and young, leaders and king. I command you all to not forget the five daily prayers and the Friday prayer. I will soon return to my land. After spending four years here I shall sail away tomorrow."
>
> When all those present had heard Sunan Panji's words they replied, "Yes, our lord Sunan, none of us will forget to pray and recite the Qur'an, and all that you have taught us we will never forsake. And if you meet Tuan Gusti, please convey our respect and greetings so that he may not forget us."[32]

Following this episode, Sunan Panji seeks out the king and speaks to him in person, reinforcing his message: "'Do not rule as you previously did. Rule according to the Qur'anic prescriptions and maintain the words of the Qur'an as your highest priority.' The king replies: 'Yes, I will never give precedence to anything above the words of the Qur'an or those of Sunan Giri.'"[33]

Before Sunan Panji takes his leave the following day, the king, like his subjects, asks the sunan to convey his respect and greetings to Sunan Giri. The concern that those newly converted would forsake Islam—depicted in this scene and others—is countered, or mirrored, by the converts' eagerness to be remembered by Sunan Giri (referred to as Tuan Gusti), the man who first introduced them to Islam. Both sides perceive that a sense of doubt, loss, and elusiveness is inherent in conversion, which highlights its stakes. Ambiguity pervades the process, in which a sense of insecurity mixes with triumphant confidence, military imposition collides with long-held beliefs, and charismatic personalities from afar encounter local kings, ministers, ascetics, and gurus.

The sense of conversion's precariousness perhaps relates to the imposed acceptance of Islam, as depicted in the "Hikayat," or, once again, reflects the Muslim community's sense of vulnerability as a minority in Sri Lankan society. There is a kind of ambivalence in the "Hikayat Tuan Gusti," a narrative that translated and transmitted the experience of Javanese conversion to South Asia, admonishing new converts to Islam, perceived as still wavering among deeds, words, and new and old beliefs, to remain Muslim but depicting them as eager to be recognized and remembered, to be accepted into the fold. The emphasis on the erection of mosques, communal prayer, and the Friday sermon (khutbah, from Arabic and Malay) points to the significance accorded to Islamizing practices, which would strengthen the emerging community, leading the individuals who had recently joined it to fortify their faith.

Sunan Giri also resorts to other means of acquiring and preserving authority— and thus the power Islam will hold over his followers—to be passed down through his line of descent.[34] Toward the end of the "Hikayat," he tells Sunan Panji to deliver iron to a blacksmith (Malay: *tukang besi*) so that the expert craftsman can produce a kris (Malay: *keris*). A kind of dagger, the kris was both a weapon and a highly charged spiritual object. It was a sacred heirloom passed down through the generations, particularly valued and guarded by the families of Java's ruling class. Sunan Panji immediately asks Sunan Giri to specify the quantity of iron required, and the latter instructs him to give the blacksmith forty *kati* so that the weight of the kris can be twenty.[35] Sunan Panji summons a blacksmith by the name of Pandita Qadiman, who hurries to meet Sunan Giri, trembling with awe and repeatedly paying obeisance and conveying his respect. After he receives the iron and is told the desired weight of the kris, Pandita Qadiman takes his leave and journeys to a place called ʿAsiqin, where he meditates and performs austerities (*bertapa*), including refraining from food, for forty days and nights. This is meant to generate the special powers needed to produce a kris, as the "Hikayat" states explicitly that the heat for welding it should come not from a burning fire but from the inner fire that these ascetic practices (Malay and Arabic: ʿamal) create. Although the "Hikayat" does not go into complex details of the art of kris making, its mention of the iron's weight and the blacksmith's retreat and austerities hint at the critical importance of measurements, materials, and especially the spiritual powers of the maker that Javanese and Malay societies thought were indispensable to producing a potent and supernaturally endowed kris.[36]

Sunan Giri is pleased with the kris, described as exceedingly beautiful, and pays the artisan forty dirhams in gold, perhaps a gold coin for every kati of iron he had received. Then Sunan Gusti endows the kris with a name, Bintang Awan, a common practice that personalizes the kris and is often related to its owner's personality, deeds, or wishes. Finally, he stores the dagger above the pulpit (minbar) in his mosque, in the niche (mihrab) in the wall that indicates the qibla, the direction of Mecca and thus of Muslim prayer.[37]

This brief scene is telling. Javanese histories link tales of great armorers with the appearance of the walis, the bearers of Islam, often depicted as patrons of the armorers' art.[38] This connection between the saints' wisdom and blacksmiths' knowledge, especially in the literature of the Pasisir period (fifteenth to seventeenth centuries), likely points to a coinciding of the arrival of Islam and a flourishing of trade and the arts on the coasts of northeastern Java (especially in Giri and Surabaya).[39] It may also have been an attempt by Javanese authors to reconcile pre-Islamic sites and objects of power with the newly emerging authority of Islam. The connections among Sunan Giri, the art and practice of kris making, and the centrality of the mosque as the keeping place of the kris suggest that the "Hikayat" was transmitted to Sri Lanka from the Pasisir region of Java, which can be said to be the cradle of Javanese Islam. This region was also the seat of power of Sunan Giri's descendants, where they ruled with political and religious command in the sixteenth and seventeenth centuries.[40]

In both these respects—as the site of early conversion and as a center of an expanding Islamic influence—the region possesses a powerful hold on the imaginations of those who recollect the Islamization of Java. I can only speculate on how much of this history was known to those reading or listening to the "Hikayat" in late nineteenth-century Sri Lanka, but it may well be that this kind of story was passed down through the generations, itself—like the kris—an heirloom to guard and revere.

LOOKING BACK TO AN EARLIER ERA OF GLOBALIZATION?

What was and is the significance of reading the "Hikayat Tuan Gusti"? Why did members of the Malay community in Sri Lanka hold it in high esteem and retell it into the twentieth century?[41] What does its reading tell us about the way Islamization was committed to memory, about the role of literary networks and the Malay community's embeddedness in both local and global contexts at this historical moment? In the final lines of the "Hikayat," Sunan Giri is preaching at his mosque on Friday and, once again, reminding his audience not to forget to recite the shahada, to pray five times a day, to recite the Qur'an, to refrain from doing evil and eating forbidden foods. The list goes on until, for the first time in the "Hikayat" and immediately before its closing lines, he speaks of the Day of Judgment, the threat of hell, and the promise of paradise. This section is laced with untranslated Arabic terms (such as *haram, mu'min, yawm al-qiyama, 'amal,* and *yatim*), indicating a Muslim ethos pervading the story, one that nonetheless required repeated reinforcement. Although admonitions to remain Muslim appear throughout the story, their detail and tone gradually intensify, reaching a climax in this final section. Here conversion and its stakes are projected on long-ago Java but also echo for contemporary listeners in Sri Lanka engaging with, and remembering, the story and its message. In this address, Sunan Giri's words—represented as direct speech—resound beyond the inner realm of the text, reaching the ears of those gathered in Colombo and Kandy, instructing and guiding them, collapsing the boundaries between past and present.[42]

Reading the "Hikayat" in early twentieth-century British-ruled Sri Lanka was not solely about remembering conversion. It was also about reaching back toward an earlier globalized age, one in which Islamic civilization was spreading into new terrain—including Southeast Asia—incorporating additional peoples and cultures into its global fold. Although that earlier period did not witness the steamship or the nation-state, textual sources represent it too as characterized by powerful forms of mobility, connectedness, and interdependence. At a time when the various religious and ethnic communities making up colonial Sri Lanka's social fabric were exploring new means of identification and expression, including emerging nationalist sentiments, the Malays—a minority even within the Muslim population of the island—could connect with a proud past through the "Hikayat" and also employ it to shape their distinct communal identity in the present.[43] That identity—including its budding political dimension—was increasingly important in the first decades of the twentieth century. In 1921, following a mass meeting in Colombo, a decision was made to establish the first Malay political association in Sri Lanka and to peti- tion the British authorities to concede a Malay seat in the legislative council. In words that resonate with the tale that the "Hikayat" narrates, of the Islamization of the Malays' forefathers, the memorandum sent to Governor William Manning urg- ing a consideration of political rights for Malays states that "the Malays of the island form a distinct and separate community, still preserving the ancient habits, cus- toms and their own language. . . . They are members of the great Malay community, spread over the Far East and counting some fifty million souls."[44]

This statement underscores a sentiment of belonging to a wider Malay world, a world to the southeast and from which many of the early ancestors of the petition writers had been sent by force. Indeed, the exilic dimension of Sri Lankan Malay history is part of a larger picture of exile and diaspora across the Indian Ocean (and beyond) under colonialism, a theme that several other chapters in this vol- ume note. In the next two chapters, respectively, Jeremy Prestholdt discusses the exile of Sultan Barghash and Nasir bin Sulayman al-Lamki, the editor of *Al-Najah,* from Zanzibar to India, while Homayra Ziad notes that a grandfather of the Indian modernist scholar ʿAbd al-Majid Daryabadi was exiled from India to the Anda- man Islands. Within the vast expanse of empire were sites of both home and exile. Exile could be brief or long, a rather pleasant learning experience (as was the case for Sultan Barghash in Bombay in 1860) or a harsh imprisonment. It could consti- tute an immediate lived reality or a distant memory. In the case of the Sri Lankan Malays, a history of displacement and exile crossed not only space but also the temporal boundary between one empire's rule and that of another. Although those living in the late nineteenth century were personally removed from the experi- ence, its echoes continued to resound in their present, as clearly evidenced in the phrasing of the plea to the governor.

Reading the "Hikayat" and other Sri Lankan texts in the present invites us to rethink the boundaries of the Malay world. It also provides clear evidence for ties, interactions, and exchanges among Muslim communities across Indonesia, Sri Lanka, South India, and elsewhere, pointing to circulation and transmission pat- terns that have often been difficult to confirm, in part because of the fragmentary nature of the available evidence. The "Hikayat" allows us to examine an important dimension of such transregional contact across Islamic societies—the participa- tion in literary networks, central to the Malay community's sense of identity for at least two centuries. Similar to the Muslims in colonial Aden whom Scott S. Reese's chapter 3 discusses, the Sri Lankan Malays were a Muslim community living in an imperial web. As such, they maintained networks—both tangible and symbolic—both across British imperial space and across empires into the Dutch East Indies. The Malay language and its texts provided key foci of contact, communication, and cohesion.

In closing, I would like to consider how the word *travel* can encapsulate the significance of the "Hikayat" and its relationships to the broader issues of literary networks, Islamization, and memory that I have raised. In a way, the "Hikayat" is a form of early travel literature. Although it shares some of the features of later literature of this genre that emphasizes discovery and detailed descriptions, the "Hikayat" has different goals and a different texture. It underscores movement and travel for the purposes of trade, acquiring knowledge, and propagating Islam, and it highlights the journeys of Shaykh Muhiddin, Sunan Giri's father, from Arabia to Southeast Asia and of Sunan Giri himself throughout his career, as well as those of sailors, merchants, and soldiers. Thinking about the "Hikayat" within the paradigm of travel writing may help us see more clearly the significance of mobility—of individuals, ideas, and beliefs—both in the narrative and in its interpretive frameworks. And the contacts, disseminations, and contractions of distance—whether physical or symbolic—that these forms of mobility allowed were certainly not first invented in the nineteenth century.

When we think about movement and travel in the Muslim world, we find their epitomes in the hajj, a theme explored in detail in Eric Tagliacozzo's chapter 5 and Homayra Ziad's chapter 11. Sri Lanka is on the route from the Malay Archipelago to Arabia, and ships filled with pilgrims used to stop at its shores on their way to the holy cities. Even before and certainly after the advent of the steamship, this annual movement of people allowed for contact between Sri Lankan Malays and pilgrims from the wide Indonesian-Malay world from which their ancestors had come. It may be that the more frequent arrival of ships as the nineteenth century progressed created a renewed sense of connection to those lands and revived awareness of a past shared with both the pilgrims and, in a broader sense, all Muslims. Attributes associated with globalization—accelerating technology, efficiency, and speed—crossed paths and interacted with perceptions of an earlier period in which Islam had dramatically extended its geographical and cultural reach. As service in the Malay regiment, with its rich literary culture, faded into the past, as distances grew smaller and the forward-moving ships and ideals of modernity seemed to prevail, so a concurrent movement back in time and space was also found, pointing to the ways in which multiple temporalities can coexist and overlap.

This travel back in time is also worth considering in assessing a text such as the "Hikayat Tuan Gusti" as a source for thinking about history and its diverse representations. Although the histories of the walis have often been regarded as fantastic, mythical tales that are either entirely fictional or at best contain a grain of barely recognizable truth, these biographies—if placed in context both in Java and, much later, in Sri Lanka—can reveal something about how authors in both places revised the past that their predecessors transmitted to them to bring it into line with contemporary needs.[45] One seemingly minor difference between Sunan Giri's biography as told in Java and the one told in Sri Lanka may hint in this direction: in Javanese versions, he eventually meets his long-lost father. In the Malay "Hikayat," Shaykh Muhiddin returns to Arabia after fathering Sunan Giri, planting a seed in faraway Java but never traveling back to meet his son. We may think of the Sri Lankan Malays as never having met their "father" or "family" in a metaphorical sense but nonetheless, like Sunan Giri, able to create a new community of Muslims.

In his introduction to the anthology *Other Routes: 1500 Years of African and Asian Travel Writing,* Tabish Khair writes that "travel, then, is not just a matter of going away. It is also a matter of coming back, even when the return never takes place in person. It is this Janus-faced aspect of travel that makes it impossible to separate the 'imaginary' elements of travel from the 'real' elements."[46] For the Malays of Sri Lanka, the "Hikayat" was a such way of returning, even if not in person and only as a journey or a pilgrimage of the imagination. The travels depicted and foregrounded in the "Hikayat" represent Sri Lankan Malays' travels to their shared past. These shared ancestry and places that used to be called home were part of a past that connected them to the communities of Southeast Asia and the global Muslim community. Finally, the journeys of Sunan Giri in the "Hikayat" reflect the travels of the story itself along transregional literary networks, the memories it carried, and the representations it transmitted and sustained.

NOTES

I thank B. A. Hussainmiya and B. D. K. Saldin for generously sharing their knowledge of the Sri Lankan Malay community with me, and John Rogers for inviting me to present a paper on the Sri Lankan Malays in Colombo. Thanks also to James Gelvin, Nile Green, Charley Hallisey, Ian Proudfoot, Bhavani Raman, and Jonathan Spencer for helpful comments and suggestions. An earlier version of this chapter (with the same title) appeared in the Asia Research Institute Working Papers Series (no. 153, June 2011).

1. These communities include, among others, the Moors of Sri Lanka and the Maraikkayars of Tamil Nadu, India. On the Moors, see M. A. M. Shukri, introduction to *Muslims of Sri Lanka: Avenues to Antiquity,* ed. Shukri (Beruwala, Sri Lanka: Jamiah Naleemia Institute, 1986), 21; Asiff Hussain, *Sarandib: An Ethnological Study of the Muslims of Sri Lanka* (Dehiwala–Mount Lavinia, Sri Lanka: A. J. Prints, 2007), 2–21. *Moor* is a contested appellation. On the controversy, see Dennis B. McGilvray, "Arabs, Moors and Muslims: Sri Lankan Muslim Ethnicity in Regional Perspective," *Contributions to Indian Sociology* 32 (1998): 433–83.

2. Merle Calvin Ricklefs, *A History of Modern Indonesia since c. 1200,* 4th ed. (Stanford, CA: Stanford University Press, 2008), 3–10.

3. On the Islamization of the Tamil region, see Susan Elizabeth Schomburg, "'Reviving Religion': The Qadiri Sufi Order, Popular Devotion to Sufi Saint Muhyiuddin ʿAbdul Qadir al-Gilani and

Processes of 'Islamization' in Tamil" (PhD dissertation, Harvard University, 2003), 19–20. On Malabar, see Sebastian R. Prange, "Like Banners on the Sea: Muslim Trade Networks and Islamization in Malabar and Maritime Southeast Asia," in *Islamic Connections: Muslim Societies in South and Southeast Asia*, ed. R. Michael Feener and Terenjit Sevea (Singapore: Institute of Southeast Asian Studies, 2009), 28–29.

4. On the relationship between trade and Islam in these regions, see Andre Wink, "*Al-Hind*: India and Indonesia in the Islamic World Economy, c. 700–1800 A.D.," in *India and Indonesia during the Ancien Regime* (Leiden, Netherlands: Brill, 1989), 48–49; Kenneth McPherson, *The Indian Ocean: A History of People and the Sea* (New Delhi: Oxford University Press, 1993), 76–78.

5. For an expanded discussion of the issues this section raises, see Ronit Ricci, *Islam Translated: Literature, Conversion, and the Arabic Cosmopolis of South and Southeast Asia* (Chicago: University of Chicago Press, 2011).

6. Sheldon Pollock, introduction to *Literary Cultures in History: Reconstructions from South Asia*, ed. Pollock (Berkeley: University of California Press, 2003), 27.

7. These twenty-first-century regional designations (and nation-state names) are clearly anachronistic, but they serve to highlight how our current divisions of the world obscure very different earlier mappings. From the mid-seventeenth century until the end of the eighteenth, both present-day Sri Lanka and Indonesia were part of Dutch Asia.

8. For evidence of a precolonial Malay presence in Sri Lanka, see Hussein, *Sarandib*, 408; B. D. K. Saldin, *The Sri Lankan Malays and Their Language: Orang Melayu Sri Lanka dan Bahasanya* (self-published, 2001), 1–4.

9. The appellations used to identify the community have shifted over time. The British, since their arrival in Sri Lanka in 1796, commonly used *Malay*, based first and foremost on the group's collective language. This name received added currency with the arrival of newcomers from the British settlements of Malaya and Singapore in the nineteenth century. Previously, the Dutch had referred to the community as the Easterners (*Oosterlingen*), another blanket term that did not hint at the diversity of their home regions, although some Dutch sources also use the designation Javanese (*Javaans*). See B. A. Hussainmiya, *Lost Cousins: The Malays of Sri Lanka* (Bangi, Malaysia: Universiti Kebangsaan Malaysia, 1987), 55–57. At present, the "Malays" are known as "people from Java" in Sinhala (*Ja minnusu*) and in Tamil (*Java manucar*) and as *Malai karar* (Malay people) among the Moors; they refer to themselves as both *orang Jawa* and *orang Melayu* (Javanese and Malay people, respectively). This shifting nomenclature, its imposition from without and adoption from within at different periods, and its relationship to the ways in which the past was understood and narrated are beyond the scope of this chapter, but I plan to study them further. Premodern Arabic writings widely use the term *Jawa*, or more often *Jawi*, to refer to all Southeast Asian Muslims. See Michael F. Laffan, "Finding Java: Muslim Nomenclature of Insular Southeast Asia from Srivijaya to Snouck Hurgronje," in *Southeast Asia and the Middle East: Islam, Movement and the Long Durée*, ed. Eric Tagliacozzo (Singapore: National University of Singapore Press, 2009), 17–64. In the case of Sri Lanka, however, *orang Jawa* seems to indicate a particular connection to Java.

10. B. A. Hussainmiya, *Orang Rejimen: The Malays of the Ceylon Rifle Regiment* (Bangi, Malaysia: Universiti Kebangsaan Malaysia, 1990): 39.

11. Shaykh Yusuf spent several years in Sri Lanka before being exiled yet farther, to South Africa, where he died and where his tomb still attracts large numbers of pilgrims.

12. Merle Calvin Ricklefs, *Jogjakarta under Sultan Mangkubumi, 1749–1792: A History of the Division of Java* (London: Oxford University Press, 1974), 102.

13. Saldin, *Sri Lankan Malays*, 8.

14. Siti Hapipa, quoted in Suryadi, "Sepucuk Surat Dari Seorang Bangsawan Gowa di Tanah Pembuangan (Ceylon)," *Wacana: Jurnal ilmu Pengetahuan Budaya* 10, no. 2 (2008): 222–26.

15. Hussainmiya, *Orang Rejimen*, 44.

16. See, e.g., ibid.

17. The syair is a form of traditional Malay poetry of four-line stanzas. It is thought to derive from a form of Arabic poetry and to have first been formulated in Malay by the Sufi writer Hamzah Fansuri in the sixteenth century. On different scholars' perspectives on the syair's origins, see Ismail Hamid, *The Malay Islamic Hikayat* (Kuala Lumpur: Universiti Kebangsaan Malaysia, 1983), 39.

18. Malay written in Arabic script is known as Jawi across much of Southeast Asia, whereas in Java, *Gundul* (which means "bald") refers to the Javanese language written in an unvocalized form of the Arabic script. Interestingly, Sri Lankan Malays have retained this Javanese term, yet they use it to describe Malay writing. This may attest to the dominance of Javanese among the early exiles.

19. Saldin, *Sri Lankan Malays,* 11–12.

20. Examples of trans-Malay works include "Hikayat Sri Rama," "Hikayat Ahmad Muhammad," "Hikayat Amir Hamzah," and "Sirat al-Mustaqim." Examples of local Malay works include "Hikayat Tuan Gusti," "Syair Syaikh Fadlun," and a host of additional syairs and pantuns.

21. On Baba Ounus Saldin's life and achievements, see B. A. Hussainmiya, "Baba Ounus Saldin: An Account of a Malay Literary Savant of Sri Lanka, 1832–1906," *Journal of the Malaysian Branch of the Royal Asiatic Society* 64, no. 2 (1991): 103–34. In addition to publishing in Sri Lanka, Baba Ounus Saldin imported books from Southeast Asia, which he often advertised in the *Alamat Langkapuri.*

22. Ian Proudfoot, "From Recital to Sight Reading: The Silencing of Texts in Malaysia," *Indonesia and the Malay World* 30, no. 87 (2002): 117–44.

23. Not all the members of the early Malay community in Sri Lanka in Dutch times were Muslims. Some who came from Bali, Ambon, and Java were not, though it is often difficult to establish their religious identity with certainty. However, the majority were Muslim, and with time Islam and the Malay language came to be common features of and to define the community. See Hussainmiya, *Lost Cousins,* 58.

24. See, for example, Russell Jones, "Ten Conversion Myths from Indonesia," in *Conversion to Islam,* ed. Nehemia Levtzion (New York: Holmes and Meier, 1979), 129–58; D. A. Rinkes, *Nine Saints of Java,* trans. H. M. Froger (Kuala Lumpur: Malaysian Sociological Research Institute, 1996); Shaik Hasan Sahib S. A. Qadhiri, *The Divine Light of Nagore* (Nagore, India: Habeen and Fahira, 1998).

25. According to tradition, Sunan Giri died in 1506 and is buried in Gresik, on Java.

26. The discussion below is based on Subedar Mursit, "Hikayat Tuan Gusti" 1897, microfilm reel 182, Hussainmiya Collection, Department of National Archives, Colombo. The author self-identifies as a retiree of the Ceylon Rifle Regiment; *subedar* refers to his rank, "chief Indian officer," in the British colonial army. The final lines (with my punctuation) read: "Tamat Hikayat Tuan Gusti yaum alsabt jam dua tengari bulan Sa'aban 21 bulan Inggris 22 Januari hijrah 1897. Menulis Subedar Mursit pension Selon Raifil Rajimit. Jua adapun aku pesan pada sekalian tuan yang suka membaca hikayat ini jangan saka qalbunya supaya dirahmatkan Allah subhan wa ta'ala dari dunya sampai keakirat." ("Thus ends the Hikayat Tuan Gusti, Saturday at 2 P.M., Sha'aban 21, the English month of January 22, 1897. Written by Subedar Mursit, a retiree of the Ceylon Rifle Regiment. I instruct all those who find pleasure in reading this hikayat: do not allow it to leave [drift from] your heart, so that you may be granted the mercy of God—may he be glorified and exalted—in this world and the next.")

27. For a recent retelling of Sunan Giri's life in Indonesian, based on the eighteenth-century Javanese *Serat Centhini,* see M. Hariwijaya, *Kisah Para Wali* (Yogyakarta, Indonesia: Nirwana, 2003), 62–102.

28. Hussainmiya, *Orang Rejimen,* 137.

29. Antoine Cabaton, "Raden Paku, Sunan de Giri (Légende musulmane javanaise): Texte malais, traduction française et notes," *Revue de l'histoire des religions* 54 (1906): 374–400. This is a much abridged version.

30. See, e.g., 'Abd al-Qādir al-Jīlānī, *Celebration of the Desires through the Narration of the Deeds ("Manaqib") of the Crown of Saints and the Convincing Beacon among Allah's Beloved Friends, Sheikh*

Abdul Qadir al-Jaelani, May Allah Bless His Secret Essence, trans. Julian Millie (Queenscliff, Victoria, Australia: Joseph Helmi, 2003).

31. Schomburg, "'Reviving Religion,'" 375–463, discusses no fewer than fourteen genres in which Tamil works on the saint were composed.

32. Mursit, "Hikayat Tuan Gusti," 96–97. All translations of the "Hikayat" are mine; I have also added punctuation, which does not appear in the Malay manuscript.

33. Ibid., 97.

34. Sunan Giri was the founder of a line of spiritual lords that lasted until 1680, while none of the other walis had successors to their authority. Ricklefs, *History of Modern Indonesia,* 41.

35. A kati equals 625 grams (1.38 pounds), or 16 *tahil*. The tahil (Javanese: *tail;* Chinese: *tael*) was widely used for weighing gold, silver, and opium. See R. J. Wilkinson, *Malay-English Dictionary* (London: Macmillan, 1959), 1149.

36. Blacksmiths and other master craftsmen (including poets) were often endowed with the title *empu,* or *mpu,* which carried magical or mystical associations. The "Hikayat" does not employ this title for the pandita. Several Malay families in Sri Lanka still possess krises brought from Indonesia by their ancestors.

37. Apparently, privileged visitors to the mosque can still view Sunan Giri's kris. In 2009 the then vice-presidential candidate Prabowo Subianto paid a visit to Sunan Giri's tomb in Gresik and was allowed to see and even touch the kris. Yoni Iskandar, "Pegang Keris Sunan Giri, Prabowo Bakal Jadi Wapres?," *Kompas,* 24 June 2009, http://nasional.kompas.com/read/2009/06/24/16561762/Pegang. Keris.Sunan.Giri.Prabowo.Bakal.Jadi.Wapres (accessed 17 June 2013). The practice of placing a kris in the mihrab deserves further research but appears to be quite unusual.

38. The walis are also often depicted as patrons of other art forms, including music and the wayang shadow theater in Southeast Asia.

39. Theodore G. T. Pigeaud, *The Literature of Java,* 3 vols. (The Hague: Martinus Nijhoff, 1967–70), 1:278, speculates on the possibility that increasing amounts of steel were traded along the coast during this period. To Tome Pires, a Portuguese traveler of the fifteenth century, Gresik, a nearby trading center, was "the jewel of Java in trading ports" (quoted in Ricklefs, *History of Modern Indonesia,* 41).

40. The main reason to believe that the "Hikayat" is of eastern Pasisir provenance is that Sunan Giri figures so prominently in it. As mentioned, the veneration of particular walis has often been region-specific.

41. In interviews with community members, B. A. Hussainmiya found that the "Hikayat" was popular in the late nineteenth and early twentieth centuries (personal communication).

42. For a similar narrative strategy of "pulling" the reader or listener into the story in a different religious tradition (the Hellenic world of the third century C.E.), see John Elsner, "Hagiographic Geography: Travel and Allegory in the Life of Apollonius of Tyana," *Journal of Hellenic Studies* 117 (1997): 28.

43. On the social and political activism of Sri Lankan Muslims in this period, including a comparison with contemporary Sri Lankan Hindu and Buddhist movements, see Vijaya Samaraweera, "Aspects of the Muslim Revivalist Movement in Late Nineteenth Century Sri Lanka," in Shukri, *Muslims of Sri Lanka,* 363–83.

44. Quoted in Hussainmiya, *Lost Cousins,* 14. Hussainmiya also discusses certain tensions between the Malay and Moor Muslim communities in this period and contends that the former "endeavoured to define their identity more clearly as the scions of an Eastern civilization rather than the inheritors of a Muslim civilization claimed by the Tamil speaking Moors as the descendents of the Arabs, and the Indians" (20).

45. In thinking about this aspect of reading the "Hikayat," I have benefited from Felice Lifshitz's "Beyond Positivism and Genre: 'Hagiographical' Texts as Historical Narrative," *Viator* 25 (1994): 95–113. In her critical discussion of historians' anachronistic use of *hagiography* to describe the lives of saints

written in the ninth to eleventh centuries in Europe, she notes that in that period, biographers departed from accepted writing models to "enmesh the saint's activities explicitly within a larger historical context . . . particularly concerning issue of burning concern such as when and how an area was first converted to Christianity" (99–100).

46. Tabish Khair, "African and Asian Travel Texts in the Light of Europe: An Introduction," in *Other Routes: 1500 Years of African and Asian Travel Writing,* ed. Khair, Martin Leer, Justin D. Edwards, and Hanna Ziadeh (Oxford: Signal, 2006), 2.

10

From Zanzibar to Beirut

Sayyida Salme bint Said and the Tensions of Cosmopolitanism

Jeremy Prestholdt

INTRODUCTION

This chapter explores concepts of space and relation at the turn of the twentieth century. Specifically, I concentrate on globalism in Zanzibari public discourse and the cognitive maps of individual perception. I focus closely on the voluminous writings of the first Zanzibari, indeed the first Arab woman, to publish her memoirs: Emily Ruete, born Sayyida Salme bint Said, a daughter of the sultan of Zanzibar. Ruete's autobiography, *Memoiren einer arabischen Prinzessin* (Memoirs of an Arabian princess; 1886), narrates a series of seeming contradictions. Ruete eloped with a German merchant and converted to Christianity, but she became a fierce defender of Islam; she was an East African woman of Omani, Persian, and Georgian descent who assimilated into bourgeois German society but found cultural solace only in Beirut. Her writings, which also include a great many letters and a treatise on Syria, are among the most detailed reflections on cosmopolitanism and global interconnectivity composed by a Zanzibari. Ruete's body of work thus provides a unique window on self-definition, the imagination of supranational space, and the constitution of a world view in the Age of Steam and Print.

The late nineteenth century was a period of expanding European empires intent on redefining political geography. Yet, as James L. Gelvin and Nile Green argue in the introduction to this volume, imperial cartographies determined only the superstructure of global interconnectivity. Multiple social imaginaries shaped the colonial world. In this chapter I outline ways of seeing that were influenced by new communication and transportation technologies but that reflected more pluralist visions of global interrelation than did the Western concept of modernity. In Zanzibar, an island entrepôt so closely connected with southeastern Arabia that it had once served as the capital of the Sultanate of Oman and Zanzibar, new fashions and transregional solidarities evidenced the reconceptualization of historical relationships, while migration, travel, and exile facilitated entirely new transoceanic networks.

To address these themes I begin with a meditation on the modes of cosmopolitanism evident in the Indian Ocean region at the turn of the twentieth century. To contextualize Ruete's itinerary and writings, I then shift my focus to how Zanzibari intellectuals interpreted the late nineteenth-century world and their place in it. For instance, increased travel and the wider circulation of print literature shaped reformist movements among Shafi'i thinkers, adherents of one of the most prominent schools of law in Sunni Islam, and Ibadis, followers of a small sect of Islam concentrated in Oman and Zanzibar. These movements in turn scrutinized local praxis in relation to ideas emanating from Algeria, Egypt, Turkey, and the Hadramawt. Circuits of information in some cases rooted in older networks of Islamic learning contributed to a pan-Islamist world view that imagined Muslim cooperation as a means to challenge European empires in East Africa and the wider Indian Ocean region.

In the second half of the essay I narrow my focus to Ruete's reflections on East Africa, western Europe, Egypt, and the Levant. Her body of work highlights the transoceanic linkages resulting from Zanzibar's central position at East Africa's interface with Arabia, South Asia, the Mediterranean, and western Europe. Penned over two decades, Ruete's observations offer a rich interpretation of the interconnected world of the late nineteenth century as well as what she saw as the substantial cultural disconnect between Muslim societies and Western metropoles. Ruete wrote nostalgically of Islam as a moral community of sentiment in the Mediterranean and Indian Ocean regions.[1] Her cognitive map traces what we might think of as an informal pan-Islamism. Rather than the pan-Islamist political vision of the Khilafat movement, which Homayra Ziad discusses in chapter 11, Ruete's work exhibits a more sentimental pan-Islamism, rooted in the perception of moral commonality across the Arabic-speaking Mediterranean and western Indian Ocean regions. She extolled a cosmopolitan, Muslim eastern Mediterranean sphere that exhibited a cultural extroversion lacking in Europe and southern Arabia. This idealized rendering of urban Levantine society, as I suggest in the final section, was the product of her personal history of alienation, dual Muslim-Christian identity, and desire for belonging. In Ruete's writings we can discern a cosmopolitanism born in the crucible of new concepts of space yet predicated on an ambiguous identity. European imperialism shaped the subjectivities of Emily Ruete and other Zanzibaris of her generation. At the same time, theirs was a world fashioned by myriad lateral connectivities and visions of alternative modes of global relation.

PERCEPTION AND THE WORLD

Studies of the economic and cultural dimensions of global integration have greatly enriched our appreciation of globalizing trends, past and present. What has received less scholarly attention is the question of how perceptions of the world as an integrated whole affect social, economic, and political realities.[2] The perceptual dimensions of global integration are often difficult to access, but the sense of the world becoming more interdependent is nonetheless a powerful social force. We might think of this cognitive realization as global consciousness, an awareness of the planet as a field of profound interrelation.[3] As a concept, global consciousness highlights the effects of communication technologies and mobility on cognition. Just as important, it emphasizes perception in the creation of linkages across space. Similar to transsocietal economic exchanges, global consciousness can be tracked across time as an ebb and flow that informs desires and actions. By focusing on changing perceptions, we may see globalization as more than a heuristic device or the measurable intensification of transnational relations. Reflection on individual and collective cognizance of planetary conditions demonstrates that globalization is also a popular spatial sensibility.[4]

Our way of perceiving and understanding the world, indeed our presumption that it is globalizing, shapes the material and digital realms that commonly draw our attention. Public and foreign policy, trade and investment are often predicated on the notion that distant places are immediately relevant to our everyday lives. Scholars have pointed to a number of similarities between globalization in the present and the economic, social, and cultural shifts of the fin de siècle. Of these similarities, profound perceptual shifts offer some of the most striking parallels. For instance, Stephen Kern has demonstrated that the combination of the telegraph, steam technology, and photography in the nineteenth century, augmented by cinema and radio in the early twentieth, had considerable effects on popular perceptions of time and space. These new perceptions transformed the arts, sciences, and diplomacy and even influenced how the First World War was fought.[5] Kern's examples point to globalism, or the operationalization of global consciousness, in multiple fields of thought. Much as at the start of the twenty-first century, globalism in the Age of Steam and Print colored interests, connections, and interventions, particularly at the level of the state.[6] Thus, at the turn of the twentieth century, global integration entailed not only shifting patterns of economic and cultural exchange but also new ways of perceiving one's relation to planetary conditions and distant events.

Late nineteenth-century European empires were the products of globalist abstraction par excellence. As T. N. Harper has noted, empires were a startling "feat of the imagination."[7] The discipline of geography offers one example of a globalist spatial imagination in the service of empire. Geography accorded well with nineteenth- and early twentieth-century imperial perspectives because these were expressly maritime and aerial and only terrestrial when necessary.[8] In the second half of the nineteenth century, a European globalist ethos also contributed to the discourse of modernity, a rhetoric that is in many ways analogous to that of globalization. In the late nineteenth century, "the modern" was, among other things, a means of conceptualizing changes of space and relation. It was also an exclusivist concept that highlighted Western interests and exceptionalism as the driving forces of global integration. But through and beyond imperial channels, modernity became a powerful and attractive discourse around the world.[9]

Before modernity became a dominant discourse, it coexisted with other globalist ways of thinking.[10] As Sugata Bose has suggested and many contributions to this collection demonstrate, the Age of Steam and Print was a time of complimentary and competing universalisms, new modes of relation facilitated by the dissemination of communication technologies, newspapers and journals in particular.[11] While the circulation of literature had a significant impact on the consciousness of many in the Indian Ocean and Mediterranean regions, nodes of commercial exchange and religious centers likewise offered focal points for communities of sentiment (see chapters 2, 4, and 9).[12] In such spaces of intense interaction, imported ideas were given local relevance and transformed. Empire created a new set of relations through which to perceive global integration, but, as both Scott S. Reese (chapter 3) and Homayra Ziad (chapter 11) show, it also offered a catalyst for global collaboration across and within older imagined communities.

Indian Ocean diasporas provide a window on the operationalization of global communities of sentiment under colonial rule. For instance, Engseng Ho has highlighted the ways in which local cosmopolitan members of the Hadrami diaspora stimulated resistance to European colonialism in the Indian Ocean region. Malabari rebellions in the 1840s and 1921 and the Aceh rising against the Dutch at the end of the nineteenth century took shape when a mobile and entrepreneurial member of the Hadrami diaspora drew on local struggles to rouse broader Muslim sentiment against empire.[13] In short, key members of the Hadrami diaspora gave direction to popular sentiments by fusing the identities of imperial subject and coreligionist with particular grievances. As important as spiritual and political leaders were, new visions of interrelation traveled farther than individual members of any diaspora. The movement of ideas and people across the colonial world—"the kinetic spaces of empire," to use Tony Ballantyne and Antoinette Burton's phrase—reached unprecedented levels at the turn of the twentieth century.[14]

In the late nineteenth and early twentieth centuries, new cosmopolitanisms emerged, subjectivities defined by the ability to see larger sets of relations stereoscopically within the minutiae of individual lived worlds and unities across landscapes of social diversity.[15] Attention to these explicitly globalist ways of seeing opens a catholic approach to the study of global integration. Since the imagination of space and of relation are intensely personal practices, by focusing on the perceptual and terrestrial experiences that coexisted with, were shaped by, and gave shape to empires, we can better appreciate the inner workings of fin-de-siècle globalisms. Considering individual concepts of space and relation also allows us to disaggregate cosmopolitan imaginations, to consider the ways in which people have held contending concepts and ideologies in dynamic tension.

In the sections that follow I will plot what we might think of as tensions of cosmopolitanism, or how world views developed within the hegemonic space of empire and within contexts of social diversity and lateral relations among colonial subjects. Emily Ruete's work is apropos to this line of inquiry because her travels from East Africa to Europe and ultimately to the Levant contributed to a way of seeing that was accommodating of Western imperialism yet critical of European culture, that reified Arabness but claimed a polyidentity. Through her itinerant life and voluminous writings, Ruete exemplified a self-conscious cosmopolitanism: the ability to see the local and the distant in stereoscope and the capacity to recognize commonality across heterogeneous social environments.

NEW COSMOPOLITANS

Zanzibar reached its apex of prosperity and regional importance between the 1830s and the seizure of the Tanzanian mainland by Germany in the late 1880s. The dramatic expansion of the island's trade with the mainland, South Asia, western Europe, and North America made Zanzibar East Africa's metropolis. It also cemented Zanzibar's position as a center of economic activity in the Indian Ocean, as Matthew S. Hopper's chapter 8 demonstrates. By the mid-1860s, ships from virtually every western Indian Ocean port could be found at Zanzibar, alongside others from the United States, Egypt, Turkey, Portugal, Denmark, France, Britain, Germany, and even Argentina.[16] New patterns of labor migration brought poor laborers from Madagascar, Yemen, Oman, and South Asia. Other South Asians— notably Vaniya, Khoja, Bhora, and Parsi, primarily from Kachchh, Gujarat, and Bombay—played a central role in the new economy as merchants and financiers.[17] Just as important, the slave trade and the rise of a plantation complex on the islands of Zanzibar and Pemba contributed to a surge in the number of slaves brought to Zanzibar Town, a population drawn from a vast region bounded by the Ethiopian highlands in the north, the Congo River basin in the west, and Lake Malawi in the south. Wealthy Zanzibaris imported small numbers of slaves from even farther afield, such as South Asia and southeastern Europe. Emily Ruete's mother, for instance, was Georgian by birth and brought to Zanzibar as a child slave.[18]

In the latter half of the nineteenth century, one of the most important facilitators of Zanzibari cosmopolitanism was Sultan Barghash bin Said (r. 1870–88),

Ruete's older brother. Barghash carried forward his father's policies of political alignment with the British, but the young sultan also strengthened ties with Istanbul and Cairo as well as Paris and Berlin. But he had not always been so open to the world. In the 1850s and 1860s, Barghash harbored a distrust of Europeans. He was disdainful of them, "even [unto] insolence," according to the British consul at Zanzibar.[19] After their father's death, Barghash's older brother Majid assumed the throne. Barghash resented Majid's deference to England in matters of Zanzibari foreign relations. Though Majid was only continuing the policies of their father, Barghash determined to overthrow his brother and expel the British. With support from several siblings, including Ruete (then Salme), he mounted a coup in 1860. The rebellion was swiftly crushed, and the British resident at Zanzibar delivered Barghash to exile in Bombay. As a result, Barghash became the first member of his family to live in western India's burgeoning industrial center.

The rebellious prince was not a prisoner in Bombay. He enjoyed a comfortable life and was exposed to a range of new technologies and ideas. The world of print media proved particularly attractive. Barghash read periodicals from across the Arabic-speaking world and gained a particular interest in Egyptian newspapers. On his return to Zanzibar, he was no longer a headstrong parochial. Both his world view and his vision for Zanzibar had changed significantly.[20] In Zanzibar he stayed abreast of events in the Mediterranean by subscribing to a number of publications. Moreover, though Barghash's English skills were limited, he tasked his personal assistant, Pera Dewji, with reading the British papers and briefing him on their contents.[21] In the mid-1870s, Barghash also began to cultivate a relationship with the Arabic-language newspaper *Al-Jawa'ib* (printed in Istanbul) and with John Louis Sabunji, the Syrian publisher of the paper *Al-Nahla,* in an effort to raise the profile of Zanzibar in the Arabic-speaking world.[22]

Barghash developed a vision for Zanzibar's modernization that had myriad repercussions. In 1875 he became the first East African head of state to visit Britain. While there, he entreated his hosts to invest in Zanzibar. He explained to a crowded lecture hall in Manchester that Zanzibaris "look to [Britain] to provide the capital and to initiate the organization which shall develop the resources of the territories under our rule."[23] Barghash dreamed of a railroad linking the east coast of Africa to Lake Tanganyika, and he published appeals to potential investors in several European papers.[24] Though he saw European capital as the key to Zanzibar's economic future, he cultivated political and empathetic ties beyond Europe as well. En route home from Britain in 1875, the sultan traveled to Egypt to meet with Khedive Isma'il. Among other things, he asked the khedive for advice on building a Western-style military.[25]

More importantly, Barghash used state funds to promote direct trade with Bombay. He purchased steamships from German and Scottish shipbuilders and inaugurated a shipping line that offered stiff competition to the British India Steam Navigation Company, which dominated the western Indian Ocean steamer routes.[26] The sultan's ships increased trade and travel between Zanzibar and Bombay exponentially. Alongside British steamers, Barghash's fleet reduced the time of travel across the western Indian Ocean, freed traders from the rhythms of the monsoon, and more completely integrated Zanzibar into a network of steamship services that streamlined transit between such distant Indian Ocean ports as Malacca, Singapore, and Aden.[27] His exile and subsequent tours of Europe and the Middle East likewise influenced his ideas about public services. Projects born of his observations in India, Egypt, and Europe included street lighting, a more effective police force, an expanded telegraph station, a free public water system, electricity generators, public clocks, and even a light tram system.

In addition to Barghash's official reforms, Zanzibar's expanding economy and increased social diversity contributed to popular trends which, like the creolized musical forms that Ann E. Lucas explores in chapter 7, evidenced a new public culture. Fashion and the intellectual landscape of Zanzibar offer telling examples of the domestication of imported objects and ideas. Among Zanzibari men, the Omani-style *kanzu,* a long, white tunic, and the *joho,* a dark overcoat, became common elements of local fashions in the second half of the nineteenth century. Indian-made European-style shoes found a large market in the city. Current Mediterranean fashions also gained popularity. At the turn of the twentieth century, many young Zanzibari men began wearing the red fez. Omani fashions also made significant inroads in women's apparel, notably among Swahilis and those of mainland descent. Arabs, Swahili, and ex-slaves wore varieties of blouses, leggings, and sandals popular in Muscat.[28]

While some migrants to the city held to the fashions of their places of birth, a Zanzibari creole aesthetic took root by the end of the nineteenth century. In addition to imported apparel, this Zanzibari aesthetic included popular accoutrements such as the Western-style umbrella, an object whose prestige was heightened by its signification of European and western Indian gentility. The most striking example of the domestication of broader aesthetic trends in late nineteenth century Zanzibar was in the domain of home decor. Like their counterparts in Muscat, wealthy Zanzibaris imported a tremendous volume of European and Indian furniture. As in Mandvi and Bombay, elites in Zanzibar filled their receiving rooms with mirrors, American wall clocks, and European porcelain. Zanzibaris' interest in imported items similar to those consumed by other urbanites across the western Indian Ocean region offers material evidence of local engagement with a transoceanic symbolic system.[29]

REIMAGINING CONNECTIVITY

Tightening connections across the Indian Ocean also altered Zanzibar's ideoscape. Much as in Southeast Asia, as Michael Laffan's chapter 1 outlines, tariqas, or Sufi orders, were notable in this respect, as was the popularity of political and reformist movements from pan-Islamism to pan-Ibadism and pan-Arabism.[30] Zanzibar became a center for Islamic learning in the latter half of the nineteenth century, drawing Shafiʿi scholars from as far away as South Africa, Yemen, and Egypt. Additionally, unlike scholars of earlier periods, most Zanzibari intellectuals traveled widely at this time. Many enjoyed close links to the Hadramawt both because of familial connections and as a result of tightening circuits of religious education. As Scott S. Reese has argued, such kinetics of empire affected the circles in which scholars moved, what they chose to read, and how they saw their societies and the larger world.[31]

Perhaps more than any other intellectual of the era, Shaykh Ahmad ibn Sumayt, a prominent scholar of the ʿAlawiyya, a Sufi order associated with the Hadrami Ba ʿAlawi family, exemplified this Shafiʿi globalism. Born in the Comoros Islands of Hadrami descent, Ibn Sumayt studied in the Hadramawt before traveling to Zanzibar at age twenty-two to take up an appointment as a qadi during Barghash's reign. Friction between the young man and Sultan Barghash soon forced Ibn Sumayt out of Zanzibar, where he was deemed persona non grata. He then traveled to Java, India, Mecca, Cairo, and Istanbul, points both within and beyond the well-trod circles of the ʿAlawiyya. After Barghash's death, in 1888, Ibn Sumayt returned to Zanzibar to take up the qadiship once again. He and many of his ʿAlawi contemporaries offer a window on what Anne Bang suggests was an ʿAlawi-Hadrami resurgence in nineteenth-century East Africa. After studying in the Hadramawt and Java, these learned men became agents of an ʿAlawi Sufi reform movement, which, as Bang has demonstrated, resulted in a greater emphasis on scripturalism. In Zanzibar and Lamu (off the coast of modern-day Kenya), men like Ibn Sumayt established ribats, or spiritual centers, that conformed to the teachings of scholars in the Hadramawt.[32] Though Ibn Sumayt did not ascribe to the reformism of the Salafi movement, his experiences in the eastern Mediterranean exposed him to contemporary intellectual trends. As a result, he assumed certain modernist attitudes, remained open to ideas that did not challenge core ʿAlawi positions, and maintained connections with a number of prominent pan-Islamists.[33] Instead of radically altering ʿAlawiyya praxis, Ibn Sumayt and others exposed to reformist intellectual trends fortified core ʿAlawi practices with the scripturalism of a longer-term ʿAlawi-Hadrami reformist sensibility.[34]

Ibadi reform movements likewise shaped public discourse in Zanzibar. In the late nineteenth century, many Zanzibaris embraced and contributed to a global Ibadi "awakening" that linked them with Oman and Algeria in less tenuous ways than in the past (see Amal Ghazal's chapter 2). Sultan Barghash, who promoted Ibadi scholars and book publishing, was a strong proponent of this renaissance, in no small part because of the challenges Ibadism faced in Zanzibar. The number and prestige of Shafiʿi ulama at Zanzibar, in contrast to the relatively small number of Ibadis there, resulted in many Ibadis embracing Sunni Islam in the latter half of the nineteenth century.[35] Barghash attempted to reverse this trend by imprisoning one of the most prominent Shafi'i ulama of the time: Shaykh 'Ali bin 'Abdullah.[36] Barghash's intimidation tactics were unsuccessful, but other efforts, notably his investments in print technology, contributed to a stronger communal identity among Ibadis in Zanzibar.

In the early 1880s, Bargash established Al-Matba'a al-Sultaniyya, or the Sultanate Press. Zanzibar thus joined the ranks of only a handful of cities where Ibadi religious texts were published, including Cairo, Tunis, and Algiers.[37] According to Philip Sadgrove, Barghash believed that stimulating Ibadi scholarship was one of the press's most important roles. Accordingly, its first publication was seventeen volumes of the *Kitab Qamus al-Shari'a*, a collection of Ibadi law and theology.[38] Through this and other scholarly texts, the Sultanate Press helped energize links among Ibadis in Oman, Zanzibar, and the Mzab Valley of Algeria. At the same time, European imperialism offered a powerful catalyst for the transformation of the *nahda* (renaissance), a broad reformist program with local and global dimensions, into a political force. As chapter 2 suggests, the Ibadi awakening gave form and direction to anticolonial rhetoric in Zanzibar, Oman, and Algeria. Using state resources and the press, successive Zanzibari sultans funded and published the work of Mzabi scholars such as Muhammad Atfiyyash, a staunch critic of French colonialism in Algeria.[39]

Barghash was the first Zanzibari sultan to establish relations with publishers in the Middle East, but later sultans, such as Hamud bin Muhammad (r. 1896–1902), deepened these ties. As a result of his close relationship with the Egyptian editor and playwright Jacob Sanua, the newspaper *Al-Tawaddud* published favorable articles about Sultan Hamud, including a biography penned by Shaykh Ahmad ibn Sumayt.[40] Sultan Hamud's successor, 'Ali bin Hamud, extended his father's relationship with the intellectual—and increasingly anticolonial—currents of the Mediterranean. Britain proclaimed Zanzibar a protectorate in 1890, and Sultan 'Ali was among the first in his family to be educated in Europe. As a result, he became firmly committed to the modernization of many aspects of Zanzibari society. Like many of his contemporaries in the Indian Ocean and eastern Mediterranean regions, he also came to resent British influence. Desirous of restoring what he saw as the "power and dignity" that the sultanate had enjoyed under Barghash, 'Ali cultivated close ties with the Ottoman sultan 'Abd al-Hamid. These ties culminated in Sultan 'Ali's official acknowledgement of 'Abd al-Hamid as caliph. In late 1907, 'Ali traveled to Istanbul to personally pledge his support. Also that year, as a further indication of his pan-Islamic ideals, he offered to mediate between Yemeni rebels and Sultan 'Abd al-Hamid, an effort that he believed necessary to check conflict within what he fancifully termed the "Islamic commonwealth."[41]

In the early years of the twentieth century, the circulation of Arabic-language periodicals contributed to a recasting of Zanzibari self-images and perceptions of the wider Arab and Muslim worlds. Many Zanzibaris subscribed to Egyptian and Lebanese publications that exemplified the contemporary intellectual currents of the Mediterranean, including *Al-Liwa, Al-Muqtataf,* and *Al-Hilal.* They also encouraged others to read these works: for instance, the reformist intellectual Sayyid Mansab bin ʿAli, with the aid of two Egyptian friends resident in Zanzibar, promoted a number of Egyptian pamphlets and newspapers there.[42] A more profound indication of the influence of reformist thinking in Zanzibar was the creation of Al-Hizb al-Islah (Reform party) in 1911, which produced the island's first fortnightly Arabic publication: *Al-Najah* (Progress). *Al-Najah* appeared regularly between 1910 and 1914 until its editor, Nasir bin Sulayman al-Lamki, was exiled to India. With reformist and pan-Islamic overtones, *Al-Najah* reflected the influence of the Salafi movement.[43]

By the early twentieth century, many Zanzibaris had come to see their relationship to other societies through new eyes. European imperialism created incentives for moral solidarity, while print and travel both breathed new life into old connections and created new links altogether. ʿAlawi-Hadrami revivalism, pan-Islamism, and pan-Ibadism offered networks that recalibrated relationships among Zanzibar, southern Arabia, and the Mediterranean. Moreover, these elements of the global ideoscape overlapped and proved mutually influential to a degree. Zanzibaris felt an impinging imperial world, but they also interpreted and recombined new aesthetic, religious, and political motifs to suit their interests. In the Age of Steam and Print, Zanzibaris drew on the intellectual currents of the Mediterranean and the Indian Ocean to develop a variety of globalist discourses, each promising new social, spiritual, or political possibilities.

CIVILIZATION, THE AUSTERE MISTRESS

Sayyida Salme bint Said ibn Sultan was among the most remarkable members of Zanzibar's late nineteenth-century generation. She did not engage in the same scholarly debates as many Zanzibari men of her time, but her world view developed from many of the same forces of globalization that affected other Zanzibari intellectuals: European imperialism and a greater familiarity with other societies and modes of thought. Like the parents of most children born in Zanzibar Town after it became the seat of the sultanate, neither Salme's father nor her mother had roots on the island.[44] Her mother, Djilfidan, was the daughter of a Circassian peasant. When Djilfidan was young, raiders killed her parents and separated her from her siblings. Sayyid Said bin Sultan, the ruler of Oman and Zanzibar, purchased the no more than eight-year-old Djilfidan and carried her to East Africa. Salme was born in 1844, her mother's only child but one of thirty-six children of the sultan. As a teenager, Salme became embroiled in a contest over succession and acted as her brother Barghash's secretary in a rebellion against their older brother Majid (see above). Majid did not punish his young sister in the aftermath of the coup. However, Salme soon found the gossip about her role in the event unbearable. With Sultan Majid's approval, she relocated to the family estate at Bububu, several kilometers outside Zanzibar Town.

Her refuge proved short-lived. The British consul at Zanzibar requested Bububu as his country retreat, and Majid asked Salme to vacate the estate. Her acquiescence enraged her coconspirators from the Barghash rebellion. She was now alienated from both family members loyal to Majid and those who aided Barghash. In the midst of this turmoil, Salme struck up a friendship with Rudolph Heinrich Ruete, an employee of one of the most prominent European trading firms in Zanzibar, the Hamburg-based Oswald & Co. Her new home in the city was opposite his, close enough so that she could peer into his living room. Salme developed a great curiosity about European customs. Rudolph indulged his new neighbor's interest by hosting parties for European residents of Zanzibar, which she eagerly observed from across the street. The unusual friendship offered Salme a reprieve from her family quarrels, and the two fell in love.

Though the young lovers attempted to keep their relationship secret, Salme was soon pregnant. The illicit relationship quickly became public knowledge. Salme's family declared that marriage was out of the question. Salme was already a pariah in Zanzibar; now her family deemed her a virtual apostate. Sultan Majid enforced greater restrictions on her movements, which made the young princess desperate to escape the confines of Zanzibar. With the aid of the British consul, who feared that she would be executed, Salme fled the city in 1866 and gained passage on a steamer bound for Aden. On discovering his sister's escape, Sultan Majid cabled the British political resident at Aden with instructions that Salme should refrain from socializing with Europeans and return to Zanzibar. The resident employed members of the Adeni 'Aydarus family and many other local elites to entreat the young princess to return home.[45] Salme refused. Her hot-tempered brother Barghash spoke of the family's disgrace and feared that her "betrayal" would be known in Muscat and ultimately "wherever Muslims live."[46] Barghash's humiliation had long-term repercussions. Once in power, he decreed that his sister was to be regarded as dead, and he refused to honor her claims to their father's inheritance.

Salme waited in Aden for nine months while Rudolph completed his business in Zanzibar. While there, she gave birth to the couple's first son. When the lovers were finally reunited in 1867, Salme was baptized Emily, and the couple hastily married. Later the same day, the young family departed for Marseilles, where they stayed briefly before making the final leg of their journey to Hamburg. In *Memoirs of an Arabian Princess*, Emily Ruete suggests that her transition to life as a German lady was relatively smooth. She quickly learned the German language and upper-class European etiquette. Yet the letters she wrote to her sister, which have only recently been made public, tell a different story. Ruete found Europe unbearable.

She thought herself morally corrupt for converting to Christianity, though she stressed that she remained a Muslim internally.[47] She avoided eating anything that might contain pork and dreaded attending church, since she saw this as a betrayal of Islam.

Ruete was appalled by much of what she saw in Europe. She wrote of German indifference to human suffering and the social distance Germans put between one another. "This is a latitude," she wrote in her memoirs, "where the weakling must perish if he is not able to offer enough resistance to the innumerable blows which, seemingly, civilization entails."[48] Civilization, she confided to her sister, was not what she expected. She wrote about its concept and practice in scathing terms; civilization was an "austere mistress."[49] Ruete found the German language difficult, and without her husband present she was often unable to communicate with others. For many months, the only person other than her husband with whom she could speak was an English maid who knew a smattering of Hindi. Ruete envied Muslims from Istanbul and Cairo, whom she believed had much more exposure to Western lifestyles. If she had been born in Cairo, she reasoned, she might have had a European governess, learned European languages, and become accustomed to eating with forks and knives, and her new life would not have been such an "upheaval."[50]

German high society was fascinated with Ruete, and her presence drew innumerable queries about Zanzibar and Islam. In her public life, she seemed to revel in her translational abilities—an interpreter of all things Arab yet fully accustomed to European ways. In private, however, the duality of her life as an Arabian princess and a German lady created an incredible strain. As a result, she sometimes concealed her identity. Rather than admit that she was an Arab or a Zanzibari, Ruete at times responded to queries about her accent by explaining that she was South American. The only comfort in her harsh new life was to recall what she wistfully termed the East, a sociogeographic category that encompassed the Arabic- and Turkish-speaking realms, including Zanzibar. She turned her clothes— the only items of her old life that she retained—into fetishes, which she hugged and kissed behind closed doors. She spent her days poring over photo albums of Egypt, Turkey, and the Levant. She bought a Lebanese cookbook, *Kitab ustadh al-tabbakhin*, and prepared "Eastern" dishes.[51]

Mementos and fantasies of the East gave Ruete some solace, but her life took a dramatic downturn in 1870 when her husband was killed in a tram accident. Ruete had lived for three years in Hamburg, given birth to three children, and now found herself entirely alone "in the big foreign world."[52] She immediately thought of returning to Zanzibar. However, instead of going home, she chose to honor her husband's wish that their children be raised as Christians in Europe. This decision pained her deeply. She confided to her sister that while she appeared "totally 'à la franca,'" in reality she was an "Arab woman to the core" and out of place in Europe.[53] Desperately searching for means to support her children, Ruete relocated to

Dresden and then to Rudolstadt, Berlin, and finally Cologne. In Berlin she offered private Arabic and Swahili tutorials. Requests for correspondence lessons soon came in from Austria, Holland, England, and as far afield as the United States. In the mid-1870s, Ruete also began composing long letters to her children, wherein she recounted her early life and experiences in Zanzibar. These would provide the bulk of the material for her memoirs. But before they were published, Ruete traveled to Zanzibar.

NARRATING ALIENATION

In 1885, after a nearly twenty-year absence, Ruete set out for Zanzibar. Her primary goal was to claim her inheritance, but she also wished to reestablish connections with her siblings. She later wrote that her greatest joy since leaving Zanzibar was arriving at Alexandria en route home. Ruete found the minarets and palm trees of the Mediterranean city exhilarating. She watched the crowd at the port with such delight that she felt as if she were in a dream. Ruete praised Alexandria and relished speaking Arabic again. "You must have been to Baghdad," one man remarked to her, surprised to meet a European who spoke impeccable Arabic. Ruete's arrival at Zanzibar was less rousing. Sultan Barghash refused to acknowledge his younger sister and forbade the family to see her. Ruete had no desire to return to her old ways. She continued to wear European clothes, and rather than sleep in town she stayed onboard a German ship. Though she spent several weeks in Zanzibar, Sultan Barghash never granted her an audience. As a result, she departed empty-handed.

Soon after her return to Germany, Ruete completed her autobiography, which was published in German in 1886 and subsequently translated into several other European languages. She earned international acclaim for the book, including the designation "Author of the World" from Le Figaro.[54] The Memoirs gained a wide and enthusiastic audience, in no small measure because nothing like it had ever appeared in print before. It was both an insightful reflection on life in Zanzibar from the perspective of a Zanzibari and a meditation on Ruete's acculturation in Germany. Most important, it seemed to promise Western readers exactly what they wanted from an Arabian princess: a firsthand account of a sultan's inner sanctum, the harem life that so fascinated Western audiences. Ruete's autobiography did indeed offer detail about the daily life of the sultan's family, but it had more critical aims as well.

The main "value of my book," Ruete explained, was to remove "misconceptions and distortions current about the East." The Memoirs, she told her readers, was an ethnography in which she drew a picture of not only "Oriental life and customs" but also the "position of women in the East." "Even in this century of railroads and rapid communication," she asserted, "so much ignorance still exists among European nations of the customs and institutions of their own immediate neighbors."

Ruete believed that hers was the authentic Muslim voice that could disabuse Europeans of their misconceptions about Islamic societies. "Having been born and bred in the East," she wrote, "I am in a position to set down the unvarnished reflection of my oriental experiences . . . to speak of many peculiarities, and lift the veil from things that are always hidden from profane eyes."[55] In her *Memoirs*, Ruete's voice is that of an intermediary between Christian and Muslim, Europe and the "Orient." She was in a unique position to make broad comparisons, but the *Memoirs* also reveals the extent to which by 1885 she had come to see the East and the North as bounded, oppositional sociogeographic entities.

While Ruete's narration of Zanzibar aims to make the Muslim metropolis, and Islam generally, intelligible to Western audiences, an equally powerful leitmotiv of her memoirs is a critique of European mores. For instance, she concludes a chapter on madrassas in Zanzibar with the opinion that European education was overly demanding and counterproductive. She later extends this critique of European schools to the civilizing discourses that underpinned European imperialism and colonization. Ruete asks her readers: Are Europeans justified in deeming others "unenlightened"? Should they be allowed to "forcibly impart" such enlightenment? Antislavery campaigns, she believed, offered a prime example of this hubris. The *Memoirs* defends Eastern slavery as less onerous than the plantation slavery with which her European readers were more familiar. Zanzibari slaves, she claims, were better off than many poor Europeans. Ruete concludes that Europeans should "concede to other peoples the right to cultivate further their national views and institutions freely and without hindrance."[56]

Ruete likewise used her autobiography as a platform to criticize Christian missions in East Africa and the construction of an Anglican cathedral (begun in 1873) in Zanzibar, a city with no appreciable Anglican population. The *Memoirs* goes so far as to claim that European civilization "is at variance with and opposed to" all of the "basic views" of Easterners. The Ottomans offer a case in point. Ruete argues that by the mid-1880s, Turks had worked to become "civilized," but she believed that such efforts only politically weakened the Ottoman Empire. Further, much like the Turkish author and publicist Ahmed Midhat, who toured Europe in the 1880s, Ruete believed that while the West was technologically advanced, it had become morally decadent.[57] The wealth and prosperity of the West produced incredible social alienation and immorality. The East, she reasoned, had been spared these social ills.

Perhaps the most charged chapters of the *Memoirs* are those devoted to challenging negative images of Arab women and gender relations in the East. Ruete stresses that European women are in most ways more subordinate than Eastern women to men. After a discussion of polygamy and concubinage, she asks her readers (with a hint of sarcasm), "Is marriage always looked upon as so sacred in Europe's moral society?" The common European practice of married men taking mistresses led Ruete to conclude that the only difference in "position" between "an oriental woman and a European one" was that "the former knows the number and also the person and character of her female rivals, whereas the latter is kept in affectionate ignorance."[58] Admitting that there were tyrants among husbands in Zanzibar just as in Germany, she concludes that domestic despots were more common in the latter. Further, Ruete's reflections on gender relations offered a springboard to raise larger critiques of such European practices as arranged marriages, discriminatory inheritance laws, and the trousseau, as well as chronic social ills including spousal abuse and alcoholism.

A final theme that emerges from the *Memoirs* is Ruete's privileging of Islam and Islamic practices as "civilizing" forces in Africa. Throughout, her charges of African barbarity provide a backdrop for the civilizational superiority of Islam, much as the moral superiority of Muslims stands in contrast to the hypocrisy of European Christians. Ruete believed that the provinciality of both Africa and Europe bound them to cultural and social extremes. The bitterness of the North created a cold morality; African indolence poisoned decency. Echoing stereotypes of mainland Africans common among elite Zanzibaris, she wrote that "Negroes" are "cowardly" and "superstitious" and must be compelled to work.[59] Ruete's self-distancing from all things African was, at least in part, a product of her upbringing in a self-consciously Arab home. Arabness, *ustaarabu* in Swahili, became an important social prestige category for upper-class Zanzibaris during Ruete's youth. Undoubtedly, this air of superiority was magnified in the royal household.[60] Ruete's chauvinism was not limited to her reflections on Africans, however. She also suggests that Zanzibaris, at least those of Arab descent, were far more sophisticated than their Omani cousins.

Written by a woman who challenged several of Muslim Zanzibar's greatest taboos, Ruete's book is remarkable for its pro-Muslim voice and advocacy of what she refers to as "oriental traditions." Perhaps Ruete took such positions because she resented European attitudes toward Muslims and regretted forsaking her family and her religion. However, what is curious about her defense of Islam, and the "Orient" generally, is that through it she reifies the spatial-cultural boundaries of East and North and claims a wide chasm between them. The warmer nature of the East, Ruete claimed, contributed to a deeper humanity among Muslims. After decades in Europe, an imagined East had become a utopia for her.

CARTOGRAPHIES OF BELONGING

Not long after the publication of her memoirs, Emily Ruete visited Zanzibar again. She was determined to make a final attempt to recover her inheritance, but she left humiliated. Three years earlier, the German government had severely strained relations with Zanzibar by seizing the mainland and forcing Barghash to renounce his claims to a number of the coast's most prosperous trading centers. By the time Ruete arrived in 1888, the new sultan, her younger brother Khalifa, was in the process of restoring positive relations with Germany. Her adoptive government feared that Ruete's presence would disrupt this détente, so the German consul shunned her. When it became clear that Germany would not support her inheritance claims, Khalifa dismissed her appeals.[61] Ruete now felt doubly betrayed, both by her adopted home and by her brother. Embittered by the incident, Ruete chose not return to Germany when she departed Zanzibar. Instead, she sailed for Jaffa in the Levant, a town that hosted a large German expatriate community. After four years in Jaffa, Ruete and her two daughters settled in Beirut. There Ruete wrote *Sequels to My Memoirs* and the miniethnography *Syrian Customs and Usages,* both of which remained unpublished for decades. Soon after Ruete's move to Beirut, her son, Rudolph Said-Ruete, took up a position at the German consulate in the city.[62] For the first time, Ruete and her children lived together in the Middle East. After three decades of alienation, she finally felt as if she belonged.

If we consider the sweep of Ruete's later writings, we find a body of work that has moved well beyond the translation of Muslim societies for Westerners. What is important for our purposes is that her later writings offer meditations on what Ruete perceived to be the contours and coherence of Indian Ocean and eastern Mediterranean cosmopolitan spaces. They reveal an introspective mental map of the world that highlights racial and religious dichotomies but also claims an Arab-Muslim spatial constant from Zanzibar to Egypt and the Levant. Like many Zanzibaris of her generation, Ruete may have been influenced by fin-de-siècle pan-Islamism, but her cognitive map tempered political vision with a strong cultural sentimentality—nostalgia for the cosmopolitan. She celebrated the cultural landscapes of Jaffa and Beirut, singling out for praise their cultural extroversion.

Ruete wrote that she felt at ease in Jaffa because she could live like a European lady, in a European community, while speaking Arabic. Here she did not have to choose to be either European or Arab; she believed that she could be both. She had found the world that she had long searched for, at once cosmopolitan and "Oriental." Beirut also offered the opportunity to live within the two worlds that she knew so well, not simply between them. She marveled at the way young people grasped Western culture. Wealthy young people, she explained, lived "alla franca [*sic*]," much as she did. They ate with forks and knives and slept in European beds. She was fascinated by local dressmakers' ability to tailor elegant ball dresses with little more than an illustration taken from a French fashion magazine.[63]

Ruete was captivated by what she perceived as the easy coexistence of things Eastern and European in Beirut. The juxtaposition of Parisian hats and the hijab pleased her. She wrote with satisfaction of a young woman in her carriage, "dressed from head to foot in the latest French fashion, with her mother or aunt next to her, still dressed in the old fashion." Ruete noted with delight that on the streets of

Beirut one could see older men having coffee and smoking a water pipe while their sons sat nearby wearing Parisian couture and speaking French. She was particularly impressed by how well many young people spoke French, noting that they used "dialectical words as little as possible." For Ruete, the city of Beirut was like an idealized mirror of her experiences. It seemed a model for the interlacing of Europe and the "Orient."[64]

Much like her memories of Zanzibar, Ruete's reflections on Beirut painted it in utopian colors. She praised Beirut as a "friendly city" where people were courteous and possessed "great intelligence." She wrote with approval that even the poor were "neat and clean." Likewise, she was keen to applaud what she perceived as Beirut's resistance to the nationalism prevalent in Europe. This, she believed, was a sign of the self-assured nature of its residents.[65] Ruete's writings from the Levant also reveal a blurring of the strong distinctions she had earlier drawn between the North and the East as sociogeographic spheres. In contrast to the *Memoirs,* Ruete's later writings focus more intently on a global Muslim cultural cosmopolitanism.

Though she had earlier criticized Turkey, Egypt, and Tunisia as having cultures too "mixed" to be the "real Orient," during her time in the Levant her perspective changed. She now commended Istanbul, Beirut, and other centers of the eastern Mediterranean for embracing certain Western influences.[66] Ruete came to see her internal identity struggle in relation to shifting identities across the Muslim world. The East that had domesticated Europe appeared the outward manifestation, indeed the resolution, of her inner conflict. Much as she had not sacrificed her sense of morality to European "civilization," she came to believe that Levantines and Egyptians had not compromised their values by internalizing elements of Western modernity. Thus, Ruete's later work has a supranationalist tone, or more precisely a cultural nationalism of the East and Islam generally. Her years in the Levant led her to see a cosmopolitan cultural continuum in the Muslim Mediterranean, one recognizable in its embrace of foreign ideas, languages, and fashions. This was a catholic sensibility that, in Ruete's estimation, many other world regions lacked.

In her final years, Ruete was no longer vehemently anti-imperialist, but she continued to argue that Easterners should be able to choose the cultural or ideological imports that suited them. In an imperial age, she developed a cognitive map of the world not dependent on imperial boundaries but instead defined by cultural cosmopolitan sentiments. Not unlike her fellow Ibadis who had been influenced by Islamic reformism and were in search of a more cosmopolitan subjectivity, Ruete developed a broader identity than the Ibadism of her youth. She was equally dissatisfied with the parochialism and the chauvinism of European Christianity. Ruete was Christian and Muslim, European and Arab, and from this unlikely position she imagined the possibility of being all of these without contradiction.

EPILOGUE

Not long after the publication of *Memoirs of an Arabian Princess*, Sultan Barghash obtained a copy. He was eager to know what his sister had written. Though it did not affect his attitude toward his sister, Barghash liked the book. It is not difficult to imagine why. The *Memoirs* probably did as much to bring attention to Zanzibar as Barghash's own efforts. He surely recognized that his sister's sympathetic portrait of Zanzibar and women's position in Muslim societies supported his attempts to win positive recognition and foreign investment for the sultanate. Perhaps Barghash realized that the sister he regarded as dead had become Zanzibar's most important voice on the global stage.

As many contributions to this collection suggest, turn-of-the-century reformism was preoccupied with reconciliation between Muslim societies and Western modernity. Emily Ruete was equally concerned with this question, in no small measure because alienation marked her peripatetic life in East Africa, Europe, and the Mediterranean. She encapsulated the contending forces of the Age of Steam and Print. More precisely, she embodied the tensions of cosmopolitanism in a world that seemed to be quickly shrinking, and she developed a world view that accommodated many European, Indian Ocean, and Mediterranean cultural sensibilities. Ruete's solitude in Europe and rejection at home forced her to seek a social environment that could relieve the inherent pressures of her position. Her writings laud spaces of plural identity, such as Jaffa, Beirut, and Alexandria at the turn of the twentieth century. Ruete was a masterful interpreter, and her travels led her to the conclusion that a flexible identity, or an easy coexistence of Western and "Oriental" symbols, was characteristic of Mediterranean cultural cosmopolitanism. Indeed, this was the ideal she searched for: the domestication of Paris on the streets of Beirut, the bricolage of Arabic and European languages. Her experiences led her to see the world in stereoscope, to translate the condition of Muslim women for foreign audiences and to draw parallels across social diversity. Ruete was the product of an imperial world, whose tensions she embodied and spent much of her life seeking relief from.

In the twentieth century, new ways of seeing shaped popular globalisms. Perhaps most important in this respect was the planetary embrace of nationalism. By the interwar period, *la tyrannie du national* affirmed exclusivist frames of self-definition.[67] One of the most difficult and paradoxical heritages of the colonial era stirred the imaginations of many in this period: the belief that people are, in Edward Said's words, "only, mainly, exclusively, white, or Black, or Western, or Oriental."[68] Modernity superimposed a particular vision of universal interrelation on the global relationships of colonized subjects. At the same time, it excluded them from many of the social, economic, and political rights championed by Western theorists of modernity. In an effort to claim these rights, many colonial subjects drew on social cartographies born in the nineteenth century, such as pan-Arabism and pan-Africanism, giving them new force and direction. Each political ideology represented a different permutation of globalism, but a sovereign-nation ideal, often with narrow parameters of belonging, ultimately supplanted them all.

Emily Ruete died in 1924, a time when both anti-imperial rhetoric and nationalist aspirations were yet in their infancy. Over the following decades, colonial subjects embraced racial identities, concepts of global community, and nationalism in an effort to address changing social and political tensions. In Zanzibar, racial thought, legitimated by the colonial state and shaped by the political imaginations of colonial subjects, encouraged the elaboration of dichotomous Arab and African identities. In the era of decolonization, this way of seeing seeded a form of nativism that defined racial and ethnic others as internal aliens. Four decades after Ruete's death, Zanzibari racial nationalism culminated in revolution and the subsequent expulsion of many people of Arab ancestry, including members of her family.[69] At the end of empire, the cosmopolitan world that Ruete dreamed of gave way to yet another way of seeing, one frequently bound to exclusive concepts of belonging.

NOTES

1. On the concept of a "community of sentiment," a social group that feels and imagines together, see Arjun Appadurai, *Modernity at Large: Cultural Dimensions of Globalization* (Minneapolis: University of Minnesota Press, 1996), 8–9.

2. As early as 1992, Roland Robertson suggested that the perception of the planet as an integrated whole is a dimension of globalization that deserves much more attention: see Robertson, *Globalization: Social Theory and Global Culture* (London: Sage, 1992). Tim Harper has similarly argued that shifts in consciousness are defining characteristics of globalization processes. See Harper, "Empire, Diaspora and the Languages of Globalism, 1850–1914," in *Globalization in World History*, ed. Anthony Hopkins (London: Pimlico, 2002), 142.

3. Though several scholars have used the term *global consciousness*, it has yet to be adequately defined. See, for instance, Edward Said, *Culture and Imperialism* (New York: A. A. Knopf, 1993).

4. Arif Dirlik, "Globalization as the End and the Beginning of History: The Contradictory Implications of a New Paradigm," *Rethinking Marxism* 12, no. 4 (2000): 4–22.

5. Stephen Kern, *The Culture of Time and Space, 1880–1918* (Cambridge, MA: Harvard University Press, 2003).

6. Jo-Anne Pemberton, *Global Metaphors: Modernity and the Quest for One World* (London: Pluto, 2001).

7. Harper, "Empire, Diaspora and the Languages of Globalism," 142.

8. Engseng Ho, "Empire through Diasporic Eyes: A View from the Other Boat," *Comparative Studies in Society and History* 46, no. 2 (2004): 241; Martin Lewis and Karen Wigen, *The Myth of Continents: A Critique of Metageography* (Berkeley: University of California Press, 1997); Anne Godlewska and Neil Smith, eds., *Geography and Empire* (Oxford: Blackwell, 1994).

9. Dipesh Chakrabarty, *Provincializing Europe: Postcolonial Thought and Historical Difference* (Princeton, NY: Princeton University Press, 2000); Arif Dirlik, *Global Modernity: Modernity in the Age of Global Capitalism* (Boulder, CO: Paradigm, 2007).

10. See, for example, Rebecca Karl, *Staging the World: Chinese Nationalism at the Turn of the Twentieth Century* (Durham, NC: Duke University Press, 2002), 195; Dilip Parameshwar Gaonkar, ed., *Alternative Modernities* (Durham, NC: Duke University Press, 2001); Antoinette Burton, *At the Heart of the Empire: Indians and the Colonial Encounter in Late-Victorian Britain* (Berkeley: University of California Press, 1998); Frederick Cooper and Ann Laura Stoler, eds., *Tensions of Empire: Colonial Cultures in a Bourgeois World* (Berkeley: University of California Press, 1997).

11. Sugata Bose, *A Hundred Horizons: The Indian Ocean in an Age of Global Empire* (Cambridge, MA: Harvard University Press, 2006), 270. Juan Cole refers to this proliferation of communication technologies at the turn of the twentieth century as the emergence of "a global information ecumene." See Cole, "Printing and Urban Islam in the Mediterranean World, 1890–1920," in *Modernity and Culture: From the Mediterranean to the Indian Ocean,* ed. Leila Tarazi Fawaz and C. A. Bayly (New York: Columbia University Press, 2002), 346.

12. On the circulation of print literature, see also Nile Green, *Bombay Islam: The Religious Economy of the West Indian Ocean, 1840–1915* (New York: Cambridge University Press, 2011); Isabel Hofmeyr, Preben Kaarsholm, and Bodil Folke Frederiksen, eds., "Print Cultures, Nationalisms and Publics of the Indian Ocean," special issue, *Africa* 81 (2011); Amal Ghazal, *Islamic Reform and Arab Nationalism: Expanding the Crescent from the Mediterranean to the Indian Ocean (1880s–1930s)* (New York: Routledge, 2010); Nile Green, "Saints, Rebels and Booksellers: Sufis in the Cosmopolitan Western Indian Ocean, ca. 1740–1920," in *Struggling with History: Islam and Cosmopolitanism in the Western Indian Ocean,* ed. Kai Kresse and Edward Simpson (London: Hurst, 2007), 125–66.

13. Engseng Ho, "Empire through Diasporic Eyes: A View from the Other Boat," *Comparative Studies in Society and History* 46, no. 2 (2004): 224, 237. On globalism in political ideology, see Ilham Khuri-Makdisi, *The Eastern Mediterranean and the Making of Global Radicalism, 1860–1914* (Berkeley: University of California Press, 2010); Mark Frost, "'Wider Opportunities': Religious Revival, Nationalist Awakening and the Global Dimension in Colombo, 1870–1920," *Modern Asian Studies* 36, no. 4 (2002): 937–67.

14. Tony Ballantyne and Antoinette Burton, "Epilogue: The Intimate, the Translocal, and the Imperial in an Age of Mobility," in *Moving Subjects: Gender, Mobility, and Intimacy in an Age of Empire,* ed. Ballantyne and Burton (Urbana: University of Illinois Press, 2009), 338.

15. Sheldon Pollock, Homi K. Bhabha, Carol A. Breckenridge, and Dipesh Chakrabarty, "Cosmopolitanisms," in *Cosmopolitanism,* ed. Breckenridge, Pollock, Bhabha, and Chakrabarty (Durham, NC: Duke University Press, 2002), 11; Edward Simpson and Kai Kresse, "Introduction: Cosmopolitanism Contested: Anthropology and History in the Western Indian Ocean," in Kresse and Simpson, *Struggling with History,* 3; Kwame Anthony Appiah, *Cosmopolitanism: Ethics in a World of Strangers* (New York: W. W. Norton, 2006).

16. Erik Gilbert, *Dhows and Colonial Economy in Zanzibar, 1860–1970* (Athens: Ohio University Press, 2005).

17. J. S. Mangat, *A History of the Asians in East Africa, c. 1886–1945* (Oxford: Clarendon, 1969); Thomas R. Metcalf, *Imperial Connections: India in the Indian Ocean Area, 1860–1920* (Berkeley: University of California Press, 2007).

18. Frederick Cooper, *Plantation Slavery on the East Coast of Africa* (New Haven, CT: Yale University Press, 1977); Abdul Sheriff, *Slaves, Spices and Ivory in Zanzibar* (London: Heinemann, 1987); Jeremy Prestholdt, *Domesticating the World: African Consumerism and the Genealogies of Globalization* (Berkeley: University of California Press, 2008).

19. Robert L. Playfair, Zanzibar consul, to C. Gonne, Bombay, 19 April 1865, L/P&S/9/42, India Office Library, British Library, London.

20. Consul Speer, "Report on Zanzibar, 1862," roll 2, vol. 4–5, United States Consulate Zanzibar, National Archives of the United States of America, Washington DC.

21. Harry Hamilton Johnston, *The Kilima-Njaro Expedition* (London: K. Paul, Trench, 1886), 30.

22. Philip Sadgrove, "From Wadi Mizab to Unguja: Zanzibar's Scholarly Links," in *The Transmission of Learning in Islamic Africa*, ed. Scott S. Reese (Leiden, Netherlands: Brill, 2004), 188.

23. "The Seyyid of Zanzibar," *Times of London*, 10 July 1875.

24. Henry M. Stanley, *Through the Dark Continent*, vol. 1 (New York: Harper Brothers, 1878), 43.

25. Randall L. Pouwels, *Horn and Crescent: Cultural Change and Traditional Islam on the East African Coast, 800–1900* (New York: Cambridge University Press, 1987), 127.

26. Jeremy Prestholdt, "On the Global Repercussions of East African Consumerism," *American Historical Review* 109, no. 3 (2004): 755–81.

27. Anne Bang, *Sufis and Scholars of the Sea: Family Networks in East Africa, 1860–1925* (London: RoutledgeCurzon, 2003), 58.

28. Laura Fair, *Pastimes and Politics: Culture, Community and Identity in Post-abolition Urban Zanzibar, 1890–1945* (Athens: Ohio University Press, 2001); Fair, "Remaking Fashion in the Paris of the Indian Ocean: Dress, Performance, and the Cultural Construction of a Cosmopolitan Zanzibari Identity," in *Fashioning Africa: Power and the Politics of Dress*, ed. Jean Allman (Bloomington: Indiana University Press, 2004), 13–30.

29. Prita Meier, "Objects on the Edge: Swahili Coast Logics of Display," *African Arts* 42, no. 4 (2009): 8–23.

30. On the expanding membership of tariqas in the late nineteenth century, see Scott S. Reese, *Renewers of the Age: Holy Men and Social Discourse in Colonial Benaadir* (Leiden, Netherlands: Brill, 2008); Abdul Hamid El-Zein, *Sacred Meadows: A Structural Analysis of Religious Symbolism in an East African Town* (Evanston, IN: Northwestern University Press, 1974).

31. Reese, *Renewers of the Age*, 7–8. Reese suggests that hagiographies and other writings by East Africans offer moral histories with which East Africans "tried to make sense of the global political, economic, and social changes enveloping them in the late nineteenth and early twentieth centuries, through the lens of their own cosmological worldview." At the same time, local scholars attempted to disseminate their ideas to broader audiences (14). Even among those who were not well traveled, most Zanzibari ulama studied with foreign-born teachers, which reduced parochialism considerably. Pouwels, *Horn and Crescent*, 149–51.

32. Bang, *Sufis and Scholars*, 151; Randall L. Pouwels, "Sh. al-Amin b. Ali Mazrui and Islamic Modernism in East Africa, 1875–1947," *International Journal of Middle East Studies* 13, no. 3 (1981): 329–45.

33. Pouwels, *Horn and Crescent*, 206; Bang, *Sufis and Scholars*, 137. Istanbul was one of the epicenters of pan-Islamism and pan-Islamic publications, so Ibn Sumayt's time in the city likely exposed him to the breadth of pan-Islamic thinkers. Cole, "Printing and Urban Islam," 355.

34. Bang, *Sufis and Scholars*, 152. Others likewise used travel as a means of reflection. See, for example, Scott S. Reese, "The Adventures of Abu Harith: Muslim Travel Writing and Navigating the Modern in Colonial East Africa," in Reese, *Transmission of Learning*, 244–55.

35. Amal Ghazal, "Seeking Common Ground: Salafism and Islamic Reform in Modern Ibadi Thought," *Bulletin of the Royal Institute for Inter-faith Studies* 7, no. 1 (2005): 119–41; Valerie Hoffman, "Ibadi Muslim Scholars and the Confrontation with Sunni Islam in Nineteenth- and Early Twentieth-Century Zanzibar," ibid., 91–118. On Arab identity and Omani-Zanzibari relations more broadly, see Thomas McDow, "Being Baysar: (In)flexible Identities in East Africa," *MIT Electronic Journal of Middle East Studies*, 5 (2005): 34–42; Erik Gilbert, "Oman and Zanzibar: The Historical Roots of a Global Community," in *Cross Currents and Community Networks: The History of the Indian Ocean World*, ed. Edward A. Alpers and Himanshu Prabha Ray (Oxford: Oxford University Press, 2007), 163–78.

36. Pouwels, *Horn and Crescent*, 117–20.

37. Philip Sadgrove, "From Wadi Mizab to Unguja," 184–211.

38. Ibid., 189.

39. Amal Ghazal, "The Other 'Andalus': The Omani Elite of Zanzibar and the Making of an Identity, 1880s–1930s," *MIT Electronic Journal of Middle East Studies* 5 (2005): 47–50; Ghazal, *Islamic Reform.*

40. Bang, *Sufis and Scholars,* 120–21.

41. Ghazal, "The Other 'Andalus,'" 50.

42. Pouwels, *Horn and Crescent,* 206–7. Popular interest in *Al-Hilal* is noteworthy because its editor was Jurji Zaydan, a staunch promoter of pan-Arabism. See Ghazal, "The Other 'Andalus,'" 51, 56–57 n. 42; Elisabeth Kendall, "Between Politics and Literature: Journals in Alexandria and Istanbul at the End of the Nineteenth Century," in Fawaz and Bayly, *Modernity and Culture,* 336.

43. Bang, *Sufis and Scholars,* 136; Ghazal, "The Other 'Andalus,'" 47–50, 53, 57 n. 48; Cole, "Printing and Urban Islam," 353. See also Shaykh Abdallah Salih Farsy, *The Shafi'i "Ulama" of East Africa, ca. 1830–1970: A Hagiographic Account,* trans. and ed. Randall L. Pouwels (Madison: African Studies Program, University of Wisconsin–Madison, 1989); Amal Ghazal, "The Other Frontiers of Arab Nationalism: Arabs, Berbers, and the Arabist-Salafi Press in the Inter-war Period," *International Journal of Middle East Studies,* 42, no. 1 (2010): 105–22.

44. The account that follows is drawn from Sayyida Salme / Emily Ruete, *Memoirs of an Arabian Princess,* in Salme/Ruete, *An Arabian Princess between Two Worlds: Memoirs, Letters Home, Sequels to the Memoirs, and Syrian Customs and Usages,* ed. E. van Donzel (New York: Brill, 1993).

45. E. van Donzel, introduction to ibid., 18–19.

46. Barghash bin Said, quoted in Heinz Schneppen, "Sayyida Salme/Emily Ruete: Between Zanzibar and Germany, between Islam and Christianity," National Museums of Tanzania, Occasional Paper no. 12 (1999), 3.

47. Salme was horrified the first time she was treated as a Christian. She remarked in disgust that when visiting Cairo's Muhammad Ali mosque en route to Marseilles, she was required to wear overshoes like the other non-Muslims. Salme/Ruete, *Letters Home,* in Salme/Ruete, *An Arabian Princess,* 412.

48. Salme/Ruete, *Memoirs,* 407.

49. Salme/Ruete, *Letters Home,* 413.

50. Ibid., 457.

51. Salme/Ruete, *Memoirs,* 385; *Letters Home,* 418.

52. Salme/Ruete, *Memoirs,* 372.

53. Salme/Ruete, *Letters Home,* 455.

54. *Le Figaro,* quoted in Donzel, introduction to Salme/Ruete, *An Arabian Princess,* 7; Dwight F. Reynolds, introduction to *Interpreting the Self: Autobiography in the Arabic Literary Tradition,* ed. Reynolds (Berkeley: University of California Press, 2001), 8.

55. Salme/Ruete, *Memoirs,* 405 fn. 98.

56. Ibid., 214.

57. Carter Vaughn Findley, "An Ottoman Occidentalist in Europe: Ahmed Midhat Meets Madame Gülnar, 1889," in *Bodies in Contact: Rethinking Colonial Encounters in World History,* ed. Tony Ballantyne and Antoinette M. Burton (Durham, NC: Duke University Press, 2005), 287.

58. Salme/Ruete, *Memoirs,* 271–72.

59. Ibid., 327–33.

60. Pouwels, *Horn and Crescent,* 129–30.

61. Salme/Ruete, *Sequels to My Memoirs,* in Salme/Ruete, *An Arabian Princess,* 520.

62. Rudolph Said-Ruete later married into a wealthy Jewish family, moved to Egypt, and took a job with a railroad company and later a bank. From 1920, he lived in London and focused his attention on political questions, particularly efforts to bridge Jewish and Muslim interests in Palestine. He renounced his German citizenship in response to German anti-Semitism. Schneppen, "Sayyida Salme/Emily Ruete," 21–23.

63. Salme/Ruete, *Syrian Customs and Usages,* in Salme/Ruete, *An Arabian Princess,* 526.

64. Ibid. See also Jens Hanssen, *Fin de Siècle Beirut: The Making of an Ottoman Provincial Capital* (Oxford: Oxford University Press, 2005); Fruma Zachs, *Making of a Syrian Identity: Intellectuals and Merchants in Nineteenth Century Beirut* (Leiden, Netherlands: Brill, 2005).

65. Salme/Ruete, *Syrian Customs and Usages,* 523–25. On sectarian tensions in nineteenth-century Lebanon see Ussama Makdisi, *The Culture of Sectarianism: Community, History, and Violence in Nineteenth-Century Ottoman Lebanon* (Berkeley: University of California Press, 2000).

66. Salme/Ruete, *Memoirs,* 310.

67. Timothy N. Harper, "Empire, Diaspora and the Languages of Globalism," 158; Anne Bang, "Cosmopolitanism Colonised? Three Cases from Zanzibar, 1890–1920," in Kresse and Simpson, *Struggling with History,* 167–88.

68. Said, *Culture and Imperialism,* 336.

69. Jonathon Glassman, *War of Words, War of Stones: Racial Thought and Violence in Colonial Zanzibar* (Bloomington: Indiana University Press, 2011).

11

The Return of Gog

Politics and Pan-Islamism in the
Hajj Travelogue of 'Abd al-Majid Daryabadi

Homayra Ziad

Today Gog has been granted a respite. Today he may intimidate, disorder, and disease our hearts, minds, and intellects, our eyes and ears, with his prosperity, his entourage, his culture and education, his sciences and arts, his doctors and engineers . . . his planes, bombs, atom bombs. But rest assured, this respite will not last forever. The curtain is on the verge of rising!

'ABD AL-MAJID DARYABADI, *SAFAR-I HIJAZ: HAJJ WA ZIYARAT
KA MUFASSAL WA MUKAMMAL HIDAYAT NAMAH*, 66–67

INTRODUCTION

In 1929, the North Indian Muslim modernist, pan-Islamist, litterateur, magazine publisher, and born-again believer 'Abd al-Majid Daryabadi (1892–1977) set sail for Mecca. An Urdu travelogue of his pilgrimage, titled *Safar-i Hijaz: Hajj wa Ziyarat ka Mufassal wa Mukammal Hidayat Namah* (Journey to the Hijaz: A detailed and complete guide book for hajj and pilgrimage), appeared that same year in forty installments of his Urdu journal *Sach* (Truth). The passage that opens this chapter may appear misplaced in the middle of a hajj narrative—what role does anti-imperialist commentary have in a deeply spiritual journey to the House of God in Mecca? But the act of pilgrimage can never be divorced from the socio-political context of pilgrims, not least in the mid-nineteenth century, when geopolitical shifts and spectacular improvements in communications and methods of travel made the hajj accessible to far greater numbers of Muslims, most significantly members of the middle classes. The mass circulation of people, most dramatically in the ritual of pilgrimage, was deeply implicated in the globalizing transformations that this volume seeks to analyze and was a means of both encountering and responding to these transformations. This chapter examines Daryabadi's travelogue in the context of the Age of Steam and Print, as a self-conscious moral response to its various disjunctures.[1]

Free-standing pilgrimage accounts emerged in South Asia during the late eighteenth century but did not become a widespread or well-defined genre until a century later.[2] With the growth of print culture and advances in long-distance transportation, between 1870 and 1950 several dozen South Asian Muslims published hajj travelogues. Far from being flat, benign travel narratives, these accounts reveal "important dimensions of Islam as a modern religion, of modes of self-presentation, and of Muslim social and corporate life."[3] In these terms, Barbara Metcalf has positioned hajj travel writing as a distinctly modern genre that follows the trajectory of the novel and the autobiography, creating a persona that emerges from individual experience and perceptions.[4] Travelogues came into being amid several modern experiments in religious self-consciousness—including pan-Islamism, the encouragement of forms of Islam that were more "scripturally orthodox," and a carrying forward of the eighteenth-century emphasis on the Prophet's example as a basis for institutional organization.[5] In fact, Metcalf suggests that hajj narratives should be examined in tandem with modern biographies of the Prophet Muhammad, "read as part of an enduring yet shifting constellation of three poles: changes in society generally, changes in concepts of individuality, and changes in the interpretation of central religious symbols . . . [most notably] the *hajj* and the Prophet."[6] In other words, hajj narratives were inherently political, drawing on iconic religious symbols to imagine new communities and sharpen identities.[7] Ronit Ricci's chapter 9, about the Malay community in Sri Lanka, also fruitfully explores the use of shared symbols and narratives to create translocal religious consciousness.

Hajj narratives of the nineteenth and early twentieth centuries are a rich and largely unexcavated resource for tracking the effects of colonial-era political, cultural, medical, and commercial developments in which the pilgrimage was implicated.[8] 'Abd al-Majid Daryabadi's travelogue is a fine example of an ambivalent response to the economic, cultural, and epistemic alienation that accompanied the Age of Steam and Print, self-consciously expressed in religious and moral terms. *Safar-i Hijaz* was written in the midst of several critical global developments that were themselves responses to the anxieties of the Age of Steam and Print. The first was the Khilafat movement, the pan-Islamic political initiative launched in 1920 by a coalition of Indian Muslim modernists and religious scholars to prevent the dismemberment of the Ottoman Empire and to ensure that Mecca and Medina would not fall under non-Muslim rule. This period also saw the acceleration of the freedom movement in India, with a call for full independence from colonial rule by 1929; the rise of the Sa'ud rulers, backed by the British government for economic reasons, and the subsequent end, in 1925, of Hashimite rule in the Hijaz; and the growth of Turkish and Arab nationalism around the Mediterranean.

In *Safar-i Hijaz*, Daryabadi differentiates the cultural memory space that he inhabits from the transcendental goal and experience of pilgrimage, which becomes a perfect site of political contestation. For example, while steam technology simplified pilgrimage, like all travel, in other ways the journey was more treacherous than ever before. The British colonial government's embrace of laissez-faire economic policies gave great latitude to shipping interests, which in turn points to how, as Eric Tagliacozzo's chapter 5 shows, lax sanitation and overcrowding on hajj steamships enabled the swift spread of cholera. Similarly, American and European industry mass-produced the basic commodities that were bought and sold in the busy markets of the pilgrimage centers and largely facilitated the experience of pilgrimage. Yet Daryabadi struggles with the realization that a European and American industrial elite dictated the world economic system that determined the logistics of the hajj at the expense of a Muslim world politically, economically, and psychically colonized. Globalization is an uneven process and its fruits unevenly distributed, and in few spaces is there the possibility of a more stark contrast between the transcendental and the material than at a pilgrimage center. In his travelogue, Daryabadi draws a direct, bitter line from Western economic hegemony to the valorizing of nationalist identity and the political and spiritual decline of the Muslim world, showing his ambivalence toward Western technology and industry. In the end, he declares that a return to the example of the Prophet and the discipline of religious law can best temper this unavoidable encounter with modernity and globalization.

It is important to note that Daryabadi's hajj narrative first appeared as a series of installments in a periodical. As Michael Laffan's chapter 1 points out, in nineteenth-century Southeast Asia, print culture, in the form of tracts and periodicals, was a means of reconceptualizing and drawing boundaries around religious identity. In much the same way, Urdu periodical culture played a crucial role in the identity politics of South Asian Muslims after the Great Rebellion (or Sepoy Mutiny) of 1857.[9]

A PILGRIM'S BACKGROUND

Daryabadi was a prolific modernist scholar. He was intellectually linked with the Aligarh school of Sayyid Ahmad Khan (d. 1898),[10] the Deobandi school of Ashraf 'Ali Thanvi (d. 1943),[11] the Khilafat movement under the leadership of Muhammad 'Ali Jawhar (d. 1931), and the early Jama'at-i Islami of Sayyid Abu'l 'Ala Mawdudi (d. 1979). Daryabadi is credited with writing nearly fifty works, including a popular Urdu translation of and commentary on the Qur'an; an English translation of and commentary on the Qur'an; a number of companion and reference works on the Qur'an; books on Sufism and Islamic culture; and two influential journals, *Sach* and *Sidq*. Daryabadi hailed from a line of religious scholars and civil servants that included Mufti Mazhar Karim (d. 1873), his grandfather, whom the British exiled to the Andaman Islands for revolutionary activities, and Mawlavi ʿAbd al-Qadir (d. 1912), Daryabadi's father, who rose to the position of deputy collector in the United Provinces of North India.

After a traditional education at home in Farsi, Urdu, and Arabic, Daryabadi studied European philosophy and logic at Canning College in Lucknow, obtained a bachelor's degree in philosophy from the University of Allahabad, and began a masters program in the same discipline at the famous Muhammadan Anglo-Oriental College in Aligarh. In time, he became a skeptic and rejected religious practice. His reconversion took place under the influence of Hindu philosophy, which led him to the Sufi poetry of Jalal al-Din Rumi (d. 1273). He was also moved by the English translation of the Qur'an by Muhammad ʿAli (d. 1951), a religious scholar and leading figure of the messianic Ahmadiyya movement founded in 1889 in British India by Mirza Ghulam Ahmad. Another major factor was the company of the Thanvi, whom Daryabadi considered a spiritual mentor.[12] He also worked closely with the Indian (later Pakistani) Qur'an exegete Amin Ahsan Islahi (d. 1998), who wrote for his journal *Sach*. Additionally, Daryabadi knew Mawdudi, at whose invitation he was present at the 1938 Pathankot meetings that led to the establishment of the Jamaʿat-i Islami, the globally influential Islamic revivalist party that was founded in 1941 and greatly influenced the religion's political development. While at one stage Daryabadi contributed to Mawdudi's Urdu journal *Tarjuman al-Qur'an* (Interpreter of the Qur'an), he later withdrew his support for the Jamaʿat-i Islami, severely criticizing Mawdudi for breaking with traditional orthodoxy and for his emphasis on political power.

As a scholar, Daryabadi is best known for his English and Urdu translations of the Qur'an. Intended for two different audiences, these translations reflect his unique training in both the Islamic and the continental European philosophical traditions. Begun in 1933, his English *Tafsir* (Commentary) was one of the first extensive commentaries on the Qur'an in English and was instrumental in the conversion from Judaism of the well-known Jamaʿat-i Islami ideologue Maryam Jameelah (b. 1934). South Asian Muslim scholars have variously hailed the commentary as a masterpiece of comparative religion, a bulwark against Orientalist representations of Islam, and a means of addressing the religious concerns of Western-educated Muslims.[13]

A major political influence on Daryabadi was the pan-Islamism of Muhammad ʿAli Jawhar (1878–1931), one of the most important leaders of the Khilafat movement, which emerged in India toward the end of the First World War. Daryabadi's family had been in British service and even recounted the story of his exiled grandfather as a tale of wrongful accusation, emphasizing that Mufti Mazhar Karim had in fact helped a British officer escape the 1857 uprising. Accordingly, Daryabadi's transition to pan-Islamism was slow, evolving from 1909 to 1925, and

driven by his reverence for Muhammad ʿAli Jawhar, whom he regarded as a political inspiration and mentor. Daryabadi honed his considerable journalistic skills
as a contributor to and editor for Muhammad ʿAli's journal *Hamdard*, which led
to the launch of *Sach*. Elected secretary of the Awadh Khilafat Committee in 1925,
a position he held for four years, Daryabadi soon became a member of the Central
Khilafat Committee. In 1927, he led the Majlis Istiqbaliyah (opening ceremony) of
the Khilafat conference. From then on, Daryabadi was consistently involved with
the conference. It was in this milieu that he sharpened his opposition to imperialism and the Westernization of the Indian intellectual sphere, an attitude reflected
in many of his writings, including *Safar-i Hijaz*.[14]

Another of Daryabadi's influential associations was his spiritual connection
with the theological seminaries in the towns of Deoband and Thana Bhavan.
Although he had undergone a formal master-disciple initiation with Husayn
Ahmad Madani, a leading Deobandi scholar and disciple of Rashid Ahmad
Gangohi, he established a strong relationship with Thanvi, turning to him more
often than to Madani for spiritual counsel. Impressed by Thanvi's Sufi scholarship,
Daryabadi established contact with him in 1927 and visited him (in the company
of Madani) in 1928. From then on, they kept up a close correspondence on a daz-
zling variety of issues. These ranged from personal spiritual guidance to "political
controversies, prominent contemporary figures in the Indian Muslim community,
long-standing theological debates . . . and topics of a more specifically Sufi interest."[15] The letters were later published in a six-hundred-page volume titled *Hakim
al-Ummat: Nuqush va Taʾaththurat* (Philosopher of the community: writings and
legacy). Muhammad Qasim Zaman posits that the language of Sufi ethics rather
than jurisprudence created a lasting link between the two men: Thanvi's insistence
on drawing theological and juridical boundaries within the Muslim community
diametrically opposed Daryabadi's emphasis on communal unity.[16] In many ways,
Daryabadi's career brings into focus the porous and shifting boundaries between
many of the faith-based movements that he was involved in before they reified into
schools.

SAFAR-I HIJAZ: AN URDU HAJJ TRAVELOGUE

Safar-i Hijaz is an integral part of Daryabadi's reformist pan-Islamic agenda,
reflected in the journal *Sach,* to create a Mecca-focused communal identity among
Indian Muslims. His goal was to encourage his readership not only to take the
pilgrimage seriously as a religious obligation on par with daily prayer but, essentially, to realize that the sacred center of the Islamic tradition lies outside India.
This was in line with Daryabadi's assertions that patriotism does not mean merging with the majority culture. He believed that as a minority community, Indian
Muslims had to maintain their distinctive cultural traditions while transcending

sectarian differences;[17] the hajj provides a perfect symbol of sectarian unity. Dary-abadi's pilgrimage took place in 1929, over the course of two and a half months (mid-March to the end of May).[18] The decision to go was the result of much soul-searching, inspired by the company of a group of Sufis in Hyderabad; permission from the shrine of Nizam al-Din in Delhi and from the madrassas at Deoband and Thana Bhavan; and logistical and spiritual advice from illustrious personalities in Azamgarh, Lucknow, and Hyderabad.[19] In the intensely personal and romantic language that gives such flavor to his travelogue, Daryabadi writes of his intention:

> This is a voyage to the land of raging sand, in the hottest of weather, with the sky as our roof, a sky with a glowing sun. This is not a trip to hotels and parks, waterfalls and greenery, but rather to dry, desolate plains, desiccated desolation, deserts that rain down fire and dust. This sinful Muslim is presenting himself at the threshold of his intercessor and tender lord. Once this servant was indeed present at the court of his master; now this escaped slave is exhausted, having given up, repentant and shame-faced. Once again, he finds his way back to his [divine] master. The atom was hopeful that the brilliance of the sun would set him dancing again, and the drop desired to savor union with the boundless ocean.[20]

Daryabadi traveled with some fanfare by train through Lucknow and Bhopal on his way to Bombay, where he expected to stay in a guesthouse for pilgrims. On reaching that city's railway station, however, he and his entourage were met by Muhammad ʿAli's brother, Mawlana Shawkat ʿAli (1873–1938), another leader of the Khilafat movement, who invited them to stay at the movement's headquarters, Dar al-Khilafah.[21] There the party waited for the departure of one of Turner Mor-rison's Mogul Line ships to Jeddah. After more than ten days in Bombay, the last few spent in an anxious to-and-fro between Dar al-Khilafah and the travel offices of Turner Morrison, the group finally left port on the steamship *Akbar*, on March 28, 1929. On April 5 the *Akbar* docked on the island of Kamaran for a mandated medical bath and quarantine, and on April 8 it arrived in Jeddah.[22]

Safar-i Hijaz appeared that same year, in forty installments in the journal *Sach*.[23] Daryabadi's travelogue has a direct, accessible, and appealing style and is inter-spersed with Persian and Urdu verse (some of it his own) and edifying tidbits from Arabic religious texts. The narrative is rhetorically pleasing for an audience with refined literary tastes. It follows the temporal pattern of the pilgrimage, while the elements of journeying, often in conditions of hardship, and the opportunity to exchange ideas and experiences with a diverse group of people allow Daryabadi to comment on a variety of social and political topics. The author speaks as a histo-rian, jurist, poet, political leader, and ardent lover of the Prophet Muhammad. At one level, his travelogue reads like a diary of experiences and events. He docu-ments each step of the way with great detail and personal impressions, catering to the varying inclinations of his readership; he even notes the weight and capacity of the ship on which he sets sail to Mecca. He also devotes space to geographical and historical description and analysis, covering the history of the Arabian Penin-sula—and Jeddah, Mecca, and Medina in particular—and includes an entire chap-ter on the various ethnic and tribal groups of the Hijaz. At the same time, the travelogue is heavy with logistical description, such as information on transporta-tion, fees, housing, and water supplies.[24] For example, Daryabadi offers practical advice on how to secure luggage, food, and other necessities for the trip, as well as how to handle money-transfer issues through the *havala* (delivery-in-trust) sys-tem. Most important, *Safar-i Hijaz* is a comprehensive manual of the rules of pil-grimage in the Sunni Hanafi legal tradition. Tying these aspects together is an evocative narrative of a personal spiritual journey, which is everywhere evident in the intimate tone in which Daryabadi shares his thoughts and reflections. This journey finds scholarly expression in a later chapter on the inner aspects of the pilgrimage, which employs the commentary of exemplary Sufi forebears to make the point that a hajj without inner work is akin to no hajj at all.

Daryabadi's biographer Tahsin Firaqi notes that in 1929, Daryabadi was a born-again believer, having been an avowed atheist only ten years earlier, and that his travelogue still reflects the exhilaration of a new Muslim. In it, he comes across as a repentant sinner whose emotions are bound up with the unfolding, uncertain destiny of the Muslim world. "His travelogue is the story of a spiritual community . . . a travelogue of love," Firaqi writes. "Majid has chosen the mountain-shattering [*alburz-shikan*] style of an Israelite prophet."[25] Rhetorically, the care that Dary-abadi puts into describing the details of the voyage reflects his contention that this is the most important trip a Muslim will make in his or her lifetime; in taking the reader through every step of the journey, he wishes to evoke a longing for the Ka'ba. His erudition and curiosity regarding history, culture, logistics, and law appeal to the educated reader. The rhetorical effectiveness of Daryabadi's travel-ogue rests in its ability to convey the high formality of the *fiqh* (legal debates) of pilgrimage with the informality of direct, authentic, individual experience.

AUDIENCE AND OBJECTIVES OF *SAFAR-I HIJAZ*

Firaqi notes the emotional impact of the travelogue on a few key intellectuals: for example, the Urdu poet, anti-imperialist, and cofounder of the Communist Party of India, Hasrat Mohani, who wrote a letter of 1933 noting that "several times my eyes filled up with tears," and the Jama'at-i Islami prose writer Mawlana Mas'ud 'Alam Nadwi, who claimed that no other travelogue affected his heart and mind as much as Daryabadi's.[26] However, Daryabadi's larger audience was the educated, Westernized Muslims of North India who constituted the political leadership of independence movements, whom he wished to reorient toward the Hijaz as a devotional center: "This voyage is not for entertainment, nor for acquiring knowledge, mastering an art, or looking at historical and archaeological sites. Nor [is it like a trip] to Kashmir or Shimla, London or Paris, Oxford or Cambridge. Nor to where there is the roaring of oratory and speeches and the passing of resolutions."[27] In his description of Medina, Daryabadi stresses the spiritual impact that the city has had on prominent members of the Muslim elite, who with all the financial and educational resources of the West at their disposal still emphasize devotion to the Prophet:

> Even in this age of Yajuj,[28] in the grip of the Antichrist [Dajjal],[29] no place in the world matches the powerful attraction of this abode. No university or college, no seminary or academy, no library or laboratory, no lecture hall of some "expert," or no circle of some professor. . . . Did not the hatim of Rampur, [the Indian Muslim ruler] Ra'is Kalb 'Ali Khan, take pride in swallowing the dirt of this road? Bhopal's Sultan Jahan Begum, that "person of heart": at whose threshold did she take pride in begging? Mir 'Usman 'Ali Khan Namdar, the crown bearer of the Asifi kingdom [of Hyderabad]: for whose alleyway does his heart yearn?[30]

These images speak to a select group who are familiar with these figures, all of whom are rulers of Indian "princely states" (Rampur, Bhopal, and Hyderabad), and with the experience of traveling overseas for entertainment or education. Similarly, Daryabadi appeals in his arguments to European Orientalists whose writings and opinions would have had some cachet with these elites. While he employs the works of Orientalist scholars to further his revivalist agenda, he does so not in homage or as an heir to that tradition but rather to resist and challenge it. In a discussion on whether the Ka'ba was the first house of worship, as the Qur'an claims, Daryabadi cites several Orientalist scholars who despite their best efforts were forced to accede to the truth of the Qur'anic statement: for instance, "[David] Margoliouth, in a drunken stupor of antagonism toward Islam, came doddering forward to express his opposition—but was cut down by his colleagues."[31] It is clear, however, that Daryabadi is chiding his readership for neglect of their religious obligations, an apathy that in his view reflects a creeping immorality among educated Muslims.[32] We see this concern throughout the travelogue, as in this colorful passage describing his fellow passengers on the *Akbar:*

> Among these fifteen hundred, there are only a hundred or so who are young, able-bodied, educated, affluent, and somewhat worldly in appearance and rank. Most of the pilgrims are elderly, weak, sick, poor, illiterate, and, having no rank or position, anonymous. They are not rejecting the world; rather, the world is rejecting them. Is the pilgrimage to the House of God now only obligatory for the hopeless? And what of those who reside in their grand structures and well-appointed homes, ride around in attractive cars, have large bank accounts and incomes of two to four thousand a month, who own large tracts of land and hold degrees from top universities in Europe and Hindustan, who are renowned barristers and doctors and engineers, successful editors, khan bahadurs, CIs [members of the Imperial Order of the Crown of India], nawabs and their offspring, members of councils, who are aficionados of theater and

cinema and dance and every Western art, who send their children to London, Paris, Berlin, Vienna, Oxford, and Cambridge—perhaps the hajj has become obsolete for them?[33]

Daryabadi reminds his readers that, like the daily prayers, pilgrimage is an individual obligation (*farz 'ayn*). But as it requires physical effort and financial expenditure, it also turns into "someone else's obligation." More important, he laments, these same careless individuals travel the length and breadth of India but neglect the one place where Muslims are required to be present: "Leave aside traveling to the Ka'ba on their foreheads; they do not even travel on their feet!"

> Readers of *Sach* must be asking, what relevance does this self-exploration have for us? Did you find anything [on the hajj] or not? . . . Tell us this, have you brought anything for us? And my response is, yes! I have brought a message for all *Sach* readers and for all men, for all women, for all boys, for the elderly and for the youth . . .: "Become supporters of God [*kunu ansar allah*]. Become supporters of religion. God does not want meetings and conferences; he wants support for the religion. The Prophet does not seek poetry and *qawwali* songs; he seeks support for the religion."[34]

Like much of his work, Daryabadi's *Safar-i Hijaz* focuses on the decline and humiliation of the Muslim world and the hopes of Islamic revival: "God knows how many Abu Jahls and Abu Lahabs exist in the world today.[35] . . . Will these 'enlightened' and 'nationalist' Abu Jahls and Abu Lahabs of the twentieth century always have respite? The emigrant [*muhajir*] of Mecca [i.e., the Prophet] had found refuge in the Qubba mosque in Medina, wherein he could call God's name and declare God's unity. Does the community [*umma*] of the Beloved contain no Qubba? And, God forbid, will they have to stumble about lost forever?"[36] It makes perfect sense that *Safar-i Hijaz* was published a few years after the end of the Khilafat movement, reflecting both the passion for pan-Islamism that gave life to the movement and the loss of face at its political failure. At the same time, the travelogue shows the reality of British economic hegemony in India. Between 1858 and 1914, the Indian economy was manipulated to make the colony a production center for agricultural raw materials and a captive market for British manufactured goods, delaying its industrialization.[37] Throughout *Safar-i Hijaz*, Daryabadi highlights the economic and spiritual subjugation of the wider Muslim world:

> Jeddah is the gateway to the Arab world, the first city of the Islamic polity [*hukumat-i islam*]. Bad or good, it is still ours. Who doesn't love what is theirs? But, oh God, you have given us permission to say this about just one presumptuous fistful of earth. Now the heart is utterly fearful, the tongue stammers, to call anything "ours." Forget Córdoba and Granada; that was a long time ago. But what about Basra, Baghdad, Aleppo, Beirut, Damascus, Jerusalem, Cairo, or Istanbul? Just yesterday these cities were ours. And not so long ago, so were [the Indian cities of] Shahjahanabad [Delhi],

Akbarabad [Agra], Hyderabad, Lucknow, Murshidabad, Azimabad [Patna], Surat, Bijapur, and Carnatic. Now do any of these still belong to us? And so how long can we continue to celebrate Jeddah?[38]

THE YAJUJ: WESTERNERS AS GOG

A common image in Daryabadi's work is Yajuj, the Muslim version of the terrifying biblical figure Gog, in Qur'anic mythology a corrupt, destructive, and rapacious people who will ravage the earth before the end of time. For Daryabadi, the West is the embodiment of Yajuj, and he classifies anything that is connected to the West or undergoing Westernization as Yajuji. Indeed, *Yajuji tamaddun* (the civilization of Gog) marks the modern era: it is a time of universal warfare, greed, injustice, and self-serving ideologies. The following passage is typical of Daryabadi's diatribes against the machinations of Yajuj:

The ocean even now is ink, blue ink. . . . However, a vision has come before our eyes, that one day this great body of water, this barren ocean, instead of lapping waves will dance with leaping fire, and the smoke will turn into clouds. This will be the day that the Yajuj, like Ravan of Lanka, will be set ablaze with the flames of his warplanes and warships, his streams of oil and petroleum wealth.[39] And when the sparks of his greed, his land grabbing, his gold worship, his imperialism and capitalism, his socialism and communism and God knows what other ism set fire to the ocean, [that will be] a version of hell on earth. . . . Today Yajuj has been granted a respite. Today he may intimidate, disorder, and disease our hearts, minds, and intellects, our eyes and ears, with his prosperity, his entourage, his culture and education, his sciences and arts, his doctors and engineers . . . his cannon and rifles and machine guns . . . his planes, bombs, atom bombs. But rest assured, this respite will not last forever. The curtain is on the verge of rising![40]

Daryabadi associates all evidence of twentieth-century industrialization with the mark of Yajuj. As a global port city and thus a vehicle of Yajuj in India, Bombay bears the brunt of his ire:

Bombay may just be the most Yajuji city in India. Those who haven't had the pleasure of being graced with a visit to London, Paris, New York, or Chicago can find a faint replica of these cities in Bombay. The same buildings scraping against the sky, brisk circulation of money, absorption in buying and selling; the same abundance of sensual pleasures, drunkenness, and self-love; the same smoke and electricity everywhere; the same din of mills, engines, and factories; the same noise of rails, trams, and motorcars; the same morning-till-evening, sunset-till-sunrise shrieking and shouting, smoke blowing, shoving, and crushing impatience of the Yajuj. . . . And in this era of Yajuj, this is what they call "progress and culture"! One can only marvel that even in the grip of Yajujiyat [Gogness], the mosques of Bombay are still respected and well attended and one still sees many practicing, faithful Muslims![41]

Of course, Daryabadi was not unaware of the irony of his situation: that while he expressed hostility toward Western industrialization, he was taking advantage of Western technology to speed his way to Jeddah. But he was not an obscurantist. He appreciated technological progress and its attendant benefits, as his astute commentary on advances in transportation illustrates.[42] His critique targets the pursuit of industrialization at any cost and globalization that benefited the West at the expense of everyone else. Yajuj had commandeered the seaways of the world, to the extreme disadvantage of the other contenders. In the following passage, Daryabadi deftly weaves both Qur'an and Hadith into his characterization of Western naval superiority:

> [Yajuj] gives permission to whomever he wishes to run ships in the ocean. And he bars whomsoever he wishes to bar from receiving the benefit of God's handiwork. . . . The seas and ports, the flags of ships, the cruisers, dreadnoughts, torpedoes, and destroyers of the admiralties and sea lords, all shout out that "the command [*amr, hukm*] belongs to Yajuj!"[43] Now, if in this context you were to hear the words of a sage that Yajuj and Majuj [the Biblical Magog] will drink the waters of the earth,[44] then surely you won't be waiting for a future age in which these words will come true . . . ?[45]

For Daryabadi, this reality was exemplified by the fact that the Mogul Line, the shipping line on which he and his party traveled, was no longer run by a Muslim-owned company. Founded in 1877, it became part of the Turner Morrison Company in 1913, though Daryabadi reluctantly acknowledges in his travelogue that the company's Bombay agent was an "honorable Englishman." He also notes that while competition had forced British-owned hajj companies to lower their fares at one time, in his day they took advantage of high demand to charge the same high price, at the expense of the pilgrims. To direct profits towards Muslim businesses, he urges pilgrims to patronize the Muslim Pilgrims Food Supply Company, a Muslim-owned shipboard restaurant, which was so poorly advertised that many pilgrims brought their own food on board.)[46]

Daryabadi's lament was not unwarranted. Frank Broeze has explained that most Indian maritime ventures established before 1914 failed, with the exception of the Mogul Line (which, as mentioned, came under the control of a British company), Bombay Steam, and the Indian Cooperative Navigation and Trading Company.[47] He contends that Indian-owned shipping foundered neither because there was no marine engineering industry in India nor because Indian shipowners lacked managerial skills or had staffing problems. Rather, their greatest challenge was competition from such powerful British maritime ventures as the Peninsular and Oriental Steam Navigation Company and the British India Steam Navigation Company, which both benefited from lucrative mail contracts with the British and Indian governments. As a result, Broeze concludes, "through the speed, regularity and large capacity of their fleets," the British shipping lines ousted the Indian- (and Muslim-) owned competition.[48]

In a similar vein, Daryabadi laments that the obligatory Islamic pilgrimage has become a source of income and prosperity only for English and American manufacturing and Western economic interests:

> The hubbub of the markets of Mecca—how can one express the heart's pain?—does not benefit Muslims. It does not add to the success of Mecca or Medina, or the Hijaz, or Egypt and Syria, or Morocco and Tripoli, or Iraq and Iran, or Bukhara and Afghanistan. No, it does not benefit any Muslim country. Rather, it is completely for the benefit of the European [farangi], the foreigner, of America and Germany, England and Italy. The goods in every shop worth lakhs of rupees:[49] these shawls and pashminas, blankets and sheets, socks and gloves, scarves and collars, sweaters and undershirts, velvets and satins, shoes and hats; these pumps and slippers, motor tubes and truck tires; these electric lanterns and gas boilers; these oil barrels and perfume bottles; these cigars and matches, jams and jellies, glasses and plates, handkerchiefs and prayer rugs, and piles of all types of attractive things. If only even a little bit of it belonged to us. If only [money] were not going directly from our pockets to the warehouses and factories, banks and treasuries of Manchester and Lancashire, Liverpool and Glasgow, Sheffield, Birmingham, Stockholm, Washington, and Chicago. Granted, there is the odd cloak from Baghdad and shoes from Delhi. But when foreigners are profiting in tens of thousands and tens of lakhs, what is a few hundred in our pocket? Who could this possibly please? Who could take pride in this?[50]

Daryabadi also draws a connection between Western economic hegemony and Islamic moral decline, noting that he never saw the notables of Mecca setting foot in a mosque. Nor did he find the level of scholarship that he expected from the Hadith scholars and jurists of the city. This again he attributes to the "diseased" hearts and "frightened" intellects of Muslims under Western intellectual and cultural siege.[51] Similarly, he blames the inefficiencies of hajj logistics in Bombay and the crowded and inadequate conditions on board the *Akbar* on the supremacist cultural attitudes of Yajuj:

> This is punishment from the Yajuji government for the following crime: that in the "enlightenment" of the twentieth century, we are leaving aside London, Paris, Rome, Vienna, Oxford, Cambridge, Glasgow and Edinburgh, New York and Washington and instead enthusiastically making our way to a sandy wilderness, a rocky wasteland. The prophetic Hadith clearly state that even in the age of Yajuj, the hajj will go on. But we did not hear how the Yajuji governments will treat the pilgrims and what the pilgrims will have to go through. Rather, we have now seen and experienced this state of affairs! It is true that for those who set forth on God's path, every pain is pleasure.... But to those tyrannical forces that today pride themselves on their strength, let it be known that this is not a test of the patience and restraint of those who walk on God's path. It is a test of the clemency of the Lord of the Heavens and the Earth himself![52]

Daryabadi takes care to document cultural attitudes, for example by noting the apathy bordering on disdain that the ships' English officers and crew display toward pilgrims (though this didn't affect Daryabadi, who thanks to his social standing and connections was offered a cabin next to the captain's).[53] Later he details the humiliating circumstances, especially for women, of the medical bath and quarantine procedures on Kamaran. He writes that the pilgrims on the island were "penned in like convicts" and suffered from every manner of illness once they reboarded the ship. An elderly lady died on board from an illness she contracted in Kamaran.[54] Elsewhere Daryabadi asks with great irony whether Muslim pilgrims really think they could be treated to twentieth-century comfort and convenience when they follow the "ancient and forgotten" laws of the seventh century. "In this age of knowledge and urbanity," he sighs, "they are seen as no better than . . . four-footed beasts."[55]

OPPOSITION TO NATIONALISM

Daryabadi was a critic of nationalism, whether expressed as a love of nation, province, region, or even language.[56] He saw it as a Western-imposed ideology, meant to weaken Muslim unity by transferring the source of ultimate identity from God to a human-made entity. Even the attainment of political power by Muslims in the nationalist mode becomes an impotent act, for the powerful make decisions not for the benefit of Islam and Muslims as a whole but for the good of their individual nations.

> Today the confession of faith recited in all places is not of faith in God but of faith in the godliness and divinity of Yajuj. Muslims are made judges in chambers of justice, and through them the decisions of Shari'a are being modified. Muslims are being made members of councils, and through the schemes and speeches of these members, Shari'a is being torn to shreds. Muslims are set up as ministers and emirs, and through their commands, Shari'a is destroyed. Muslim universities and schools are established, and in the treatises and articles of Muslim experts, Shari'a is mocked. An ardent love of nation is set aflame among Muslims, and the result is that Turks worship Turkness, Egyptians Egyptianness, and Indian Muslims leave aside their Islam and begin to grow proud of their Indianness.[57]

To drive this point home, *Safar-i Hijaz* zeroes in on episodes that provide perfect models of Muslim unity. One such is Daryabadi's experience at the Prophet's Mosque in Medina. He notes that what were once four separate prayer arenas, for followers of each Sunni school of Muslim jurisprudence (madhab), had been consolidated into one and that at every prayer time an imam from a different school of jurisprudence would lead the prayer. He mentions with approval that in the course of one day every Muslim would have to pray behind an imam of each school, thus keeping the unity of the umma intact:

The division of legal schools into four is purely for the sake of convenience and ease, and not to break the umma into pieces or to turn each one against the other. The division of prayer into four congregations does not have the same pleasure and beauty as reading prayers together and giving respect to one imam. There is also no separate congregational arrangement for the Shiʿas, but I have seen small groups of Shiʿas praying in the *rawdah* [grave of the Prophet] behind their own imam. However, Shiʿas such as Chaudhri Muhammad ʿAli Radawlvi join our congregation without hesitation. If only such ecumenicism were common among the Shiʿas![58]

It is noteworthy that he calls this a "praiseworthy innovation" (*bidʿa hasana*) of the Nejdi rulers of the Hijaz and expresses a wish that they would engage in other efforts at engendering unity.[59] Similarly, in a discussion on the correct intention for visitations in Medina—the legal debate hinges on whether the pilgrim should intend to visit the grave of the Prophet or the Prophet's Mosque—he tries to reconcile conflicting opinions by invoking Hanafi legal scholars who present the most ecumenical perspectives on the matter. He prefaces this discussion by noting that

> the human being's love of contention twists around what is perfectly straight. It is clear that the goal should be visitation of the Prophet. Of course, it is not possible to [see the Prophet] with our material gaze. Thus, focusing on a part of the structure with which [the visitor feels that] the Prophet had the closest relationship, the greatest nearness, will make the visitation that much more important and beloved. . . . Any difference of opinion that occurs beyond this is not a difference of fundamentals [*usul*] or creed [ʿ*aqida*] but a matter of taste.[60]

The Prophet Muhammad then becomes the rallying point for all Muslims, each of whom, despite variations in theology, ritual, and etiquette, is essentially a "Muhammadi."

> I saw the different sects of Bohra—Daʾudi and Sulaymani—and other Muslim sects, reading prayers and engaging in visitation in their own particular ways. But the court of the mercy of the worlds is the center of every confession. Differences of opinion are external, not internal; they are differences in the path, not in the goal. Whether it is Imam Abu Hanifah or Imam Shafiʿi, Hazrat Jilani or Khwaja Ajmeri, each of them is a conduit to the threshold of prophecy. On entering the sacred enclosure, on reaching the door of the Prophet, there is no Hanafi, no Shafiʿi, no Maliki, no Hanbali, no Ashʿari, no Maturidi. There is no [Sufi] Qadiri, no Chishti, no Sabiri, no Mujaddidi. There is no *muqallid*, no non-*muqallid*.[61] Everyone is merely a Muhammadi. At the time of the Prophet, what religion did his companions adhere to? Were they anything but Muhammadis? . . . Today, when good fortune has brought you to the door of the Prophet and you have faith that your Prophet is eternally alive, what audacity and idiocy that, in the presence of the Prophet, you attach yourself to some other prophet, and take pride in that attachment! No doubt in the darkness of the night, every bit of light is a blessing. But when you are standing before the sun, at least for now snuff out your candles and torches. And if you can, become Muslims anew, renew your Islam,

strengthen your covenant and oath, and pledge allegiance at the hand of him whose hand is the hand of the Omnipotent and allegiance to whom is allegiance to the creator of the worlds![62]

In the course of his pilgrimage, Daryabadi sent a letter to 'Abd al-'Aziz ibn Sa'ud (1876–1953), then the king of Nejd and the Hijaz, who became the ruler of Saudi Arabia in 1932, offering suggestions about how he and other custodians of the holy sites might honor the unity of the Muslim community.[63] In it, Daryabadi contends that every Muslim persuasion has equal rights to the holy sites of Mecca and Medina and that the most generous-minded attitude toward the rites and practices of each is necessary. In the interest of unity, even the persuasions considered wayward or false should be granted space in which to engage in their rituals and leniency toward their claims, until they adopt the correct fundamentals.[64] Daryabadi here refers to a contentious issue his travelogue addressed earlier: the appointment of sentinels to monitor and prevent reprehensible innovation in worship at the graves of the ancient cemetery of Jannat al-Baqi' in Medina.[65] To him, this imposition was rendered more unbearable by the fact that the graves were in a dismal state of filth and disrepair: "Apparently, in the Nejdi definition, throwing trash on the graves of the pure ones does not come under the category of reprehensible innovation." While he acknowledges that many Muslims engage in unorthodox behavior (dance, intoxication, decoration, prostration) at grave sites in the name of adoration, the opposite extreme, dishonoring the graves of the pious in the name of purification, is equally reprehensible.[66] In his letter, he offers Ibn Sa'ud the names of Indian scholars well versed in questions surrounding the etiquette of visitation, who would provide the rulers of the Hijaz with sage advice on a more ecumenical approach. These scholars included members of the Ahl-i Hadith, Nadwat al-'Ulama, and 'Usmaniya University, as well as the shaykh al-Islam of Hyderabad. "In this way," Daryabadi writes, "we could largely do away with the bitterness that a rather large group of Indian Muslims has developed with regard to the attitudes of the Hijazi rulers."[67]

For all its emphasis on the ideal of unity, this incident highlights the unavoidable fractures of pan-Islamism. While Daryabadi condemns nationalism as an ideal, national and regional connections necessarily mediate all of his experiences: the group with which he travels, the contacts he has in each city, the places in which they stay (mainly guesthouses set up by Indian Muslim princely states),[68] and the political lens through which he views the Muslim world. He does not speak the language of the Hijaz and is made painfully aware of this fact as soon as he lands in Jeddah: "They can speak neither Farsi nor English nor Urdu!," he exclaims and soon realizes that even the few phrases of Arabic that he can muster are considered "formal" (*nahwi*) and are a source of great amusement for the locals.[69] Indeed, the provincialism of the Hijaz is in stark contrast to the cosmopolitan character of Daryabadi's experience in India, and he can't help but strike an elitist note when comparing the crude infrastructure of Mecca, Medina, and surrounding towns with the urban sophistication to which he is accustomed.[70]

Often, Daryabadi writes as a foreigner to the Hijaz, an Indian staking his claim to the holy cities. He lauds the establishment of Indian religious schools in Mecca in the early twentieth century, one financed by a wealthy woman called Sulat al-Nisa Begum of Calcutta, and goes into considerable detail regarding the history and funding of each. He emphasizes the fact that these institutions have deep roots in the city and even makes a fund-raising call for one, providing an address where money can be sent.[71] In this way, Daryabadi illustrates that Indian Muslims are not strangers to the city, playing the nationalist card to impress upon his readers an obligation to support Indian claims to religious and institutional authority in Mecca. In the same vein, he makes a theological gibe at the expense of the political leadership of the Hijaz, whose support of these institutions is less than satisfactory—a gibe that further expresses a sense of entitlement to a piece of this holy ground.[72] In discussing the decrepit state of Jannat al-Baqi' and the Prophet's Mosque, as well as logistical concerns, Daryabadi is not shy in his criticism of Sa'udi rulers: "At the very least, after seeing [the terrible state of Jannat al-Baqi',] the average Muslim would hardly be left with any fond memories of the Sa'udi government. And this is hardly the last item in its long list of crimes."[73] He goes on to detail other instances of negligence, such as the absence of carpets in the Prophet's Mosque during much of the year, the tattered state of the carpet when it is laid out, and the unreliability of the electric lights in the holy cities.[74]

Of course, Daryabadi is quick to couch his criticisms in the discourse of Muslim unity. They are for the good of the Sa'udis: the real enemy is not Nejd but Yajuj. For although they may be mistaken in their religious attitudes, the Nejdi and Hijazi Arabs still fall within the circle of Islam.

> Today is not a time for war with Hijazis and Nejdis, or between Hanafis and Hanbalis, or between the people of innovation and the people of Sunna. Now is the time for unity in the fight against the innumerable armies of Yajuj, who under infinite names, marks, disguises, and veils, from every corner and every side, are attacking God's religion, the Prophet's law, the message of Islam. . . . Jihad is not called for against those [Muslims] who knocked down the mausoleum of 'Uthman or demolished the grave of [the Prophet's daughter] Fatimah al-Zahra. Rather, jihad must be waged against those who oppose the very religion of 'Uthman and Fatimah, who, let alone targeting the grave of 'Uthman, have destroyed the very memory of 'Uthman . . . and who create contempt and disrespect for Fatimah in the heart![75]

Daryabadi's pan-Islamism champions a normative set of identities that make one Muslim at the expense of regional identification. It is in this vein that he writes of cultural symbols such as the Taj Mahal (although built by a Muslim emperor) and the Eiffel Tower as "child's play" in comparison with the Ka'ba, which has endured for millennia and is a sacred building for people around the world.[76] Similarly, he asks his compatriots to turn their backs on poetry and *qawwali* devotional music and become "supporters of God."[77] He champions the creation of a polity that draws on collective experience and consciousness to establish a normative, universal Islam. It is important to note that by the 1920s, the deepening of sectarian divisions (not least because of the Ahmadiyya movement) had become one of the most pressing issues facing Muslim intellectuals in India. Daryabadi's utopian vision should certainly be read in this context.

PILGRIMAGE AS PANACEA

Based on his own experience, Daryabadi counsels that a return to religious commitment can best temper the unavoidable and crushing encounter with modernity and globalization. For the Westoxicated Muslim, the commitment of pilgrimage is the optimal means of finding a path back to the fount of the tradition, adoration (*muhabbat*) of the Prophet. However, not only love but also discipline makes pilgrimage meaningful—a spiritual connection with the holy cities can take place only through a renewed commitment to following Islamic law, to moral discipline rooted in love of the Prophet. In his narrative, Daryabadi himself models the perfect pilgrim, overcome by emotion yet keenly aware of the rules and regulations that determine proper interaction with the sacred. In a chapter on the etiquette of visitation, he expresses frustration at the lax commitment to law engendered in the name of love of the Prophet, which in his words makes

> every forbidden thing [haram] allowed [halal] and every weakness a virtue. Are they
> not aware that love in their own lives takes on such a variety of forms? The love of
> one's wife is different from the love of one's children. And the kind of love that is
> shown to children, who in their right mind would show this kind of love to their
> mother and father? While the child is young, we hold him in our laps, tickle him, and
> play with him. And when the child reaches the age of maturity, we treat him with
> respect and show him a completely different manner of love. Now, if we began to
> tease, tickle, and play in this way with our elders and our parents, would this be con-
> sidered proof of our love or proof of utter idiocy and madness?[78]

By demonstrating that every relationship has different rules of engagement and, later, that the connection to the Prophet is the highest form of relationship, Daryabadi argues for the necessity of a unique and more formal etiquette in the latter case. To make this easier for his readers to understand, he incorporates relevant excerpts, with translation, from Hanafi legal works on hajj rituals (*manasik al-hajj*)—for example, 'Allamah Rahmatallah Sindhi's *Lubab al-Manasik* and Mulla 'Ali Qari's *Sharh Lubab al-Manasik*—all of which stress fear, awe, and neediness as the proper emotional responses to the Prophet's grave site. Lest his readers think that "these commands are merely those of dry jurists," Daryabadi offers similar injunctions from the tradition of the Sufis known as the "people of the heart" (*ahl-i dil*).[79]

Daryabadi is always keenly aware of his audience. It is rare that he presents laundry lists of legal jargon. Rather, he skillfully weaves information on legal obligations into his travel narrative, and without sacrificing detail or clarity. In this way, he humanizes and simplifies the logistics and religious obligations of the pilgrimage.[80] His discussion of misperceptions about the ritual of donning the simple cloth sheet (ihram), for example, occurs in a deeply emotional passage on his experience of leaving the home of the Prophet, a transitional moment.[81] Similarly, he elucidates the rituals of Mina in a chatty travel diary in which he goes off on amusing tangents, such as the undervalued merits of having a solid roof over one's head![82]

CONCLUSIONS

Daryabadi's discourse paints the new realities of nationalism and the global economic system as a tale of conflicting moralities. He draws a direct line from Western economic hegemony to the valorizing of nationalism and the economic, political, and spiritual decline of the Muslim world. These exogenous, pervasive theopolitical projects have implications that must be countered by marshaling the indigenous spiritual and political resources of Islam. In *Safar-i Hijaz*, the hajj becomes the symbolic center of this struggle. In his study on pilgrimage, Alan Morinis defines it as "a journey undertaken by a person in quest of a place or a state that he or she believes to embody a valued ideal." He notes that the pilgrimage destination serves as "an intensified version of some ideal that the pilgrim values but cannot achieve at home."[83] This model certainly works for Daryabadi, for whom the pilgrimage center of Mecca embodies the qualities that every Muslim community should nurture. Most crucially, these are leadership by way of sectarian unity, renewed devotion to the Prophet's example, and commitment to God through disciplined attentiveness to religious law and financial and physical hardship.

Mecca's role as a symbol goes beyond its connection to the House of God. Daryabadi singles out the city and its environs as one of the few Muslim spaces territorially, economically, and culturally unfettered by Yajuj, the West. In fact, the stream of characters that populate his pilgrimage narrative attest to a deeper reality: the hajj was not only a symbolic but also an effective center for a variety of religious responses to the epistemic rupture of the Age of Steam and Print. In one of the many ironies that accompany globalization, the powerless inevitably transform and redeploy the tools of hegemony. Developments in steam travel enabled Muslims, most significantly from the educated middle classes, to make the hajj in ever greater numbers. The result was a furious circulation of ideas converging on the Hijaz and the consequent rapid growth of Sufi, pan-Islamist, and other reformist and anti-imperialist movements. In much the same way, religious scholars quickly adopted print technology to close ranks against Western cultural and ideological hegemony (but also to sharpen competing Muslim identities), and the printed pamphlet became a ubiquitous tool of debate and protest. As James Gelvin and Nile Green note in their introduction, the European post-Enlightenment definition of religion as a private matter provided some autonomy from imperial interference for religious activities. In India, Queen Victoria's Proclamation of 1858 "to the princes, chiefs, and people of India" (announcing her assumption of control over the Indian colonies) enshrined this idea, declaring that all religions would enjoy the equal and impartial protection of law and maintaining that authorities would not interfere in the religious belief or worship of any subject. Thus the religious realm became a space for the exercise of creative agency. Daryabadi took advantage of this, and his skillful deployment of the ideologies and communicational resources of his time provide a window onto some of the decisive concerns of global Muslims in the Age of Steam and Print.

NOTES

Unless otherwise noted, all translations in this chapter are mine.

1. A brief and salient introduction to Daryabadi's travelogue may be found in Sugata Bose, *A Hundred Horizons: The Indian Ocean in the Age of Global Empire* (Cambridge, MA: Harvard University Press, 2009), 221–31.

2. The genre arguably came into existence with the 1787 travel account of Rafi' al-Din Muradabadi, a disciple of the renowned reformist scholar Shah Wali Allah (d. 1762). See Barbara D. Metcalf, "The Pilgrimage Remembered: South Asian Accounts of the *Hajj*," in *Muslim Travellers: Pilgrimage, Migration, and the Religious Imagination*, ed. Dale F. Eickelman and James Piscatori (Berkeley: University of California Press, 1990), 86.

3. Ibid., 85.

4. Ibid., 87.

5. C. A. Bayly, *The Birth of the Modern World 1780–1914* (Oxford: Blackwell, 2004), 354–55.

6. Metcalf, "The Pilgrimage Remembered," 88.

7. For a useful review of the symbolic use of the hajj in relation to South Asian pan-Islamism, see Saurabh Mishra, *Pilgrimage, Politics and Pestilence: The Haj from the Indian Subcontinent, 1860–1920* (Delhi: Oxford University Press, 2011).

8. For the impact of colonial-era transitions on the hajj accounts of the Indian pilgrims Amir Ahmad Alawi and Nawab Sikandar Begum, see Mushirul Hasan and Rakhshanda Jalil, *Journey to the Holy Land: A Pilgrim's Diary* (Delhi: Oxford University Press, 2009); Siobhan Lambert-Hurley, *A Princess's Pilgrimage: Nawab Sikandar Begum's "A Pilgrimage to Mecca"* (Delhi: Women Unlimited, 2007).

9. On the speedy adoption of lithographic print culture by Indian religious scholars and its impact on the use and development of the Urdu vernacular, see Barbara D. Metcalf, *Islamic Revival in British India: Deoband, 1860–1900* (Delhi: Oxford University Press, 2005), 199–203, 209.

10. The Aligarh movement was one of the main educational reform drives among Indian Muslims after the Rebellion of 1857. Under the intellectual and political leadership of Sayyid Ahmad Khan, it led to the establishment of the Muhammadan Anglo-Oriental College at Aligarh (later Aligarh Muslim University), which became a center of the Indian and Pakistan independence movements.

11. Deoband was the site of Dar al-'Ulum, a theological academy founded in 1867 by the religious scholars Rashid Ahmad Gangohi and Mawlana Muhammad Qasim Nanotvi, among others. It spearheaded a reformist religious movement across India and in South Asian Muslim diaspora communities around the world.

12. Salim Qidwai, 'Abd al-Majid Daryabadi (Delhi: Sahitya Academy, 1998), 11–16.

13. Tahsin Firaqi, 'Abd al-Majid Daryabadi: Ahwal wa Athar (Lahore: Idarah-yi Thaqafat-i Islamiyyah, 1993), 585–88.

14. 'Abd al-Majid Daryabadi, Ap Biti (Lucknow: Maktabah Firdaws, 1978), 260–64.

15. Muhammad Qasim Zaman, Ashraf 'Ali Thanwi: Islam in Modern South Asia (Oxford: Oneworld, 2008), 100–101.

16. Ibid., 101.

17. It is worth noting that this is not an unusual view; by the 1930s, it was the formal position of the Indian National Congress and of Muslim religious and political leadership.

18. Daryabadi, Ap Biti, 331.

19. These included Mawlavi Zafar al-Mulk 'Alavi, Mawlana Sayyid Sulayman Nadvi, and Professor Harun Khan Sherwani of Hyderabad's 'Usmaniya University. Daryabadi, Safar-i Hijaz: Hajj wa Ziyarat ka Mufassal wa Mukammal Hidayat Namah (Lucknow: Nasim Book Depot, 1967), 31.

20. Ibid., 30.

21. Ibid., 33–35.

22. Ibid., 68, 82.

23. Ibid., 22.

24. Ibid., 41, 44.

25. Firaqi, 'Abd al-Majid Daryabadi, 440.

26. Hasrat Mohani and Mawlana Mas'ud 'Alam Nadwi, quoted in ibid., 442–43.

27. Daryabadi, Safar-i Hijaz, 29–30.

28. See below for more on the concept and implications of Yajuj.

29. Dajjal, or "the one who deceives," is a key figure in Islamic eschatology and is mentioned in Hadith literature. Comparable to the Antichrist, he will appear before the Day of Judgment pretending to be the Messiah and will wreak havoc in the world before Jesus Christ finally defeats him.

30. Daryabadi, Safar-i Hijaz, 99–100.

31. Ibid., 248–49. Margoliouth (1858–1940) was a Laudian professor of Arabic at Oxford and in the 1900s and 1910s authored several famous works on the Prophet Muhammad and early Islamic history.

32. Ibid., 25.

33. Ibid., 63.

34. Ibid., 27–28.

35. Muslim sacred history represents the Meccan Quraysh leaders Abu Jahl (Amr ibn Hisham) and Abu Lahab ('Abd al-'Uzza) as two of the most vociferous opponents of Muhammad's prophethood and message.

36. Daryabadi, Safar-i Hijaz, 171.

37. Sugata Bose and Ayesha Jalal, Modern South Asia: History, Culture, Political Economy (Lahore: Sang-e-Meel, 1998), 97–102.

38. Daryabadi, Safar-i Hijaz, 90.

39. Ravan is a demonic villain and king of Sri Lanka in the Sanskrit epic the Ramayana.

40. Daryabadi, Safar-i Hijaz, 66–67.

41. Ibid., 37.

42. See, for example, his comments on ships and railroads in ibid., 47, 105.

43. This is a play here on the Qur'anic expression in 3:154: "The command [amr] belongs to God entirely."

44. This is a reference to a Prophetic Hadith.

45. Daryabadi, *Safar-i Hijaz*, 66.

46. Ibid., 61–62.

47. Frank Broeze, "Underdevelopment and Dependency: Maritime India during the Raj," *Modern Asian Studies* 18, no. 3 (1984): 429–57.

48. Ibid., 443.

49. The Urdu term *lakh* denotes a sum of one hundred thousand.

50. Daryabadi, *Safar-i Hijaz*, 225–26.

51. Ibid., 90. For example, Daryabadi spent some time with a direct descendant of Muhammad ibn ʿAbd al-Wahhab, a man whom he was told was one of the finest scholars of the Nejd. But Daryabadi was thoroughly unimpressed by his level of scholarship (92).

52. Ibid., 49.

53. Ibid., 60.

54. Ibid., 69–76. Pilgrims' complaints to the Hajj Committee about conditions at Kamaran bore fruit a few years later, in 1931, when the quarantine was no longer deemed mandatory (72). For more on hajj quarantines, including at Kamaran, see ch. 5.

55. Daryabadi, *Safar-i Hijaz*, 83.

56. Firaqi, *ʿAbd al-Majid Daryabadi*, 447.

57. Daryabadi, *Safar-i Hijaz*, 177–78.

58. Ibid., 151–52.

59. Ibid., 151.

60. Ibid., 113.

61. A *muqallid* is someone who adopts wholesale the legal decisions of a particular school of Muslim jurisprudence.

62. Daryabadi, *Safar-i Hijaz*, 167–68.

63. Mawlana Manazir Ahsan, an early-to-mid-twentieth-century scholar from the Deoband madrassa, translated the letter into Arabic from Urdu. Though the emir of Medina had invited Daryabadi to be present at an event with the king, he was too unwell that day to attend and had a friend deliver his note. The friend reported that the king handed it to his secretary and said, "Remind me of this during the hajj season." Ibid., 174.

64. Ibid.

65. Jannat al-Baqiʿ houses the graves of many of the Prophet's relatives and companions. In 1925, Ibn Saʿud destroyed the mausoleums in the cemetery in the name of religious purification. Its treatment by subsequent Saʿudi governments has been a continuous source of contention and debate in the Muslim world.

66. Daryabadi, *Safar-i Hijaz*, 162.

67. Ibid., 174–75.

68. For example, Ribat Tonk, Ribat Bhopal, and Ribat Hyderabad in Medina. Daryabadi's party was put up in one of the Hyderabadi buildings at the request of Akhtar Yar Jang Bahadur, the authorized agent (*muʿtamad*) of religious affairs of the last nizam of Hyderabad. Ibid., 107–8.

69. Ibid., 85.

70. Here Daryabadi also follows a trope in South Asian hajj accounts that portray the inhabitants of the Hijaz as lacking piety and competence.

71. Daryabadi, *Safar-i Hijaz*, 374.

72. Ibid., 372, 373.

73. Ibid., 163.

74. Ibid., 164.

75. Ibid., 175–76.

76. Ibid., 251.

77. Ibid., 27–28, 177–78.

78. Ibid., 130.

79. Throughout the book, Daryabadi points his readers toward accessible *manasik al-hajj* works that are comprehensible within the framework of Hanafi law. Others include Rashid Ahmad Gangohi's *Zubdat al-Manasik*, Mawlavi Shah Ilyas Barni's *Sirat al-Hamid* (a travelogue written for a Sufi audience), Mawalvi Shah Sulayman Ashraf's *Kitab al-Hajj*, Mawalvi Munavvar al-Din's *Al-Hajj wa'l Ziyarah*, and Mawalvi Abu'l-Khayr Khayrallah's *Khayr al-Manasik*. See Daryabadi, *Safar-i Hijaz*, 218.

80. As an example, see his discussion of the obligations at Mina, near Mecca. Ibid., 328–37.

81. Ibid., 200–201.

82. Ibid., 328–37.

83. Alan Morinis, introduction to *Sacred Journeys: The Anthropology of Pilgrimage,* ed. Morinis (Westport, CT: Greenwood, 1992), 4.

12

Taking ʿAbduh to China

Chinese-Egyptian Intellectual Contact in the Early Twentieth Century

Zvi Ben-Dor Benite

INTRODUCTION

In 1935 two rather unusual publications appeared, one in Cairo and the other in Shanghai. The first was an Arabic edition of the *Analects* of Confucius (551–479 B.C.E.), the *Lun Yu*. Published in Cairo as *Kitab al-Hiwar li Kunfushiyus* (Confucius's book of dialogues), the Arabic *Analects* appeared at the end of a yearlong series of lectures and discussions about China, its society, and its religions held at Al-Azhar University, the leading Islamic educational institution in the world.[1] The book was published by the famous Salafiyya Press (Al-Matbaʿa al-Salafiyya), a publishing house that at the time gave voice to an "entire movement that sought to revive the Arab-Islamic heritage and the memory of the pious ancestors."[2]

Meanwhile, in Shanghai, the second book, *Huijiao zhexue* (Islamic philosophy), appeared. The title is a bit misleading, for it is not exactly a work on Islamic philosophy but rather a translation of *Risalat al-Tawhid* (Essay on theology, or The theology of unity) by Muhammad ʿAbduh (1849–1905), which was first published in Cairo in 1897 and went on to gain a considerable degree of fame in the following decades.[3] Contrary to what one might expect, it was not an Islamic press that published this book, which "can be seen as the manifesto of modernist Islam."[4] Its publisher was Shanghai's Commercial Press (Shangwu yinshuguan), one of the largest modern presses in China at the time. Among other tomes, that year it released a biography of Benjamin Franklin, a book by Mohandas Gandhi on Indian independence, and a study in Japanese of Western civilization and its philosophy.[5] ʿAbduh, then, was in good—if not specifically Islamic—company when he made his Chinese debut.

Paired together, these two literary events raise intriguing questions. It seems that something was afoot between China and Egypt at that moment—but why so late? As is well known, thanks to major transformations in communication and transportation, the Middle East was already well integrated into the world system decades before. How and why did 'Abduh come to China and Confucius to Cairo in the same year? Why at this particular time and not before? Furthermore, what was the ancient Chinese philosopher doing on the list of an Islamic press, and why was the *Risalat* presented as "Islamic philosophy" to a clearly non-Islamic audience? Above all, what was the context in which the entire affair took place?

This chapter tells the tale of these two translations as part of the greater story of the emergence of circuits of (Islamic) intellectual exchange between China and the Middle East, particularly Egypt, during the first half of the twentieth century, and presents some of the broader historical and cultural aspects of that exchange. The purpose here is not to inquire into the impact of the introduction of Confucian philosophy in Cairo or of 'Abduh's thought in China. That kind of intellectual history requires a much greater space than the limited scope of this chapter, and it is doubtful if such an approach is possible. I will focus, rather, on the historical context in which these translations were produced and present their publication as key moments in that context. Since the modern intellectual history of Chinese Islam is still quite unknown, this chapter proceeds first with the necessary background.

CHINESE ISLAM AND THE MIDDLE EAST BEFORE 1900

China's establishment of contacts with the Middle East was a late but dramatic development, like many other major changes that the country experienced when it integrated into modern global routes of transportation and communication. Coming out of their near-complete isolation of the preceding centuries, Chinese Muslims established strong ties with many parts of the world, including the Middle East, rather quickly. From the late nineteenth century on, they were exposed, as were many Chinese generally, to foreign knowledge and technology. This group specifically saw a dramatic and profound transformation in access to knowledge and information from the Islamic world. Until that time, Chinese access to Arabic texts—crucial for acquiring knowledge about the greater Muslim world—was limited, almost nonexistent. Lack of knowledge of Arabic, which meant lack of people able to translate Arabic texts into Chinese, was the key obstacle that blocked Chinese Muslims from learning about the Muslim world. Visitors to a southern Chinese mosque in the late 1840s reported that they met "one old man, who sometimes comes to the mosque[,] . . . a copy of the Koran in his possession, but he [seems] unable to read the text intelligently."[6] Another observer described an encounter with a Muslim Chinese official: "Some Arabic sentences were familiar to him, but the Chinese organs of speech can scarcely pronounce the Arabic well."[7]

Concrete knowledge about the Middle East was another critical issue. Two early modern texts by Chinese Muslims about the geography of the Middle East illustrate this well. *Qingzhen Jiaokao* (Investigation of Islamic teachings; 1732) is a geography of the Middle East and the Indian Ocean, based almost entirely on Chinese sources from the twelfth and fourteenth centuries.[8] More concrete and updated knowledge of the Middle East came only in 1861, when the Yunnanese imam Ma Dexin (1794–1874), the most influential Chinese Muslim cleric of the nineteenth century, produced his *Chaojin Tuji* (Record of pilgrimage), about his hajj.[9]

Trips such as Ma's were still rare occurrences in the mid-to-late nineteenth century, but his journey signified the beginning of a new era in Chinese Islamic–Middle Eastern connections. In his brief account, Ma details the journey he made to Mecca in the 1840s through Indian Ocean trade routes, on both land and sea. After spending eight years at Cairo's Al-Azhar University, he wrote his travelogue in Arabic and had two of his disciples translate it into Chinese, which he had taught them. This was part of a sizable project of translating and producing new Chinese Islamic knowledge—in Chinese and Arabic—that several of Ma's disciples in Yunnan undertook following his return. But this episode too was brief and limited in scope and distribution, as most of the texts never left the province of Yunnan.[10]

The Yunnanese story tells a lot about the general historical backdrop. Until shortly before Ma's hajj, China's integration was limited and slow and affected only specific regions—mostly the port cities, such as Canton. Integration truly began after Chinese defeats in wars with Britain and other Western powers and the creation of treaty ports and other forms of colonial settlement in the 1840s and 1850s. The timing of Ma's trip, the first significant Chinese hajj of the modern period, was therefore not a coincidence. Furthermore, one must take into account the devastated conditions of the major centers of Chinese Islam throughout most of the nineteenth century. Beginning in the 1780s, the Manchu-Qing advent in and conquest of the heavily Muslim Central Asian territories that came to be known as Chinese Turkestan placed a tremendous amount of pressure on Muslim communities inside China. Tensions between the Chinese state and its Muslim subjects were high and affected relations between Muslim and non-Muslim communities all over China, particularly in areas heavily populated by Muslims. The northwestern Chinese Muslim communities engaged in an on-and-off violent struggle with the state and their non-Muslim neighbors for most of the nineteenth century. In the southwestern province of Yunnan, tension between Muslim and non-Muslim communities developed into a full-scale rebellion, which lasted from 1856 to 1873. Violence did not reach the Muslims of the eastern Chinese territories, but elites in those provinces suffered a dramatic decline in social standing.[11]

The violence that engulfed Chinese Muslim communities during most of the nineteenth century left many of them socially and economically devastated and without leadership. Ma's ascent to a position of leadership came during the last stages of the rebellion in Yunnan. He knew when to switch sides and make a deal with the Qing government. But even this did not leave him immune to harassment and death. In the aftermath of the rebellion, the newly appointed anti-Muslim governor-general of Yunnan murdered Ma, together with three other Yunnanese Muslim leaders.[12] The situation in other Muslim communities was even worse than in Yunnan, and millions lost their lives in decades of ongoing violence.[13]

But before his tragic death, Ma set the pattern for the next few decades for early connections with the Middle Eastern centers of Islamic learning—most notably Al-Azhar. Typically, these were based largely on a single important imam traveling alone or with a small entourage to the Middle East and returning to China with books and information about Islam and the Middle East. Wang Haoran (1848–1919), Wang Jingzai (1879–1949), and Ma Songting (1895–1992), three of modern China's so-called Four Great Imams (si daming ahong), visited the Middle East and Al-Azhar in the 1900s, 1920s, and 1930s, respectively. But it was only after Ma Songting's visit that larger groups of Chinese Muslims began arriving at Al-Azhar.

INTEGRATION AS RECUPERATION

The devastation of China's Muslim communities in the nineteenth century helps us to see why the integration of Chinese Islam into global networks occurred only in the first half of the twentieth century. Slow and limited as it was in the beginning, once it started the situation changed dramatically. In the early 1900s, a missionary on a reconnaissance tour among Chinese Muslims noticed that "in China the Mohammedans at Peking seem to be making special efforts in the establishment of schools, and the [successful] Ali Riza Effendi, . . . a graduate of Al Hazar [sic] University, has for the last two years been teaching in and organising the Moslem schools of Peking."[14]

The Ottoman sultan 'Abd al-Hamid II (1842–1918) apparently sent 'Ali Riza to China, but significant changes in Chinese Islam in the period were mostly due to Chinese rather than Ottoman initiatives. In 1906, Wang Haoran (1848–1918), the most important imam in China at the time, traveled to Egypt and Turkey to ask for support in laying the ground for reforming the Chinese Islamic education system. His return in 1908 with the abovementioned envoy and, more important, numerous Islamic books ("A thousand!") and teaching materials marks the beginning of the new Chinese Islamic education system, whose center was in Beijing. Most of the leading Chinese imams during the next thirty years came out of this institution.[15]

Wang's story of returning from the Middle East with "a thousand" books is an exaggeration. But it does express the desperate thirst for Islamic knowledge among Chinese Muslims at the time. In certain respects this thirst had always existed among Muslim elites in China.[16] But in the wake of the nineteenth-century devastation it was far more acute. Thus, integration with the Middle Eastern heartlands of Islam also meant an opportunity for cultural recuperation after years of violence and isolation. Otherwise, Wang would not have so happily reported on his return with books from the Middle East. As more and more Chinese Muslims visited the Middle East, more and more knowledge and information arrived in China. While most Chinese Muslims still did not have access to Arabic, increasing numbers now did, and major translations of Islamic works of all sorts undertaken by these intellectuals beginning in the late 1910s enriched Chinese Islam.

One should not forget that these early contacts and reformist initiatives were not forged in a political or cultural vacuum. They were part of a more general transformation that China and its society underwent from the late nineteenth century on. While many Chinese Muslims took part in the general effort to reform or otherwise change China, many did so with the view that Islamic modernization should be part of the national effort to modernize. Thus, Chinese Islam saw the emergence of its own modernizing elites, who struggled to forge a modernizing agenda for the Muslims of what was now the Chinese republic.[17]

This new elite expressed itself through the new Chinese Muslim press. Just as a deluge of newspapers, the new main means of communications, transformed the general Chinese public sphere at the time, so too, a bit later, did it transform Chinese Islam.[18] *Yue Hua* (Crescent China)—which carried a title in Arabic as well, *Nazrat al-Hilal*—was its lead periodical, which was sent to communities in China, elsewhere in Asia, and in Africa.[19] Appearing every ten days until the 1937 Japanese invasion of China, *Yue Hua* was part of a much larger wave of Chinese Islamic journalistic endeavors that began in 1904.[20] By the 1930s, more than a hundred Muslim newspapers and all sorts of periodicals were coming out in almost every province of China.[21] The largest among them, such as *Yue Hua,* were global in their approach and frequently included notices and news about worldwide issues, particularly if they had an Islamic angle. *Yue Hua* also regularly published translated essays on a variety of topics from the *Al-Manar* journal of Rashid Rida (1865–1935) and the *Al-Fath* journal of Muhibb al-Din al-Khatib (1886–1969).[22]

The rise of the Chinese Islamic press was not limited to journals. In 1922, Ma Kuilin (d. 1943), the imam of the old and strong Muslim community of Niujie Mosque in Beijing, founded the Qingzhen Shuwushe (Islamic press). This press was intensely active for three decades—publishing numerous works on Islam and translations of Islamic materials—until it was closed in 1956, most probably by a governmental order.[23] Other presses published numerous Islamic texts, such as "manuals of prayer," in this period as well. The big change was not only the volume of new books but also the marked presence of Arabic. Many of these texts were bilingual, and still more carried bilingual titles in Arabic and Chinese. Others taught the basics, at least, of Arabic: "primer[s] of Islam's alphabet" and Arabic-Chinese dictionaries.[24] It is not a coincidence, then, that in this period the complete Qur'an appeared in several different Chinese translations in a short span of time.[25] Beyond conveying their messages, their burgeoning press was the main crucible in which Chinese Muslim modernizing elites forged their ideas. It was also the main receptacle for ideas and messages from the greater Islamic world, particularly the Middle Eastern centers. Most important, connections with Egypt and Al-Azhar produced immediate and direct change that one can easily gauge.

China and Egypt established more formal contacts when the two governments, sharing a sense of comradeship forged under the yoke of Western imperialism and colonialism, signed several mutual agreements. In this context, Chinese Muslims were seen as a bridge between the two countries. In the wake of the aforementioned imam Ma Songting's visit to Egypt, King Fu'ad (1868–1936) donated money to build an Islamic library in Beijing (Chinese Fude Tushuguan, Fuad Library) and financed the travel and lodging of Chinese students in Cairo.[26] Newspapers and books, a rising degree of access to Arabic, and increasingly frequent visits of individuals now connected Muslim China to the larger Muslim world.

Chinese Muslim intellectuals did not see the connections with the Middle East as something new. Rather, they perceived this burst of activity as a renewal of Chinese Islam's ties with the Arab world and a return to its Arab roots. Chinese Muslims have long held that their origins date back to Muhammad's days and that their ancestry is Arab. This self-understanding is the basis for their supposed exilic existence in China, which has always insisted on a direct, if imagined, link to the heartlands of Islam.[27] Now the physical connection between China and the Middle East—that is, Egypt—enabled the first instance of Arabization of Chinese Islam and offered the chance to "purify" it of its "Turco-Persian" features. In this regard, the fact that Chinese Muslims were able to establish meaningful connections with the Arab world in the twentieth century worked hand in hand with the idea that the modernization of Chinese Islam meant, among other things, a return to its Arab origins.[28]

Furthermore, these intellectuals understood the movement toward Chinese Islam's supposed Arab roots as something that would benefit China as a whole. Sun Shengwu (1894–1975), a leading Muslim thinker, declared that these "renewed" connections were a continuation of the "intimate relationship" (miqie guanxi) that had always existed between the Chinese and the Arab civilizations "since Muhammad's time." This new phase marked the bringing together again of two of the "three main currents of Eastern civilization" (dongfang wenhua de san da zhuliu): "the Chinese, the Indian, and the Arab." (Note here the erasure of the Persian and the Turkic cultures, both Islamic.) China had benefited from these contacts before, when "Arab science" had arrived along with the Mongols. At this stage in history, however, it was the job of the Chinese Muslims to bring these civilizations together, Sun argued.[29] In other words, the renewal of connections between China and the heartlands of Islam was a major global event—the coming together of two of the world's greatest civilizations.

Written in 1939 and summarizing "thirty years" of "Chinese-Arab" relations, Sun's words are significant. The fact of the matter was that Chinese Muslims were the most active—indeed, almost exclusively—in forging relationships and exchanges between China and the Middle East. But Sun rejected the notion that these activities interested only their community. In his view, they were instrumental in bringing together two of the world's greatest civilizations. He tied these activities specifically to the republican period, when "transportation [between China and the world] was increasingly improving." China's Muslims, by his account, took advantage and headed to "the Arab world."[30] Moreover, by invoking the distant past of Chinese-Arab (read: Islamic) relations, Sun seems to suggest that in the modern period, renewing the cultural exchanges between China and the Arabs is to be the "historical role" of China's Muslims. And how nice it sounds: China's Muslims, products of past Chinese-Arab ties, were now the key players in bringing these two civilizations together again.[31] This was nothing less than another chapter in a glorious history of transcivilizational relationship in which they played a key and long-standing role.

CHINA SEEN FROM EGYPT

When the imam Wang Jingzai stayed at Al-Azhar in 1923, he attracted a great deal of attention. I. Ra'uf and H. Lutfi-Ramzi, who met him when was lodging at the Al-Kilsani tekke (a Sufi lodge) in Cairo, published a report on this rare encounter in the newspaper *Al-Ahram*. They specifically say that they are writing the story to raise interest in China among the "scholars of Egypt," whom they encourage to meet the imam. They heard about him in the "journals and newspapers of Cairo" and went to ask him about China. The detailed report, too long to include here in full, is based on numerous questions the two asked the imam, whom they describe as "a man in his sixties . . . thin, with no beard, and long mustache . . . who offered us real Chinese tea in a Chinese cup." He introduced himself as "the imam of Tianjin and a journalist," who had left China "to travel and learn about the Muslim lands and about the new ideas in the Middle East" (*al-afkar al-jadida al-mawjuda fi al-sharq al-awsat*).

Wang answered questions: "There were about seventy million Muslims in China. . . . The followers of Buddha are few, and most of the people follow the teaching of Confucius, who was not a prophet but a reformer." He also reported that since the founding of the republic, China "had awakened" and begun demanding its colonized territories back. When asked for his impression of the Egyptian ulama, Wang responded that he had met none so far. "But," he added, "I did hear about Muhammad 'Abduh[,] . . . who is one of the greatest men of this world. . . . I am not interested in politics, but I have translated many books about the history of ancient and modern Egypt, [topics] that are not known" in China. The interview concludes with a request by the two Egyptian interlocutors: could the imam deliver a lecture on China to the Egyptian intelligentsia? Wang agreed but said that since his Arabic was not good he would have to "write the lecture first and read it aloud."[32] It is not clear whether he ever delivered this lecture, but it is evident that in 1923 the presence of a Chinese Muslim in Cairo was a curiosity of sorts, something to be reported in the newspapers. As for China itself, it was seen as one of the "unknown" (*ghair ma'arufa*) "distant countries" (*min al-bilad al na'ina*).

Before the mid-1930s, Middle Eastern Islamic sources said little—in fact, close to nothing—about Chinese Islam, and virtually all of their information about it came from or was filtered through Western sources. During its first eight years, from 1926 to the end of 1933, *Al-Fath* published only two short items on China. The first was a little notice, fewer than one hundred words, on "Islam in China," adapted from a "famous" but unidentified "French book."[33] It says that "Islam spread in China slowly, leisurely [*ruwaydan ruwaydan*], thanks to marriage with Chinese [women], adoption, and the guidance of slaves. . . . Five hundred years ago, one of the kings of China deemed it a 'pure and true religion' [*dinan haqqan naqiyan*]." The anonymous author, probably al-Khatib, the paper's publisher, also provides Chinese words transliterated into Arabic for "pure and true religion," *tshing tshang kiao,* echoing the then-prevalent Western transliteration system for Chinese characters.[34] The phrase *Pure and True* (*Qingzhen jiao*) was the main designator for Islam in China, used mostly by Muslims but also by non-Muslims.

The second item on China in *Al-Fath* arose from a more colorful circumstance. "Islam in the Lands of China after the Great War" contains information transmitted to the newspaper by Dr. Khalid Sheldrake (b. 1888).[35] This man, an English physician born Bertram William Sheldrake, was a convert to Islam and the founder, in 1930, of England's branch of the Western Islamic Association. Deeply committed to the idea of global Islamic unity, he had an intense interest in Islam in China. In 1934 he named himself "King of Islamistan," an entity that was supposed to exist in Xinjiang.[36] It is not clear if he ever made it to Xinjiang to take the (nonexistent) throne. But before he disappeared, he passed through Shanghai, where he made contact with the city's China Muslim Society and sent a report on it to *Al-Fath.*

These articles seem random, and in some respects they are. Moreover, both are the products of Western informants—a French scholar and an English convert—rather than Chinese Muslims. But things changed rapidly as more concrete knowledge about China and its Islam came to the Middle East. In particular, students, known in China and Egypt as the Chinese-Azhari Delegations (*al-Bi'that al-Siniyya al-Azhariyya*), began arriving at Al-Azhar in the early 1930s as part of the agreement between their government and Egypt.[37] They attracted a good deal of interest, particularly from organizations such as the Jam'iyyat al-ta'aruf al-Islami (Association for mutual Islamic acquaintance), established and headed by Muhibb al-Din al-Khatib. Born in Syria and having settled in Cairo in the early 1920s, al-

Khatib was focused at the time on a mixture of pan-Arab and pan-Islamic ideas. He was part of an important circle of thinkers, among them the more famous Shakib Arslan and Rashid Rida.[38]

THE DYNAMICS OF TRANSLATION

Two years after the arrival of the first Chinese delegation in Cairo, probably soon after its members were able to communicate well in Arabic, the Jam'iyyat al-ta'aruf al-Islami sponsored a series of lectures on China, mostly on Islam there. *Al-Fath* sequentially printed these lectures, which presented China, its history, and its main belief systems (or religions, if you will)—Confucianism, Buddhism, and Daoism—in almost every issue from July through October 1934 and soon thereafter offered them in a special book printed by the Salafiyya Press. The lecturer and the author of this publication was Ma Jian (1906–78), a native of Yunnan of learned background who in Egypt called himself Muhammad Makin. Makin, who translated the Qur'an into Chinese in the 1950s, was the head and most prominent member of the Chinese Muslim delegation to Egypt.[39] The book significantly has a bilingual title, in Arabic and Chinese: *Nazrah Jami'ah ila Ta'rikh al-Islam fi al-Sin wa-Ahwal al-Muslimin fiha: Zhongguo Huijiao Gaiguan* (General view of the history of Islam in China and the conditions of its Muslims).[40] Soon after its publication, *Al-Fath* began advertising the book in Chinese as well as Arabic characters. Thus, a little more than a decade after Arabic first appeared next to Chinese in mass media in China, Chinese appeared in mass media in Egypt.

Publishing such materials on Chinese Islam was understandable and necessary, given the strong pan-Islamic orientation of the intellectuals involved. Yet *Al-Fath* surprised its readership by hosting another publication—this time on something Chinese but not Islamic: Confucius and Confucianism. Makin, also the author of this new project, must have been very busy that year. Soon after his lectures on China and Chinese Islam ended and the book went to print, he turned to translating the *Analects* (though in both cases he took care to mention that he undertook the China-related projects during the "summer vacation"). As with the lectures on Chinese Islam, *Al-Fath* proceeded almost immediately with the serialized publication of Makin's translation. These appeared in installments often a page or two in length starting in November 1934 and ran throughout 1935. Makin accompanied the translation with a short biography of Confucius. Once these were finished, they were bound in a book, which the back cover of *Al-Fath* advertised for months, in Chinese alongside Arabic.[41] All told, for more than eighteen months, one journal, *Al-Fath*, published in each issue at least one item relating in some way to China, and the jam'iyya sponsored a series of lectures on the country. For a Middle Eastern journal dedicated to Islam, this was a huge amount of material devoted specifically to China.

How and why was all this undertaken? We have many jottings and other clues in the records that reveal how much interest Makin's Middle Eastern interlocutors, the aforementioned intellectuals among them, expressed in China. Al-Khatib, for instance, writes in his foreword to Makin's lectures that his colleague Rida, the editor of *Al-Manar,* had been so enthusiastic about them as to declare after the first that "for many years he had not heard a lecture from which he had learned so much as from this one."[42] Another China enthusiast was Shaykh Ibrahim al-Jibali (b. 1878), the son of a distinguished scholarly family at Al-Azhar and the author of a general explication of Islam and other works on the Qur'an and Islamic theology.[43] He was the man who had encouraged Makin—with whom he had developed an intimate master-disciple relationship—to translate Confucius into Arabic. As we shall see, he was also the person behind translating ʿAbduh into Chinese. He apparently had an impressive taste for knowledge and in 1936 headed an Azharite delegation to India, from which he reported in a letter: "Many hundreds of officials, journalists and ordinary visitors have asked us why Al-Azhar delegated us to visit this country. Our answer has been that Al-Azhar, that venerable university of the Orient, sought to strengthen the bonds of friendship and affection with Muslims of distant countries in order to promote intellectual and scholastic cooperation."[44]

This passage seems to nicely characterize the mood and the attitude among Al-Azhar scholars toward Muslims from "distant countries." Indeed, the relationship between al-Jibali and Makin allows us a rare vista of the dynamic of exchange and interaction between Chinese Muslims and Middle Easterners at Al-Azhar. In his preface to his translation of Confucius, Makin recounts the origins of the venture as lying in the shaykh's interest in Chinese "wisdom," which he wished an Arabic-speaking audience could access. Makin's account shows us what kind of interactions he had with his Middle Eastern interlocutors, who were clearly interested in the Chinese background of the young Muslim student:

> One of these days the Honorable Shaykh Ibrahim al-Jibali asked me about the wisdom of the wise man of China the great Confucius [*hikmat hakim al-Sin al-akbar* "*Kunfushiyus*"], and I promised to provide the Honorable with translations into Arabic of some of his sayings; alas, the many classes [I am taking here] did not allow me [to continue], and I was late in carrying out this long overdue promise, until the Honorable Teacher Sayyid Muhibb al-Din, the editor of *Al-Fath,* asked me to produce a glance through the ethics of China and its wisdoms [*Adab al-Sin wa hikamha*]. . . . So I translated it during the summer break at Al-Azhar University.[45]

And so Confucius was translated. Al-Khatib's and Rida's involvement—through attending the lectures, supporting al-Jibali, and corresponding with Chinese Muslims—reveals that al-Jibali, a senior teacher at Al-Azhar, was not alone in expressing an interest in the "wisdom" of the Chinese. We can assume that many others were highly interested as well. The symbolic highlight of this interest was the great praise Makin received for all his translations and lectures. One of the May 1937 issues *Al-Fath* published his picture and labeled him "the Perfect Muslim" (*al-Muslim al-Kamil*), "Sayyid Muhammad Makin al-Sini, the author of the articles on China . . . and translator of the *Book of Dialogues* of Confucius" (*sahib maqalat al-Islam fi al-Sin . . . wa mutarjim Kitab al-hiwar li Kunfushiyus*).[46]

Why were China, Confucius, and Chinese Islam so interesting in Cairo? In his foreword, al-Khatib avers that knowledge of the history of Chinese Islam "and the circumstances of how it arrived in China" are vital to the project of acquaintance (*taʾaruf*) among Muslims, particularly in the context of the then-current awakening (*yaqza*) of Islam throughout the world.[47] It is possible to think of the Islamic interest in Confucianism as an extension of the *taʾaruf* project and as a way for Muslims to learn how their religion interacts with a dominant non-Muslim civilization, in this case not Western but Chinese. It is clear that the leading intellectuals at Al-Azhar in the 1930s, such as al-Jibali, Rida, al-Khatib, and Arslan, designed their cultural projects "to strengthen the bonds of friendship and affection with Muslims of distant countries in order to promote intellectual and scholastic cooperation," as al-Jibali said. This also meant learning about Confucius.

Now came ʿAbduh's turn, which deserves greater attention. Al-Jibali's interactions with Makin are an interesting case that reveals how the dynamics of exchange worked on the ground. We learn from Makin's writings that the shaykh served as his mentor at Al-Azhar and was his guide to Islamic knowledge in Arabic. Al-Jibali was intimately involved in another translation project of Makin's. Shortly after arriving at Al-Azhar, Makin began translating materials from Arabic into Chinese. As he relates (this time in Chinese), he had been looking for a "new book" in Islamic thought when he met al-Jibali. The encounter was quite beneficial for the two. The honorable shaykh introduced the Chinese student to ʿAbduh's *Risalat al-Tawhid*, which Makin ended up translating. As he says in a letter to *Yue Hua*, "When I first saw Professor Shaykh Ibrahim elGibali[48] of the Institute for Islamic Philosophy [*Huijiao zhexue yuan*] at Al-Azhar, I asked him whether or not there was a new book on [Islamic] theology [*renzhuxue*].[49] The honorable professor promptly introduced this book and recommended that I study it by myself. During my free time from classes, I always read it, caught the general meaning [*dayi*], and sent the honorable professor requests to explain questions, doubts, and difficulties [*zhi wen yin nan*]." Makin goes on to describe the intensive process of studying with the "modest" and encouraging al-Jibali until "that summer vacation," when he translated the book into Chinese "for the people of China."[50] Note here that the intended audience was not necessarily only Muslims.

It is not at all surprising that al-Jibali recommended that Makin start his studies in "new" Islamic theology with ʿAbduh. A reformer with strong convictions about Islam's place in the world and in human history, ʿAbduh was the thinker whose influence on leading reform-minded figures at Al-Azhar at that time was most crucial. His most influential disciple, Rida (who by then was gravitating away from his master's pan-Islamic vision toward a more pan-Arabic one), was still alive and quite active at Al-Azhar, as was Arslan.[51] These Muslim intellectuals were the most globally minded in the Middle East then. They expressed this perspective through learning and teaching about the world and its history as they viewed it—a tone that 'Abduh first set. Makin, a Muslim from the "distant" country of China, was therefore a perfect candidate for Islamic dialogue with them. The *Risala*, a pan-Islamic text conceived and written as a reintroduction of Islam to Muslims in turbulent times, was a good basis for starting this dialogue. It is not surprising that Makin ended up not only studying the *Risala* but also translating it into Chinese and publishing it in China. We can now better understand his afore-quoted Arabic preface to the *Analects* of Confucius. When he says that al-Jibali asked him about Chinese *hikma*, this was probably when the shaykh was helping him read 'Abduh. Makin, therefore, was both a student and a teacher at the time. However, whereas Confucius's *Analects* was introduced in Cairo as "wisdom"—a reasonable enough categorization that reflected at least one possible view—'Abduh's journey to China involved a redefinition of his project.

PRESENTING THE *RISALA*: TAWHID AS PHILOSOPHY

Like Confucius's Arabic translation, the *Risala* was first serialized in a magazine, *Yue Hua*, in 1933 and 1934, and then came out as a book. The two publications have different titles. The *Yue Hua* series is simply called "Huijiao Renzhuxue dagang" (Principles [or outline] of Islamic theology), more or less loyal to the original Arabic albeit failing to convey the monotheist message of *tawhid* (unity of God).[52] However, the book has a very different name: *Huijiao zhexue* (Islamic philosophy).[53] I suggest that the change in the title—introducing the *Risala* as "philosophy"—should draw our special attention.

The scope of this chapter does not allow for a full discussion of 'Abduh's reception in China, but a few highlights are necessary. To begin with, we know that Makin refers to the *Risala* in an introduction to the book in *Yue Hua* as "theology." Thus the use of the loaded term *philosophy* (*zhexue*) in the title suggests that this deviation from the original was deliberate. A comparison with the French translation of the *Risala*—the only other in a non-Islamic language at the time—might help to highlight the significance of the choice of this term. One might think that Makin simply translated *theology* as *philosophy*, but that does not make much sense. Support for this point comes from another Chinese translation of the *Risala*, published a little more than a year later by Ma Ruitu (1896–1945), an imam from Beijing who translated the book completely independently. His version carries the title *Huijiao renyi lun*, which could be translated as "Islamic discourse of knowing the One." With *knowing the One* (*ren yi*), Ma Ruitu clearly wanted to convey the

important theological value of the Islamic concept of tawhid (making the One)—
whose primacy he was known for insisting on—and its strong transitive value.[54]
His use of *renyi* brilliantly succeeds in rendering *tawhid* into Chinese, and it is
more loyal than Makin's title to traditional Chinese Islamic vocabulary, which uses
the verb *ren*—"to know, to identify, recognize, and acknowledge"—in explaining
the way in which humans know Allah.[55]

Let us also keep in mind that Makin, now fluent in Arabic and steeped in
Islamic studies at Al-Azhar, was well aware of the Arabic term *falsafa* (philosophy)—
a possible reason behind naming the *Risala* "philosophy." As we shall see below, he
translated *falsafa* from Arabic into Chinese as *zhexue*. Perhaps he did not fully
appreciate the major problems that modern Arab and Muslim intellectuals had
encountered when they engaged this medieval term, but surely he knew of some
of the debates in Cairo on its nature.[56] Furthermore, we know, for instance, that
during his discussions with al-Jibali about the translation of Confucius, al-Jibali
spoke of *hikma* (wisdom) and not *falsafa* (philosophy). In light of this, Makin's
choice to define the book as philosophy seems even more intriguing.

Finally, we must also take into account that the *Risala* "was not about theology
[but] about Islam and Muslims in the modern world."[57] The French translation
undertaken in 1925 bears the title *Rissalat al Tawhid: Exposé de la religion musulmane*.[58] Indeed, even if one does not entirely agree with the contention that the
Risala is theology, the term *exposé* seems to fit the contents of the book better, and
in Chinese it has many equivalents. A title such as "An explication of Islam" is fitting, particularly if the book is intended for a wide audience. (Let us recall that in
his aforementioned letter to *Yue Hua* about the book, Makin says he translated it
for the "people of China"—that is, not only Muslims.) Indeed, at the time, numerous Islamic tomes in Chinese did have titles such as *Explication, Exposition*, and
Introduction of Islam. All told, the different titles suggest that Makin intended his
book to present Islam to a general Chinese readership in a certain way and that
this goal mandated the choice of terminology. In short, his use of the term *philosophy* as opposed to *theology* for the *Risala* was deliberate and purposeful.

A few words on *philosophy* in the Chinese context are in order. At the time,
zhexue was a relatively new word in Chinese. It had migrated from Japan, where in
1874, Nishi Amane (1829–97), a scholar of Western thought, combined two existing terms—*kitetsu* ("love of wisdom"; Chinese: *xizhe*) and *gaku* ("study, learning,
or science"; Chinese: *xue*)—to invent *tetsugaku*. *Kitetsu* fits the original meaning of
the Greek word *philosophia* better. But Amane, who was wrestling with the issue of
translating *philosophy*, wanted his new term to sound more "scientific" (that is,
Western), which is why he added the *gaku* and dropped the *ki* ("love" or "fond-
ness"; Chinese *xi*). The general thrust behind this was a sense of inferiority vis-à-
vis the West, which, unlike the East, had "philosophy." Thus the thought systems of
the East, Confucianism chief among them, were now designated philosophies, in

the Western sense of the word.⁵⁹ In China, where the sense of defeat was far more acute than in Japan—thanks to the Opium Wars, the 1894–95 Sino-Japanese War, the failure of the Boxer Rebellion, the failure of 1911 revolution, numerous international humiliations, and above all the loss of many large territories to the West and to Japan—*zhexue* was adopted in the early twentieth century as code for modern, Western thinking. The standard view was that this mode of thinking was superior to any other in rigor and comprehensiveness, which China, an Eastern country, lacked. This triggered a response that posited Chinese thought, most notably Confucianism, as an equivalent to Western philosophy.

Zhongguo zhexue shi (History of Chinese philosophy), the first book on its subject, came out in 1916. It main message is that Confucians are philosophers. It is important to note that in both China and Japan, the consolidation of the terms *zhexue* and *tetsugaku* was fraught with debates about the status of Eastern thought, for lack of a better term, vis-à-vis Western philosophy.⁶⁰ This context allows us to understand the significance of the presentation of the *Risala* as "Islamic philosophy." For Makin, its publication was an Islamic intervention in the Chinese debate about philosophy and the possibility of Chinese (read: non-Western) philosophy. In his preface, Makin declares that "*tawhid* is the basis of Islamic philosophy" and presents ʿAbduh as a "leading Islamic philosopher" who, he takes care to mention, "spent time in Paris." "Everyone inside and outside the faith [*jiaonei jiaowai*]" should read ʿAbduh, he declares.⁶¹ Conversely, Ma Ruitu presents ʿAbduh simply as an "Islamic revivalist" [*huijiao zhi zhenxing zhe*] and not as a philosopher.⁶²

There is more that may further explain why Makin was so keen to present the *Risala* as Islamic philosophy. In the 1920s and early 1930s, the Chinese intellectual scene was deeply engaged in a debate about China's future. Briefly put, until World War I, modernity-oriented and reform-minded intellectuals considered Western civilization the model that New China must follow. However, after the Great War, a controversy over Western values erupted. Leading modernist intellectuals such as Liang Qichao (1873–1929) began arguing that adopting the science, technology, and philosophy, particularly materialism, of Western civilization would lead China to a catastrophe similar to what had just occurred in Europe. Liang argued forcefully that in the wake of European failures, China must not desert its "traditional" principles altogether and replace them with Western ideas. Rather, he called for "harmonizing and blending" Western science and technology with Chinese spiritual traditions. The reason the West had failed, Liang observed, was its inability to balance between "exaggerated idealism and spirituality" on one hand and "overemphasis on materialism" on the other. Unlike the West, China was always able to balance between these two extremes, and deserting Chinese tradition would mean losing this ability, which would lead to catastrophe. Chinese intellectuals, therefore, must have a "sincere purpose of respecting and protecting our civilization." Furthermore, Liang viewed this harmonizing project as benefiting not only China but also the rest of the world. He hoped that the "young people" of China would "put our civilization in order and supplement it with others' so that it will be transformed and become a new civilization."[63]

ʿAbduh—"neither a traditionalist nor a liberal" and "a Muslim reformer who was critical of both traditionalist religious authority and colonial modernity," as Samira Haj understands him—can be presented as a Muslim counterpart to Liang's call.[64] Like Liang in China, ʿAbduh sought to reconfigure Islamic tradition against the backdrop of Europeanization, in his case, of Middle Eastern society. Furthermore, Liang expressively hoped that "China's young people" would "extend this new civilization to the outside world so that it can benefit the whole human race."[65] This wish is crucial. It affirms a panhuman ideal as the new project's ultimate goal—the creation of a global civilization that is to benefit all. In the Risala, ʿAbduh repeatedly "posits that Islam was designed to benefit humanity and to facilitate man's welfare and happiness on this earth and beyond."[66] Liang, to be sure, was less concerned with life beyond earth, but it makes sense that Makin might have considered ʿAbduh's presentation of Islam's contribution to human civilization as the key element in the Risala with which Chinese intellectuals "inside and out the faith" should become familiar. In other words, in presenting the Risala as Islamic philosophy, Makin might have sought to make Islam part of Liang's new project. Let us recall Sun Shengwu's aforementioned words about the historical role of Chinese Muslims in bringing the Chinese and Islamic civilizations closer again. Indeed, one of Makin's next big projects was translating Abu Rida's 1938 Arabic version of T. J. Boer's History of Philosophy in Islam into Chinese.[67]

CONCLUSION

This chapter presents the story of two translations as the culmination of a viable circuit of exchange between China and the Middle East (Egypt, to be precise). Reading these stories—of a Chinese and an Arabic translation—next to each other does more than just expose the circulatory nature of the exchange of ideas between China and Egypt. Contrary to what may seem coincidental to an unsuspecting eye, the near-simultaneous appearance of ʿAbduh in China and Confucius in Cairo was not random. The intellectual worlds that placed al-Jibali and Makin together both produced and reverberated with their intense encounter. In this regard, the road to these translations exposes the dynamic of exchange and interface between the "local and regional" and "the supra-regional, even the global," to borrow Sanjay Subrahmanyam's words on a different, much earlier period of intense exchanges and other connections.[68]

Chinese Muslims played a key role in the formation and growth of the circuit of exchange discussed here, and this fact dictated much, particularly timing. In the nineteenth century, repeated waves of violence overwhelmed the Chinese Muslim communities of western China, geographically speaking the best suited to form connections with the Middle East. The Chinese Muslim communities of eastern China were simply too far from the Indian Ocean routes of communication. This explains why the first two notable travels to the Middle East were those of Ma Dexin from southwestern China in the 1840s, before the eruption of violence, and of Wang Haoran in the early 1900s. It took few more decades and (Chinese and Egyptian) governmental involvement for truly viable links to form. In this regard, the Muslims of China stand out from the many other Muslim communities with which this volume is concerned. They were distant, extremely vulnerable to the circumstances in China, and depended on the support of a non-Muslim government. A stable Chinese government with interest in the Middle East formed only in the late 1920s.

If Muslims were the pumping heart of this circuit of exchange, Islam, better yet Islamic knowledge, was its main commodity. However, just as Muslims traveled not in a vacuum but in a Western-dominated world, so did Islam. The presumed target audience of the knowledge coming to China from the Middle East was not necessarily exclusively Muslim, but all of China. The Chinese Muslims involved in this exchange understood themselves as people whose historical role was to bring the Chinese and Arabic civilizations together again. Perhaps even more than that, as the tale of Muhammad 'Abduh in China suggests, they were participants in an effort to rethink Chinese cultural and intellectual relationships with Western culture and civilization. Were these translations responses to Liang Qichao's call for "China's young people" to "put our civilization in order and supplement it with others' so that it will be transformed and become a new civilization"? Was the Chinese 'Abduh intended to be such a supplement? Was Ma Jian / Muhammad Makin trying to help bring about a "new [global] civilization"? This possibility is quite fascinating, but it remains only a possibility: World War II, the rise of Communist China, and perhaps even the rise of secular regimes in the Middle East put an end to it. Connections between China and Egypt did not end, but they radically transformed. Ma Jian / Muhammad Makin's later career illustrates this well. The man who headed a Chinese Muslim delegation to Al-Azhar in the 1930s served in the 1950s and 1960s as a professor of Arabic in Beijing and as one of China's most skilled Arabic-Chinese translators, facilitating, among other things, the conversations between Gamal Abdel Nasser and Zhou Enlai during the Bandung Conference.[69]

NOTES

Grants from the Carnegie Foundation of New York and the Gerda Henkel Stiftung generously supported research for this essay. I am eternally grateful to Nile Green and James Gelvin for suggesting that I take another look at the question of Muhammad 'Abduh in China.

    1. Muhammad Makin, *Kitab al-Hiwar li Kunfushiyus* (Cairo: Al-Matba'a al-Salafiyya, 1935).

2. Henri Lauzière, "The Construction of *Salafiyya*: Reconsidering Salafism from the Perspective of Conceptual History," *International Journal of Middle East Studies* 42, no. 3 (2010): 382.

3. For a concise account of the *Risala* (within a biography of ˈAbduh), see Mark J. Sedgwick, *Muhammad Abduh* (Oxford: Oneworld, 2010). The *Risala*'s first edition had no recognized publisher. Its second edition is *Risālat al-tawhīd*, ed. Muhammad Rashīd Ridā (Cairo: ˈIsā al-Bābī al-Halabī, 1938).

4. Sedgwick, *Muhammad Abduh*, 70. By that time there were only three other translations of the book, in French, Urdu, and Javanese.

5. Sun Yuxiu, *Fulankelin* (Shanghai: Shanghai Shangwu yinshuguan, 1935); M. K. Gandhi, *Gan di*, trans. Tan Yunshan, (Shanghai: Shanghai Shangwu yinshuguan, 1935); Somei Ryō, Chin Sei, and Ra Jōbai, *Tōzai bunka oyobi sono tetsugaku* (Shanghai: Shangwu yinshuguan, 1935).

6. Elijah Coleman Bridgman and S. W. Williams, "Hsiang Fan, or Echoing Tomb, a Muhammadan Mosque and Burying-Ground near Canton," *Chinese Repository* 20 (1851): 83–84.

7. Karl Friedrich August Gützlaff, *Journal of Three Voyages along the Coast of China, in 1831, 1832, and 1833* (London: Westley and Davis, 1834), 224–25.

8. Sun Ke'an, *Qingzhen Jiaokao* (Taipei: Guang wen shuju, 1975 [reprint]).

9. Ma Dexin, *Chaojin Tuji* (Yinchuan, China: Ningxia Renmin Chubanshe, 1988 [reprint]).

10. For collections of Ma's writings, see Ma Fuchu, *Mashi yishu wuzhong* (Yinchuan, China: Ningxia Renmin Chubanshe, 1988); Yang Guiping, *Ma Dexin sixiang yanjiu* (Beijing: Zongjiao Wenhua Chubanshe, 2004).

11. For Manchu-Qing military activities in Central Asia, see Peter Perdue, *China Marches West: The Qing Conquest of Central Eurasia* (Cambridge, MA: Belknap, 2005). For the violence in northwestern China, see Jonathan Lipman, *Familiar Strangers: A History of Muslims in Northwest China* (Seattle: University of Washington Press, 1997). For southwestern China, see David Atwill, *The Chinese Sultanate: Islam, Ethnicity, and the Panthay Rebellion in Southwest China, 1856–1873* (Stanford, CA: Stanford University Press, 2006). For goings-on among Muslims in eastern China, see Yoshinobu Nakada, "Shindai Kaikyōto no issokumen," *Tōyō gakuhō* 36 (1953): 66–86.

12. On Ma's career, whereabouts, and death during the rebellion, see Atwill, *Chinese Sultanate*, 120–25, 187–89.

13. Lipman, *Familiar Strangers*, 98–156.

14. Marshall Broomhall, *Islam in China: A Neglected Problem* (London: Morgan and Scott, 1910), 295.

15. Yi Boqing, "Wang Haoran Ah-heng zhuan," *Yue Hua*, 1934–35, anthologized in *Zhongguo yisilanjiao shi cankao ziliao xuanbian: 1911–1949*, ed. Li Xinghua and Feng Jinyuan (Yinchuan, China: Ningxia Renmin Chubanshe, 1985), 608–17. All translations are mine unless otherwise noted.

16. Zvi Ben-Dor Benite, *The Dao of Muhammad: A Cultural History of Muslims in Late Imperial China* (Cambridge, MA: Harvard University Asia Center), 83–84, 95–96.

17. On modernization and Chinese Islam, see Zvi Ben-Dor, "From 'Literati' to 'ˈUlama': The Origins of Chinese Muslim Nationalist Historiography," *Nationalism and Ethnic Politics* 9, no. 4 (2003–4): 83–109.

18. Barbara Mittler, *A Newspaper for China? Power, Identity and Change in Shanghai's News Media, 1872–1912* (Cambridge, MA: Harvard University Press, 2004); Christopher Reed, *Gutenberg in China: Chinese Print Capitalism, 1876–1937* (Vancouver: University of British Columbia Press, 2004).

19. In 1936, the cover of this newspaper boasted a map of world with all the locations that received it—from China and India to East Africa. It is not clear whether recipients outside China were able to read the Chinese newspaper, but at least they had a subscription to it.

20. For information on early Chinese Muslim newspapers, see Ben-Dor, "From 'Literati' to 'ˈUlama,'" 85–90.

21. Rudolf Loewenthal, *The Religious Periodical Press in China* (Beijing: Synodal Commission in China, 1940), 215.

22. Zvi Ben-Dor Benite, "'Nine Years in Egypt': The Chinese at Al-Azhar University," *HAGAR: Studies in Culture, Polity and Identities* 8, no. 1 (2008): 105–28.

23. The history of this press needs further research. All we know now is that it was closed in 1956, probably because of the various campaigns against unwanted elements that the Chinese Communist Party initiated that year.

24. See the comprehensive list by Claude Pickens, *Annotated Bibliography of Literature on Islam in China* (Hankow: Society of Friends of the Moslems in China, 1950).

25. For a short survey of these translations, see Françoise Aubin, "Les traductions du Coran en chinois," *Etudes Orientales* 13–14 (1994): 81–88. For a fuller list, see Lin Song, *"Gulanjing" zai Zhongguo = The Holy Quran in China* (Yinchuan, China: Ningxia Renmin Chubanshe, 2007).

26. Masumi Matsumoto, "Rationalizing Patriotism among Muslim Chinese: The Impact of the Middle East on the *Yue Hua* Journal," in *Intellectuals in the Modern Islamic World: Transmission, Transformation, Communication,* ed. Stéphane Dudoignon, Hisao Komatsu, and Yasushi Kosugi (London: Routledge, 2006), 117–42.

27. Ben-Dor Benite, *Dao of Muhammad,* 12–19.

28. On Arabization in the Chinese context, see Ben-Dor Benite, "'Nine Years in Egypt,'" 124–28. Marris Gillette first identified this phenomenon of Arabization and discusses it in its 1980s and 1990s context in her *Between Mecca and Beijing: Modernization and Consumption among Urban Chinese Muslims* (Stanford, CA: Stanford University Press, 2000), 68–113.

29. Sun Shengwu, "Sanshi nianlai de Zhong-Ah wenhua guanxi," *Huimin Yanlun Banyuekan* 1, no. 3 (1939), reproduced in Li and Feng, *Zhongguo yisilanjiao,* 1768–76.

30. Ibid., 1771.

31. On the Chinese Muslims as the descendants of Arabs and Chinese, see Ben-Dor Benite, *Dao of Muhammad,* 204–13.

32. This interview is reprinted in a special section on China in Shakib Arslan, *Hadir al-'Alam al-Islami,* vol. 2 (Cairo: Maktabat 'Isa al-Babi al-Halabi, 1933), 268–70.

33. This was probably the oft-cited Henri Marie Gustave d'Ollone, Pierre Gabriel Edmond de Fleurelle, Lepage, Henri Eugène de Boyve, A. Vissière, and E. Blochet, *Recherches sur les musulmans chinois* (Paris: E. Leroux, 1911).

34. "Al-Islam fi al-Sin," *Al-Fath,* first year (1926), no. 9: 9. (Note that the initial weekly dating system changed after a while.)

35. Khalid Sheldrake, "Al-Islam fi Bilad al-Sin ba'd al-Harb al-'Uzma," *Al-Fath,* 27 June 1929, 9–10.

36. "China: Sheldrake's Islamistan," *Time,* 13 August 1934.

37. Ben-Dor Benite, "'Nine Years in Egypt'"; Li and Feng, *Zhongguo yisilanjiao shi,* 736–37; Yufeng Mao, "A Muslim Vision for the Chinese Nation: Chinese Pilgrimage Missions to Mecca during World War II," *Journal of Asian Studies* 70, no. 2 (2011): 373–95.

38. C. Ernest Dawn, "The Formation of Pan-Arab Ideology in the Interwar Years," *International Journal of Middle East Studies* 20, no. 1 (1988): 67–70; Nimrod Hurvitz, "Muhibb ad-Din al-Khatib's Semitic Wave Theory and Pan-Arabism," *Middle Eastern Studies* 29, no. 1 (1993): 119.

39. Ma Jian, *Gulanjing = al-Qur'an al-karim: bi-al-lughah al-Siniyah* (Beijing: Zhongguo shehui kexue chubanshe, 1981); see also Li Zhenzhong, *Xuezhe de zhuiqiu: Ma Jian zhuan* (Yinchuan, China: Ningxia Renmin Chubanshe, 2000).

40. Muhammad Makin al-Sini, *Nazrah Jami'ah ila Ta'rikh al-Islam fi al-Sin wa-Ahwal al-Muslimin fiha: Zhongguo Huijiao Gaiguan* (Cairo: Al-Matba'a al-Salafiyya, 1934).

41. Makin, preface to *Kitab al-Hiwar li Kunfushiyus.* For an advertisement, see, e.g., *Al-Fath* 422 (14 Sha'ban 1353 [2 November 1934]): 22.

42. Muhibb al-Din al-Khatib, "Muqadama," in Makin, *Nazra Jami'ah,* 4.

43. The general explication is Ibrahim al-Jibali, *Haqiqat al-Islam wa-Mahasinuhu* (Cairo: Al-Matba'a al-Haditha, 1933). The others, published posthumously, are Jibālī, *Shifā' al-ṣudūr bi-tafsīr Sūrat al-Nūr* ([Cairo?]: Maṭba'at al-Irshād, 1936); Jibālī and Muhammad Muwaffaq Bayānūnī, *Al-Islām*

dīn al-fiṭṭrah (Aleppo: Maktabat al-Hudá, 1972); Jibālī, *Min al-adab al-Nabawī* (Cairo: Majallat al-Azhar, 2006).

44. Al-Jibali, quoted in Yunan Labib Rizk, "Al-Azhar Goes to India," *Al-Ahram Weekly* 731 (24 February–2 March 2005): 24. Al-Jibali wrote a long book about this trip, *Al-Baʿta al-Azhariyya ila al-Hind* (Cairo: Matbaʿat Hijazi, 1937).

45. Makin, preface to *Kitab al-Hiwar,* 6.

46. "Muhammad Makin al-Sini al-Muslim al-Kamil," *Al-Fath,* 27 May 1937, 47.

47. Al-Khatib, "Muqadama," 3–4.

48. Makin transliterated this name into Chinese and Latin letters, simulating the way the words sound in the Egyptian dialect.

49. Here Makin uses a very old and traditional Chinese Islamic term, which in the seventeenth century meant "knowing God" in the Sufi sense of the Arabic word *maʿarifa.*

50. Ma Jian, "Jiaoyi: Renzhuxue dagang," *Yue Hua* 5, no. 27 (25 September 1933): 11. This translation, with my major amendments, is based on Matsumoto's in "Rationalizing Patriotism," 131.

51. Indira Falk Gesink, *Islamic Reform and Conservatism: Al-Azhar and the Evolution of Modern Sunni Islam* (London: Tauris Academic Studies, 2010), 165–96.

52. Matsumoto, "Rationalizing Patriotism," 130–31.

53. Muhanmode Abudu, *Huijiao zhexue,* trans. Ma Jian (Shanghai: Shangwu yinshuguan, 1935).

54. Muhanmode Abudu, *Huijiao renyi lun,* trans. Ma Jian (Shanghai: Zhonghua Shuju, 1937).

55. Ben-Dor Benite, *Dao of Muhammad.*

56. On these debates, see Samira Haj, *Reconfiguring Islamic Tradition: Reform, Rationality, and Modernity* (Stanford, CA: Stanford University Press, 2009).

57. Sedgwick, *Muhammad Abduh,* 64.

58. *Rissalat al Tawhid: Exposé de la religion musulmane: Traduite de l'arabe avec une introduction sur la vie et les idées du cheikh Mohammed Abdou,* trans. B. Michel and Moustapha Abdel Razik (Paris: P. Geuthner, 1925).

59. H. Gene Blocker and Christopher I. Starling, *Japanese Philosophy* (Albany: State University of New York Press, 2001), 4; John C. Maraldo, "Japanese Philosophy," in *Companion Encyclopedia of Asian Philosophy,* ed. Brian Carr and Indira Mahalingam (London: Routledge, 1997), 738–40.

60. For the only discussion on this issue in English, see Ori Sela, "Qian Daxin (1728–1804): Knowledge, Identity, and Reception History in China, 1750–1930" (PhD dissertation, Princeton University, 2011), 339–46.

61. Ma Jian, "Xu" (preface), in Abudu, *Huijiao zhexue,* 1.

62. Ma Ruitu, "Xu" (preface), in Abudu, *Huijiao renyi lun,* 2.

63. A sizable collection of translations of essays pertaining to this debate is in William Theodore De Bary and Richard Lufrano, eds., *Sources of Chinese Tradition,* vol. 2, *From 1600 through the Twentieth Century* (New York: Columbia University Press, 2000), 351–95. Liang's essay, "Travel Impressions of Europe," is on 378–79.

64. Haj, *Reconfiguring Islamic Tradition,* 67–108.

65. Liang, "Travel Impressions of Europe," 379.

66. Haj, *Reconfiguring Islamic Tradition,* 84.

67. T. J. de Boer, *De wijsbegeerte in den Islam* (Haarlem: De Erven Bohn, 1921), translated by Muhammad ʿAbd al-Hadi Abu Rida as *Taʾrikh al-Falsafa fi al-Islam* (Cairo: Matbaʿat Lujnat al-Taʾlīf wa-al-Tarjamah wa-al-Nashr, 1938), translated by Ma Jian as *Huijiao zhexue shi* (Shanghai: Shangwu yinshuguan, 1946).

68. Sanjay Subrahmanyam, "Connected Histories: Notes towards a Reconfiguration of Early Modern Eurasia," *Modern Asian Studies* 31, no. 3 (1997): 745.

69. Li, *Xuezhe de zhuiqiu,* 67–81.

CONTRIBUTORS

ZVI BEN-DOR BENITE is a professor of history, Middle Eastern, and Islamic studies at New York University. He received his PhD from the University of California, Los Angeles. He is the author of *The Dao of Muhammad: A Cultural History of Muslims in Late Imperial China* (Harvard East Asian monographs, 2005) and *The Ten Lost Tribes: A World History* (Oxford, 2009).

ROBERT CREWS is an associate professor of history and the director of the Center for Russian, East European and Eurasian Studies at Stanford University. He is the author of *For Prophet and Tsar: Islam and Empire in Russia and Central Asia* (Harvard, 2006) and coedited (with Amin Tarzi) *The Taliban and the Crisis of Afghanistan* (Harvard, 2008) and (with Shahzad Bashir) *Under the Drones: Modern Lives in the Afghanistan-Pakistan Borderlands* (Harvard, 2012). In 2009 he was named a Carnegie Scholar.

JAMES L. GELVIN is a professor of modern Middle Eastern history at the University of California, Los Angeles. He has written extensively on the region, particularly Greater Syria (contemporary Syria, Lebanon, Jordan, Israel, and the Palestinian territories) in the late nineteenth and early twentieth centuries. He is the author of *Divided Loyalties: Nationalism and Mass Politics in Syria at the Close of Empire* (University of California Press, 1998), *The Modern Middle East: A History* (Oxford, 2004, 2007, 2011), *The Israel-Palestine Conflict: One Hundred Years of War* (Cambridge, 2004, 2007), *The Arab Uprisings: What Everyone Needs to Know* (Oxford University Press, 2012, 2014), and numerous articles and chapters in edited volumes.

AMAL GHAZAL is an associate professor in the History Department at Dalhousie University. She has been researching Arab intellectual networks in the late Ottoman and interwar periods. Her research extends to the Middle East and North and East Africa. She is the author of *Islamic Reform and Arab Nationalism: Expanding the Crescent from the Mediterranean to the Indian Ocean (1880s–1930s)* (Routledge, 2010).

NILE GREEN is a professor of South Asian and Islamic history at the University of California, Los Angeles, and the founding director of the UCLA Program on Central Asia. A specialist on the Muslim communities of South Asia, Iran, and Afghanistan, he has written books including *Indian Sufism since the Seventeenth Century: Saints, Books and Empires in the Muslim Deccan* (Routledge, 2006), *Islam and the Army in Colonial India: Sepoy Religion in the Service of Empire* (Cambridge, 2009), *Bombay Islam: The Religious Economy of the West Indian Ocean, 1840–1915* (Cambridge, 2011; winner of the Albert Hourani Prize from the Middle East Studies Association and the A. K. Coomaraswamy Prize from the Association for Asian Studies), *Making Space: Sufis and Settlers in Early Modern India* (Oxford, 2012), and *Sufism: A Global History* (Wiley-Blackwell, 2012).

MATTHEW S. HOPPER is an associate professor in the History Department at California Polytechnic State University, San Luis Obispo. He completed his PhD in history at UCLA in 2006 and was a postdoctoral fellow at the Gilder Lehrman Center at Yale University in 2009. His writing has recently appeared in *Annales, Itinerario,* and the *Journal of African Development.* Yale University Press will publish his book on the history of the African diaspora in eastern Arabia in 2014.

ILHAM KHURI-MAKDISI is an associate professor of Middle East and world history at Northeastern University. She received her PhD in history and Middle Eastern studies at Harvard University in 2004. She is the author of *The Eastern Mediterranean and the Making of Global Radicalism, 1860–1914* (University of California Press, 2010), as well as a number of articles and book chapters on the history of the Left in the Arab Mediterranean region, global migrations, and theater in the late nineteenth century.

MICHAEL LAFFAN is a professor of history at Princeton University. He received his PhD in Southeast Asian history from the University of Sydney in 2001. He is the author of *Islamic Nationhood and Colonial Indonesia: The Umma below the Winds* (RoutledgeCurzon, 2003) and *The Makings of Indonesian Islam: Orientalism and the Narration of a Sufi Past* (Princeton, 2011). The latter explores the links between Indonesian Muslim reformers and Dutch colonial scholars and their shared role in setting the parameters for contemporary Southeast Asian Islam and its study.

ANN E. LUCAS is an American Council of Learned Societies postdoctoral fellow in the Department of Music at Brandeis University and a research fellow with the Center for Middle Eastern Studies at Harvard University. She holds a PhD in ethnomusicology from the University of California, Los Angeles, where her research covered the history of Persian music from circa 1100 through the 1950s. She is the current chair of the Special Interest Group for Historical Ethnomusicology within the Society for Ethnomusicology and is on the board of the Manoochehr Sadeghi Foundation for Persian Classical Music. Her recent publications include "Between Heaven and Hell: The Relationship between Music and Islamic in Persian Sufi Treatises, c. 1040–1800," in the *Asian Music Journal.*

JEREMY PRESTHOLDT is an associate professor of history at the University of California, San Diego, and the author of *Domesticating the World: African Consumerism and the Genealogies of Globalization* (University of California Press, 2008). His work has appeared in a number of edited volumes and journals, including the *American Historical Review, Journal of World History,* and *Public Culture.* His current research addresses globalism and the culture of politics in coastal Kenya.

SCOTT S. REESE is a professor of history at Northern Arizona University specializing in Islamic Africa, comparative Sufism, modern Muslim discourses of reform, and the construction of world systems in space and imagination since 1500. He is author of *Renewers of the Age: Holy Men and Social Discourse in Colonial Benaadir* (Brill, 2008), along with numerous articles and chapters in edited volumes, and the editor of *The Transmission of Learning in Islamic Africa* (Brill, 2004).

RONIT RICCI is a lecturer in the School of Culture, History, and Language at the Australian National University. She holds BA and MA degrees in Indian languages and literatures from the Hebrew University of Jerusalem and a PhD in comparative literature from the University of Michigan. Her recent publications include "Islamic Literary Networks in South and Southeast Asia" (*Journal of Islamic Studies,* 2010), "The Ambiguous Figure of the Jew in Javanese Literature" (*Indonesia and the Malay World,* 2010), and *Islam Translated: Literature, Conversion, and the Arabic Cosmopolis of South and Southeast Asia* (University of Chicago Press, 2011).

ERIC TAGLIACOZZO is an associate professor of history at Cornell University, where he primarily teaches Southeast Asian studies. He is the author of *Secret Trades, Porous Borders: Smuggling and States along a Southeast Asian Frontier, 1865–1915* (Yale, 2005), which won the Harry J. Benda Prize from the Association of Asian Studies. He is also the editor or coeditor of *Southeast Asia and the Middle East: Islam, Movement, and the Longue Durée* (Stanford, 2009), *Clio/Anthropos: Exploring the Boundaries between History and Anthropology* (Stanford, 2009), *The Indonesia Reader: History, Culture, Politics* (Duke, 2009), and *Chinese Circulations: Capital, Commodities, and Networks in Southeast Asia* (Duke, 2011). Oxford University Press will publish his forthcoming book, *The Longest Journey: Southeast Asians and the Pilgrimage to Mecca.*

HOMAYRA ZIAD is an assistant professor of religion at Trinity College. She holds a PhD from Yale University. She is working on two books: one on the intersections of spirituality and literary aesthetics in the writings of the late Mughal Sufi Khwaja Mir Dard, and another on Islam and humor. Her research interests include the history of religious ideas in Muslim India, the cultural and intellectual history of Islam in America, Sufi ethics and theology, Qur'anic studies, and women's religious authority.

INDEX

CPSIA information can be obtained
at www.ICGtesting.com
Printed in the USA
FSHW010905031020
74426FS